FIELDING'S
PORTUGAL

Other Fielding Titles

Fielding's Amazon
Fielding's Australia
Fielding's Bahamas
Fielding's Belgium
Fielding's Bermuda
Fielding's Borneo
Fielding's Brazil
Fielding's Britain
Fielding's Budget Europe
Fielding's Caribbean
Fielding's Europe
Fielding's Far East
Fielding's France
Fielding's Guide to the World's Most Dangerous Places
Fielding's Guide to the World's Great Voyages
Fielding's Guide to Kenya's Best Hotels, Lodges & Homestays
Fielding's Guide to the World's Most Romantic Places
Fielding's Hawaii
Fielding's Holland
Fielding's Italy
Fielding's London Agenda
Fielding's Los Angeles Agenda
Fielding's Malaysia and Singapore
Fielding's Mexico
Fielding's New York Agenda
Fielding's New Zealand
Fielding's Paris Agenda
Fielding's Portugal
Fielding's Scandinavia
Fielding's Seychelles
Fielding's Southeast Asia
Fielding's Spain
Fielding's Travel Smarter Book
Fielding's Vietnam
Fielding's Worldwide Cruises

FIELDING'S PORTUGAL

The Most Authoritative Guide to the Charm and Romance of Portugal

A. Hoyt Hobbs & Joy Adzigian

Fielding Worldwide, Inc.
308 South Catalina Avenue
Redondo Beach, California 90277 U.S.A.

Fielding's Portugal
Published by Fielding Worldwide, Inc.
Text Copyright ©1994 A. Hoyt Hobbs and Joy Adzigian
Icons & Illustrations Copyright ©1994 FWI
All rights reserved. No part of this book may be reproduced, transmitted or utilized in any form or by any means, electronic or mechanical, including photocopying, recording, or by any information storage and retrieval system, without permission in writing from the publisher. Brief extracts for review purposes for inclusion in critical reviews or articles are permitted.

FIELDING WORLDWIDE INC.

PUBLISHER AND CEO **Robert Young Pelton**
PUBLISHING DIRECTOR **Paul T. Snapp**
PUBLISHING DIRECTOR **Larry E. Hart**
PROJECT DIRECTOR **Tony E. Hulette**
ACCOUNT EXCUTIVE **Beverly Riess**
ACCOUNT SERVICES MANAGER **Christy Harp**

EDITORS
Linda Charlton **Kathy Knoles**

PRODUCTION
Tina Gentile   **Chris Snyder**   **Craig South**

COVER DESIGNED BY **Digital Artists**
COVER PHOTOGRAPHERS — Front Cover **Chad Ehlers/Tony Stone Worldwide**
Background Photo, Front Cover **Grame Norways, Tony Stone Worldwide**
Back Cover **Dallas & John Heaton/Westlight**
INSIDE PHOTOS **Portuguese National Tourist Office**

Although every effort has been made to ensure the correctness of the information in this book, the publisher and authors do not assume, and hereby disclaim, any liability to any party for any loss or damage caused by errors, omissions, misleading information or any potential travel problem caused by information in this guide, even if such errors or omission are a result of negligence, accident or any other cause.

Inquiries should be addressed to: Fielding Worldwide, Inc., 308 South Catalina Ave., Redondo Beach, California 90277 U.S.A., ☎ *(310) 372-4474*, Facsimile *(310) 376-8064*, 8:30 a.m.–5:30 p.m. Pacific Standard Time.

ISBN 1-56952-046-1
Library of Congress Catalog Card Number
94-068340
Printed in the United States of America

Dedication

We gratefully dedicate this book to
Susan Schneider,
our muse for Portugal and life.

Letter from the Publisher

In 1946, Temple Fielding began the first of what would be a remarkable new series of well-written, highly personalized guide books for independent travelers. Temple's opinionated, witty, and oft-imitated books have now guided travelers for almost a half-century. More important to some was Fielding's humorous and direct method of steering travelers away from the dull and the insipid. Today, Fielding Travel Guides are still written by experienced travelers for experienced travelers. Our authors carry on Fielding's reputation for creating travel experiences that deliver insight with a sense of discovery and style.

Unforgettable. That's what you'll say after a vacation in Portugal the Fielding way. Hoyt Hobbs and Joy Adzigian have been traveling through Europe for the past 20 years, searching for the dramatic, the little-known, the romantic attractions, and the pristine beaches that make Portugal one of the most entertaining countries in Europe. In Fielding's *Portugal*, Hoyt and Joy have created the perfect balance of entertainment and education, all in a historical context. You won't forget Portugal. Not with Fielding.

Today the concept of independent travel has never been bigger. Our policy of *brutal honesty* and a highly personal point of view has never changed; it just seems the travel world has caught up with us.

Enjoy your Portugal adventure with Hoyt Hobbs, Joy Adzigian, and Fielding.

RYP

Robert Young Pelton
Publisher and C.E.O.
Fielding Worldwide, Inc.

ABOUT THE AUTHORS

Hoyt Hobbs and Joy Adzigian

Hoyt Hobbs and Joy Adzigian have traveled extensively throughout Europe and North Africa since 1973. They first visited Portugal in 1976 while living in the south of France, and were enchanted by the gentle beauty of the country and the warmth of its people. Portugal's quaint villages, graceful architecture, stunning beaches and savory cuisine drew them back again and again.

The couple wrote their first guidebook in 1979—to Egypt—when, after numerous trips, they had been unable to find a guidebook to their liking. Popular guides conveyed too little understanding of history and culture, while more scholarly books obscured interesting information within reams of detail. Reviewers applauded their balanced approach. *The Library Journal* said: "...with only this book [one can] enjoy a more comprehensive, efficient, and informative tour...than is possible with any of the classical travel guides." According to *Traveler's Book Society* "...the level here is almost exactly right for the intelligent traveler....This is a book to travel with as well as to use in planning a tour...." "This book is a model of specific, useful, honest travel advice and concise, vivid historical exposition," noted the *Chattanooga Times*, adding that "you ought to buy this book at once." In 1981 their Egypt guide was selected for publication as the first of the Fielding's country guides. Now they have applied their successful and informative approach to Portugal.

Dr. Hobbs, an Associate Professor of Philosophy at Long Island University, is widely read in history, architecture and cultural history; Joy Adzigian, a stylist and producer, brings a background strong in literature, art and design. Both are serious about food and wine and relish making fresh discoveries. They report the findings of their Portuguese explorations in this lively, comprehensive guide.

The authors are married and live in New York City.

ACKNOWLEDGMENTS

A project such as this could never have been completed without substantial assistance from a large number of people and organizations. It is a great pleasure to have an opportunity to publicly thank some of them.

We especially wish to thank Jorge Felner da Costa, director, ICEP/Portuguese National Tourist Office for his generous cooperation and interest in this project, and Sergio Lopes, director, USA. TAP/Air Portugal for his kind attention and support.

We are exceedingly grateful to João Custódio of Enatur Pousadas de Portugal, Gloria Mello of TAP/Air Portugal, and Luis Reis of the Association of Hotels du Charmes for their gracious and enthusiastic assistance.

Abundant thanks to Manuel Ferreira Enes, José Almeida, and Ruth Santiago for their many kindnesses on our behalf. We are grateful to our good friends Pamela Dailey and Arthur Krystal for timely and astute editorial assistance.

Our debt to and affection for Maria João Ramires of ICEP/Portuguese National Tourist Office in New York is beyond measure. We were as constantly awed by the grace, efficiency and bubbling good humor with which she worked countless miracles as we were by her generous nature and warm friendship.

Dr. and Mrs. Albert H. Hobbs laid all the groundwork for this book with a lifetime of lessons. Lastly, we thank our friends and family for their patience and we want them to know that, for better or worse, we are available again.

Fielding Rating Icons

The Fielding Rating Icons are highly personal and awarded to help the besieged traveler choose from among the dizzying array of activities, attractions, hotels, restaurants and sights. The awarding of an icon denotes unusual or exceptional qualities in the relevant category.

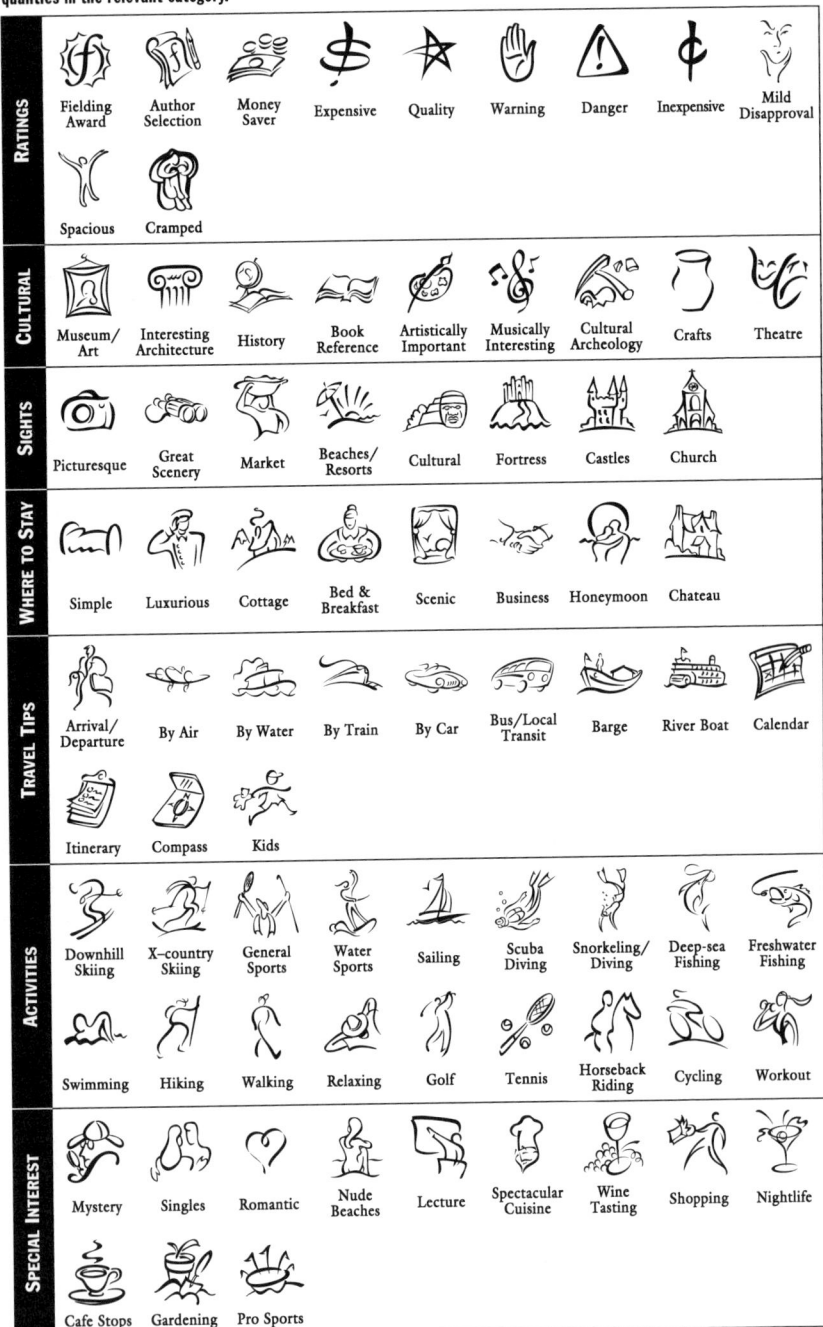

TABLE OF CONTENTS

ABOUT THE AUTHORS ... ix
ACKNOWLEDGMENTS ... xi
LIST OF MAPS ... xxi
FIRST OF ALL ... 1
    1995 ... 1
    Using This Guide ... 2
    Using Our Rating System ... 2
    Prices ... 3
    Changes ... 4
PRACTICAL MATTERS ... 5
    Travel to Portugal ... 5
    Costs ... 11
    When to Go: Climate and Seasons ... 12
    Holidays and Special Events ... 13
    Passports ... 14
    Car Rental ... 15
    Customs Allowances ... 16
    Clothes and Packing ... 17
    Accommodations ... 18
    Money ... 23
    Travel in Portugal ... 24
    Restaurants ... 27
    Shopping ... 29
    Tipping ... 30
    Time Zone and Official Hours ... 31
    Mail, Telephones, Electricity and Measurement ... 31
    Sports ... 33
    Student Travel ... 35
    Female Travelers ... 36
    Crime ... 36
    Books ... 37
THE LAND AND THE PEOPLE ... 39
WHERE TO GO ... 45
    The Top Sights ... 45
        Beaches ... 47
        Castles ... 48
        Charming Villages ... 49

Itineraries 50

HISTORY 53
Prehistory Through the Birth of Portugal (9000 B.c.–a.d. 1139) 53
The Burgundian Dynasty (1140–1385) 56
The House of Avís (1385–1588) 58
Spain and the House of Bragança (1580–1910) 59
The Republic (1910–1976) 61

ART AND ARCHITECTURE 63
Roman to Romanesque 64
Gothic and Manueline 66
Neoclassic and Baroque 67
Sculpture 68
Painting 70
Azulejos 71

FOOD AND DRINK 73
Food 74
Drink 76

THE SIGHTS OF PORTUGAL 79

LISBON 81
Historical Profile:
The Story of Lisbon 81
Lisbon 85
What to See and Do 89
Where to Stay 103
Where to Eat 108
Shopping 112
Entertainment 113
Directory 115
Excursions 116

ENVIRONS OF LISBON 119
Historical Profile:
The Rise and Fall of the House Of Avís 119
Environs Of Lisbon 126
Alcobaça 126
Where to Stay 129
Where to Eat 129
Directory 129
Excursions 129
Batalha 129
Where to Stay 132
Where to Eat 133
Excursions 133
Fátima 133
Cascais 134

Estoril	134
Where to Stay	135
Where to Eat	137
Leiria	138
Mafra	138
Where to Stay	139
Nazaré	139
Where to Stay	140
Where to Eat	141
Óbidos	142
Where to Stay	143
Where to Eat	144
Queluz	144
Where to Stay	146
Where to Eat	146
Setúbal	146
Where to Stay	147
Excursions	148
Sintra	149
Where to Stay	153
Where to Eat	154
Shopping	155
Directory	155
Excursions	156
NORTHERN PORTUGAL	157
Historical Profile:	
The Birth of Portugal	157
Northern Portugal	162
Almourol Castle	164
Aveiro	164
Where to Stay	166
Where to Eat	168
Directory	168
Bom Jesus	169
Braga	169
What to See and Do	170
Where to Stay	172
Where to Eat	173
Directory	174
Excursions	174
Barcelos	174
Bravães	175
Viana Do Castelo	175
Where to Stay	176
Where to Eat	176

Bragança	176
Where to Stay	179
Where to Eat	180
Bravães	180
Buçaco Forest	180
Coimbra	180
What to See and Do	182
Where to Stay	187
Where to Eat	188
Directory	189
Excursions	190
Condeixa	190
Where to Stay	191
Directory	192
Luso	192
Figueira Da Foz	194
Where to Stay	194
Where to Eat	195
Conimbriga	195
Figueira Da Faz	195
Guimarães	195
What to See and Do	196
Where to Stay	199
Where to Eat	200
Excursions	200
Leiria	200
Peneda-gerês National Park	200
Where to Stay	201
Porto	202
What to See and Do	206
Where to Stay	208
Where to Eat	210
Directory	212
Excursions	213
Mateus	213
Tomar	214
Where to Stay	217
Where to Eat	219
Excursions	219
Viana Do Castelo	220
Viseu	220
What to See and Do	222
Where to Stay	223
Where to Eat	224
Directory	224
Excursions	225

EASTERN PORTUGAL 227
Historical Profile:
The End of the Monarchy and its Aftermath 227
Eastern Portugal 235
Arraiolos 236
Borba 236
Castelo Branco 238
Castelo De Vide 238
Elvas 238
- What to See and Do 239
- Where to Stay 240
- Where to Eat 241
- Directory 241
Estremoz 241
- Where to Stay 243
- Directory 243
- Excursions 243
- Vila Viçosa 244
Évora 245
- What to See and Do 247
- Where to Stay 251
- Where to Eat 252
- Directory 253
- Excursions 253
- Evoramonte 253
- Monsaraz 254
- Redondo 255
Evoramonte 256
Flor De Rosa 256
Guarda 256
- Where to Stay 257
- Where to Eat 258
- Excursions 258
- The Southern Forts 258
- The Northern Forts 260
Marvão 261
- Where to Stay 262
- Where to Eat 263
- Excursions 263
- Portalegre 263
- Flor De Rosa 263
- Castelo De Vide 264
- Castelo Branco 264
Monsanto 265
Monsaraz 265
Redondo 265

THE ALGARVE 267
Historical Profile:
When Portugal Ruled the World 267
The Algarve 273
Sagres 276
Where to Stay 278
Where to Eat 279
Directory 279
Salema 280
Where to Stay 280
Where to Eat 280
Praia Da Luz 281
Where to Stay 281
Where to Eat 281
Lagos 282
Where to Stay 283
Where to Eat 285
Alvor 286
Where to Stay 286
Where to Eat 287
Portimão/Praia Da Rocha 287
Where to Stay 288
Where to Eat 290
Armação De Pêra 290
Where to Stay 291
Where to Eat 292
Directory 292
Albufeira 292
Where to Stay 293
Where to Eat 295
Excursions 296
Vilamoura 296
Where to Stay 296
Quarteira 297
Where to Stay 298
Faro 298
Where to Stay 299
Where to Eat 300
Directory 301
Excursions 301
Olhão 301
Where to Stay 302
Tavira 302
Where to Stay 302
Where to Eat 303
Directory 304

The Southwest 304
   Porto Covo 304
      Where to Stay 305
      Where to Eat 305
   Vila Nova De Milfontes 306
      Where to Stay 306
   Almograve 306
   Odeceixe 307

THE PORTUGUESE LANGUAGE 309
HOTEL QUICK REFERENCE LIST 317
SPECIAL RESTAURANTS 337
INDEX 345

LIST OF MAPS

Portugal xxii
    Lisbon 86
Northern Portugal 163
Central Portugal 237
Southern Portugal 275

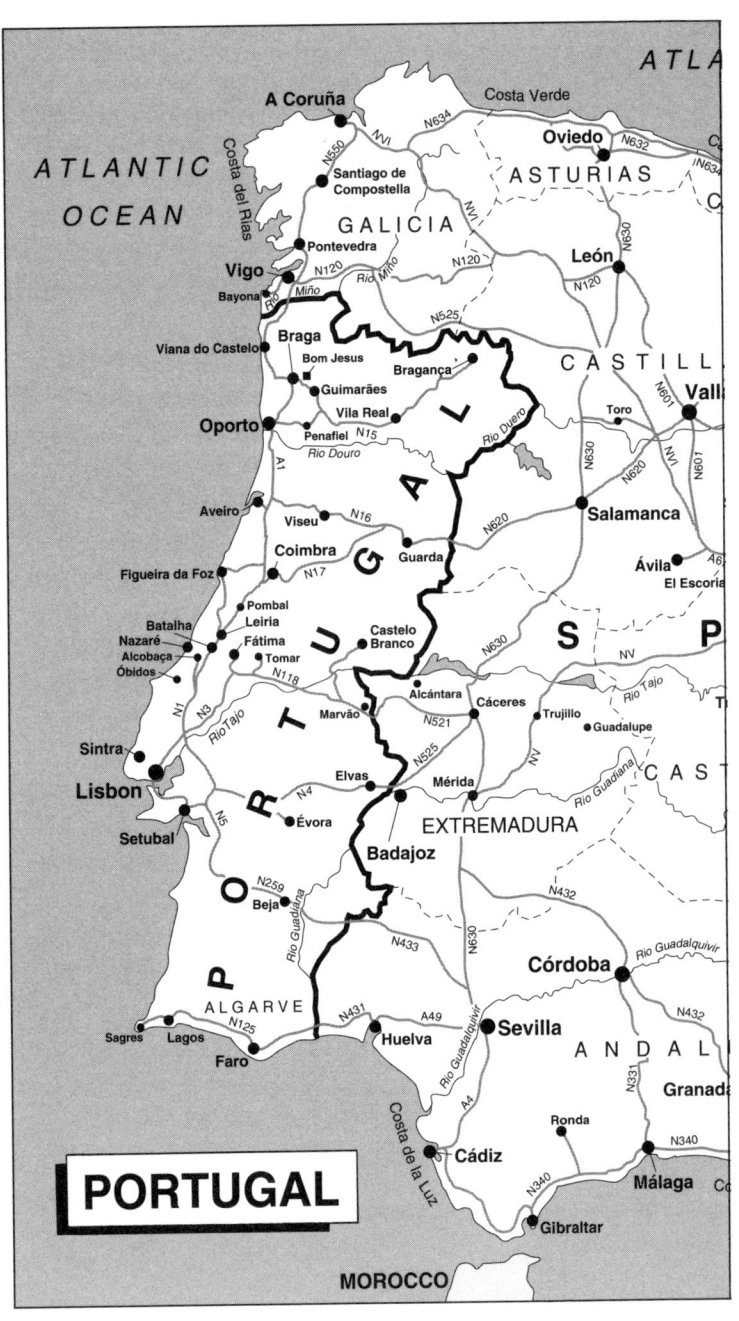

FIRST OF ALL

We've written this book to introduce you to the best of Portugal—the best hotels, restaurants, cities and villages, beaches, art, architecture and shopping.

If you're an independent traveler, our descriptions and itineraries will help you decide what's the best of the best for you. If you're an undecided traveler, we'll give you reason to go. Even an armchair traveler will find enough background information and descriptions of sights to amount to a vicarious trip.

For Americans, Portugal has long been Western Europe's best-kept travel secret. While Europeans have flocked to its extraordinary beaches and graceful palaces for decades, to most Americans it's still a fresh discovery, a rare and wonderful surprise. You're not too late. Portugal has changed little over recent decades—except in some good ways, such as raising its hotels to world-class levels. Portugal remains unspoiled, its prices the lowest in Western Europe, its people warm and unaffected, its sights pleasantly unfamiliar.

For most travelers, Portugal's history is equally unknown, a circumstance which, in the visitor's imagination, leaves palaces anonymous, ancient fortresses unmanned, and historical changes in fortune unexplained. We take time—much more than the average guide book allows—to discuss Portugal's history, famous people, and culture, and individual monuments, because nothing enriches a trip more than understanding what you're seeing.

1995

In 1995 Americans will find even more reason to visit Portugal. Lisbon's designation as Europe's Cultural Capital last year prompted the refurbishment, renovation, and improvement of the city's major historical and cultural monuments. Among others, the venerable

Museum of Ancient Art was remodeled and all its exhibits redisplayed, and both the Tower of Belem and Belem Monastery now glisten for the first time since Vasco da Gama sailed by.

Visitors will also enjoy the benefits of a veritable explosion of hotel building and remodeling resulting from a low-interest, about-to-expire loan program provided by the European Economic Community to encourage tourism in its less affluent member nations. Not only will there be more hotels to choose from in 1995, but existing ones will be substantially refreshed.

As a final enticement, Portugal offers Americans more affordable prices than it has for over a decade. Worldwide economic problems took their toll on Portugal whose tourist industry responded by lowering hotel rates for this year. In addition, a dollar will buy a third more in Portugal today than it did just two years ago—all of which adds up to a very affordable vacation.

USING THIS GUIDE

Following introductory chapters on trip preparation and historical and cultural background, we divide the country into five areas, beginning with a chapter on Lisbon, the point of arrival for 92 percent of all visitors to Portugal. This is followed by chapters on Lisbon's environs, northern Portugal, eastern Portugal, and the Algarve in the south. Each chapter describes an area whose most attractive sights can all be easily visited during a three or four day stay in one centrally located city or town.

USING OUR RATING SYSTEM

Apart from giving you information about what is available to see and do in Portugal and background about its history and culture, the most valuable help we can provide is an evaluation of sights, monuments, hotels and restaurants. For easy reference, we codify our opinions within a star system:

★★★★★ Outstanding anywhere in the world
★★★★ Exceptional, among the best in the country
★★★ Superior for a particular area of the country
★★ Good, a clear step above the average
★ Above average

For hotels and restaurants we include additional information by assigning each a price category (explained under "Prices" below) and, in the case of hotels, specifying the services offered. We award a hotel or restaurant an extra star (or even two) if the quality of its service, style and/or cuisine sufficiently surpasses that of its higher-priced competitors in the same class. Conversely, we award fewer stars to establishments charging higher prices than their accommodations or food merit. Read our descriptions of each hotel or restaurant to understand its rating.

We also designate (with a script "*f*") a "Fielding's choice"—our very favorite hotels and restaurants.

Unlike the stars assigned hotels by the Portuguese government which rank establishments by the number and variety of services such as TVs, minibars, saunas or conference rooms available, our stars evaluate comfort, attractiveness and quality of service, all of which the government system ignores. We assign a class-category to indicate the quantity of available services. A **Luxury** or a **1st-class** hotel will provide every possible facility and service; a **2nd-class** hotel will offer a restaurant and room TV, but usually not saunas, conference rooms or other infrequently used extras; and a **3rd-class** accommodation, while often as pleasant as hotels given higher class designations, may begin and end with a comfortable room.

As in many European countries, the Portuguese government also assigns from one to four stars to unofficial hotels, variously called *residentials, pensões, hostals,* or *estalgems,* which provide a smaller range of services from similarly rated official versions. Such accommodations might lack an elevator, overnight desk staff, or an on-premises restaurant. To many travelers the absence of such features may be of little concern, and the otherwise fine accommodations may be well worth consideration. We include these lodgings with our hotel listings, and distinguish them with the letters "R," "P," "Hs," or "E" for *residential, pensõe, hostal or estalgem.*

We don't believe that an endless Yellow Pages of hotels and restaurants is not what most tourists to a foreign country want or need. Instead we've selected and c scribed a range of good hotels in all price ranges with locations con. 1ient for a sightseer. Because Portugal offers such an abundance of good hotels, we tell you about bad hotels only when a desirable location might tempt you to book them.

PRICES

Because daily international currency fluctuations prevent us from telling you the exact dollar costs of the hotels and restaurants we review, we group their prices into more stable general categories: **Very Expensive**, **Expensive**, **Moderate** and **Inexpensive**.

Price Category	Hotel (a double room for 2 persons)	Restaurant (full meal for 1, +house wine)
Very Expensive	$200+	
Expensive	$100-$200	$30+
Moderate	$50-$99	$15-$30
Inexpensive	Less than $50	Less than $15

CHANGES

Although we've researched and inspected hundreds of hotels and restaurants over many visits, we're aware of the constantly changing landscape—improvements, declines, or even closings that may have occurred too recently to be reflected in our reviews. If you locate some treasure we've missed, we'd love hearing about it; similarly, if you receive bad food or inadequate service in any of the establishments we recommend, we certainly want to know about that. While no hotel or restaurant can score perfectly every time, rude service is never acceptable. We welcome your comments and suggestions. Write us c/o Fielding Worldwide, 308 S. Catalina Avenue, Redondo Beach, CA 90277.

Most important, have a wonderful trip!

PRACTICAL MATTERS

TRAVEL TO PORTUGAL

BY PLANE

Three airlines currently fly directly from the U.S. to Portugal: TAP (Air Portugal), TWA and Delta. All depart from New York (or Newark) and land in Lisbon, where connections to other cities can be made. TAP and TWA leave every day in summer, Delta three times a week. TAP also provides direct service from both Boston and LA twice weekly. Air Canada joins TAP in providing frequent service from both Montreal and Toronto in Canada. Flight time from New York or Boston is a little more than 6 hours, an hour more from Canada, and six more from LA.

British Airways arranges connecting flights through London to Lisbon; Air France provides the same service through Paris; and KLM stops over at Amsterdam. All can fly directly from their stop-over to Faro, in the Algarve, Porto or Lisbon. In addition, charter flights abound.

Since airfares were deregulated, competition has led to complex, changing rates along with exotic giveaways and deals. Like specials at the supermarket, prices change continually, so that only a travel agent will know what is available at a given time. However, some principles are constant.

Prices change with the seasons and are most expensive from June through August and during Christmas and Easter, least expensive both from November to the middle of December and from the second of January through the first half of March, and fall between these two extremes at other times.

Whatever the season, first-class fares will be the most expensive way to fly by a factor of three or four times the least expensive. For that price, a traveler is provided free stopovers, extra leg room, and quiet. Meals are more elaborate, and drinks and headsets are free—though the high fare covers such generosity many times over. Most carriers, although not TAP, also offer a class of fares between first class and economy, called "Business Class," "Preference Class," or some such designation, with about the same benefits as first class, except for a tad less room and at about half the price.

Most of us cram into tourist, economy, or coach class. The names vary but not the fact that this is the low end, both of comfort and cost. Here rates grow complex.

In addition to regular economy (tourist, coach, or whatever-the-name) fares, there are also discount economy fares. "Excursion" fares are lower in cost—economy-class travel with required minimum and maximum stays that happily correspond to the duration of most vacations. APEX (Advanced Purchase EXcursion) fares are special excursion fares that require full payment for tickets two weeks or so before departure. All excursion fares carry an expensive penalty for changing a reservation, and APEX fares involve a penalty for cancelling the trip. But savings, which can be half what a regular economy ticket would cost, lead most tourists to opt for such arrangements.

Stand-by fares, once the bargain-hunters treasure, have been discontinued by most airlines (Virgin Atlantic to London is an exception), because of inconvenienced and sometimes irate travelers. A true bargain hunter might, however, call airlines to check the current status.

Charter flights were once great bargains. They were also risky—if the charter company failed, the price of the paid-in-advance ticket could be lost. Since scheduled airlines have lowered their fares, the savings on charter flights today are less than they used to be, although still real. Generally there is little or no flexibility in dates of travel, and advance payment is always required. If you cancel your trip, you forfeit the entire price of the ticket, but the charter company may cancel its flight, up to ten days before scheduled departure, as long as it refunds your money. So if your charter leaves as scheduled, you can be sure it will be full—the company would have cancelled otherwise. Still, we have seen one-way flights from New York to Lisbon for a very tempting $200. For more information ask your travel agent, check the travel section of the newspaper or try **Council Charter**, *205 East 42nd Street, New York, New York 10017* (☎ *212-661-0311 or 800-223-7402*).

Ticket consolidators can provide tickets as cheaply as most charters with less risk. These firms sell at discounts the tickets that airlines were unable to at higher fares. Thus, space will not be available for every flight, and never for popular times. But discounts range from 20 percent and more off standard fares. A sampling of consolidators is: **Access International,** *101 West 31st Street, New York, NY 10016* (☎ *212-465-0707; 800-825-3633*), **Travel Avenue,** *180 North Des Plaines, Chicago, IL 60661* (☎ *800-333-3335*), **UniTravel,** *Box 12485, St. Louis, MO* (☎ *800-325-2222*), **Council Charter,** *205 E. 42nd St., New York, NY* (☎ *800-800-8222*) and **Sunline Express Holidays, Inc.,** *607 Market St., San Francisco, CA 94105* (☎ *800-SUNLINE*).

Although requiring a nominal membership fee, joining a travel club is another way to save because such organizations buy tickets in volume. Try **Moment's Notice**, *425 Madison Avenue, New York, NY 10017* (☎ *212-486-0503*); **Discount Travel International**, *114 Forrest Avenue, Narberth, PA 19072* (☎ *215-668-7184*); or **Worldwide Discount Club**, *1674 Meridian Avenue, Miami Beach, FL 33139* (☎ *305-534-2028*) for more information.

More offbeat for the venturesome or desperate, is generic air travel. **Airhitch** is the best known (*2901 Broadway, Suite 100, New York, NY 11025,* ☎ *212-864-2000*). You register by paying a small fee and specify a range of departure dates and a preferred destination, along with alternatives. About a week before your first desired departure you are offered at least two flights meeting those specifications. If you do not accept any, your fee is forfeited; otherwise you pay the balance minus the fee. Savings can be great, as low as the lowest charters, with less money risked up front. Write or call for details and other variations on this theme.

After paying, the question remains of what to take with you. Each economy passenger is allowed two pieces of luggage, neither of which can exceed 70 pounds, and whose combined dimension (length, width, plus height) measures no more than 62 inches for one piece and 55 for the other; plus one carry-on with dimensions totaling no more than 45 inches, and one shoulder bag. Higher classes of fares are allowed more. These limits apply to adults and to those children paying at least half of the adult fare; children paying less than half-price fares are permitted less. If you must take more than what the airline allows, come early to the check-in and expect to pay for overweight.

Seats in the rear of a plane rock and shake more than those further forward. Tall travelers should request seats behind the door or the emergency exit, as these provide the most leg room. All told, the last row of seats is the worst, not even reclining fully. Note that foreign flights are not subject to the nonsmoking regulations of our domestic ones, so request whichever section is appropriate. One food tip is to ask for a special dietary meal both at reservation time and again when you confirm. The special diet can be kosher, low sodium, low cholesterol, or any other, but such meals generally will be prepared with more care than your seatmate's.

BY CAR

There is no very convenient way to drive to Portugal from any European country except Spain, for the route involves traveling the long breadth of Iberia. But numerous border crossings link Portugal with Spain, and customs formalities no longer exist. The most common crossings are at Spain's Tuy in the north, Badajoz in the center and Ayamonte in the extreme south; all of which remain open 24 hours. Bringing a car from elsewhere in Europe is more conveniently done by traveling along with it on a car-train.

BY TRAIN

The only direct train from France to Porto then Lisbon is the *Sud Express* that leaves Paris' Gare d'Austerlitz around noon and arrives the next morning. Other trains stop first in Madrid for a change there. They leave Paris every evening, arrive at Madrid 13 hours later, where one transfers across Madrid from Chambartín to Atocha Station for the Lisboa Express, and nine hours more to Lisbon. The most modern of these trains are the luxurious TALGO and the Puerto del Sol which depart from Paris' Austerlitz station. In Madrid the Lisboa Express leaves at 1:50 and 11pm. Part of the reason this leg of the trip takes nine hours is that trains have to be changed at the Portuguese border because of wider-gauge Spanish rails. Note that sleeping accommodations must be reserved well in advance. Trains can also be picked up south of Paris, through Biarritz for Madrid, and through Perpignan for Figueres and Barcelona on Spain's east coast, for connections west. In most cases the train costs as much as a plane and sometimes more.

In the other direction, the Lusitania Express leaves at Lisbon at 9:45 p.m. for arrival at Madrid's Chamartin Station at 8:55 a.m. The Luiz de Camões, in the daytime, is faster by a couple of hours.

If a car is part of your baggage, it can be loaded on one Paris train in the evening, while passengers take another the following morning so that both will arrive in Lisbon on the next day. Reservations are imperative. Contact **Chemin de Fer** in Paris or **French National Railroads**, *Rockefeller Center, 610 Fifth Avenue, New York, NY 10020* (☎ *212-757-1125*).

PACKAGE TOURS

A package tour combines travel and hotel costs in a single price. Since the packager deals in volume, he books flights and rooms more cheaply than individuals can. Even after the packager's profit, the combination should cost less than the same arrangements made individually. On the minus side, the hotels provided are seldom the best choices in the price range and the itinerary may be rigid. Note that the prices cited for packages generally are *per person* in a double occupancy room. Figure the costs of the tour you would arrange for yourself and see if the savings of a package tour makes it worthwhile. On your own, you can find accommodations more interesting than what the package offers, our book is filled with suggestions for you, but you will have to work to make selections and reservations. Of course a travel agent can make the reservations you want for no additional charge.

Travel sections of newspapers often advertise package tours. Travel agents will know many more. In choosing a package tour it is important to find out whether you will be charged for price increases that occur after you've booked. Some companies guarantee the price at booking time will not be raised. You should also ask whether you'll receive a full refund if any part of the package promised should become unavailable.

Package tours come in three distinct kinds with three levels of ascending price. "Independent packages," called FITs in the industry, allow the most freedom since they involve only a combination of hotel and flight arrangements, sometimes with a car as well. More familiar are "escorted tours," those where you join a group to travel together, often by bus, under the direction of a leader. Activities are ensemble; all problems are the leader's responsibility. Such tours are the most carefree way to travel, but throw you in with a group of strangers and restrict your freedom to do what you want when you wish. The third type, a variation on the second, is a "special interest tour." The difference from other escorted tours is that the leader is an expert on Portuguese art, wine, food, or whatever the specialization of the company. Such a tour provides an education impossible to gain on one's own. Since the expenses include a fee for the leader, this sort of tour will cost more than other package tours, probably bringing the price to about what individual arrangements would cost.

Major airlines flying to Portugal generally offer independent packages, as do a few specialty companies:

Delta Dream Vacations, (☎ *800-872-7786*).

TAP, (☎ *800-324-3520*).

TWA Getaway Vacations, (☎ *800-439-2929*).

American Express Vacations, Gadabout, Petrabax and Odysseys Adventures offer FITs, as well as the escorted tours listed below.

Here is a list of a number of companies that offer escorted tour programs who will be pleased to send information about their offerings:

Abreu Tours, Inc., *317 East 34th Street, New York, NY 10016* (☎ *212-661-0555 or 800-223-1580*).

American Express Vacations, *local American Express offices, or 300 Pinnacle Way, Norcross, GA 30071* (☎ *800-241-1700*).

Cosmos Tours, *95-25 Queens Boulevard, Rego Park, NY 11374* (☎ *800-221-0090*).

Getaway Vacations, Inc., *10 East Stow Road, Marlton, NJ 08053* (☎ *800-GETAWAY*).

Globus-Gateway Tours, same address as Cosmo Tours, above.

Odyssey Adventures, *537 Chestnut St., Cedarhurst, NY 11516* (☎ *516-569-2813 or 800-344-0013; FAX 516-569-2998*).

Petrabax USA, *21 E. 26th St., New York, NY 10010* (☎ *212-689-8977 or 800-854-0103.*

Portuguese Tours, *Box 729, Elizabeth, NJ 07207* (☎ *800-526-4047*).

Sun Holidays, *26 Sixth Street, Suite 603, Stamford, CT 06905* (☎ *800-243-2057, FAX 203-323-3843*).

TAP, *399 Market Street, Newark NJ 07105* (☎ *800-336-6690; in NY, 800-324-3520*)

Tour Directions International, Inc., *70 West 36th Street, Suite 1004, New York, NY 10018* (☎ *212-564-3236 or 800-423-4460; FAX 212-629-5934*).

Trafalgar Tours, Merged with Petrabax, USA, above.

Special interest tours include the following:

Swan-Hellenic Tours, *77 New Oxford Street, London WC1A* (☎ *071-831-1616*) does art tours.

The Texas Connection, *217 Arden Grove, San Antonio, TX 78215* (☎ *512-225-6294*) organizes a crafts tour.

Thomson Holidays, *London House, Hampstead Road, London NW1* (☎ *071-387-1900*) offers wine tours.

Adventure Gold Holidays, *815 North Road, Westfield, MA 01806* (☎ *800-628-9655*) arranges golf tours.

Marens International, *2121 Ponce de Leon Boulevard, Suite 715, Coral Gables, FL 33134* (☎ *305-441-1555*) provides history tours.

Easy Rider Tours, *P.O. Box 228, Newburyport, MA 01950* (☎ *800-488-8332; FAX 508-463-6988*) organizes nine different bike tours from spring through early autumn.

COSTS

Despite the loosening of government price controls on Portuguese hotels and restaurants and the falling U.S. dollar, Portugal remains the best travel buy a North American tourist can make.

Comfortable double rooms in moderately priced hotels in tourist areas cost about $75 during July or August and will include a continental breakfast in the price. The same room in a town less frequented by tourists will be a third less. Count on $15 per person for an adequate dinner with wine. Budget about $135 per day for a couple to travel modestly in Portugal in July or August, not including transportation—either getting to or around the country. This is less than half the cost of travel in France or Italy.

> **TIP:** Most hotel prices drop by 25-33 percent before and after July and August, and decline even more in winter, though Easter and Christmas weeks are exceptions. Many hotels in Lisbon, however, have this backwards, offering their lowest prices in high summer.

Hotels drop their prices by at least 20 percent for any time other than July and August; and most lower their prices by up to 33 percent during the winter. So anyone who visits at these quieter times can budget about $115 per day, with the same caveat about adding the cost of travel mentioned above. Portugal's museums are also great bargains at any time of the year for they never cost more than 400$00. Only Portuguese gasoline is equal in cost to the rest of Europe—a significant expense at almost $40 a tank full.

WHEN TO GO: CLIMATE AND SEASONS

In latitude Portugal sits opposite that part of the United States stretching from Boston to Baltimore, but because of proximity to the Gulf Stream, Portugal enjoys a Mediterranean climate. Palms flourish all year even in Lisbon—because Portugal is blessed with mild weather all year.

There are temperature differences, however, of about 10 degrees between the mountainous north and the southern Algarve beaches (see the chart below). In summer the thermometer often tops 90 and rain is uncommon. Spring and autumn bring mid-70s temperatures, accompanied—especially in autumn—by brief showers in the center and south of the country and steady rain in the north. Winter frost is rare and snow unknown except in the highest mountains where few tourists go. Portuguese winters compare to spring in the U.S. northeast, with 50- or even 60-degree temperatures during the day, dropping to the 40s at night.

AVERAGE DAILY TERMPERATURES DAY (NIGHT)

	Lisbon	North	Alentejo	Algarve
January	56 (46)	49 (33)	54 (42)	59 (48)
February	58 (46)	50 (34)	56 (42)	61 (48)
March	63 (50)	56 (38)	61 (47)	64 (52)
April	67 (53)	61 (41)	67 (49)	68 (55)
May	72 (55)	67 (47)	72 (52)	72 (57)
June	78 (60)	75 (52)	81 (57)	78 (64)
July	83 (63)	83 (56)	86 (61)	84 (67)
August	82 (63)	82 (56)	86 (61)	84 (67)
September	79 (62)	75 (52)	81 (59)	79 (65)
October	72 (58)	64 (46)	72 (56)	74 (61)
November	64 (52)	54 (39)	61 (48)	66 (54)
December	58 (47)	47 (34)	55 (42)	61 (48)

For Portugal's best weather, schedule your visit for spring (April through the first half of June) or early fall (September through October). If you enjoy the sizzle of July and August, remember that those are the months when vacationing Portuguese—along with most of the rest of Europe—crowd resorts and fill hotels. Book peak-time lodgings in the Algarve no later than January. If possible, consider mild winter for a relaxed, relatively tourist-free Portuguese experience.

HOLIDAYS AND SPECIAL EVENTS

The dates of holidays are important because businesses, certainly, and sights, possibly, will be closed; but holidays also offer the best opportunities to view and take part in the local color of the country.

National Holidays All offices closed.

January 1, Ano Novo (*New Year's Day*).

February 7, Carnaval.

April 14, Sexta-feira Santa (*Good Friday*).

April 16, Páscoa *(Easter).*

April 25, Dia da Liberdade (*Liberation Day*).

May 1, Dia do Trabalito (*Labor Day*).

June 10, Dia da Portugal e da Camões (*Portugal and Camões Day*).

August 15, Dia da Assuncão (*Assumption Day*).

October 5, Dia da Republica (*Republic Day*).

November 1, Todos os Santos (*All Saints' Day*).

December 1, Restauração da Independencia (*Independence Day*).

December 8, Imaculada da Concepção (*Immaculate Conception*).

December 25, Dia de Natal (*Christmas*).

Various regions and towns celebrate their own festivals at appointed times during the year. See the discussion of the town in question for details, but they line up as follows:

1st half of January: *Porto and Aviero.*

2nd half of January: *Aviero; Évora.*

March Carnival: *Throughout the country.*

April, Easter Week: *Especially festive in Braga.*

1st half of May: *Barçelos Fair; Fatima pilgrimage.*

May: *Music festivals throughout the Algarve.*

Late June: *Lisbon's St. Anthony fair; Porto's St John's Fair.*

June, last week: *Évora's São João Festival.*

July-August: *Estoril's music fair.*

August, !st weekend: *Redondo Folk Festival.*

1st half of August: *Folk Festival of Gualterianas in Guimarães.*

2nd half of August: *Colorful "Lady of Agony" festival in Viana do Castelo; Agriculture and folk fair in Viseu.*

1st half of September: *Dona da Nazaré festival in Nazaré.*

2nd half of September: *Folk festivals throughout the Algarve.*

October 12-13: *Fatima pilgrimage.*

There are also recurring fairs and market days, discussed in detail in the section on the relevant city.

Lisbon: *Tues. and Sat. "Thieves" Market.*

Cascais: *Wed. and Sat. market.*

Sintra: *2nd and 4th Sat. of the month market.*

Malveira: *Thurs. market.*

Barçelos: *Thurs. market.*

Estremoz: *Sat. market.*

Lagos: *1st Sat. of the month market.*

Loulé: *Sat. market.*

PASSPORTS

The single requirement for the average tourist entering Portugal is a valid passport. No shots are needed. A visa is necessary only when stays will exceed 60 days or for employment in the country. Visa applications and information are available at the nearest Portuguese consulate.

U. S. State Department passport agencies are located in Boston, Chicago, Honolulu, Houston, Los Angeles, Miami, New Orleans, New York, Philadelphia, San Francisco, Seattle, Stamford (CT) and Washington D.C. Federal or state courthouses also issue passports, as do many post offices.

Unexpired passports can be renewed by mail, providing that no more than 12 years have elapsed since the date of issue and the applicant was at least 18 years old at the time. Enclose the expired passport and two full-face photographs, two inches square, taken against a light background. Sign them on the back center, include a completed application form, obtainable at one of the offices listed above, and a check or money order payable to the U.S. Passport Service for $55. Processing can take up to a month during the busy summer season, after which you will receive your old passport, cancelled, and a new one valid for ten years.

First passports and replacements for those already expired must be applied for in person at one of the offices listed above. Usually the process involves two trips, one to submit the forms and a second to pick up the passport. Proof of citizenship must be presented, which can be a previous passport, a copy of a birth certificate, or a Certificate of Naturalization or of Citizenship. A proof of identity is also required that may be satisfied by a driver's license or other ID with your picture on it. Credit cards are not sufficient proof of identity, but a friend of two-years' standing is. You will also need two full-faced photographs, two inches square, taken against a light background. The fee is $55 for adults eighteen and over, or $30 for minors. A $10 charge is added if you apply in person. It can take up to six weeks for a first-time passport to arrive.

Though not promised, renewals in person usually can be managed on an emergency basis in 24 hours at State Department offices. Frequent travelers may request double the normal 24 pages at no extra cost.

CAR RENTAL

Car rentals may be done either on the spot or by making arrangements before departure. Because comparison shopping is easier from home, it's the way to find the best prices. Reserving in advance from the U.S. also saves about 17 percent, locks in the lowest rate and prevents the possibility of no cars being available. All major U.S. rental companies have Portuguese subsidiaries. Your travel agent can make arrangements, or you can call directly for prices or reservations. Lesser known companies act as brokers to find the least expensive European rental for the type of car you specify. Generally, Auto Europe will have the lowest prices. Note that Portuguese rentals will bill at 17 percent more than the price charged because of the IVA tax.

Although the legal driving age in Portugal is 18, most Portuguese rental agencies require a driver to be at least 23. Check in advance. Estimate about $350 per week for a compact car with air-conditioning and automatic transmission, or about half that price for a smaller, manual-drive car without AC.

Avis: ☎ 800-331-2112.
Auto Europe: ☎ 800-223-5555, or ☎ 800-458-9503 in Canada.
Budget: ☎ 800-472-3325.
Dollar (**EuroDollar** in Europe): ☎ 800-800-6000.
Europe by Car: ☎ 800-223-1516 or ☎ 212-581-3040.
Foremost Euro-Car: ☎ 800-423-3111, in California ☎ 800-272-3299.
Hertz: ☎ 800-654-3001.
Kemwel: ☎ 800-678-0678.

National: ☎ 800-227-3876

In addition, most rental companies and major airlines offer fly/drive packages that bundle airfare and car rental prices, frequently with very attractive savings.

Renting a car for foreign use raises the issue of insurance. Rentals generally include collision insurance in the price—though this should be checked when comparing costs—but often leave a deductible of $1000 or more for damage to the rented car. In such a case, a collision damage waiver should be considered even though it can add $10 per day or more to the rental fee. Note that insurance policies covering damage waivers on rental cars at home generally do not apply to overseas rentals, although rentals charged to credit cards often do.

A major credit card is sufficient for renting any car, but the lack of such plastic makes difficulties, here or there. Some companies will not rent at all to cardless clients; others require substantial deposits or prepaying.

An International Driving Permit is strongly recommended, for it is understood throughout Europe. Branches of the American Automobile Club can supply one. Bring along two passport-sized photos, a valid driver's license and a $5 fee. Incidentally, AAA has reciprocal arrangements with automobile clubs in Portugal that provide similar services for AAA members from the U.S. **Automovel Clube de Portugal** is located at *Rua Rosa Arango 24 in Lisbon* (☎ *01-736-121*).

A good map of Portugal is a necessity when driving, such as Michelin map #440. Old, haphazardly developed cities can be mazes of tiny, one-way streets. If aiming for the center, follow signs saying "*Centro.*"

CUSTOMS ALLOWANCES

Portugal permits visitors to bring with them any items intended for personal use. This can include one carton of cigarettes and one liter of alcohol per adult. Expensive equipment, such as cameras and computers, should be registered with U.S. Customs before leaving to ensure that they are not charged duty on return. A proof of U.S. purchase will also serve.

On your return home, U.S. customs does not charge duty on a resident's first $400 of purchases for personal use or on gifts that accompany the traveler, providing his last allotment was claimed one month or more before. A family is permitted to pool its individual allotments as they wish. One carton of cigarettes is also duty-free for each adult, as are 100 cigars (not Cuban, of course), one liter of alcohol, and one bottle of perfume (if sold in the U.S, more otherwise). The next $1000 of personal merchandise or gifts is taxed at 10 percent. Above that amount, rates vary. Save receipts in case of questions. Antiques with proof from the seller that they are over 100 years old are duty-free, as are one-of-a-kind artworks.

Packages mailed home, unless clearly marked "American Goods Returned" or "Unsolicited Gift under $50" will be assessed a duty when delivered. In either case, they do not count as part of your customs allotment.

CLOTHES AND PACKING

Most travelers bring more clothes than they need or use, and since living out of a suitcase means having to carry it, the best advice about packing is that less is better.

Remember that, except at resorts, you'll be visiting cities and towns where most people are dressed for work. You might be on vacation, but everyone else is heading for the office. Although Portugal is less formal than other European tourist destinations, jackets, shirts and—except in the hottest weather—ties are the norm for men and skirts or dresses are customary for women.

Street clothes tend towards more somber hues than many Americans wear. Yet black, grey and navy—standard for Europeans because they withstand wear—also work well for tourists. Given the lack of one-hour cleaners, a spill on a brightly colored dress or jacket might retire it for the rest of your trip.

A pair—or two, for alternating—of comfortable leather walking shoes is preferable in town to sneakers, which are primarily seen on school children. Use insoles inside to take the battering of medieval cobblestones rather than your uncushioned feet.

For most of the year, raincoats with linings are ideal—single garments that fend off cool, cold or rain. Natural fiber clothing is best year-round—it's lightweight, packs well, and both holds warmth in winter and permits circulation in summer.

Of course at resorts and on holiday or summer weekend trips, Portuguese men and women can be spotted in that universal fashion statement—jeans, polo or tee shirts and sneaks.

Do not be overly concerned about forgetting something. Portugal is a civilized country where almost anything forgotten or lost can be replaced. Still, it's convenient to have things at hand rather than having to search for them in a store. The following can prove useful:

- Small sewing kit
- First aid kit
- Sunglasses
- Travel alarm
- Penknife
- Ziplock bags
- Safety pins
- String
- Sunscreen

Camera film is expensive in Portugal, but bringing your own risks fogging from airport x-rays (despite disclaimers to the contrary).

ACCOMMODATIONS

The best hotels in Portugal can be a special treat, but even lower classes of accommodation will be squeaky-clean and good values. The Portuguese are natural hosts, which your acquaintance with any hotel's staff, from managers through porters and maids, will confirm. In almost every case you will receive more for your hotel dollar than at home.

Because Portugal contains some of the most interesting as well as some of the most quietly elegant hotels in the world, a stay at one can provide a memorable experience—at least the equal of a visit to a special museum or church. With rare exceptions, extraordinary accommodations in Portugal fit into even modest budgets if mixed with money-saving stays at lower-priced hotels. Indeed, Portugal is the only country in Western Europe in which you can fashion an itinerary to include stays at deluxe hotels exclusively and expect costs to average about $150 per night for two people.

How you decide to combine and trade off stays at more and less expensive lodgings are personal and budgetary choices made easier in Portugal by the range of comfortable rooms is available in every price-range, even the least expensive.

Pousadas are one way Portugal eases your decisions. Copying the lead of Spain's paradors, Portugal instituted a system of state-run hotels in 1940 and called them pousadas—for the Portuguese word for "place of repose." The system accomplished two goals. It attracted tourists (both within and outside of Portugal) to beautiful though undeveloped areas of the country while simultaneously making use of an oversupply of historic buildings whose private owners could not afford their upkeep.

By preserving irreplaceable structures while offering tourists a chance to eat and sleep in the palaces, castles and convents in which they could ordinarily only sightsee, the program has become a huge success. So much so that entirely new hotels have been built in scenic areas that lack historic buildings. The system overall is a mix of old and new, sometimes providing magnificence such as the Santa Marinha in Guimarães with its grand azulejoed halls or Santa Maria in Estremoz with its palatial elegance; other times offering views instead of splendor, such as the mountain panorama of São Laurenço in Manteigas, the sea and rugged coast seen from the do Infanto in Sagres or the quiet lagoon vista of the do Ria in Aveiro. Thirty-seven pousadas now dot the country, about half of which either partially or entirely are incorporated in historic monuments.

Because pousadas are deservedly popular, reservations are always wise. Some are so small—such as the 10-room castle at Obidos—that reservations become essential, at least five months in advance for the summer season. In recent years, the parent company ENATUR, has consistently upgraded the level of cuisine in pousada dining rooms. Rather than the bland international selections of past years, pousadas now feature regional specialties, providing visitors with a convenient way to sample local delicacies, often in stunning surroundings.

Though never inexpensive, pousadas tend to be less costly than other hotels of similar ratings because they are managed by a quasi-government corporation. A night's pampered stay in a 15th-century castle for about $100 strikes most people as a bargain indeed. A list and brochure is available from the **National Tourist Office of Portugal** (☎ *212-354-4403, FAX 212-764-6137*) or from the booking agent for the U.S. and Canada, **Marketing Ahead, Inc.** at *433 Fifth Avenue, New York, New York, 10016* (☎ *212-686-9213, FAX 212-686-0271*). Reservations can be made directly through: **Empresa Nacional de Turismo** (ENATUR), *Avenida Santa Joana a Princese, 10A, Lisbon 1700* (☎ *01-848-1221; FAX 01-80-5846*), Marketing Ahead, or any travel agent.

Turismo de Habitaçãos provide another sort of special tourist accommodation in which the government, through tax breaks, encourages owners of country manor houses to open their homes to guests. As no real quality control exists, offerings range from virtual palaces with magnificent grounds to rather ordinary country houses, although prices generally provide an accurate clue to the luxury level. A more serious difficulty with the scheme is that no central registry exists to provide information about availability and prices, let alone pictures of the houses. One can start by contacting the National Tourist Office of Portugal (☎ 212-354-4403; FAX 212-764-6137) for lists and prices. More offerings are available from **Tourism do Espaço Rural**, *Avenue António Augusto de Aguiar 86, 1099 Lisboa* (☎ 01-575-015) for manor houses in the center and south of the country, or **TURIHAB**, *Praça da República, 4990 Ponte de Lima* (☎ 058-942-239; FAX 058-741-444) for houses in the north. Bookings can be made through **Alta Tours** in San Francisco (☎ 1-800-338-4191; FAX 415-434-2684).

Not all the wonderful hotels in Portugal are pousadas or manor houses. We would as soon stay at the Palácio de Setais in Sintra as at any hotel in the world; the São Paulo near Évora will match many pousadas and outdo most; the Infante de Sagres in Porto is an utterly distinguished hotel; and several special little hotels in the Algarve are more elegant than the beautifully situated pousada in Sagres. So, even if the idea of a pousada seems wonderful and it should—check our descriptions of an area's other hotels before automatically booking into the closest pousada.

An easy way to assure yourself of a grand hotel experience is to put yourself in the hands of the Hotels de Charme. This year-old association groups 16 of Portugal's best hotels country-wide and takes the guesswork out of choosing accommodations—every member hotel boasts extraordinary service, luxury, history or location. The association is comprised of some exceptional pousadas, some traditionally grand institutions and some wonderful small hotels. In fact, 11 are on our list below of the best hotels in the country. Call or write Luis Reis, Director of the Hotels de Charme, at Praça do Príncipe Real, *11-r/c, 1200 Lisbon, Portugal* (☎ 351-1-347-0146; FAX 315-1-346-1976).

Advanced booking is always recommended if a stay at a particular hotel is important to you. It is essential for small hotels, most Turismo do Habitaçãos, and accommodations in the Algarve in summer. All good rooms in the Algarve for July and August are booked by the end of February. The crush of summer tourists is intense; don't attempt to go without a reservation. At other times and places it is perfectly possible to drive into a town and find acceptable lodgings—although not always your first choice. If nothing seems available, the local tourist office should be able to help.

Here's a list of Portugal's most extraordinary hotels (all in the expensive range):

The Best

Palácio Seteis, Sintra
Pousada Santa Marinha, Guimarães
Hotel São Paulo, Redondo near Évora
Pousada Santa Maria, Estremoz
Infante de Sagres, Porto
Hotel da Lapa, Lisbon
Hotel Albatroz, Cascais

Special

Vila Joya, Albufeira (Algarve)
Buçaco Palace, Buçaco, near Coimbra (but see the description)
Vilalara, Armanção de Pêra (Algarve)
Pousade de Palmela, Palmela
Pousada do Infante, Sagres (Algarve)
Pousada de São Lourenço, Manteigas (but see the description)

HOTEL TYPES

Whether pousada, manor house or just familiar hotel, virtually every public accommodation in Portugal is officially rated by a system of stars based on measurable features such as the percentage of rooms with private baths, air conditioning, etc., though not rated for such immeasurable qualities as comfort, efficiency and friendliness of service. Thus, although official ratings provide a rough guide to price and quality, they should be read in conjunction with our descriptions and alternative star-system (see, *Introduction*, "Ratings.") The government also separates accommodations into hotels, pensions and inns. A white and blue metal plaque outside an establishment will indicate its official rating and type—"H" a hotel, "P" a *pensõe*, and "E" an inn (*estalgem*). These distinctions make a difference to government bureaucrats, but no difference to travelers since all provide maid service, have reception desks and offer at least breakfast—services expected in any hotel. Relatively new on the scene are apartment-hotels, which combine the comfort of apartment living with the services and daily booking convenience of a hotel. We indicate their extra feature with an "A."

First-class and luxury hotels all include TVs in every room and those universal minibars. Hotels of this class also provide a concierge, that is, a kind of ombudsman to help with almost any problem. He (or she) can locate tickets for almost any event, confirm travel arrangements or make them, recommend restaurants and shops, and deal with emergencies. Their knowledge and expertise are always impressive and make otherwise difficult chores effortless. The concierge should be tipped according to the number of requests you've made but at least 100$00 each. Second-class hotels include TVs, but not always minibars. TVs are unusual in hotels ranked lower than second-class.

Our reviews will take note of extras such as TVs or air conditioning only if they are unusual amenities for a hotel of a given class.

Don't hesitate to ask to see a room before you register. Europeans do it all the time, and hotels don't consider it an unusual request. Desk staff at most Portuguese hotels speak English. If not, a single room is *um quarto individual*, a double is *um quarto duplo*. *Con banho* means with bath. Few double rooms contain a large bed for two (*de casal*), though one can request one. A single rooms will cost about 75 percent of the price of a double. The quoted price for a room in Portugal includes taxes and a surcharge for service.

Free accommodations are sometimes possible to arrange through a system of international house exchanges. Although your lodging is in a fixed location, you can use it as a base for side trips; and sometimes cars are even included in the exchange. Such trades are easiest to arrange when your own home is located in or near an area of potential interest to foreign visitors. Of course the odds of an agreeable arrangement improve when inquiries are initiated well in advance. Several companies specialize in helping with such arrangements for a fee of $35-$60:

International Home Exchange/Intervac U.S., *Box 590504, San Francisco, CA 94119* (☎ *415-435-3497*).

Vacation Exchange Club, *Box 650, Key West, FL 330441* (☎ *800-638-3841*).

For those willing to base in the same spot, an option is renting an apartment or villa. For a fee the following firms will help you find one:

At Home Abroad, *405 East 56th St., Suite 6H, New York City, NY 10022* (☎ *212-421-9165*).

Interhome, Inc., *124 Little Falls Rd., Fairfield, NJ 07004* (☎ *201-882-6864*).

Overseas Connection, *31 North Harbor Dr., Sag Harbor, NY 11963* (☎ *616-725-9308*).

Rent a Home International, *7200 34th Ave. NW, Seatle, WA 98117* (☎ *212-421-9165*).

Vacation Home Rentals Worldwide, *235 Kinsington Ave., Norwood, NJ 07648* (☎ *201-767-9393*).

Villas International, *605 Market St., Suite 510, San Francisco, CA 94105* (☎ *415-281-0910*).

MONEY

Portuguese money is called *escudos*. Each escudo is divided into 100 centavos, and prices are written in the form 0$00, with escudos to the left and centavos to the right of the dollar sign. (Actually, this is rather silly, because centavos barely circulate.) Coins exist in denominations of 5, 10, 20, 50, 100 and 200 escudos, with banknotes of 500, 1000, 5000 and 10,000 escudos. Both 100 and 200 escudo coins have brass centers and can be detected by a thickness greater than coins of lesser value, which vary in worth simply with size. Currently, one U.S. dollar buys 170$00 escudos, which is to say that 100 escudos is worth about 60 cents, but this is certain to fluctuate. Incidentally, the "Travel" section of the Sunday *New York Times* quotes rates for buying and selling escudos in this country, not in Portugal. These figures are low by 20 percent compared with what you will find when you arrive.

Safety argues for carrying traveler's checks, rather than cash because they can be replaced if lost or stolen. Of course, traveler's checks usually cost one percent or more to buy, but not always. Currently American Express Traveler's Cheques are free at American Automobile Association offices for members, and Thomas Cook Traveler's Cheques are free when travel arrangements are made through that agency. Inquire about other such promotions. If possible, exchange money at banks or official *cambios*—hotels, restaurants and stores give less favorable rates. Fees are charged for each transaction which argues against numerous small exchanges, but try not to convert more money than you will use, since converting back to dollars involves another exchange premium.

For some reason exchange rates are terrible in the U.S., so do not buy foreign money before your trip. At most, purchase a small amount for the first day. Although escudos are hard to find in the U.S., **Thomas Cook Currency Service** in *New York at 630 Fifth Ave.*

(212 757-6915) is an exception. Yet this should not be necessary, for the cambio in Lisbon's airport greets every international flight.

Popular credit cards are widely accepted in Portugal, although Visa and MasterCard are recognized more generally than Amex or Diners cards. Most restaurants, except very inexpensive ones, accept them, as do all first class and luxury hotels, except for La Réserve in the Algarve. Incidentally, payment by credit card ensures the best possible exchange rate.

Cash machines are becoming popular in Portugal, but, although discussions underway to link the Portuguese Multibanco system with the American CIRRUS and PLUS systems may succeed soon, at present they do not accept American bankcards. Advance arrangements with your bank to procure a special PIN number however will allow you the use of Visa and Mastercharge to receive cash advances on Portuguese ATMs.

TRAVEL IN PORTUGAL

Getting from one city to another in Portugal is no more difficult than getting around anywhere else. You have the same choices—car, plane, train or bus.

BY CAR

When you drive in Portugal you will discover at first hand how good U.S. roads are. Portuguese national highways are two-lane roads that would be considered fair country roads in the U.S. The only true, six-lane highways are the main Lisbon to Porto road, an extension that crosses this main artery to link Aveiro part way to Viseu, and one that covers about two-thirds of the Algarve.

The quality of a Portuguese road and whether it is multilaned is indicated by its letter designation. "A" followed by a number, as in A-1, means an *auto-estrada*, a well-paved six-lane highway. A1 linking Lisbon to Porto charges tolls (*peajes*) and stiff ones at that (e.g., $15 for the 200 mile trip from Lisbon to Porto). The rest are free. These roads will also have an "E" designation, since the major arteries in Europe are being systematically numbered throughout the European Economic Community. Although the tolls may be high, there are compensating savings in time and gas, for these highways do not pass through low-speed-limit villages. Nor do they incorporate much scenery or offer chance views of quaint villages and people.

"N" followed by an Arabic numeral means a highway, a national road (*Estrada Nacional*). These are one lane in each direction over most of their length and pass through towns and villages where speeds must be reduced in half or more. The number of digits in its designation tells how minor a road is. That is, N203 would be a worse road than N10, acceptably paved but slower going, generally with more curves. The problem with roads that are one lane in each direction becomes painfully obvious when one gets stuck behind a slow-moving vehicle. To help with such problems these roads become three-laned up steep hills, allowing an opportunity to pass.

All roads are well marked with self-explanatory international highway symbols. Except for *auto estradas*, Portuguese roads present astonishing hairpin curves, especially over the mountains, but sometimes on perfectly flat terrain. These curves are usually well marked, and preceded by signs indicating an appropriate speed, but stay alert.

Speed limits are 120 kilometers per hour (75 mph) on *auto estradas*, 100 (62 mph) on national highways, 90 (55 mph) on other roads, unless otherwise marked, and 60 (38 mph) or 40k in towns. Note that distances and speed limits in Portugal will be measured in kilometers, approximately five-eighths of a mile. When passing, leave the left blinker on throughout your time in the passing lane, then signal right to return. Truckers will let you know when it is safe to pass them by signaling with their right blinker, but be careful not to confuse this with a truck's impending righthand turn.

You will quickly discover that the Portuguese are helpful and sweet in the normal conduct of their lives and business, but, as a psychologist friend reminds us, everyone needs some outlet for hostilities. The Portuguese find theirs in driving. Technically they are perfectly capable drivers, and in general they steer fine machines, but they seem compelled to pass any vehicle that has the affrontary to be ahead of them and will do so under risky circumstances. Need we add that they seem unaware of the speed limits? No wonder the Portuguese consistently earn the highest average accident rate in Europe. You must drive defensively in Portugal. Be aware that a car may pass you at any moment, even if the road behind seemed empty a moment before. Most of all, be alert at the rise of every hill for some maniac driving in your lane straight toward you.

Portuguese authorities are serious about punishing drunken drivers, so don't take chances. And seatbelts must be worn outside of towns.

Gas is a major expense in Europe, costing three times what it does in the U.S. Posted gas prices are initially deceptive for Americans because they are quoted by the liter (slightly more than a quart), as opposed to per gallon. "Fill her up" is *Encha o dispósito, por favor*, non-leaded is *sem chumbo*. Stations are plentiful and remain open late throughout the country.

BY PLANE

Portugal is so small that flying from one part of the country to another is rarely called for, nor does one see much of the color of the country from 10,000 feet in the air. The only time a flight need be considered is if traveling from Lisbon to Porto without stopping in between or when traveling directly to the Algarve during the summer traffic congestion.

Both Porto and Faro in the Algarve are served by Portugalia commuter flights from Lisbon that leave hourly, require no advance reservations and cost under $100.

BY TRAIN

Trains beat planes when the distance is 200 miles or less, which is to say almost everywhere in Portugal, because train stations are located downtown while airports are not. Trains also follow more scenic routes than cars and buses. British-built to the finest wide-gauge standards 75 years ago, the Portuguese national rail system (CP) can today be called adequate at best since service was drastically cut in 1990 and equipment upkeep seems to have stopped at about the same time. Still, there remains a romance about a train ride, and costs generally are very low.

IR trains make fewer stops than **Regional** trains; **IC** trains are faster still because they stop only at large cities. **Serviço Alfas** are the fastest of all, include dining facilities and are first-class only, but command a ticket supplement. They travel from Lisbon to Porto in under three hours for about $40, and to the Algarve in four and a half hours for about $50. There are regular car trains to Porto, and to the Algarve's Faro in summer only, which require advance reservations. Your car must be at the station an hour before departure.

Fares depend on the caliber of train and whether accommodations are first- or second-class. Tickets purchased on the train are levied a hefty fine. So many types of discounts are offered that any tourist paying full fare has simply not asked about them—roundtrips, senior citizens, families, youths, and certain days of the week are all assigned one discount or another. Reservations are always advised.

If planning a substantial amount of train travel, the best buy is a pass allowing unlimited rides during a fixed period. **Eurail** and **In-**

terail passes are valid on Portuguese trains, as well as for the rest of Europe, but for such passes to prove worthwhile a great deal of mileage must be used and, since they provide only first-class travel, they cost more than some alternatives. **Eurail Flexipasses**, issued for fewer train days at lower prices, generally prove more suitable. For those 26 or younger, a **Eurail Youthpass Flexpass** for second-class travel is cheaper still. All Eurail passes must be purchased in the traveller's home country through a travel agent or directly from **Rail Europe** located at *610 Fifth Avenue, New York, NY 10020* (☎ *800-345-1990*).

For train buffs, CP offers a rather expensive ride on a 19th-century train through the northern mountains, complete with train crew dressed in authentic costume. Contact the Portuguese National Tourist Office for dates and other details. Alternatively, several regularly scheduled trains run on narrow gauge rails in the north, chugging slowly through the mountains with every bit as much scenery and romance: the Corgo line from Régula to Vila Real, the Tuy line to Bragança and the Douro line from Porto to Pocinho are all atmospheric, as is the wider-gauge rail from Valença in the extreme north to Porto.

BY BUS

A bus is usually the cheapest form of travel, often beating the cost of trains by about a third, and buses go where trains do not. Each city, village and hamlet contains a depot—addresses will be found in the "Directory" section for each city— and the ticketing procedure is familiar. Pay as you board for a short trip or purchase a ticket in the station for a longer trip. Estimate about $6 per 100 k of ride. Although there is no provision for reservations, arriving early accomplishes the same thing.

The government owned Rodoviára Nacional (RN) covers all but the far north of the country, which is divided up between 50 private companies. Schedules can be obtained at any major depot and at some hotels.

RESTAURANTS

Restaurants in Portugal serve filling meals at about the price of restaurants at home, and if the cost is sometimes slightly greater, the portions will be too. Dining hours are about what we are used to—7pm to 10pm for dinner. The Portuguese delight in eating out generates an abundant supply of restaurants, and, fortunately, few places where bad food is served at too-high prices.

Because the quality of available ingredients is outstanding throughout Portugal, even modest restaurants provide delicious meals. Vegetables are grown for flavor, not for their capacity to survive early picking and travel; humble chicken retains the taste we have all but forgotten; and bread always tastes homemade. With rare exceptions, Portuguese food is of a homey sort—hearty and tasty, generally either stews or plainly-done meat or fish. The flavor will be savory, but, surprising for the country that introduced eastern spices into western cuisine, the seasoning tends toward the bland. Best are fresh fish—especially sardines—that melt your heart as they melt in your mouth, roast chicken, breads to bring out the peasant in anyone, and wines of surprisingly high quality for impressively low prices. At many inexpensive restaurants the price of a meal with wine will hover in the $30 range for a couple.

While decent restaurants proliferate in Portugal, a few special ones stand out as memorable. Some are simple seafood restaurants on the coast that remind us of what truly fresh fish can taste like. Others attempt and succeed at more complex dishes. Our choices for the best restaurants in Portugal include three in Lisbon, two in the Algarve, one near Coimbra, and another in Fátima (near Tomar).

Vila Joya near Albufeira in the Algarve

La Réserve in Santa Bárbara de Nexe (in the Algarve hills behind Faro)

Casa da Comida in Lisbon

Tágide in Lisbon

Conventual in Lisbon

Tia Alice in Fátima

Ramalhão in Montemor-o-velha near Coimbra

All are expensive—in the range of $100 for dinner for two—and worth it. To whet your appetite, see the discussions in the relevant city section.

Although, on average, Portuguese restaurant prices are reasonable, if you want to trim dining costs still further, look for a restaurant specializing in *frango assado* or *churrascera*. Almost any such establishment will serve half of a delectable roast chicken, usually with *piri piri* (hot sauce) on the side and a pile of tasty french fries for about $10 with house wine. Another way is to keep your eyes peeled for stands selling steak sandwiches, *pregos*. There are also abundant pizza places. And all restaurants offer an *ementa do dia* (menu of the day) that provides a full meal at about 75 percent of the cost of ordering separate dishes. Finally, check our city by city restaurant reviews for the best inexpensive dining in the area.

Wine is important to the Portuguese, so the house wine (*vinho da casa*) will generally prove pleasant. Their Sagres beer is eminently palatable.

When the meal is over, *a conta, por favor* will bring the check.

SHOPPING

Ceramics, embroidered rugs, linens, antiques, woven baskets and flea market finds all call to the tourist's wallet in Portugal.

Only the rare traveler can resist bringing ceramics home from Portugal. The pieces are delightful and range from elegant Vista Alegre productions to charming folk pieces. Vista Alegre wares approach the finest French and English bone china, however prices are rigidly controlled by the factory so they are hardly cheaper in Portugal than at home. Purchases are possible at the factory shop outside of **Aveiro** from a grand selection.

Delightful traditional ceramics in different styles and designs are available throughout the country. These include blue on white or polychrome copies of 16th- and 17th-century designs, sold all over but made in **Condeixa** near Coimbra where the supply is greater and prices lower than elsewhere. All are hand-painted and unbelievably inexpensive given the quality of the work. **Caldas da Rainha,** also near Coimbra, is known for darker colors and especially for charming articles in the shape and color of vegetables and fruit. **Barçelos**, in the north, produces red roosters sold throughout the country, but also charming figurines available only locally. Painted glazed tiles, called *azulejos*, can be purchased individually or in the form of lovely scenes composed of separate painted tiles. The best buys on the scenes are in the **Algarve**.

Arraiolos, near Èvora, is the source of Portugal's needlepoint carpets; **Portalegre**, near Mavão in the Alentejo, produces fine hand-made embroidered tapestries. Several **Lisbon** shops carry beautiful lacework and embroidered linens from Madeira, although cheaper Chinese copies have demoted these from the buys they once were. Nonembroidered linens, however, are outstanding in **Lisbon**, both for quality and price.

Woven baskets, brass and copperware are produced mainly in **Loulé** in the Algarve. Befitting the largest producer of cork in the world, cork objects of every sort imaginable are sold throughout the **Alentejo**, the center of Portugal.

Lisbon is known for filigree goldwork and fine silver. Leatherwork of decent quality and reasonable prices is sold in the capital as well. Antique furniture and especially antique ceramics are available in many areas, but the largest concentration of fine antique shops collects in the Bairro Alto in **Lisbon**. Of course, old port wines proliferate in **Porto**, but are sold even in supermarkets throughout the rest of the country.

The most entertaining shopping is to be found in local flea markets, such as the **Feira de Ladra** (Thieves' Market) in Lisbon. Among the tons of dross, including cheap pots and pans and cheap shirts, hide the folk pieces of undiscovered artisans. In our discussions of each city, we'll tell you what to look for there and where to find it.

One unfamiliar complication to shopping in Europe is the Value Added Tax, added to purchase prices to equalize disparities among the countries of the European Economic Community and the larger world. In Portugal the IVA (as it is known there) is a whopping 17 percent, with 33 percent for luxuries. Needless to say, such a supplement can turn a bargain into a bad buy. You will discover, however, that many small shops do not bother to collect the tax. Larger, more established emporia will collect it, but for expensive items costing $500 or more foreigners are entitled to a refund if they carry the article home. Refund forms will be supplied by most stores or obtained at airport refund offices. Receipts and forms must be stamped by a customs official, who will ask to view the article. It takes a month or more for the refund to arrive or be reflected on your charge card.

TIPPING

Hotels and restaurants in Portugal automatically add an amount for service to the bill. Still, 10 percent is a normal tip for underpaid wait-people in Portuguese restaurants. At hotels above third-class levels, it's gracious to leave some bills from the hotel payment for the staff, and $1 per night in the room for the maid. The concierge, doorman and porter should be tipped for specific services, say the equivalent of 100 escudos per bag carried, or a like amount for hailing a cab. In an elegant restaurant where a captain orchestrates the meal and a sommelier presents the wine, the captain should receive 5 percent of the total bill, the waiter 10 percent and sommelier the equivalent of $2.

Cab drivers expect a 10 percent tip. Ushers are not tipped, but washroom attendants should be given 50$00 or so. Anyone who opens a church or lights it merits 200 escudos. A guide expects 100 escudos per person. Hairdressers generally receive a 10 percent tip.

TIME ZONE AND OFFICIAL HOURS

Clocks in Portugal run six hours ahead of Eastern Standard Time in the U.S. Daylight saving time is observed in Portugal from the last week in March to the end of September, so that during October the difference from E.S.T. declines to five hours.

Shops in Portugal open at 9:30 or 10am, close for lunch from 1pm until 3pm, then remain open until 7pm every weekday. The few **department** stores stay open through the lunch period, while shopping centers may remain open until midnight. **Businesses** follow the regime of shops except for closing earlier, at 5:30 or 6pm. **Banks** open at 8:30am and do business until 3 or 3:30pm. Some large branches open Saturday until 1pm, as do most shops. **Museums** generally unlock their doors at 10am, close for lunch from 12:30 until 2pm, then reopen until 5pm. A few in big cities remain open through the lunch hour. Most are open every day except Monday. **Restaurants** open from 1 until 4 for lunch, then from 7 until 10pm, sometimes until 11pm, for dinner. Of course, there are always exceptions.

The afternoon closings of shops, businesses, museums and monuments in Mediterranean countries, including Portugal, can be an avid tourist's bane, leaving him with nothing to do except eat, rest or sit at an outdoor bar during midday. August, the vacation month for most Portuguese, can further complicate a tourist's itinerary. Some museums and many restaurants distant from the resort areas close altogether or curtail their hours. The only rule is to check before setting out.

MAIL, TELEPHONES, ELECTRICITY AND MEASUREMENT

Post offices (*Correios*), usually located in the center of towns, open from 8 (or 9am) until 12:30, and again from 2:30 until 6pm, Monday through Friday. Main offices in large cities remain open during the lunch hours and reopen Saturday morning. The mail is generally reliable, taking about a week or ten days for delivery to the U.S. Airmail postage to the U.S. costs 130$00. Letters addressed to you can be sent to any Portuguese city along with the words *Lista do Correios*. Such mail will be held until you pick it up. Sometimes it will be filed, however, by your first name rather than your last, so ask for both names. There is a 20$00 charge. American Express will also hold mail free for a month for card-holders or for those who carry Amex Traveler's Cheques.

Portugal's telephone system is adequate, if sometimes slow. A local call costs 20 escudos from a phone booth. To dial another province preface the area code with 0. The 0 is unnecessary when calling from abroad. To call Portugal from the U.S. or Canada, dial 011 for international calls, 351 for Portugal, then the local Portuguese telephone number. To call the U.S. or Canada from Portugal, dial 097, for overseas, then 1 for the U.S. or Canada, plus the local area code and number. Calls from Portugal to the U.S. cost about twice what they do in the other direction, but if you use any of the international calling cards offered by U.S. long-distance telephone companies, the cost drops to about the same as calling from home. To call the U.S. using an **AT&T** calling card dial *05-017-1233* for an American operator; using an **MCI** calling card dial *05-018-120-33*.

Using credit calling cards precludes the exorbitant bills that hotels often charge for long-distance calls. The alternative of using public pay phones means dealing with Portuguese-speaking operators. At telephone or post offices, however, an agent will place the call for you.

Portuguese measures are metric, as in most of the world. Distance is measured in kilometers, volume in liters, and weight in grams.

Metric	U.S. Standard
1 kilometer	5/8 mile
1 liter	1.02 quarts
100 grams	3.5 ounces
100 kilometers	62 miles
4 liters	1.1 gallons
1 kilogram	2.2 pounds

Electricity in Portugal runs at 220 or 240 volts, compared with 110 in the U.S. Unless an appliance has a 220 volt switch, it is likely to burn out in an Iberian socket when run at twice its power. Inexpensive converters are readily available in the U.S. Make sure you also buy an adapter for European sockets, which accept thin tubes, rather than our wider prongs.

Temperatures are given in degrees centigrade rather than Fahrenheit

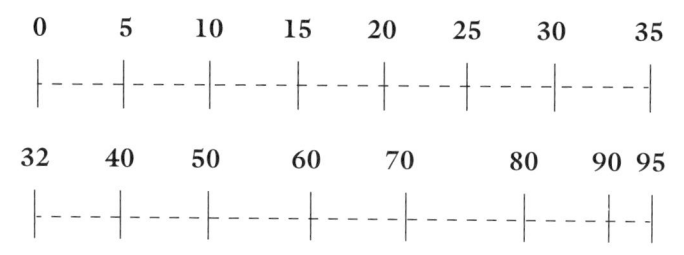

```
  0      5     10     15     20     25     30     35
  |------|------|------|------|------|------|------|

 32     40    50     60     70            80    90 95
  |------|------|------|------|-------------|------|--|
```

SPORTS

GOLF

Golfing is splendid in Portugal. Her scenic courses certainly are the best in continental Europe. Links proliferate in the Algarve and around Estoril outside of Lisbon. Figure about $40 for green fees unless the links are connected with your hotel and included in the price, and about $12 to rent clubs. Choice courses would be:

Estoril Palácio Golf Club, 1 k inland from Estoril, is Portugal's oldest. The par is 69, placing a premium on accuracy, but the greens are less challenging. Mimosa and eucalyptus scent the air in these foothills of the Sintra mountains. The course is associated with the Estoril Palácio Hotel, which provides tennis too. For information: *Estoril Golf Club (Av. da República, Estoril, Portugal 2765;* ☎ *01-268-0176).*

Estoril Sol Golf, on N6-8, the Estoril to Sintra Road, provides nine holes, but numerous tee combinations in a pine forest carpeted by lush grass. Two holes are played virtually out of a lake and another incorporates a thirty-foot cliff. For information: *Lagoa Azul (Linhó, Portugal;* ☎ *01-293-2461).*

Campo de Palmares near Lagos in the Algarve is a championship course that hosted qualifying rounds for the 1985 World Cup. The course ranges over sand dunes and wooded hills. So magnificent is the view from the 17th tee that it is difficult to concentrate on one's game. For information: *Campo de Palmares (Lagos, Portugal 8600;* ☎ *082-762-953).*

Quinta do Lago in the Algarve at Almancil offers four nine-hole challenges ranked with the best in Europe, to combine in any number of 18-hole courses. Although not the most scenic in Portugal, the area offers many other activities in addition to golf. For information: *Campo de Golf da Quinta do Lago (Almansil, Portugal 8100;* ☎ *089-396-002).*

Vilamoura Golf Club near Amansil is so stunning with its ocean views and pines that it can distract from the golf. Now with a total of 63 holes, its par 73 course is one of the most challenging in the country. The club forms part of a huge resort development offering every imaginable sport. For information: *Club Golf de Vilamoura (Vilamoura, Portugal 8100;* ☎ *089-321-652).*

Clube de Golf do Vale de Lobo, also near Amancil, presents not one, but three different 18-hole courses. All are challenging in different ways and located in a self-contained resort that adds fine tennis. For information: *Clube de Golf do Vale de Lobo (Vale de Lobo, Portugal 8100;* ☎ *089-363-939).*

TENNIS

Tennis is not a national sport, but the Portuguese, being good hosts, provide ample numbers of courts for visitors. Most of the courts are hard-surfaced, with occasional synthetic grass and rare clay alternatives. Many first-class resort hotels will have facilities. Courts rent for about $10 per hour. Some choices in the sunny Algarve are:

Roger Taylor Tennis Clinic, in Vale de Lobo, provides tennis camps as well as individual play. The 12 hard courts include six lit at night. Located in the Vale de Lobo resort complex, golf, swimming and squash are also available. Arrangements may be made through *Roger Taylor Tennis Holidays, Ltd. (85 High Street, Wimbledon, London SW 19, 5EG, England;* ☎ *089 947 97 27).*

Vilamouratênis in Vilamoura opened in 1991 in a big way with 13 hard courts, some clay courts and several stadium courts. This resort offers everything for the tennis lover. For information: *Vilamouratênis (Vilamoura, Portugal 8125;* ☎ *089 321 25).*

HIKING

Portugal offers abundant wilderness for hikers, including two special national parks and one magical forest. Peneda-Geres national park, located in the center of the extreme north of Portugal is perhaps Europe's finest, incorporating all that a nature lover could ask. It combines luxurious forests, steep scenic hills, rushing rivers, archaeological sites, and is the haunt of boars, deer, eagles and wild horses. The Serra da Estrela is Portugal's highest mountain range, reaching over a mile in the air, 2000 feet above the tree line. Only scattered villages dot the course of the 40-mile long range, allowing plenty of space to commune with nature. Most magical of all, although not far from the madding crowd, is the Serra da Sintra. True, one cannot get lost for long without coming upon one's fellows, but for a day or an afternoon, there is a dark magic about these forests that affects almost everyone including Lord Byron, who passed a summer here and called it the finest spot in Europe.

STUDENT TRAVEL

Any student or person of student age or inclination seeking information on student travel should contact the **Council on International Educational Exchange** (**CIEE**). In addition to its headquarters at *205 East 42nd Street, New York, NY 10017* (☎ *212-661-1414*), branches are located near many large universities. The organization stores reams of information on work, study, education and travel programs for students. In addition it issues **Youth International Educational Exchange Cards** and **International Student Identity Cards**, each of which discount transportation costs and museum entries, and provide many other benefits. To apply for a card, send two passport-type pictures, a proof of birth date, and a $10 dollar fee. You need to be under 26, but not necessarily a matriculating student. The same organization can provide information about work abroad and provide books on the procedure if you dial extension 1130.

To gain entry to youth hostels' cheap dormitory accommodations an International Youth Hostel Federation membership card is necessary, although you need not be young. A first-time card good for one year costs $25, less for teens and those 55 or older. It is available to anyone—student or not— through **American Youth Hostels**, *Box 37613, Washington, DC 20013* (☎ *202-783-6161*).

In Lisbon run to the Turismo Social e Juvenil in the Truicoop Building on Rua Pascual do Melo for information about the special facilities and discounts available to the young and young at heart.

For study abroad, contact **Experiment in International Living**, *Kipling Road, Box E10, Brattleboro, VT 05301* (☎ *802-257-7751*). If you'd like to read up on the subject first, it is covered extensively in two books—*Academic Year Abroad* and *Vacation Study Abroad*, both published by **The Institute of International Education** *(809 UN Plaza, New York, NY 10017;* ☎ *212-883-8200)*.

Young people, 26 or under, are eligible for an especially inexpensive version of the Eurail Pass called Eurail Youthpass. See the discussion under "Travel by Train" above. The young will find living in Portugal cheaper than any other European country and much cheaper than being on their own at home. The only pleasure they might miss is the convenience of hitchhiking. Europeans generally show little consideration for those attempting the joys of the road.

FEMALE TRAVELERS

The situation for women in Portugal has changed dramatically since the repressive Salazar days when bare arms and short skirts were criminal offenses. Topless sunbathers on Portuguese beaches now constitute a non-event. In fact, sexual harassment probably is less of a problem in Portugal today than at home, but that is not to say that female travelers will experience no problems.

Naturally, problems are greater for women alone. But other than in large cities or in resorts used to foreigners, a woman will experience only shy curious looks, nothing more. It is only where tourists are a common event that some men become emboldened. The situation is complicated when ignorance of the language means not knowing how to respond; still, the cold shoulder is understood internationally. Rape is infinitely rarer in Portugal than in the U.S., (when it occurs it makes the front page of national newspapers) but harassment can be unpleasant and can be avoided by taking the same precautions as at home.

CRIME

When Portugal was a dictatorship under Salazar, the crime rates approached zero. Today, true democracy brings its worldwide accompaniments—drugs and thievery. Compounding the change in politics, Portugal admitted almost a million emigrants from Africa in the 1980s, some of whom now form an underclass. Crime does exist today, but at about the levels of the U.S. a quarter of a century ago. That is to say, it is unlikely to be noticed by any visitor. You will feel completely secure, but that can cause rash behavior; for safety's sake, take the same precautions as at home.

More often than any of us would like, unfortunately, criminals prey upon tourists. As travelers we carry expensive cameras and probably more money than local citizens on their way to work, making ourselves good marks for pickpockets and purse snatchers. Just as we can spot a foreign visitor by his attire and attitude, so do we become easily identifiable in a foreign land. The question is not how to stop robberies, for we cannot solve that one at home, but how to decrease the odds that we will be chosen.

Thieves congregate where the tourists are, which means that Lisbon and the Algarve experience the highest crime rates; the rest of the country is remarkably safe. In those two locales be a more difficult mark by carrying as little as possible, thus leaving your hands free, and by holding pocketbooks or cameras close to the body. Most important, stay alert, especially at night, and avoid deserted areas. Such precautions should be sufficient.

Cars pose another problem. Windshield stickers indicate a rented car that may contain valuable luggage or cameras. In the Algarve or Lisbon, empty your car before parking, or, at least be scrupulous in hiding visible signs that luggage waits inside.

Thefts in hotels are extremely rare, and violent crimes are a tiny percentage of U.S. figures. Statistics show that traveling in Portugal is far safer than traveling in the U.S. Be alert, take reasonable precautions, and no untoward event should interrupt your trip.

The emergency police number anywhere in Portugal is *115*.

BOOKS

Nothing enhances a trip more than understanding what you see, so read all you can before you go and while in Portugal. A very selected list follows of informative books that can give the visitor a sense of the variety of the country.

Written by a writer of Portuguese extraction, John Dos Passos, *The Portugal Story: Three Centuries of Exploration and Discovery*, is a readable history.

Another good history that covers a wider scope is H.A. Livermore, *A New History of Portugal*.

The best art surveys are unfortunately not so readable. There is George Kubler and Martin Soria, *Art and Architecture in Spain and Portugal and Their American Dominions: 1500 to 1800*, and R.C. Smith, *The Art of Portugal 1500-1800*.

For pictures and readable text, try Alice and Helmut Whol, *Portugal*.

The best on wines is Jan Read's little book, *The Wines of Portugal*.

Marion Kaplan writes most entertainingly and anecdotally, about the history and people of Portugal in *Portugal of the Portuguese*.

For discussions of food and recipes, the best is Jean Anderson, *The Food of Portugal*.

Hans Christian Andersen's *A Visit to Portugal, 1866* remains interesting and enjoyable.

THE LAND AND THE PEOPLE

Children

As countries go, Portugal is tiny—about the size of the state of Indiana. It occupies the western fifth of the Iberian Peninsula in a rectangle 137 miles wide (at its widest) by 350 miles long—the length of it could be driven in one very long day. Yet Portugal manages to fit great geographic variety into its small package. Wildflowers, forests, mountains and rolling hills contrast with the generally more ascetic landscape of its larger neighbor Spain.

The northern third of the country consists of tall mountains lining a narrow coast of hills. Mountains continue all the way south in a thin line that follows the eastern border to form a natural barrier against a neighbor that threatened through most of Portugal's history. About a third of the way down, at the latitude of Coimbra, the aptly named Serra da Estrelas (Mountaines of the Stars) rise in a series of precipitous peaks to Portugal's highest elevations, averaging almost a mile in height—with one peak thrusting above the tree-line 6532 feet in the air. Then, at the southern end of Portugal, mountains fan again across the width of the country to create a climactic barrier for the Algarve beaches, sealing out the cold and damp to produce their balmy weather.

Between the Minho River that forms the northern border with Spain and the parallel Douro river 200 k south of it, the land rises in mountainous granite covered in dense vegetation. This plateau is known as Trás-o-Montes, beyond the mountains, where Portugal remains least changed from ways of life several hundred years old. Small villages nestle in warmer valleys where lyre-horned oxen still pull wooden wheeled carts. The Douro River slices through this granite plateau on its way to the sea. Along its banks grow the grapes for port wine, before shipping west down the river to the natural port aptly named Porto, and the sea.

South of the Douro dense mountains continue in the east, but the land drops low along the coast. Castles and fortified walls in the mountains still defend villages from the Spanish as they have for eight centuries, while sheep graze and farmers raise grapes for the fine wines of the Dão region. Rice paddies on the low western coast stretch for uninterrupted miles, protected from sea salt by dunes anchored by pines.

The substantial river Tagus (*Tejo*, in Portuguese) cuts the country roughly in half lengthwise, widening into an estuary beside Lisbon before it empties into the sea. Its alluvial banks raise olives, grapes, vegetables and wheat. Rice grows on spreading plains where horses and black fighting bulls roam. On the coast, both north and south of Lisbon, cliffs surround sand beaches and quaint fishing villages.

South of the Tejo spreads the vast department of the Alentejo, comprising almost a third of Portugal. Flat and poorly watered by nature, artificial irrigation has transformed it into the granary of Portugal. Geological flatness is broken by clustered stands of eucalyptus and cork oaks—one-third of all those in the world—from which Portugal sells more cork products than any other country. Away from these isolated forests, rolling hills cradle houses dazzlingly whitewashed, topped by orange tile roofs that grow ornate, eccentric chimneys. Occasional windmills turn in the breeze.

The southernmost part of Portugal is called the Algarve, named from the Arabic word for west, for this was the western extremity of the Moors' territory. The ancient volcanos of the Monchique mountains separate the Algarve from southern Alentejo, and are tall enough to constitute a barrier that allows the Atlantic waters to temper weather and produce a semitropical climate for the coast. Vegetation is lush with camellias and citrus groves. Rolling sand beaches and sandbars on the eastern coast turn to spectacular cliffs on the west framing smaller beaches. The Algarve ends in the sheer windswept bluffs of Capo de São Vicente, the southwestern extremity of Europe. Not surprisingly, tourists have discovered the mild climate, beautiful beaches, and crystal ocean and arrive in droves each summer.

By virtue of occupying the southwest corner of Europe, Portugal owns 520 miles of coastline, most of it in beaches bathed by a mild climate thanks to the warmth of the Atlantic's Gulf Stream that passes by. These tepid waters produce mild winters but summer temperatures of over 100 on the coast, though subdued by continual sea breezes, while the inland plains of the Alentejo grow stifling and airless in midsummer when temperatures of 120 are not unknown. Hence, palms and agave can be spotted almost anywhere along the coastline, except in the extreme north.

Indeed, Portugal appears to be a Mediterranean country, akin in climate and flora to Italy or Greece, despite the fact that this sea never touches its shore. More than France and even Spain, Portugal exudes that warm languor the Mediterranean calls to mind.

Forests of eucalyptus trees cover the rolling hills that spread inland from the coast to perfume the air with their distinctive scent. Mature eucalyptus are not familiar round-leafed versions but bear narrow leaves spreading away from thin trunks. They are grown for timber, for they mature without care in quick time. To the south the hills are covered by huge stands of evergreens and by corpses of low spreading trees of green-grey leaves—the famed cork oaks of Portugal, evident by the naked strips of trunk where the product has been removed.

Olives are cultivated throughout the country, but especially in the north, sufficient to make Portugal the sixth largest producer of that oil in the world. Except for their trunks being covered by bark, these low spreading, green-grey leafed trees might be mistaken for corks. The north is also the place to see the low-lying vines of wine grapes, most often in small plots rather than in spreading vineyards.

Profusions of bougainvillea, camellias and geraniums, along with orange, lemon, fig and carob trees makes the southern Algarve tropical in feeling. Where the land spreads on the eastern side of the Algarve sugarcane and rice grow.

The last census in 1981 gave Portugal a population of just under 10 million, including the islands of Madeira and the Azores. Today the population probably approaches 11 million. This number incorporates almost a million expatriates from the African colonies of Angola, Guinea and Mozambique who returned in 1975 to raise the country's population by 10 percent in six months. Portugal boasts only one metropolis—Lisbon, in which one Portuguese in 10 lives, and one additional true city—Porto, with a population of a third of a million. In Portugal a family of visiting tourists can raise the population of towns by percentage points.

Despite major efforts to industrialize, Portugal remains a country of farmers. One in five still earns his living from the land. Sixty percent of Portugal's industry concentrates in Lisbon and Porto, leaving the majority of the country either empty or in farms. Fishing remains a major industry, with sailors routinely harvesting catches off the Newfoundland Banks in North America as they have since time immemorial, as well as from local seas. Portugal is one of the largest producers of tungsten and mines significant quantities of uranium, but must import all its petroleum, and has built the usual ugly refineries in Porto and Sines.

Despite great economic advances through the 70s and 80s, Portugal is a poor country with many of its people still living without indoor plumbing. None of this will be apparent to the visitor, however, as he passes scattered old houses of indeterminate age and inescapable charm throughout the countryside, separated by gleaming new buildings owned by Portuguese who left the country to find their fortune and proclaimed it in their houses when they returned. In particular, most visitors from the U.S. are impressed by all the new cars they see in Portugal, lending a feeling of prosperity. When we asked a native how so many can afford them, he answered in perfect English "Have you ever heard of leasing?"

The Portuguese tend to be short and stocky, but seldom fat, with black hair and olive complexions. Yet there are occasionally taller, blue-eyed and sometimes red-haired Portuguese, probably the descendants of some Viking raider or passing northern European crusader from long ago.

As a people the Portuguese seem surprisingly quiet, always dignified in contrast to southern Spanish exuberance. A streak of melancholy lies just beneath the surface, and emerges in their music. An outstanding trait is an extreme courtesy—*Disculpe*, "excuse me" is likely to be the Portuguese word most often heard. We have never seen a Portuguese display anger (other than when he changes into another creature behind the wheel of his car), despite chaotic and frustrating circumstances, usually when dealing with uncomprehending tourists. The Portuguese go far out of their way to help anyone who asks for help, seem to love all dogs and children, and may be the sweetest people on earth.

But even the Portuguese realize full well that their language seems Greek to everyone else, and strive hard to understand a visitor in his own language. All have studied a second language, and the chances are that anyone under forty will understand English, for this has been taught in the schools for the past three decades. Older citizens will know some French. All Portuguese understand Spanish, though can become offended when a Spaniard speaks to them in his language while a guest in their land. Centuries of conflict are not readily forgotten. Of course they do not take the same offense when a tourist tries Spanish should English fail.

The Portuguese work so hard that it is difficult to find one at rest, outside of old men in local bars in the evening. In particular the women in the countryside seem always on the move, often with heavy bundles on their heads. Both sexes show the depths of their feelings when they cry during *fado* songs. But most outstanding is their simple sincerity, plain on their faces and in their eyes.

WHERE TO GO

The walls of Óbidos

Portugal is small enough to make all the major sights accessible in a two-week whirlwind tour. But why hurry if you don't have to? Whether traveling by car, bus or train, take time to stroll around, lie on the beach, and feast at leisure in one of the fine restaurants. Three weeks (or even four) would approach an ideal—sight-seeing combined with relaxation. Because fine beaches can be reached from anywhere in Portugal, travelers are permitted great flexibility in their plans.

THE TOP SIGHTS

As befits the capital, **Lisbon** ★★★★ is the most visited city in Portugal. While other European cities may be more grand, Lisbon has a character of its own, with enough sights to merit a week's visit.

And surrounding Lisbon are elegant beaches at **Estoril** and **Cascais** ★ fourteen miles west; lovely **Queluz Palace** ★★★ six miles northwest; the magical forests of **Sintra** ★★★★, described below, ten miles further along; the imposing monastery of **Mafra** ★★★ standing nearly twenty miles to the north; and **Batalha** ★★★★★, described next, close enough for a day-trip.

Portugal's most elegant spot is certainly the monastery at **Batalha** ★★★★★. For the 100 years it took to build this edifice, doting kings spared no expense to create a marvel. The ensemble of buildings comprises an unusually harmonious whole, graceful in every detail. Batalha is an easy day-trip from Lisbon that should not be missed. A visit can also include the nearby village of **Alcobaça** ★★★ which has a fine monastery of its own containing the romantic tombs of Inês de Castro and her lover, Pedro the Cruel. **Fátima** ★ of the miracles is ten miles east, and the grand beach of **Nazaré** ★★ lies less than twenty miles west.

Évora ★★★★, due east of Lisbon, does not offer any one must-see sight, but a number of attractions contained in the lovely package of the town itself, and more wait nearby. Because Évora is located at Lisbon's latitude, a traveler could leave the capital early one morning, see Évora's sights before dark, stay the night in Estremoz at one of Portugal's most elegant pousadas, and spend the next day touring the fortified towns of **Estremoz** ★, **Evoramonte** ★, and lovely **Elvas** ★★.

If you have an extra day, you could also include the embroidered carpets of **Arraiolos**, the antiques of **Borba** and the village of **Marvão** (discussed below).

Although **Marvão** ★★ is a fortified hilltop village of which Portugal possesses scores similar in age and condition, it differs by being the most charming. A stroll through the village provides enough mood for a half-day's sojourn. Marvão is a breeze of a day-trip from Évora, or can be reached directly from Lisbon in five hours by car.

Sintra ★★★★, a mere 30 k from Lisbon, ranks near the top of any tourist's list both for its enchanted mountain site, and for its three castles—one from the 10th-, another from the 16th-, and one unbelievable fantasy from the 19th-century. Spend the night and there's time to add the baroque royal palace of **Queluz** ★★.

Tomar ★★★, 80 miles north of Lisbon, holds one special sight. Its monastery consists of a mysterious 12th-century church of the Knights Templar, graced by sublime cloisters. What makes a visit even more appealing is proximity to **Almourol** ★★—Portugal's most romantic castle—sitting, as in a fairy tale, on the waters of the Tejo river. And less than half an hour away is the pilgrimage site of **Fátima ★**.

Coimbra ★★★ is the major city on the road from Lisbon to Porto and offers plenty to do both in the city and around it. Coimbra contains the old buildings of Portugal's first university, a fine museum, and several interesting churches tumbling down a steep hill. **Condeixa ★**, 11 miles south, sells lovely ceramics at good prices and retains Roman ruins on its outskirts at **Conimbriga**. Twenty-five miles west is the resort of **Figueira da Foz ★**, with the Vista Alegre china factory and shop on its outskirts.

Because of its one perfect square, travel to **Viseu ★★**, 60 miles further north. A stately cathedral stands on one side, a fine museum on another, and a perfect Portuguese baroque church graces the opposite end. If only the space between them were not a parking lot! A trip to Viseu can also be combined with **Guarda ★**, a village situated in the center of a score of medieval fortified hilltop villages, each more atmospheric than the next.

Porto ★★, is a city that still feels and looks like a 19th century town. For its attractive buildings and vivacity, it seems a kind of Portuguese Paris. Yes, there is port wine to be tasted, and plenty of it.

Braga ★, 50 kilometers of expressway north of Porto, is a city of baroque churches, parks and—at Bom Jesus—a flight of stairs that must be seen to be believed. By backtracking 12 miles one reaches **Guimarães ★★★**, site of the country's oldest surviving castle where the first King of Portugal was born. Plus, there is a dramatic renaissance palace and the most magnificent of all the pousadas, the grand Santa Marinha.

From Porto or Braga, **Bragança ★★** is an exquisitely scenic 120 mile trip. Its old churches stand in lonely isolation behind mountains in an almost forgotten area of the country—a glimpse of an older way of life.

BEACHES

Portugal's southern extremity, the **Algarve ★★★**, consists of 200 k of the finest beaches in Europe. The water is an unpolluted blue-green; beaches are the finest white sand; and cliffs behind form exquisite rock formations and picture-postcard coves. Such perfection naturally attracts hordes of sunseekers, yet the Algarve's prices are surprisingly low—generally lower than the less entrancing resorts along Spain's coast. Best of all, there remain areas at both ends of the

Algarve that the crowds have not yet discovered. The Algarve is an easy day's travel from either Lisbon or Évora.

Fine beaches are also available near **Setubal** within an hour's drive south of Lisbon. There are elegant resorts only a half hour west of Lisbon at **Estoril** ★, with a casino, and at neighboring **Cascais** ★. Further north, near Batalha is the famous beach of **Nazaré** ★★, exciting, but crowded during the summer. About 20 miles west of Coimbra stretch long lovely beaches at **Figueira da Foz** ★. Half-way between Coimbra and Porto, less than 100 k west of Viseu, is the beach town of **Aveiro** ★★, situated on a huge lagoon and divided by canals. But perhaps the most dramatic beaches in the country are cuts in the cliffs that line the western coast south of the refinery town of Sines, lining most of the way to the Algarve. Their virtue and vice is that they are so far undiscovered, for that means accommodations are simple at best. We describe them in the Algarve chapter.

CASTLES

No country in the world retains more castles of great age than Portugal. Here even a castle glutton can sate his appetite.

Let's start with the oldest, none of which retain anything but ruins inside but are truly magical spectacles from a distance.

On the highest land in **Leiria**, 80 miles north of Lisbon, stands a fortified castle still commanding the plains that was erected early in the 12th century by Afonso Henriques, the first king of Portugal. It is worth a drive when visiting nearby Batalha. In **Guimarães**, north of Porto, soar reconstructed 11th-century towers of the first castle of Portugal, where the parents of Afonso Anriques lived and in which he was born, to make it the cradle of the country. But the most magical castle of all is **Almourol**, perfectly situated on an island in the Tagus River, near Tomar. Built by the Knights Templar, this is the one castle lovers fantasize about.

After expelling the Moors, Portugal was still not secure. She had neighboring Spain to worry about, and so, during the 13th century, she built a series of fortresses along the border. Twenty or so still ring the town of **Guarda**, 85 miles east of Coimbra. These were never palaces, but stout redouts built to withstand sieges. Today their strong walls, generally with nothing inside them, allow the imagination to man the barricades. **Monsanto**, north of Évora, is probably the most dramatic.

More modern fortresses, that is to say 17th century, include the extensive "Vauban" style walls of Almeida, near **Guarda**, and Elvas, near **Évora**, that spread for miles. These are more than just massive walls to keep unwanted visitors out, but designs for enticing the enemy into cross fires.

For pure fun visit the "cute" little fort, *fortaleza*, on the **Cape of São Vincente** in the Algarve.

The palaces are something else again. Most impressive is the National Palace at **Sintra**, 200 years in the making, and unrestored. The restored Palace of the Dukes of Bragança, in **Guimarães** north of Porto, is a splendid 15th-century structure with elegant fittings. The palace at **Queluz**, near Lisbon, delicate and lovely, is a fitting contrast to the baroque munificence of the palace at **Mafra**. Try to include Pena Palace, also at **Sintra**, on your itinerary. Here the adjective "Victorian" takes on new meaning.

Passing the night in a castle or palace is even more enjoyable than just looking. The pousada of Rainha Santa Isabel in **Estremoz** is built inside the former grand palace. Pousada do Castilo in **Óbidos** provides a more rustic, medieval castle feel. Pousada Castelo de **Alvito**, 85 miles from Lisbon near Beja in the Alentejo, is housed in a 15th-century Gothic fortress.

And while a monastery is not a palace, some are splendid enough to make the distinction academic. The grandest is Santa Marinha pousada in **Guimarães**. More intimate and older (14th-century) is the privately owned Hotel Convento de São Paulo, near **Évora**. The dining room of Pousada de **Palmela** is the former rectory of a 15th-century monastery, high on a hill.

Even if you don't stay in a palace, it is possible to eat in one. The restaurant in **Lisbon**'s Castelo São Jorge is run by the pousada people, who also serve meals in the kitchen of **Queluz** Palace overlooking gardens, 20 miles from Lisbon. Last, the little fort, *fortaleza*, on the **São Vincente cape** in the western Algarve presents meals in a fortress setting.

CHARMING VILLAGES

Outside of a few cities and resort areas, Portugal consists of nothing but countryside dotted with charming villages. Of course some of these villages are more charming than others, but those on the tourist circuit may well be peopled by more gawkers than natives. For example, **Óbidos**, lost in time, charms everyone with its steep tiny streets and hilltop castle, and is a favorite of the tourists. You will not be alone there. **Marvão**, in the northern Alentejo, sites granite houses amid granite boulders for a unique picturesqueness, but you will not be alone there either. **Sintra** is deservedly famous as well, but provides enough surrounding forests to swallow up the touring throngs.

Our picks for the most picturesque place to visit would be **Buçaco** and **Sintra** forests on a quiet day;17th-century **Amarante,** near Porto, peacefully overlooking the Tâmega on any day; and always **Bragança**, lost in time behind the Trâs-o-Montes in the north.

ITINERARIES

The five itineraries that follow offer different tastes of Portugal in trips of five to 11 days. They comprise sight-seeing and travel through the countryside, but do not include stops at the beach. In particular, none incorporates a stay at any of the truly beautiful beaches of the Algarve, which are pleasant all year and provide fresh fish even when the air is too cool for swimming. Given that beaches line the west and south of the country and Portugal is narrow west to east, at almost any time during a trip one can break away to the ocean. The best beaches, those of the Algarve, are readily combined either with a visit to Lisbon or Évora. For example, in the "Lisbon, Évora, Marvão and Tomar" or "The Best of Portugal" itinerary, instead of travelling to Évora on day 4, you can head south to the Algarve instead. After sufficient sun and sand, one can continue to Évora and rejoin the itinerary.

LISBON, 5 days

This tour covers the highlights of Lisbon and leaves time for shopping and strolling.

Day 1: Travel to Lisbon and settle into a hotel.

Day 2: Castello de São Jorge, the Alfama, the Cathedral and the Rossio.

Day 3: São Roque, Igreja do Carmo, shopping in the Chiado, and a visit to the Calouste Gulbenkian museum. If time allows, add the Estufa Fria in the Parque Eduardo VI.

Day 4: The Belém Tower, Hieronymite monastery, Carriage Museum, and Museum of Popular Art (all located in the suburb of Belém, 3 k from the center), stopping en route at the Museu Nacional de Arte Antiga.

Day 5: Departure.

LISBON AND ITS ENVIRONS, 7 days

This trip adds the elegance of Batalha and enchantment of Sintra to the best of Lisbon.

DAY 1: Travel to Lisbon and settle into a hotel.

DAY 2: Castello de São Jorge, the Alfama, the Cathedral and the Rossio.

DAY 3: The Belém Tower, Hieronymite monastery, Carriage Museum, and Museum of Popular Art, stopping en route at the Museu Nacional de Arte Antiga.

DAY 4: São Roque, Igreja do Carmo, shopping in the Chiado, and a visit to the Calouste Gulbenkian museum. If time allows, add the Estufa Fria in the Parque Eduardo VI.

DAY 5: Travel to Batalha for the monastery, visiting Alcobaça on the way.

DAY 6: Travel to Sintra for its palaces, visiting Queluz on the way.

DAY 7: Departure.

LISBON, ÉVORA, MARVÃO AND TOMAR, 7 days

DAY 1: Travel to Lisbon and settle into a hotel.

DAY 2: Castello de São Jorge, the Alfama, the Cathedral and the Rossio.

DAY 3: The Belém Tower, Hieronymite monastery, Carriage Museum, and Museum of Popular Art, stopping en route at the Museu Nacional de Arte Antiga.

DAY 4: Travel to Évora and settle into a hotel; Roman temple; Cathedral and mansions.

DAY 5: Travel to Tomar, visiting Elvas and Marvão on the way; settle into a hotel.

DAY 6: Convent of Christ; return to Lisbon, visiting the castle of Almourol on the way.

DAY 7: Departure.

Note: If additional time is available, instead of returning to Lisbon on day 6, continue to Batalha, visiting Alcobaça on the way. On the return to Lisbon visit Sintra and Queluz, if time allows.

LISBON AND NORTH, 11 days

DAY 1: Travel to Lisbon and settle into a hotel.

DAY 2: Castello de São Jorge, the Alfama, the Cathedral and the Rossio.

DAY 3: The Belém Tower, Hieronymite monastery, Carriage Museum, and Museum of Popular Art, stopping en route at the Museu Nacional de Arte Antiga.

DAY 4: Travel to Batalha, visiting Sintra and Alcobaça on the way; settle into a hotel.

Note: If the Batalha pousada is full, accommodations generally are available in Leiria 10 k north.

DAY 5: Tour the monastery; travel to Tomar, visiting the castle of Almourol on the way; tour the monastery; settle into a hotel.

DAY 6: Travel to Viseu, visiting Coimbra on the way; settle into a hotel.

DAY 7: Cathedral; Museu Grão Vasco; tour of the village; travel to Braga; Cathedral; settle into a hotel.

DAY 8: Museu Biscainhos; tour of the town; Bom Jesus; travel to Porto,; settle into a hotel.

DAY 9: Cathedral; São Francisco; Palácio Bolsa; tour of the port lodges.

Day 10: Travel to Lisbon; settle into a hotel.

DAY 11: Departure.

Note: If an extra day is available, travel to Guimarães instead of Porto; settle into a hotel. On day 9 walk the town, the castle, the Ducal Palace, and travel to Porto, settling into a hotel. Days 9 and 10 above become days 10 and 11.

THE BEST OF PORTUGAL, 11 days

DAY 1: Travel to Lisbon and settle into a hotel.

DAY 2: Castello de São Jorge, the Alfama, the Cathedral and the Rossio.

DAY 3: The Belém Tower, Hieronymite monastery, Carriage Museum, and Museum of Popular Art, stopping en route at the Museu Nacional de Arte Antiga.

DAY 4: Travel to Évora and settle into a hotel; Roman temple; Cathedral and mansions.

DAY 5: Travel to Tomar, visiting Elvas and Marvão on the way; settle into a hotel.

DAY 6: Convent of Christ; travel to Batalha, visiting the castle of Almourol on the way; settle into a hotel.

Note: If the Batalha pousada is full, accommodations are generally available in Leiria 10 k north.

DAY 7: Tour of Batalha monastery; travel to Viseu; settle into a hotel; Cathedral; Museu Grão Vasco; tour of the village.

DAY 8: Travel to Braga; settle into a hotel; Cathedral; Museu Biscainhos; tour of the town; Bom Jesus.

DAY 9: Travel to Sintra, visiting Porto along the way; settle into a hotel.

DAY 10: Visit the three castles of Sintra; travel to Lisbon; settle into a hotel; São Roque, Igreja do Carmo, shopping in the Chiado, and the Calouste Gulbenkian museum, if time and energy allow.

DAY 11: Departure.

HISTORY

The tomb of Inês de Castro in Alcobaça's Santa Maria Monastery

PREHISTORY THROUGH THE BIRTH OF PORTUGAL (9000 B.C.–A.D. 1139)

c. 9000 B.C.	Neolithic occupation.
c. 1300 B.C.	Iberians inhabit the peninsula.
c. 1000 B.C.	Phoenician traders and settlements.
900 B.C.	Celts inhabit Portugal.
206 B.C.	Rome invades Iberia.
138 B.C.	Rome defeats Virianthus.
19 B.C.	Augustus completes the conquest of the peninsula.
c. A.D. 400	German Swabians migrate to Portugal.
A.D. 450–585	Swabians battle the Visigoths.
A.D. 711	Muslims invade from Morocco.

A.D. 1095   Henri of Burgundy is named the Count of Portucale.
A.D. 1139   His son, Afonso Henrique, titles himself King of Portugal.

Evidence reveals that Portugal has been inhabited for at least 100,000 years, and down through "Stone Age" cultures from 10,000 B.C., although nothing so far has been found as splendid as the cave paintings done by their kin in Spain or France. But it is not until the third century B.C. when Romans encountered a people they dubbed Iberians that the historical record of the Portuguese may be said to begin.

We know that the Iberians had settled throughout the peninsula at least seven or eight hundred years before the Romans arrived to name them. It was believed at one time that they migrated from North Africa, for archeologists assumed that all civilizations spread outward from a common Middle-East origin. However, the experts have revised those opinions today, and now maintain that the Iberians were a race indigenous to the Iberian peninsula who borrowed certain ideas and practices from people across the Straits of Gibraltar.

The Romans found a second tribe sharing the peninsula with the Iberians—Celts. Originally they may have migrated south from Brittany, though it is more likely that an indigenous people borrowed burial and building practices from northern neighbors. Origins aside, archaeologists have so much trouble distinguishing Celts from Iberians that they coined the term "Celtiberian" to apply equally to both.

Phoenicians also visited Portugal before the Romans came, searching for tin to manufacture bronze. They established a trading post to conduct their business on a hill overlooking the mouth of the Tejo (Tagus) River, the forerunner of Lisbon. They were followed by people from Carthage, originally a colony of Phoenicia, but afterward the successors of that trading empire. Then the Carthagenians' general Hannibal attacked Rome, and Romans came to the Iberian Peninsula to sever his supply lines.

The Romans confronted various tribes, including a particularly warlike bunch living in the south who called themselves Lusitanians, after which the Romans named a province, "Lusitania"—which became Portugal's original name. Lusitanians were already familiar to the Romans, since many of them had joined Hannibal as mercenaries in his attempt to conquer Rome. So when the Romans returned the favor by invading Portugal, her generals were not surprised by the fierce resistance they encountered. In fact, the Lusitanian chief Virianthus defeated every Roman army sent against him for three decades until three of his own soldiers, bribed by the Romans, murdered him as he slept.

It took Rome longer to subdue Iberia than any of their territories except Britain. They prevailed only after 200 years of struggle in 19 B.C., then set out to civilize the peninsula with roads and buildings. When they left, 400 years later, their Latin language began a slow evolution into Spanish and Portuguese.

Roman decline, by the dawn of the fifth century A.D., allowed German tribes to divide up its Empire. Swabians grabbed latter-day Portugal. Visigoths swept in 40 years later, subduing or evicting all the other German tribes who had arrived in the peninsula ahead of them, except for those Swabians entrenched in Portugal. The Swabians resisted for a century and a half before the Visigoths incorporated them into a Germanic state comprising all Iberia.

The Germans enjoyed their conquest for only two centuries, although long enough to plant their new religion of Christianity ineradicably throughout Iberia. Their undoing was Moroccans from across the Straits of Gibraltar who were eying Portugal and Spain hungrily. In 711 a small army of well disciplined Muslims landed on the Spanish coast, then swept through the peninsula. Only scattered enclaves of Swabians and Visigoths remained unsubdued in the extreme north, but from these confines they launched a stubborn reconquest that persisted for five centuries.

During their half-millennium of control, the Moors, as the Spanish called them, introduced a civilization superior in science and culture to that of any country in Europe. They prized literacy and art, and encouraged the cultivation of olives, rice and citrus fruits. Not only did the Moors build in a sophisticated style, they introduced the techniques of paper-making from China, resurrected the secret of making glass, and taught advanced glazing techniques for pottery. They also brought their tolerance for any "people of the Bible," that is, for Muslim, Christian and Jew alike.

Above all else, this Islamic influence distinguishes Spain and Portugal from other European nations. Sadly, however, Islamic religious tolerance did not take hold with the Christians when they reclaimed Spain and Portugal.

Both native Celtiberians, Visigoths and their Swabian allies bided their time in northern enclaves throughout the Islamic domination of the rest of the peninsula. Their reconquest advanced at a snail's pace until Alfonso VI came to the throne of Spanish Castile. Alfonso managed to capture Toledo as well as Lisbon, raiding as far as the southern coast of Spain. His victories so frightened the Moors that they called on Morocco for assistance. Alfonso, in turn, cried to France for help to beat back the so-called infidel. A division of knights answered the call, including Henri, a younger son of the Count of Burgundy. Henri helped turn the tide and was rewarded with the hand of one of Alfonso's illegitimate daughters, and the dowry of a large northwestern territory, then known as *Portucale*, from which the modern name of the Portugal derives.

Being a feudal state, Portucale was ruled by Henri on behalf of the King of Castile. Ambitious Henri struggled to gain his independence but died young, leaving a three year-old son and a widow under thirty. His wife moved in with a new man, then refused to render feudal homage until compelled by force. His mother's living arrangements had estranged the young son from his mother, so he claimed that his mother's fealty did not include his. In time that son, Afonso Henrique, came of age, assumed his father's title, fought his mother in battle and refused to pay the expected homage until defeated by the next king of Castile. Then another invasion by Moroccans pressed hard on Castile, although Afonso Henrique stemmed their advance in his territory. That success and the continued distraction by the Moors, enabled the Count to title himself Afonso I, the King of Portugal in 1139. From that moment on, with only a 60-year hiatus, Portugal has been independent of Spain, ruled by a royal house bred of a French noble and an illegitimate Spanish princess.

THE BURGUNDIAN DYNASTY (1140–1385)

1107–1185	The span of Afonso Henrique.
1185–1211	Sancho I completes most of the reconquest of Portugal.
1211–1223	Afonso II, the Fat, attacks the power of the Roman Catholic Church.
1223–1248	He is replaced by his brother Sancho II, who wins the last Moorish strongholds.
1248–1279	Afonso III completes the mopping up.
1277–1325	Dinis I revitalizes agriculture and founds the University of Coimbra.
1357–1367	Pedro I, the Cruel, breeds an illegitimate son from whom the succeeding House of Avís descends.
1367–1383	Fernando I rules with the scheming Leonor Telles.
1385	João, Master of the House of Avís, seizes the throne.

Initially Afonso's kingdom consisted only of the northern third of modern Portugal; the rest of the country was controlled by Moors.

But Afonso managed to retake Lisbon, already a major city because of its harbor. He also recaptured much of the south, although some of it was won back. After his death in 1185, his son and grandson carried on the campaign, regaining all of modern-day Portugal except for scattered pockets of Moors, mopped up by 1249. Thus did Portugal become the first unified country in Europe, three and a half centuries before Spain managed the same feat. Afonso Henriques had founded the first of Portugal's dynasties, and illegitimate children of his descendents would found the rest. No wonder Afonso Henriques is known as the father of his country.

The first king after pacification was complete was Dinis I. He granted land to the common farmer, who previously had subsisted as a serf, thus earning the sobriquet *Dom Dinis Labrador* (Lord Dinis the Farmer). In addition, he founded Portugal's first university, originally in Lisbon but later moved to Coimbra, where it remains. During his reign the majority of the great Portuguese fortresses were completed that still guard the eastern border majestically against Spain. He married a woman later canonized as Saint Isabel. With all this he had time to write respectable poetry, and proved to be the best monarch of this Burgundian line.

Two reigns later Pedro I, the Cruel, occupied the throne. He came honestly to his cruelty for his father had ordered the murder of the woman Pedro loved. In revenge, Pedro personally killed the assassins, then buried the body of his beloved in the greatest Portuguese tomb, inside the church of Alcobaça, north of Lisbon. Between murders Pedro found time to sire a number of illegitimate children, one of whom he installed as the abbot of the religio-military order of Avís, an organization something like the Knights Templar. That abbot would one day seize the crown.

Fernando I succeeded Pedro. His early death left his heiress daughter Beatrice under the control of his widow, Leonor Teles. Leonor openly took up residence with a courtier, then married off Beatrice to the King of Castile. Many were upset, both at Leonor's morals and her politics, especially when she sent heralds through the land announcing that the King of Castile ruled Portugal. This prompted the Master of the House of Avís to hie to the palace and kill Leonor's paramour. Then he incited a crowd to proclaim him Regent and, finally, King. Thus did João I, formerly the abbot Master of the Order of Avís, become King of Portugal in 1385, and the founder of its second dynasty.

THE HOUSE OF AVÍS (1385–1588)

1385–1433	The reign of João I.
1394–1460	The life of Prince Henry the Navigator.
1419	Discovery of the Madeira Islands.
1431	Discovery of the Azores.
1487	Bartolemeu Dias rounds the Cape of Good Hope.
1495–1512	The reign of Manuel I, the Fortunate.
1497–1498	Vasco de Gama reaches India.
1500	Pedro Álvares Cabral discovers Brazil.
1519–1521	Magellan circles the globe.
1580	The last king of the Avís line dies.

It was one thing for João to declare himself king, quite another to convince the rival King of Castile to give up his own, rightful claim to Portugal. The two met in a decisive battle on the plains of Abjubarrota north of Lisbon where João miraculously won the day. In celebration he constructed the great monastery at Batalha nearby.

João I was fortunate to marry a special woman, the English Philippa of Lancaster, who raised four exceptional boys. When old enough they joined in an invasion of Ceuta on the Moroccan coast. Most of the credit for their successful conquest was paid to one son—Dom Henrique, who devoted the remainder of his life to encouraging maritime exploration. For which enterprises he became known to the English-speaking world as "Prince Henry the Navigator." He financed expeditions that discovered Madeira and the Azore Islands, still territories of Portugal today, and voyages that made their way down most of the African coast. The reason for these explorations was that European tastes for eastern spices had drained the continent of gold, Henry was pursuing more.

His older brother succeeded their father as King in 1433, but died five years later mourning yet a third brother who had been captured in Morocco. The fourth, and last, brother traveled to the corners of Europe, something seldom done in those times.

Two reigns later, João II received Columbus to hear his plan to sail west to India, but declined to back him when Bartolemeu Dias rounded the Cape of Good Hope, giving Portugal its own route to India.

João II died without heirs, bringing the throne to the son of an adopted child of Prince Henry the Navigator. Manuel I, called the Fortunate, presided over many of the great Portuguese discoveries. Vasco de Gama reached India, establishing Portuguese colonies, and Pedro Cabral discovered Brazil. Portugal grew rich, allowing Manuel to build extensively in a flamboyant style named for himself. Splendid examples survive in the Belém Tower and the Hieronymite Monastery, both in Lisbon's suburb, the Convent at Tomar and parts of the great monastery at Batalha. Intricate designs displayed the exotic flora and fauna discovered by the Portuguese on their explorations.

For a brief moment, tiny Portugal had become the richest country in Europe, thanks to its overseas colonies. It manned outposts throughout Africa, in India and in the Far East from which it imported the spices, tea and coffee that Europeans soon found indispensable. For a time money flowed into Portugal in seemingly inexhaustible supply, like the waves of the sea. But, one by one, these outposts were seized by more powerful nations, or they at least ended Portugal's monopoly. The inexhaustible funds were soon exhausted.

Manuel married the daughter of the Spanish monarchs Ferdinand and Isabella, hoping that his son would grow up to rule a united peninsula, but he paid a terrible price. The Spanish required that Portugal expel her Jews and institute an inquisition like their own, thus ending the history of Jews in Portugal. Manuel's scheme came to nought, as it happened, for his bride died in childbirth and the infant son expired soon after. Manuel remarried, producing an heir who continued the practice of marrying Spanish royalty and sent his sister to marry the new King of Spain. The exchange gave Spain a future claim on the Portuguese throne. The next Portuguese monarch, Don Sebastião, died pursuing chivalric fantasies in Morocco, leaving no heirs. The only remaining Portuguese in line for the throne was his uncle, a cardinal, who died in 1580 childless.

SPAIN AND THE HOUSE OF BRAGANÇA (1580–1910)

1580–1640	Spain rules Portugal.
1640–1656	The Duke of Bragança recaptures the throne.
1706–1750	Architecture flowers under João V.
1750–1777	The indolent José I cedes governing to Prime Minister Pombal.
1755	Lisbon is razed by the Great Earthquake.
1808–1812	The Peninsular War.
1808–1821	The court goes into exile in Brazil.
1825–1836	Civil war erupts over the succession.
1908	King Carlos I and his heir are assassinated.
1910	Manuel II abdicates, ending the monarchy.

As the result of all the Portuguese and Spanish intermarriages, when the last Avís died childless, Felipe II of Spain gained the throne of Portugal. To ensure popular acceptance, he agreed that the Portuguese government would be run by Portuguese. While this arrangement lasted, Spain ruled Portugal, but 60 years later Felipe's descendent appointed Spaniards to government positions, inciting the Portuguese.

The most powerful Portuguese noble of the time was the Duke of Bragança, who the Spanish feared as a rallying point for rebellion. They foolishly tried to seduce him with power by giving him control of the Portuguese army. He turned his troops against the Spanish in 1640, conquering all of Portugal in a matter of weeks. Thus did João IV found the Bragança dynasty, Portugal's last.

Half a century later, after independence had been consolidated, João V came to the throne. Supported by gold and diamonds discovered in the colony of Brazil, he built ostentatiously throughout Portugal. Especially splendid is the palace at Mafra, near Lisbon, and the library at Coimbra, an ideal of its type. His son, José I, lacking all ambition, trifled while a favorite minister named Pombal ruled the country. In 1755, Lisbon was leveled by a cataclysmic earthquake. Pombal stepped forward to resurrect the city, which still bears his orderly stamp.

Since 1386 Portugal had been tied by treaty in a "strong, perpetual and true league of friendship" with England. When Napoléon declared war on England, this treaty embroiled Portugal in a conflict that otherwise did not affect her. Napoléon's troops invaded in 1808 to deprive the English of Portuguese bases, and England sent the future Duke of Wellington the next year to drive them out. By this time there was no royal court in Portugal, for all the blue-bloods had run as fast as silk slippers could take them to ships bound for the colony of Brazil. Wellington chased the French from Portugal by 1811, and from Spain two years later, but the royal court had found the weather and society of Rio de Janero more congenial than Lisbon, and remained abroad for another decade.

By the time a king returned to Portugal in 1821 he found a constitution had been drafted in his absence that rejected absolute rule. Monarchies through most of Europe had been replaced by republics by this time. Voices shouted for political freedoms enjoyed elsewhere, but fell on deaf royal ears in Portugal. In 1908 the King and his heir were assassinated. The King who followed would be the last—an uprising by the navy sent him into exile in 1910, making Portugal at last a republic.

THE REPUBLIC (1910–1976)

1910–1926	Liberal governments replace one another.
1926	A military coup installs General Carmona.
1928	Salazar enters the government.
1932	Salazar becomes Prime Minister.
1968	Incapacitated, Salazar is replaced.
1968–1974	Marcelo Caetano takes over.
1974	The flower revolution brings socialism.
1975	The African colonies are given independence.
1976	A new constitution is enacted.

With no tradition or principles of democratic rule, Portugal had a stormy time with republican government, switching ministers and parties several times a year. At the same time the economic situation deteriorated, exacerbated by the cost of joining the Allies in World War I. The situation had grown desperate by the 1920s. In 1925 three separate military coups were attempted; in 1926 one succeeded.

The military government drafted a civilian economics professor, António de Oliveira Salazar, to solve crushing economic problems. At first he succeeded brilliantly, so much so that he became Prime Minister by 1932. He then promulgated a new constitution in which only his party could field candidates. Salazar had become dictator, in fact, if not in title. He kept Portugal out of World War II, from which it profited greatly, but by the 1960s, economic troubles brewed again. At the same time, independence movements in Portugal's African colonies of Angola, Mozambique and Guinea could not be quelled. During this crisis, Salazar suffered an incapacitating stroke from which he never recovered, and finally died in 1970. His replacement was a party faithful, Marcelo Caetano, who tried to hold on to the African colonies with 50,000 Portuguese troops, a huge drain for the small country. Still it was too few to silence the African independence movements. Before long almost everyone except the government could see that the expensive military enterprise was not working.

It was the army who finally revolted, in 1974, filling the streets of Lisbon with flower-draped tanks in the so-called "Flower Revolution." A realistic general who recognized the futility of military colonization in Africa became president, freeing the colonies as his first official act. Much strife remained before Portugal could settle into orderly political processes—a communist government that had to be ousted by a popular uprising, and governments that changed themselves capriciously. During the 1970s Portugal seemed the most politicized of countries, but now appears set on a moderate socialist course.

ART AND ARCHITECTURE

The nave of the church at Batalha Monastery

Architecture, the outstanding Portuguese art form, is exemplified in both modest homes as well as grand palaces. Every southern village is filled with tiny houses, brilliantly whitewashed, whose doorways and windows wear playful cerulean blue or ochre outlines. In northern towns you will be drawn to that one house in an ordinary row covered in wildly patterned tile. Called *azulejos*, these bold glazed tiles reveal a passionate side of the Portuguese.

The same love of display can be observed in more august edifices, such as palaces and cathedrals. Like other European countries Portugal spared no expense to create grand palaces of the finest materials. She erected splendid cathedrals of imposing size and sumptuous marble and gilt. However, Portuguese grand buildings differ from their French and Italian counterparts in remaining inviting, despite their grandeur. You can (almost) imagine living in a Portuguese palace, for there is an engaging quality about its human scale that survives the beauty.

The best Portuguese architecture adds distinctive touches to styles common throughout Europe. Especially characteristic is the 16th-century Manueline, a lightening formal Gothic frameworks with intricate decoration of flora, fauna and instruments of the sea. And hardly a city or town fails to provide at least one plaster building of pleasing proportions whose details are picked out by darker stone—the Portuguese translation of the Baroque style. Portuguese architecture, like her people, is little known but most appealing.

ROMAN TO ROMANESQUE

Many influences contributed to form the Portuguese aesthetic. First were the Romans, who left a special souvenir of their occupation—a lovely second-century temple in the center of **Évora**. In fact, an entire Roman city has been excavated at **Conimbriga** which contains the largest private houses so far discovered from Roman times, and fine mosaics.

Although the Moors controlled Portugal from the eighth through the 12th century, few of their buildings survive. This does not mean their presence had no lasting impact. Brightly colored tiles in a profusion of patterns (*azulejos*), and elegant paired windows separated by a delicate column (*ajimeses*), are aesthetic remains of the Moors. Even when the Christians took back Portugal, the Moorish influence continued, for quite often Moors were hired to design or decorate Christian buildings. A splendid example of such *mudejar* architecture survives in the 10th century church of **São Pedro de Lourosa** outside **Olivera do Hospital** near Coimbra. Predating the time of towering cathedrals, its low ceiling rests on horseshoe arches atop ancient Roman columns, but its delicate *ajimese* windows are a delight to behold.

The 12th century ushered in the Romanesque architectural style, with an emphasis on barrel-vaulted ceilings, supported by round Roman arches. Portugal possesses two exceptional examples. *Sé Velha* (Old Cathedral) in **Coimbra** was designed in the middle of the 12th century as a fortress church, since it was wartime and Coimbra defended the front. An imposing facade with a single window is topped by triangular merlons to protect rooftop defenders shooting at attackers. Massive piers support the ceiling while Byzantine columns define the galleries (the impressive altar and cloisters, however, were added a century later). This church "in armor" epitomizes medieval times.

In **Tomar** the magnificent *Convento do Cristo* is surrounded by sturdy 12th-century walls. All of the convent is wonderful, but the centerpiece is the oldest part, the 12th-century *Charola*, a 16-sided church of the Knights Templar modeled on the Mosque of the Rock in Jerusalem. Inside, an octagon rises an impressive two stories to a dome resting on the polygon of the building walls.

In **Bragança**, miraculously, a civil building remains from the 12th century—the *Domus Municipalis*, City Hall. Its five sides are pierced by multiple Romanesque round arches, playing against circular medallions that ring the roof. Since the interior of the structure is composed of one huge room, the wonder is how the city government could function.

Castles survive from the hoary times of warfare with the Moors. The oldest is the castle in **Guimarães**, whose 10th century perpendicular walls and towers precede the founding of Portugal. But the most romantic castle is **Almourol**, perfectly situated on an island in the Tagus River near Tomar. Approachable only by boat, it looks as a fairy castle should, with stout walls and soaring towers. High on a hill in **Leiria**, Afonso Henriques, the first King of Portugal, constructed another castle in the early 12th century. Although sticklers point out that the castle was modified later, it looks magical nonetheless.

These early fortresses, designed to protect territory captured from the Moors, were followed by more fortresses once Portugal became embroiled with neighboring Spain. Between the 13th and 14th centuries, Portugal walled itself in with an immense number of fortified keeps. Always placed high to command the surrounding countryside, they generally consisted of a double outer wall enclosing a square massive tower (a *Torre de Menagem*, "Tower of Homage") topped with merlons. A fantastic line of 20 still watch over the Estrela mountains on the eastern border with Spain.

By the 16th century, Portugal was using the ideas of the French architect Vauban to create fortresses in a star shape, whose rays would concentrate attackers into massed targets hard to miss. Dramatic examples survive at **Almeida** in the Estrela mountains and at **Elvas** near Évora. Portugal retains so many imposing castles beckoning from hilltops across the terrain (over 50), that by rights the world should refer to "castles in Portugal," rather to "castles in Spain."

GOTHIC AND MANUELINE

Toward the end of the 12th century, the Gothic design for churches began its sweep through Europe. Round arches became pointed to reach up to ever-higher ribbed vaults resting on thin supports—to give a heavenly upward thrust to buildings.

A typical Gothic church is the 14th-century *Santa Maria de Vitoria* in the monastery at **Batalha**. The monastery was commissioned by João I, the founder of the house of Avís, in gratitude for God's help in defeating the Spanish. Complete with rose window, buttresses, pinnacles and mammoth outside door (unfortunately, except for the central *Christ in Majesty*, only copies of the original statues remain), the plain interior sweeps upward to a forest of ribs in the vaulting. This is flamboyant Gothic at its most harmonious.

The other buildings of the monastery are magnificent Gothic structures as well, though decorated in a new style. As Portugal grew rich from her overseas colonies during the reign of Manuel I, "the Fortunate," an original Portuguese style developed celebrating the sea and the foreign flora and fauna that Portugal had discovered. The term *Manueline* refers not to building plans or structures, but to the decoration, its profusion, and the representation of ropes, knots, ship's masts, palm trees, acorns, leaves and flowers, or even playful designs. Decoration became a wonder of its own, a feature on which light could leap and gambol.

The very first Manueline building is the *Church of Jesus* at **Setúbal**. Inside, huge pillars unexpectedly twist in spirals to support a flamboyantly ribbed ceiling. The *Royal Palace* at **Sintra** shows off Manueline wings against a rich mudjar center. But the *Hieronymite Monastery* at **Belém**, outside Lisbon, represents the culmination of the style. The church interior is a grotto of tapering columns rising to webs of crossed vaulting. The cloister outside is a study-piece of sophisticated decoration.

For a harmonious mix of Gothic structure and Manueline decor see *Santa Maria de Vitoria* monastery at **Batalha**, noted before, whose *Claustro Real* (Royal Cloister) and the *Capelas Imperfeitas* (Unfinished Chapels) employ rich decoration that plays well against a simple Gothic structure. Yet the most famous example of the Manueline is the often-pictured window surround of the nave in the *Convent of Christ* at **Tomar**. Amid the masts, knots, seaweed and chains, a window can barely be discerned. This was the apex of Manueline exuberance.

NEOCLASSIC AND BAROQUE

The Manueline style lasted only 100 years. A neoclassical reaction against extravagant decoration held sway by the late 16th century. *São Vencente de Fora* in **Lisbon** is simple and classically perfect in its coffered ceiling. Lovely *azulejos* (painted tiles) cover the walls, some depicting the capture of Lisbon from the Moors. At **Coimbra** *Santa Clara a Nova* suggests the Parthenon of Rome. Although harmonious, it shows tastes moving again toward profuse adornment.

In the beginning of the 18th century, King João V promised to build a monastery if God would grant him an heir. When God fulfilled his part of the bargain, João erected the sumptuous palace/monastery at **Mafra**. Availing himself of huge deposits of gold and emeralds discovered in Brazil, João lavished millions on this palace. He ordered a German architect, known to the Portuguese as João Frederico Ludovice, to design a Baroque masterpiece whose walls run two miles in circumference, and whose every inch is covered in marble.

But this change of style again was followed by a reaction. After an earthquake leveled much of **Lisbon** in 1755, Prime Minister Pombal took up the challenge of restoring the city. Classically simple open squares and boulevards created a style named after its producer —*Pombaline*—, and survive to this day. The epitome of the style is Lisbon's grand *Praça do Comércio*, elegantly lined with buildings encircling a statue of the King.

By the end of the century, a busier style became dominant, exemplified by the Baroque *Royal Palace* at **Queluz**, ten miles outside Lisbon. Although inspired by Versailles, its feel is different, thanks to a rose stucco facade and the delicacy of an interior decorated for a queen, rather than a king. Yet the crowning achievement of the Portuguese Baroque is a single flight of stairs. But what a flight it is! Built to bring pilgrims to the church of *Bom Jesus*, in the outskirts of **Braga**, this staircase is perfectly harmonious despite splitting into two parts and folding back on itself. One doubts that it has an equal in the world.

In the 19th century, Portugal like many other countries adopted the Victorian style, but did so in an unusual way. In 1836 the queen of Portugal married the Duke of Saxe-Coburg-Gotha, a German. His cousin then married the queen of Belgium, while another cousin, Albert, married Queen Victoria of Britain. Although little known, it was Victoria's cousin-in-law Fernando of Portugal who first built in the style that would become so closely associated with her as to be called "Victorian." For an afternoon of pure fun visit the original Victorian building, the *National Palace of Pena* at **Sintra**. No other decor attempts to mix such varied patterns within a structure combining Moorish elements with vaguely Gothic additions, and oriental motifs.

At the turn of the present century Portugal developed its own version of the art deco style that would also travel through Europe and the Americas. Unfortunately, very little of it has been preserved. What remains may be stumbled upon and enjoyed—as in the case of a little house along the main canal in the city of **Aveiro**.

We moderns have created a new architecture of simple shapes formed of solid materials and glass. Portugal also supports a thriving modern architectural community today. Two especially interesting examples are the post-modern shopping mall called *Amoreis* in **Lisbon**, and the clever modern glass addition to the top of a 19th-century building at the corner of Castilho and Herculano streets.

SCULPTURE

Sculpture in Portugal pops up everywhere, but not everywhere does it attain a high quality. The surprise lies in its delicacy, a refinement stemming from French aesthetics rather than the robustness of her perennial enemy Spain.

Of the early sculpture, everyone's favorite are the tombs of Pedro I and his beloved Inês de Castro in the monastery in **Alcobaça**. The story behind them adds some spice. While still a prince, Pedro fell in love with the Spanish Inês, but his father had her murdered because he mistrusted her Spanish connections. When Pedro came to the throne, he viciously killed her assassins, then moved Inês' body to Alcobaça. There he constructed his own tomb facing hers so she would be his first sight on resurrection. Thus, these tombs lie foot-to-foot in opposite transepts of the church. Inês' effigy, borne by six angels, looks beautiful enough to explain Pedro's passion. The carving of the Last Judgment at Inês' feet is sublime. Pedro's tomb is emblazoned with an intricately designed wheel of fortune at his head and scenes of his last moments at his feet. The tombs are not to be missed.

The place to study the range of Portuguese sculpture is in the *Museu Machado de Castro* in **Coimbra**. The wing to the right on the ground floor traces the art of sculpture up to the Renaissance. Take a close look at an early limestone knight. It may be only two feet high, but the man in heavy armor astride his equally sturdy steed is an imposing sight. In the left wing is displayed the genius of Nicolas

Chanterene. A Walloon by birth, Chanterene's French aesthetic made him the great sculptor of the Manueline period. His *Virgin Reading*, and *Entombment of Eight Personages* provide a foretaste of the exceptional sensitivity he exhibited in such masterpieces as the tombs in **Coimbra's** *Monastery of Santa Cruz* of Afonso Henriques and Sancho I, the first two kings of Portugal. Unretouched, they still exude strength in restful sleep. Chanterene is largely responsible for the imposing west door of the church at the *Hieronymite Monastery* at **Belém** in the outskirts of Lisbon, which includes a statue of Prince Henry the Navigator and effigies of Manuel I and his queen. The overall harmony of conception is remarkable for a time when the placement of statues was dictated by architecture.

Chanterene aside, sculptors are largely unsung in Portugal and attributions to individuals must remain dubious because most pieces were produced in workshops. Here and there, however, an exceptional artist can be picked out. In the late 16th century two Portuguese brothers Gaspar and Domingos Coelho produced a lovely work in **Portalegre**. They placed rectangular panels in an arched frame in the high altar of the *Cathedral* to produce a pleasing classical aberration during a time of gilded excess.

By the 18th century, rococo gilded wood ran riot through churches. *São Francisco* in **Porto** is the outstanding example, although the tiny chapel of *São Lourenço* in the Algarve's **Almansil** will do as well. Both look as if the carvers covered every inch with gilded wood and were not satisfied, so they topped their work with more intricate gilding. And, in **Aveiro**, near Porto, the chancel of the church of *Convento de Jesus das Barrocas*, now a museum, includes a remarkable marble mosaic, only outdone by the astonishing marble chapel of São Baptista in *São Roque* in **Lisbon**.

One last sculpture deserves mention because every visitor to **Lisbon** sees it—the statue of José I in *Terreiro do Paço* square. Construction of the grand monastery at Mafra, discussed above, required so much carving that a school was established to train sculptors. Joaquim Machado de Castro emerged as its most gifted pupil. To ensure that his rebuilding of Lisbon would receive royal commendation, Prime Minister Pombal wanted a statue of his King displayed centrally and called upon de Castro to set this "pretty" king atop a small horse. The bronze work is of the highest order, amazingly intricate in detail. To say the least, the conception does not seem flattering; yet José was apparently pleased to see himself portrayed as a chubby, effete boy on a pony.

PAINTING

Paintings in Portugal, little known or reproduced, come as fresh surprises. Portugal has bred scores of competent artists whose work is admirable, and, in the 15th century it produced one certified genius—Nuno Gonçalves.

To explore the scope of this small nation's painters, proceed directly to the *Museu Nacional de Arte Antiga* in **Lisbon**, which exhibits both native and foreign works. The second floor displays great works by foreign artists, including a fine *Temptation of Saint Antony* by Bosch, the splendid *Saint Jerome* by Dürer, and the magnificent *Twelve Apostles* by Zurbáran. Portuguese paintings take up the third floor.

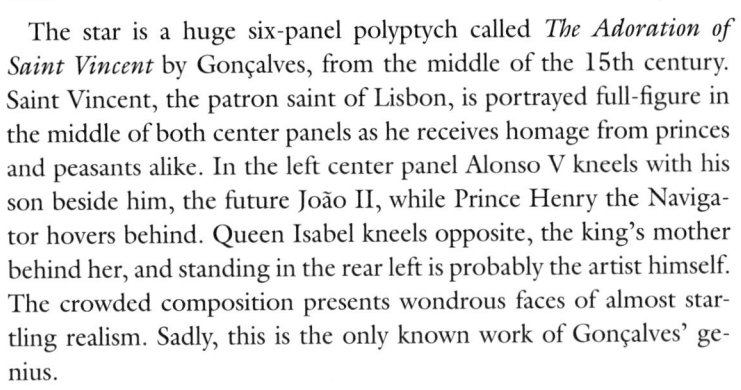

The star is a huge six-panel polyptych called *The Adoration of Saint Vincent* by Gonçalves, from the middle of the 15th century. Saint Vincent, the patron saint of Lisbon, is portrayed full-figure in the middle of both center panels as he receives homage from princes and peasants alike. In the left center panel Alonso V kneels with his son beside him, the future João II, while Prince Henry the Navigator hovers behind. Queen Isabel kneels opposite, the king's mother behind her, and standing in the rear left is probably the artist himself. The crowded composition presents wondrous faces of almost startling realism. Sadly, this is the only known work of Gonçalves' genius.

Gonçalves' talent soars above his contemporaries whose works are displayed on the same floor. In fact, aside from Gonçalves, most 15th-century painting in Portugal slavishly imitated the Flemish artist Jan van Eyck (who visited Portugal in 1428). The exceptions are works by untrained painters who substituted feeling for academic instruction to produce delightful primitives.

By the next century, however, Portugal found its stride. The great Manueline painter Jorge Afonso (died 1540), whose altar painting of *Christ Appearing to the Virgin* in the church *Madre de Deus* in **Lisbon** is a balanced portrayal of peaceful faces. In the ambulatory of the *Templars' church* in **Tomar**, hangs his *Resurrection*, with Christ floating above the city of Lisbon.

Gregorio Lopes (died 1550) is famed for his backgrounds which make intricate frames for unexceptional figures. The *Museu Nacional de Arte Antiga* in **Lisbon** displays his striking *Virgin and Child with Angels*. Another artist, Cristovão Figueiredo (c. 1500- 1555) painted faces as well as anyone, as his *Entombment* in the same museum proves. But perhaps the most haunting painting in the museum is by an unknown artist—*Portrait of a Lady with a Rosary*, worthy of Zurbarán.

"The Grand Vasco," Vasco Fernandes was born in (about 1542) and practiced in Viseu, the best place to see and appreciate his work. *Museu Grão Vasco* holds his masterpieces—five altars from the cathedral. *Saint Peter on his Throne* is a tour de force of spatial illusion, while *Calvary* crowds peasants and German soldiers in an assemblage for the eye to wander over and the mind to contemplate.

Domingos António de Sequeira (1768-1837) was Portugal's Goya, and like Goya an exile because of his liberal political views. He won a gold medal in Paris by besting Delacroix and Gericault, among other luminaries. Much of his finest work is displayed in the *Museu Nacional de Arte Antiga* in **Lisbon**. *Saint Bruno at Prayer*, simple and intense, employs bold foreshortening. *Count do Farrobo* is perceptive and forceful. The *Portrait of the Viscount of Santarem and Family* is complex, subtle in tone, and arresting. His charcoals are luminous. Sequeira indeed was a master, and a fitting culmination for Portuguese art.

In 1955 Portugal received one of the greatest gifts of art that has ever been donated. Calouste Gulbenkian, an Armenian from Turkey, brokered oil for Iraq to become one of the wealthiest men in the world. He was an avid collector who lived his last 15 years in Portugal, and left a museum in **Lisbon** to house his treasures when he died in 1955. The *Calouste Gulbenkian Museum* ranks with the major museums of the world, and constitutes the finest collection amassed by a single person. Oriental carpets and ceramics, European paintings from the 12th through the 20th century and art nouveu Lalique glass all make this a museum to savor.

AZULEJOS

Portugal's most eye-catching contribution to the world of art is the glazed-tile scenes that cover church and palace walls, and even house facades. The Portuguese acquired a taste for such tiles after conquering northern Morocco early in the 15th century. At first, the tiles were imported both from Morocco and Moorish Spain, but by the late 16th century the Portuguese were manufacturing their own versions. The original tiles were drawn in deep blue tones on white, causing them to be named azulejos, from *azul*, meaning "blue."

A national craze for the tiled scenes soon developed, and by the 17th century yellows and greens had joined the original blues. Biblical themes gave way to classical scenes, sylvan pictures and even landscapes. Church, palaces and manor house all were covered in the latest style. This huge demand ultimately led to the mass-production of azulejos, causing an inevitable decline both in quality and panache. As a result, the artform fell out of favor, until recently when the Portuguese learned all over again to appreciate the old tiles, bidding them up in auctions or in antique shops.

Sixteenth and 17th-century originals remain in churches and palaces around the country, adorning walls that would otherwise be bare. Painted tiles may not be high art, but the unsuspecting visitor, coming upon a room or church nave covered with naive scenes in cheery blue, feels the irresistible delight of this Portuguese specialty.

The best of azulejos include the 16th-century tiles from Spain that cover the walls of the *Palácio Real* in **Sintra**. The tiles in the *Church of the Convento dos Lólos* in **Évora** from 1711 were done by António de Oliveira Bernardes, one of the great practitioners of the craft. For the apex of sumptuous tile-art see *São Francisco* in **Porto**. But for a special treat, spend a night or two in the grand azulejo corridors of *Pousada Santa Marinha* in **Guimarães** or in the more intimate halls of the *Hotel Convento São Paulo* near **Évora**. You'll be glad you did.

FOOD AND DRINK

Homemade bread

Visitors will find lots to like about Portuguese food, and much that is familiar. Meals are served at the times we are used to, as opposed to the late hours of neighbor Spain, and encompass expected fish, meat, starches and vegetables. Seafood can be relied on to be wonderful, simple grilled chicken will be a treat and all the breads are guaranteed to be delicious.

Most Portuguese restaurants bill what moderate dining establishment charge at home. All are government rated by a system of graphic "forks" indicating a price, service level and range of offerings, with four and five forks signifying the high end. A plaque outside the establishment displays its rating. Note that this governmental evaluation does not take in to account how good the food tastes, while our stars most assuredly do.

Like the Spanish, the Portuguese sauté in olive oil, rather than Northern European butter, and use garlic generously. (Say *sem alho* to request no garlic.) In general, seasonings lean to the bland (spicy *piri piri* sauce excepted). In most restaurants the simply prepared dishes, broiled meats and fish, will surpass those in sauces.

Breakfast (*pequeno almoço*) is a light meal, consisting of bread or a roll (*bolo*), tea (*chá*) or coffee—*café solo* (black), or *café com leite* (with milk).

A full, three- or four-course, lunch (*almoço*) may be eaten in any restaurant. But for those not so hungry or looking to save escudos, there are other options. Sandwiches and simple platters can be munched in a *cervejaria* (beer hall). *Pastelarias* (pastry shops) also serve sandwiches, fried envelopes of meat or seafood (*rissóis*) and a sort of small pizza, in addition to sweets. And, still for pre-dinner, there are tapas-type bars, called *tascas*, serving delectables after work.

Restaurants open for dinner (*jantar*) at seven and close at ten, later in Lisbon. A *menu do dia* will offer a multicourse meal at a set price lower than the à la carte regular menu. The *Prato do dia* is the daily special, and always fresh.

FOOD

Bread lovers will think they've reached heaven in Portuguese restaurants. Corn bread (*pão de milho*) is not sweet or coarse, but fragrant with the aroma of corn. If you have never had barley bread (*pão do centeio*), here is your chance. *Pão de broa* is a rye bread beyond compare. There are scores of other breads, some regional, some available nationally, and every one is delectable.

The bread will be served before you order your meal along with some side-dishes to nibble. These are part of a cover-charge (*couvert*) imposed by almost all Portuguese restaurants that can range from a dollar, at inexpensive establishments, up to seven or eight dollars at the most expensive.

The menu (*lista* or *ementa*) will start with appetizers, either individual choices, such as *presunto* (proscuitto-type cured ham), or a combination (*acepipes* or *entrada*) that includes more wonderful bread.

Soups (*sopas*) are prepared in a great variety and can be hearty enough for a light meal. The most famous is *caldo verde*, a potato soup containing spiced sausage and lightly cooked kale. Tomato soup is a delicate combination of stock with chunks of tomato, rather than the creamed version produced in the U.S. *Sopa a alentejana* is the most garlicky of garlic soups, usually arriving with an egg poached in the broth. *Sopa de mariscos* is a seafood bisque; *caldeirada*, a seafood chowder. Hearty bean soup is *sopa de feijões*. The Portuguese also make their own version of *gazpacho*, and if it is *a alentejana*, it will have ham or sausage added. For something lighter try *canja de galenha*, chicken and rice soup.

In most restaurants fish (*peixe*) is the best entree choice. Broiled or fried, its freshness makes the taste a revelation. *Sardinhas assadas* are the world's best grilled sardines. Just sprinkle with lemon, or add oil and vinegar. Equally delectable is red mullet (*salmonette*), sea bass (*robalo*) or mackarel (*cavala*). Less assertive, but still tastier than what we are used to, are hake (*pescada*) and sole (*lenguado*). Shellfish are wonderful, although more expensive. If your budget allows, splurge on a big plate of *camarãoes* (large shrimp). Baby clams (*amêijoas*) can be spectacular.

Incredibly, the fish that appears most often on the menu is dried *bacalhau*, or codfish. Why, with some of the best fresh fish in the world do the Portuguese pine for salted cod? If you see it in shops it looks like an animal flattened by a truck. So dry it has to be cut with a saw, it is soaked in water overnight before it can be eaten, which does not exactly infuse it with flavor. Yet the Portuguese love their bacalhau and have found hundreds of ways to prepare it, although just about every recipe is as bland as the fish it incorporates. Baked cod with potatoes could attract only the Portuguese, though *bacalhau dourado*, in a tomato, onion and garlic sauce, or *lisbonense*, in a cream sauce are tastier. *Bacalhau á Bras*, which also goes by a score of other names, is a famous specialty that scrambles the cod with egg and onion to produce a bland but not unpleasant combination. Most people who visit Portugal feel an obligation to try its national dish, but remember there is no requirement that you order it more than once. And spiced codfish cakes (*pastéis de bacalhau*) can be extraordinary.

Another seafood combination is *Cataplana*, clams stewed with sausage and bacon in a sort of double wok. This one is certainly flavorful, though the delicate taste of the clams is overwhelmed by the stronger pork products.

Meat (*carne*) and poultry (*ave*) can be interesting. The flavor of a simple grilled chicken (*frango assado*) is totally unlike the taste of our own mass-produced fowl. Try one *piri-piri*, with a peppery red sauce that kicks. Portuguese pork (*porco*), is famed throughout Europe for it comes from pigs fed on flavorful chestnuts—simply done it can be delicious. Suckling pig (*leitao*) is invariably good. Lamb (*cordiero*) or kid (*cabrito*) cooked over wood is well worth seeking out. Portugal's *chouriço* is a tasty smoked sausage similar to the Spanish chorizo. On the other hand, beef is generally better avoided. It does not form a regular part of the Portuguese diet, so they neither produce nor prepare it well.

In local restaurants, the more ambitious the dish the less successful it generally proves to be. For example, a national specialty is *porco a alentejana*—pork marinated in wine and spices to which clams are added. As with clams cataplana, while the flavor is tasty, the delicate bivalve cannot stand up to the pork and spices.

Portuguese cheese (*queijo*) is delicious, especially milky goat *serra*, mild *Castelo Branco*, and *alentejo*, made from sheep's milk. *Cabreiro* is a goat cheese—*beja* means it is salty, *serpa* that it is sharp. *Flamengo* is similar to Gouda.

Desserts (*sobremesas*) include Europe's universal flan (*flã*); others tend to cloying sweetness. If such is your fancy, try *pudim Molotov*, a moist meringue with caramelized sugar topping. Another unusual dessert is clotted egg yolks swimming in a sugar sauce called *trouxas de ovos*, although it goes by other regional names. *Arroz doce*, rice pudding is generally available and good. Fruit (*fruta*), especially oranges or peaches in season, will generally prove an excellent choice.

Finish your meal with a cup of the best coffee (*cafě*) in the world, as flavorful as, but avoiding the bitter taste of, espresso.

DRINK

Do not judge Portuguese wine by Mateus—those omnipresent flagons of semisparkling, slightly sweet rosé wine—or by Lancers in the pottery bottle. Portugal can do much better, and at prices that will gratify.

In the center of the country, around the city of Viseu, the large production area of **Dão** bottles superior reds and whites in quantity. Here wine is aged for five–seven years in oak to create smooth vintages of great body, similar to burgundy. These are good, modestly priced wines. Allow at least five years for the reds, but make sure the whites are no older than five years or so. The largest bottler is SOGRAPE whose "Grão Vasco" is reliable, but J.M. Da Fonseca's "Terras Altas" ranks a level higher. Pinhel, nearby, produces wines of similar character but with more finesse. A good Pinhel can stand up to a second growth French wine at a third or even a quarter of its price.

Portugal's best wine comes from the coast just north of Lisbon. **Colares**, near Sintra, grows grapes on vines anchored in 20 feet of sand dunes. At the turn of the century this sand warded off the attack of *phylloxera* that destroyed all vines throughout Europe, forcing a grafting of traditional European vines to American roots resistant to the plague. In all of Europe, only the wines of Colares still grow from native root stock. The reds of Colares are dry and rich in tannin. but, unfortunately, the vineyards are rapidly giving way to seaside bungalows, causing supplies to dwindle and prices to rise.

The best whites come from *Buçelas* and *Carcavelos*, whose territory is unfortunately small. They are light, dry, and fruity.

South of Lisbon near the city of *Setubal*, J.M. da Fonseca produces two reds, "Periquita" and "Palmela." There are wine connoisseurs who dismiss "Periquita" as ordinary, but we have found it satisfactorily smooth, if light, and an exceptional buy. "Palmela," a lighter bordeaux type wine despite its burgundy bottle, is also a good value.

East of Lisbon the Alentejo produces a great deal of wine, generally high in alcohol content. For a treat try a fine old *Redondo* red.

Of all the affordable Portuguese wines, the best value in a red is *Esporão* from the Alentejo; and for whites our favorite is a complex young *Bairrada*. The one wine to be avoided at all costs is a *Convento Tomar* white, unless you appreciate the taste of petroleum.

Otherwise, there seldom is cause for concern about Portuguese wine. The house wine (*vinha da casa*) inevitably will be a pleasant accompaniment to a meal, and the pousada chain's house brands are good.

For a different experience, try one of Portugal's **green wines** (*vinhos verdes*). These are grown in the extreme north where cool temperatures shorten the growing season. Grapes are picked young—"green"—hence the name. A chilled white will be light and dry, even astringent; the reds, also chilled, are an acquired taste. *Monção* holds first place among the regions producing such wine.

Portugal's most famous wine is **port**, named for Porto, the place from which it has been shipped since the 18th century. Port is an intensely rich, fortified wine—brandy is added to arrest grape fermentation and raise the alcohol content to 20 percent. At their best and oldest they enter the mouth with a smooth sweet taste, then fill the palate with a most delicate aroma that lasts for savoring. They are best sipped after dinner like a brandy, or before as an aperitif.

A vintage port (on average only one year in five produces such a beverage) is not ready for drinking until ten years old, and becomes special and a characteristic tawny color only as it approaches twenty years. People either love its mix of rich flavors or find them cloying. Graham's is an outstanding bottler. Crusted port is a blend of different years; it is lighter than vintage port and ready for drinking in five years or so. The most accessible of the ports is called tawny; it is matured in casks rather than bottles until it is delicate and pale maroon in color. A twenty year-old tawny will be a treat. Try Fereira for the best. Darker-colored ruby port is a younger, cheaper version. White ports are gaining in popularity; dry and chilled they make a nice aperitif. Taylor, Cockburn, and Sandeman each bottles acceptably dry versions.

The other famous Portuguese fortified wine is **Madeira**, from the island of that name, so rich it suggests a syrup.

Most of the wine in Portugal is sold as *vinho da casa*, house wine, or *vinhos da região*, regional wine, and will be better than it costs. It can be red (*tinto*), white (*branco*), or rose. Beer (*cerveja*) can be excellent; try Sagres brand. Water is *água*.

Boa apetite!

THE SIGHTS OF PORTUGAL

A view along Lisbon's Rua Augusta to the Triumphal Arch of the Praça do Commércio

We divide Portugal into five packages so its sights can be presented conveniently. The idea is that each area be small enough for touring from one base, or two in the case of the larger areas of eastern Portugal and northern Portugal. Of course there is nothing wrong with changing locations for the fun of new surroundings.

Prefacing each of these five chapters is a short historical profile describing one of the major historical periods in Portuguese history to add life to the sights.

The first section is all about **Lisbon** ★★★★ because almost everyone begins there. Next comes the **Environs of Lisbon**, an area that can be visited either as day trips from a Lisbon base or by moving as you go. Some of the finest sights in the country surround Lisbon. The magical forest of *Sintra* ★★★★ holds two palaces not to be missed, another lovely palace stands at *Queluz* ★★★, and a monumental one at *Mafra* ★★★. The finest building in Portugal waits at *Batalha* ★★★★★, the finest sculpture in a lovely church at *Alcobaça* ★★★, and the holiest spot at *Fátima* ★. A quaint castle abides at lovely *Óbidos* ★★. There are elegant beaches at *Estoril and Cascais* ★★, a beautiful one at do *Guincho* ★★, and a lively one at *Nazaré* ★★.

Northern Portugal which starts at cosmopolitan *Coimbra* ★★★ (including ceramic shopping), 125 miles north of Lisbon, reaches up to *Porto* ★★★, almost 200 miles north of Lisbon. It covers the mysterious templar church in *Tomar* ★★★, the magical castle of *Almoral* ★★, baroque *Braga* ★★ with the extraordinary staircase at Bom Jesus, charming *Viseu* ★★ and historic *Guimarães* ★★★. There is scenery in the enchanted forest of *Buçaco* ★★ as well as in the national park of *Peneda Gerés* ★ and behind the mountains at *Bragança* ★★, elegant beaches at *Viana do Castilo* ★★, fine lagoon beaches at *Aveiro* ★★, unspoiled beaches at *Figuera da Foz* ★★.

Eastern Portugal runs from Évora at roughly Lisbon's latitude, but 100 miles east, up to the ancient fortresses surrounding *Guarda* ★★, about 200 miles north. It encompasses the strange fortress of *Marvão* ★★, elegant *Évora* ★★★★ and *Estremoz* ★★★, carpets at *Arraiolos* and bric-a-brac and antiques at *Borba*. There are also wild landscape beaches along the southern coast, but those are packaged in the Algarve chapter.

The Algarve, of course, consists primarily of beaches, but splendid ones. We place this section last so that it can be found from anywhere in the country when it's needed.

LISBON

A Lisbon street car

Historical Profile: The Story Of Lisbon

As the River Tagus nears the Atlantic Ocean it opens into an estuary lake before narrowing again for a final nine mile run to the sea. Lisbon, situated on the inland side of this lake, overlooks the best harbor in the country, protected by land barriers against both the elements and seaward attack.

Lisbon is older than Rome, older—in fact—than any western European capital. It owed its initial growth and importance to its fortunate geography. As long ago as the 12th century B.C. Phoenician sailors were attracted by the harbor to build the first settlement atop

São Jorge, the highest part of what later became Lisbon. They called their settlement *Alis Ubbo* (the Serene Harbor), from which the present name of the city derives.

After the Second Punic War in 201 B.C., Romans replaced the Phoenicians, and established Lisbon as the capital of their province of Lusitania. Various Germanic tribes, the most powerful being the Visigoths, followed the Romans before the Moors conquered Lisbon in 714 enroute to subjugating the peninsula, and held it for the next 400 years.

Obsessed with recapturing Lisbon, Afonso Henriques, the first king of Portugal (see "Historical Profile: The Birth of Portugal" on page 157), enlisted knights on their way to the Second Holy Land Crusade with promises of spoils and land. An army of Portuguese, English, Normans, Dutch and Germans lay siege to fortress Lisbon in 1147. With a reported population of 20,000 families, Lisbon was by that time the second-largest city in Western Europe. Four months into the siege, Afonso Henriques accepted the starving Moors' call for a truce, but only as a ploy to overrun the city while its guard was down. Satisfied with their spoils, most of Afonso's foreign entourage continued on to Palestine, but some accepted his offer of Portuguese land. An Englishman, for example, Gilbert of Hastings, was consecrated as the first bishop of Lisbon. A century later, in recognition of the city's importance, King Afonso III moved Portugal's capital from Coimbra to Lisbon, where it has remained ever since.

Lisbon's harbor became prominent again in the 16th century, when Portugal undertook great voyages of discovery. Vasco de Gama sailed to India from Lisbon's Belém suburb in 1497, ushering in a golden age for all of Portugal, but especially for its capital. He had given the Portuguese a virtual monopoly on the eastern spices that Europe craved for meat that often was slightly rancid. For the next two centuries, comparatively tiny Lisbon enjoyed greater revenues than any other city in Europe. In the first 25 years after the spice cargos began flowing into its harbor, Lisbon's population of 50,000 doubled, a century later, it tripled.

This sea-born wealth permitted King Manuel I to build as no king had been able to build before or since. His architects created a style, the Manueline, whose elaborate decorative carvings paid homage to the newly discovered flora and fauna of India and the Spice Islands. You can still see the preeminent example in Lisbon's Belém suburb—the Heronymite Monastery. However, Manuel spent so lavishly that his successors were left with debts they could not repay for a century.

In 1531 and again in 1597 severe tremors shook Lisbon, harbingers of the worst earthquake ever to hit a European city. Catastrophe finally struck in 1755 while most of the citizens of Lisbon were collected in churches to celebrate All Saints' Day. The earth shook; buildings fell; fires erupted throughout the city. Citizens who ran to the open harbor to escape the flames were swallowed by a tidal wave four stories high. Although the epicenter of the earthquake lay below Lisbon, it sent tremors as far away as Scotland and even Jamaica. In a few hours, Lisbon lost between a quarter and a third of its population. The city had been decimated and destroyed.

The king, José I, was fortunate enough to have been vacationing in Belém, for his Lisbon palace collapsed, as did most of his ministers. Only one kept his wits, and demonstrated courage and initiative for which he later received the title of the Marquis of Pombal. He collected the dead and towed their bodies out to sea, to prevent plague; he stationed soldiers to stop looting; and tore down the remains of damaged buildings and whole structures to create the first rational urban renewal in Europe.

On the site of the king's ruined palace, Pombal cleared a grand plaza, the Praça do Comércio (Commercial Square), where he placed a statue of King José prominently. Inland from the plaza, he replaced the former medieval maze of streets with parallel avenues containing stores and factories devoted to and named after single trades—names which, for the most part, remain in use today. Around the plaza and along the new avenues he erected a series of harmonious buildings financed by a citywide four percent tax. But seduced by the immense resources he controlled, Pombal grew into a dictator, and ultimately was charged with embezzlement and dismissed from office.

Ironically, the square that Pombal created as a tribute to his king was the stage for the event that sealed the fate of the monarchy a century later. In 1908 both the king and his heir were murdered by anti-monarchists' bullets as their carriage pulled into the Praça do Comércio. Two years later monarchism ended for good after a naval bombardment of Lisbon's palace. And two-thirds of a century after, in 1974, tanks with flowers in their guns rolled down Pombal's grand avenues to depose the government of the dictator António Salazar during Portugal's "Flower Revolution."

The first act of the new revolutionary government was to liberate the Portuguese colonies of Angola, Mozambique, Guinea and Cape Verde, which impacted Lisbon as greatly as the earthquake two centuries before. Portugal was forced to incorporate three-quarters of a million *retornados*, people of Portuguese descent fleeing independent Africa for their official homeland. Its population swelled by 10 percent in a matter of months. The effects of such massive immigration on such a small country are still visible; especially in Lisbon where almost half of these retornados remained to raise the city's population by a quarter almost overnight. Shantytowns sprang up in Lisbon's outskirts and spread across the south bank of the Tagus, replaced over the years by blocks of low income housing projects. Today Lisbon, like most major urban areas, has its share of visible poverty and occasional beggars. Not enough, however, for a New Yorker to notice, for only another earthquake could change Lisbon's character and appearance from that of an 18th-century city.

Despite the fact that so little remains from before 1755, Lisbon looks older than all the other Western European capitals. The heart of the city is Pombal's 18th-century urban renewal, unchanged in structure since his day. Elsewhere in the city's center, steep hills make avenues and tall buildings impractical, thus preserving ancient alleys lined by 18th-century originals that all but touch across the lanes. Palaces and mansions may be preserved in other cities, but only Lisbon managed to save whole blocks of ordinary 18th century houses—now blackened by age.

One reason Lisbon retains its old look is that industrial development is recent. Portugal somehow managed to avoid the Industrial Revolution of the previous century, which generated factories and housing for an exploding middle class to change the landscape of cities throughout most of Europe. Lisbon still exhibits both faces of an 18th-century city—imposing expanses designed for royalty, and crowded warrens of lower class housing.

With a population today of just over one million, Lisbon is the smallest capital in western Europe.

In addition to its own attractions, Lisbon is fortunately situated so that much of the variety of the country can be covered in day trips by car, bus or train from the capital. On the other hand, we would urge a tourist to move as he travels, so he can relax in some of the lovely accommodations surrounding Lisbon.

Just 70 miles north of Lisbon is the most sumptuous collection of buildings in Portugal, the graceful Gothic monastery at

Batalha ★★★★★. Southwest of Batalha spreads the well-known fishing village and glorious beach of **Nazaré** ★★. Typically described as a "picture-postcard spot," it is rather difficult to see the village today amid the crowds of tourists. A few kilometers away the moving medieval tombs of Pedro the Cruel and his lover Inês de Castro are housed in **Alcobaça** ★★★, while twenty miles south of Alcobaça stands the adorable medieval walled town of **Óbidos** ★★. Twenty miles north of Lisbon stretch the arms of a sumptuous Baroque monastery at **Mafra** ★★; royal palaces at verdant **Sintra** ★★★★ and **Queluz** ★★★ are even closer. Fine beaches wait at **Cascais** ★ and **Estoril** ★, ten miles west. **Setúbal** ★ lies on the sea 30 miles south of Lisbon and contains the first Manueline church, while nearby beaches beckon. Including three days for Lisbon, eight days should cover the sights of the area, all within one hundred miles of the capital and described in the following chapter.

LISBON ★★★★

Population: 826,140
Area code: 01; zip code: 1100

The autoestrada A-1 from **Porto** *and* **Coimbra** *also rings the* **airport**, *7 k north of the city. It bends west along the southern edge of the airport where it is called Av. Craveiro Lopes. Just before the racetrack, turn right at the large interchange to travel along Av. Campo Grande with a center island. At the second traffic circle (the Pr. Duque de Saldanha) bear rightward along the wide Pereira de Melo for 3 blocks until it enters the circle of the Pr. Marquês de Pombal, with a park to the right. Turn south (left) along Av. de Liberdad, lined with flowers, to skirt the Pr. dos Restauradores and enter the Pr. Rossio. Take the rightmost of the parallel streets heading south toward the river, R. do Aurea, which ends in 6 blocks in the huge plaza of Praça do Comércio with the best chance for parking.*

From **Setúbal** *and* **south**, *the soaring span of the Ponte 25 da Abril is crossed to become Av. de Ponte in the city. Exit at the first opportunity. Follow the river east along Av. 24 de Julho, which leads in 3 miles to the huge Praça do Comércio with parking.*

From **Cascais** *and* **Estoril** *by the coastal N-6 Belém is entered along Av. Marginal, which changes its name to Av.*

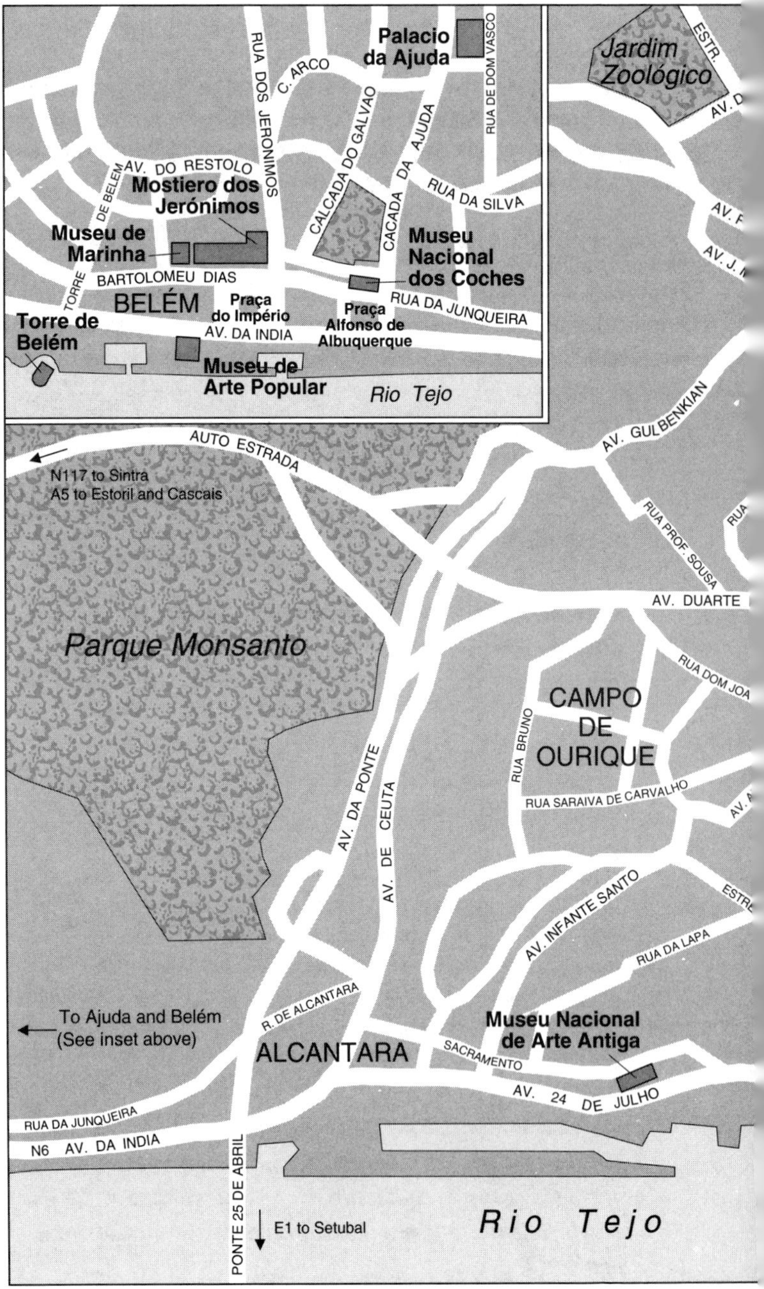
Palacio da Ajuda
Jardim Zoológico
RUA DOS JERONIMOS
C. ARCO
RUA DE DOM VASCO
CALCADA DO GALVAO
CACADA DA AJUDA
AV. DO RESTOLO
DE BELÉM
Mostiero dos Jerónimos
RUA DA SILVA
Museu de Marinha
Museu Nacional dos Coches
TORRE
BARTOLOMEU DIAS
BELÉM
Praça do Império
Praça Alfonso de Albuquerque
RUA DA JUNQUEIRA
Torre de Belém
AV. DA INDIA
Museu de Arte Popular
Rio Tejo
ESTR.
AV. D
AV. F
AV. J.
AUTO ESTRADA
N117 to Sintra
A5 to Estoril and Cascais
AV. GULBENKIAN
RUA PROF. SOUSA
RUA
AV. DUARTE
Parque Monsanto
RUA DOM JOA
CAMPO DE OURIQUE
RUA BRUNO
AV. DA PONTE
AV. DE CEUTA
RUA SARAIVA DE CARVALHO
AV. INFANTE SANTO
ESTR
RUA DA LAPA
R. DE ALCANTARA
To Ajuda and Belém (See inset above)
Museu Nacional de Arte Antiga
ALCANTARA
SACRAMENTO
AV. 24 DE JULHO
RUA DA JUNQUEIRA
N6 AV. DA INDIA
PONTE 25 DE ABRIL
E1 to Setubal
Rio Tejo

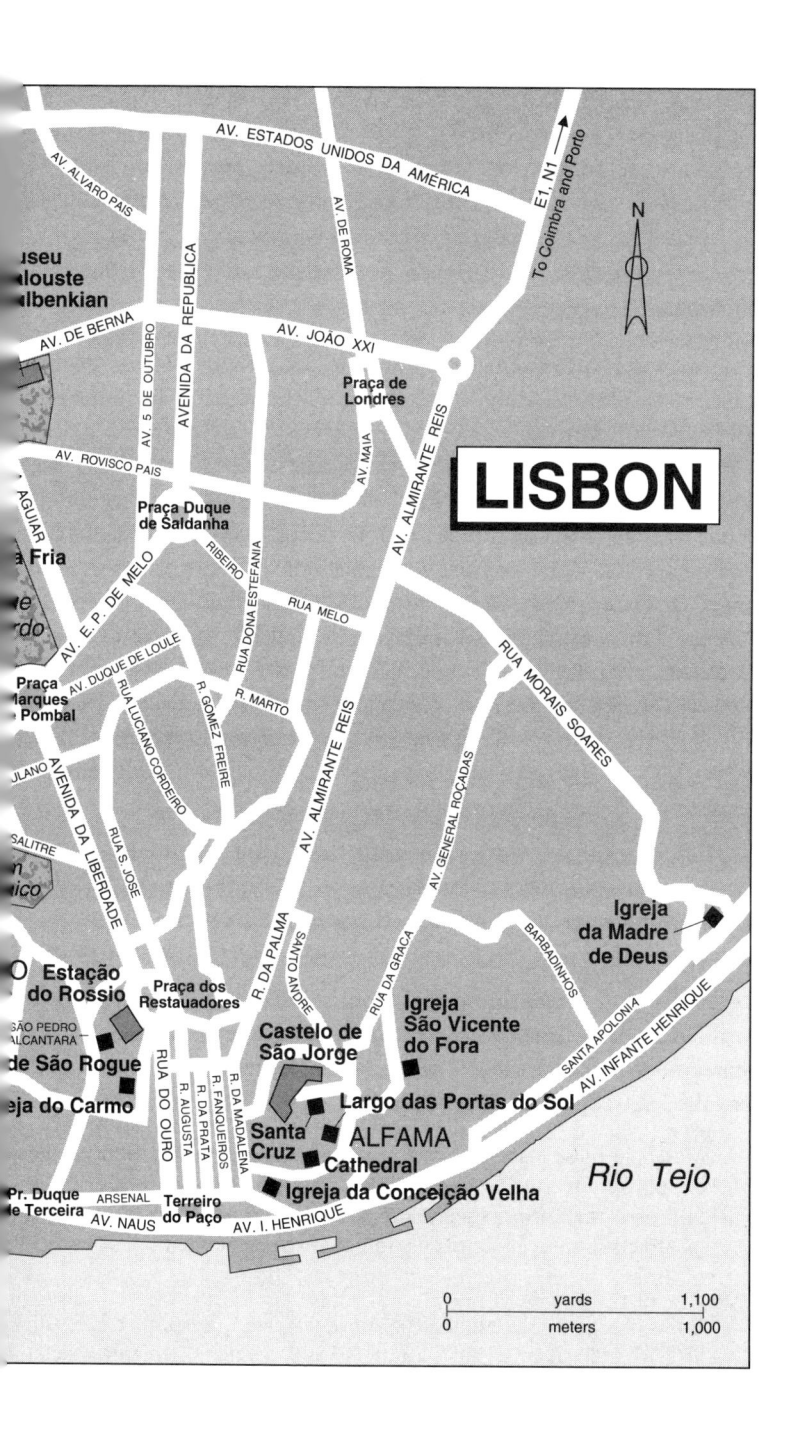
LISBON
AV. ESTADOS UNIDOS DA AMÉRICA
E1, N1
To Coimbra and Porto
N
AV. ALVARO PAIS
AV. DE ROMA
AVENIDA DA REPUBLICA
AV. DE BERNA
AV. JOÃO XXI
AV. 5 DE OUTUBRO
Praça de Londres
AV. MAIA
AV. ALMIRANTE REIS
AV. ROVISCO PAIS
Praça Duque de Saldanha
RIBEIRO
RUA DONA ESTEFANIA
AV. E. P. DE MELO
RUA MELO
RUA MORAIS SOARES
AV. DUQUE DE LOULE
RUA LUCIANO CORDEIRO
R. GOMEZ FREIRE
R. MARTO
AVENIDA DA LIBERDADE
RUA S. JOSE
SALITRE
AV. GENERAL ROÇADAS
Igreja da Madre de Deus
BARBADINHOS
R. DA PALMA
SANTO ANDRE
RUA DA GRAÇA
Estação do Rossio
Praça dos Restauadores
Igreja São Vicente do Fora
Castelo de São Jorge
SANTA APOLONIA
AV. INFANTE HENRIQUE
de São Rogue
RUA DO OURO
R. AUGUSTA
R. DA PRATA
R. FANQUEIROS
R. DA MADALENA
Largo das Portas do Sol
Santa Cruz
ALFAMA
Cathedral
Rio Tejo
Igreja da Conceição Velha
ARSENAL
Terreiro do Paço
AV. NAUS
AV. I. HENRIQUE
0 yards 1,100
0 meters 1,000

> de India and finally to Av. 24 de Julho as it follows the river. In a few miles it deposits traffic in the huge Praça do Comércio with parking.
>
> By the inland road and from **Sintra** along N-7, the autoestrada becomes Av. Duarte Pacheco, then changes its name to Av. Joaquim de Aguiar before reaching the large traffic circle of Pr. Marquês de Pombal. From there follow the Porto directions.

Lisbon is a canyon emptying into the wide Tagus (*Tejo* in Portuguese). A valley called the Baixa (slang for "lowland"), beginning at the river with Pombal's Praça do Comércio, leads north over an orderly grid of avenues for seven short blocks to the Praça Rossio, the heart of town. On either side hills rise. To the east (right, if facing inland) stands the steep bluff of São Jorge crowned by the castle of the same name. As the bluff descends southward toward the river, the most characteristic quarter of the city, the Alfama, spills down its sides. To the west (left) of the Baixa, another hill rises to the Bairro Alto (the High Quarter), an area of shops and restaurants. Lisbon's better stores perch on its southern slopes in a quarter named Chiado. Further north, past the Rossio, the grand avenue of Liberdade parades to the plaza of the Marquês de Pombal fronting the large park of Eduardo VII. Beyond sprawls modern Lisbon.

The area within this canyon is all the average visitor to Lisbon needs to traverse—with the exception of Belém, the sight-filled suburb four miles further west along the river.

Lisbon's delights are best savored on foot. The city's old yellow streetcars and buses imported from England, whose stops are marked by large signs with clearly posted routes, provide easy respites for the foot-weary. Even more convenient are Lisbon's taxis—the least-expensive in western Europe.

> Meters in these black cars with green-blue roofs start at 130$00, and are unlikely to run beyond 500$00 (about $3.00) for local trips. A 10% tip is the norm. When their roof lights are lit, taxis can be hailed on streets, but are more readily found in stands beside hotels or monuments.
>
> Buses charge by the number of zones traversed, starting at 125$00. Streetcars do likewise but start at 105$00. *Módulos*, ten-trip tickets, cut both these costs in half. Even cheaper are 1000$00 special 4-day tourist passes purchased at the Santa Justa elevator just south of Pr. Rossio.

WHAT TO SEE AND DO

Lisbon's pleasures extend beyond traditional sights. They include walking the lanes of the **Alfama** ★ to taste city life as it was two centuries ago, and strolling the Baixa along wide avenues.

The most pleasant of the traditional sights is the **Castelo de São Jorge** ★★, both for the ramble along its walls and for perfect views of the city, river and sea below. The architectural highlights of the city are the **Mosteiro dos Jerónimos** ★★★★ and the **Torre de Belém** ★★, both Manueline masterpieces in the suburb of Belém. Lisbon contains the two best art museums in Portugal—the **Museu Nacional de Arte Antiga** ★★★★ for Portuguese painting, Bosch, Durer and Zurbarán, along with collections of silver and gold; and the **Museu Calouste-Gulbenkian** ★★★★ for special Islamic art, superb 18th-century French painting, and an enormous collection of Lalique arte nouveau.

Also in Belém, the **Museu de Marinha** ★★ (Maritime Museum) presents some interesting displays, while the **Museu Nacional dos Cochas** ★★★ (Coach Museum) is probably the best of its kind anywhere. Lisbon has no magnificent churches, but a collection of pretty ones. The **Cathedral** ★★ conveys a Romanesque feel, **São Roque** ★★ has one amazing chapel, **Igreja do Carmo** ★★ (whose ceiling fell in the earthquake) conveys a strong sense of olden times, but best of all, is **Igreja da Madre de Deus** ★★★ for its beautiful *azulejo* tiles.

The uninspiring **Museu do Arte Popular** ★ in Belém is worth a visit for its survey of craftwork from all the provinces of Portugal. An unexpected treat is the **Estufa Fria** ★, the so-called "cold greenhouse," in Parque Eduardo VII at the end of Av. de Liberdade, for its lush collection of tropical plants amid artificial waterfalls and grottoes.

Covering the sights of Lisbon requires a minimum of three days.

The most expeditious way to tour Lisbon is by combining visits to sights located in adjoining areas. Begin at the Castelo de São Jorge, at the top of its hill, meander down through the Alfama, and end with a tour of the Cathedral at the bottom. Or wander through Pombal's Praça do Comércio and explore the avenues leading to the Praça Rossio. From here, take an excursion up to the Bairro Alto and return along Av. de Liberdade to finish at the Parque Eduardo VII and its botanical Estufa Fria.

A taxi or bus trip to the suburb of Belém yields the Mosteiro dos Jerónimos, the Torre de Belém, the Museu de Marinha, and the Museu Nacional dos Cochas, all within walking distance of one another. Include the Museu do Arte Popular if interested. The Museu Nacional de Arte Antiga, located enroute to Belém, can readily be included in one long day. Because neither lies near other sights, both the Museu Calouste Gulbenkian and the church of Madre de Dios, with its wonderful azulejo tiles, require separate outings.

São Jorge Hill

Castelo de São Jorge ★★

Open daily 8 a.m. to sunset. Admission: free. Although it's best to taxi up to the castle, before walking down through the Alfama, bus #37 and trolleys #12 and #28 also stop nearby.

It was on this hilltop that the Phoenicians first settled, though no one records who lived here before. Remains of a later Roman city are still being excavated, but the massive perimeter walls of the castle (and probably its ten towers) were raised by Visigoths and restored and strengthened by the Moors. The ruined 13th-century palace built inside the walls served as the principal palace of Portuguese kings for over 300 years, not replaced until the 16th century when Manuel I built a new one—later destroyed by the great earthquake of 1755—in the lower city. Afterwards the São Jorge palace became a prison, abandoned and fallen to ruin in the present century.

Within the walls remains a haphazard garden populated by rare white peacocks, black-necked swans, ducks, ravens, chickens and the occasional flamingo. Walk the ramparts for the best orientation to the city. Southeast, spilling down the hill, is the aged Alfama quarter. To the east, in a valley, spreads the orderly avenues and plazas of Pombal's Baixa, with the Praça do Comércio beside the river. The Av. de Liberdade stretches straight as an arrow north to the large park of Eduardo VII. The Bairro Alto rises directly east of São Jorge hill. Even further east, and south, the graceful bridge of the American-built Ponte 25 da Abril, whose 3323 feet of single span—the longest in Europe and second longest in the world—curves gracefully cross the Tejo.

Alfama ★

From São Jorge Castle walk to the church of Santa Cruz at the southeast corner of the grounds. Continue east behind its apse and follow R. de Santa Luzia going right downhill until it bends and narrows to stairs that enter the open plaza of Largo das Portas do Sol. If coming from the lower town, taxi directly to Largo das Portas do Sol. Trolleys #28 and #12, as well as bus #37 also stop there. The route described below can be followed in reverse from the Cathedral, though it is uphill all the way.

The famed Alfama quarter—whose name probably derives from the Arabic word *al Hamman* (the baths)—presents an interesting historical contradiction. Traditionally home to the city's upper crust, its affluent residents fled at the onset of the great earthquake of 1755 to wait out the aftermath in the safety of country estates. The poor of Lisbon, on the other hand, had nowhere to go and many had lost their homes. They rushed to the abandoned Alfama and moved in, for this quarter had sustained less damage than any other because of the hill's granite base. When the rich returned, they chose not to live near the poor, so, ironically, the greatest number of old patrician houses survive in this poor section of Lisbon today.

The Alfama presents a slice of life from the 18th century. Buildings squeeze against one another, wash hangs from windows, braziers in doorways waft the scent of food, and children, animals and activity abound. Catch a glimpse of this earlier time in the mornings or late afternoons when the neighborhood is busiest. (But for safety's sake avoid the area after dark.) Before the cataclysm, most of Lisbon would have looked the way the Alfama does today.

The best introduction to the quarter is the Plaza of **Largo Das Portas do Sol**, named for a long-vanished gate which, erected during Moorish rule, was positioned to face the rising sun. On the right, at the southern end of the plaza, is the **Fundacão Ricardo do Espirito Santo Silva ★ ★**. This museum of decorative arts, housed in a 17th-century former palace of the Counts of Azurara, contains a remarkable collection of 17th- and 18th-century furniture and accessories displayed in rooms around a courtyard as they were used, rather than as in a museum. The furniture was donated by Sr. Ricardo do Espírito Santo, head of the bank of the same name and possibly the richest man in Portugal. The foundation supports a school in its annex where students study old crafts, such as wood inlaying. *(Open Tuesday-Saturday 10 a.m. to 1 p.m. and 2:30-5 p.m.; Admission: 500$00. ☎ 86 2184)* **Santa Luzia**, opposite, has tiles inside depicting the palace that occupied the site of the Praça do Comércio before the earthquake.

Walk west from the museum (across the plaza) to descend the steps of Beco de Santa Helena on the right. Halfway down take the first left along Beco do Garces then left again to ascend R. do Picão, which enters **Largo do Salvador**. At number 22 is a rare remaining 16th-century mansion, formerly belonging to the Counts of Arcos. Its balcony is later Baroque. Return to the southern end of the largo to take the small **R. da Regueira**, which forks left of the R. do Picão on which we entered. It is a street of small shops and restaurants. At **Beco das Cruzes**, the first alley on the right, an 18th-century house rises with carved ravens supporting an overhanging second story. A few feet down Beco das Cruzes an *azulejo* panel surmounts a door on the left, and beyond it an old arch crosses the street. Back on R. da Requeira again, a few steps sees it opens to a fountain on whose left are the steps of the **Beco do Carneiro**—so narrow that houses almost touch across the alley. There's a lovely view from the top.

Return to the fountain to follow **R. de San Miguel** (opposite Carneiro) where tiny antique shops line the way. **Beco da Cardosa**, the second left, is worth ascending for a short way to see 16th- to 18th-century houses branching off its blind alleys. Proceed a few steps along R. de San Miguel to the church of **San Miguel** which contains some fine Baroque woodwork. Largo de San Miguel (which fronts the church) is crossed by **R. de San Pedro**, the quarter's most animated street. Walk along it to the right into **Largo de San Rafael**, with its one remaining tower from the 14th-century city walls. West of the largo, R. de João da Praça leads in two blocks to the **Cathedral** of Lisbon.

Cathedral ★★
Open daily 9 a.m. to noon and 2:30-6 p.m. Open Mon., Wed. and Fri. to 7:30 p.m. Admission: 100$00 to the museum and cloisters. From the northern end of the Praça do Comércio go east two blocks to R. da Madalena which runs north-south. Three blocks north at the church of Madalena turn right on R. de Santo Antonio da Sé for three short blocks. (Another route is described in the Alfama section above.) Bus #37 and trolleys #28 and #11 stop at the Cathedral. After capturing Lisbon from the Moors in 1147, Afonso Henrique ordered a cathedral built for his English bishop. By the end of that century a Romanesque cathedral was completed, including defensive capabilities for a city that did not yet feel safe from attack. Over the centuries Gothic additions and, later, Baroque decorations were appended. But after the cathedral suffered great damage in the 1755 earthquake it was reconstructed to its earlier style, producing the bare but imposing church on view today.

The facade is particularly harmonic, with massive crenulated towers and solid walls leaving only small Romanesque apertures for the rose window, bells and entry portals. It is all quite stately. Inside, a pure Romanesque barrel vault rests on plain pillars that lead to a simple lantern at the crossing. The aisles paralleling the nave, however, are surmounted by an elegant Gothic triforium. Yet, somehow the reconstruction removed the life from the cathedral, leaving it cold.

To the left, upon entering, a baptismal font dating from 1195 is said to have christened Saint Anthony of Padua. The church altar is 18th-century; behind it is a fine 14th-century Gothic ambulatory. The third chapel on the right (south) contains endearing 14th-century tombs of Lopo Fernandes Pacheco, a close friend of Afonso IV, and his wife, María Vilalobos. The carving is simple, with pains taken for small things, such as the hair, but gross caricatures for their clothing and the dogs at their feet. Just to the right is the entrance to a lovely, though damaged, 13th-century cloister. On the right in the south transept is the entrance to the sacristy, which serves as the treasury. It contains relics of Portugal's patron Saint Vincent in a lovely mother-of-pearl casket.

Santo António da Sé, on the site of the birthplace of Saint Anthony of Padua, is west of the Cathedral facade.

BAIXA

This is the "new" Lisbon, built by Pombal after the great earthquake. Straight lines and ordered vistas reflect the rationalism of the 18th century—one of Pombal's rules was that buildings could include no overhangs or curves. The intent was to construct a commercial district anchored at either end by large plazas for public gatherings. Despite the office buildings and banks that have replaced the old shops, and the herd of cars that now fills the formerly dramatic expanse of the Praça do Comércio, the Baixa remains more or less as Pombal envisioned it.

Praça do Comércio ★

The Baixa begins by the river at the Praça do Comércio. Most Lisboetas call it "Tereiro do Paço" (Terrace of the Palace), still memorializing the royal residence on this site before the earthquake. This huge square opening to the wide river lapping at its steps harkens to Venice. The plaza is closed on three sides by pink arcades housing government offices, including courts at its north end. Here, by waiting a while on weekdays, formally robed barristers and judges can be seen.

In the center of it all stands an equestrian **statue of José I**, king during Pombal's era. Machado de Castro cast this large work in the finest 18th-century style, reminiscent of statues of the French Sun King. As it happened, Dom José fell ill during the statue's creation so he did not sit for his portrait, which perhaps explains the ornate helmet and visor that all but obscures his face. A bronze medallion in the front depicts Pombal. When Pombal was removed from office in disgrace, the craftsman who made the medallion was ordered to destroy it. Unable to melt down his own work, he hid it instead, and later it was found and replaced.

The northeast corner of the plaza was the spot where King Carlos I and his heir were gunned down in their carriage by assassins.

Rossio

A handsome **triumphal arch** in the northern arcade of the Praça do Comércio leads out to a series of parallel avenues, each built and named for a trade—*Sapateiros* (Cobblers), *Prata* (Silversmiths), *Aurea* (Goldsmiths). The center Rua Augusta is now a pedestrian mall. All the streets lead north over seven short blocks of stores and banks to the main square of the city known as the **Rossio**, although its official name is Praça Dom Pedro IV.

The statue in the center of Pedro IV which lends the official name to the square is actually of Maximilian, the French emperor of Mexico. A ship transporting the statue to Mexico from France had sailed into Lisbon as word arrived of Maximilian's death. The Portuguese were able to buy the now useless statue for a pittance, and changed only a few details to adapt it for their own king.

Before the 1755 earthquake, this plaza was the city center for bullfights and autos-da-fe, witnessed by cheering crowds. The palace of the Inquisition stood at the north end, replaced in the middle of the 19th century by the present **Teatro Nacional**. Two central Baroque fountains imported from France are surrounded by flower stalls and always animated cafes.

To the left of the Teatro Nacional stands the main train station of Lisbon, the **Estação de Rossio**. Its 19th century lobby mimics either the

Manueline or the Moorish with such exuberance that it is difficult to tell which. North of the station is the **Pr. dos Restauradores** whose central obelisk commemorates those who rose against the Spanish in the 17th century to regain independence for Portugal. In the northwest corner of the plaza stands the huge **Palácio Foz** which now serves as the Direcão-General do **Turismo** (☎ *346 3314),* and provides maps along with answers to tourist questions—including where to find a room when none seem available.

From the northern end of the plaza flows the grand avenue of Lisbon, **Av. da Liberdade**, straight (but uphill) for one mile to the large Eduardo VII park. This boulevard was laid out in the 19th century for promenades by the well-to-do. Originally it was walled and gated for their protection. The gates and walls are gone today but the promenade is composed of playful mosaics on the sidewalks, and presents vistas bordered by palms and water gardens. Because the hotels and office buildings that line it are of no great interest, a taxi is a good way to reach the park at its end.

The park, **Parque Eduardo VII**, is named for Queen Victoria's son who visited Lisbon several times, partly to shore up the shaky monarchy of Carlos I who, despite these efforts, was assassinated. At the northwest (far) corner of the park visit the tropical lushness of the **Estufa Fria** ★. Called the "Cold Greenhouse" because wooden shutters, instead of glass, maintain the temperature. Inside are an acre of plants, ferns and flowers connected by paths, tiny bridges, fountains, ponds and streams. The Estufa Quente (Hothouse) nearby maintains desert flora, and well deserves its name in the summer. *(Open daily 9 a.m. to 6 p.m.; to 5 p.m. in winter; admission: 57$00.)*

BARRIO ALTO

One block back toward the river from the Rossio, narrow R. de Santa Justa heads west to the Santa Justa Elevator that rises conveniently up the steep slope of the Bairro Alto. This wonderful cast-iron lift is an 1898 design of Gustave Eiffel, the man responsible for another famous monument in Paris. A one-way ride costs 30$00. Alternatively, the funicular (for the same fare) will take you up to fine city views from the terrace of São Pedro de Alcantara. The funicular entrance is just north of the Office of Tourism in the Pr. dos Restauradores. Either of these routes permits you to walk downhill through the barrio. If you prefer an uphill hike, walk west from R. da Conceição in the Baixa up C. de São Francisco and take a right (northward) turn at the top. After a deep breath, follow the directions below in reverse.

The curves of the steep slope defeated Pombal's efforts to construct his usual grid of orderly avenues in this quarter. Today the hill is a place for cafes and, especially on its southern side, called the Chiado, the site of Lisbon's best stores. In 1988 terrible fires destroyed a score of shops including Lisbon's two largest department stores. The area has not completely recovered, although plenty of establishments remain.

Igreja do Carmo ★★

> *Open Monday-Saturday 10 a.m. to 1 p.m. and 2-5 p.m. Closed Sunday and holidays. Admission: 150$00. The Santa Justa elevator stops at this church. (If arriving by the funicular, visit Igreja São Roque first, then go south down R. Oliveira to the pleasant Largo do Carmo, with this church at its end.)* Construction on this Carmelite church began at the end of the 14th century, although problems with its foundation delayed completion for years. It was finished in the finest Gothic style to become the second largest church, after the Cathedral, in Lisbon. Then the great earthquake toppled its ceiling. For some reason the church was never rebuilt, so it serves today as dramatic evidence of that cataclysm. Past the entry comes a startling grassy sward and the Church's skeletal walls, apse and arches. All is quiet inside, and moving. The former apse functions as a dull archaeological museum.

South of the church R. Garret cuts across lined with better shops. They continue on surrounding streets down the slope of the Chiado. For the church of São Roche, go west through the square in front of Igreja do Carmo, then north along R. Oliveira to Largo Trindade Coelho faced by the classical facade of São Roque. (Or, from the funicular, follow São Pedro de Alcantara south from the terrace for one block.)

Igreja São Roque ★★

> *Open daily 10 a.m. to 5 p.m. The museum is closed on Monday Admission: 25$00, free on Sunday.* An unremarkable 16th-century exterior encases an elegant Baroque interior that includes what may be the most sumptuous and costly chapel in the world.

The nave's flat wooden ceiling is a trompe l'oeil vault painted with scenes of the Apocalypse. Four ornate chapels line each side. Proceeding down the right side, note lovely *azulejos* and a fine painting in the third chapel. Continuing around, the chapel of São João Baptista is last on the left before the high altar, and unique in the world. In 1742 King João V commissioned a chapel of semiprecious stones to be built in Rome. Upon its completion, it was blessed by the Pope, dismantled, transported on three ships and reconstructed again in Lisbon in 1750. Lapis lazuli dominates, but there are elements of rare green porphyry, amethyst, jade and several sorts of marble. What appears to be a painting above the altar is also of stone, a finely detailed and polished mosaic, as are the others in the chapel. Note the chandeliers and their "chains."

After a look at the sacristy *azulejos,* located to the left of the São João Baptista chapel, exit the church for an inspection of its treasures in the **Museu de São Roque**, to the right of the church entrance. One bowl hefts at more than 30 pounds of gold, a miter is covered in Brazilian diamonds, and a pair of gilded silver candlesticks together approach one ton.

Running west from the north end of the church is **R. Dom Pedro V**, where Lisbon's best antique shops crowd together for four blocks.

BELÉM

Belém is a 20-minute taxi ride for 8 k west of the center of Lisbon along the river. It is served by buses #12, #14, #27, #28, #29, #43 and #49, and trolleys #15, #16 and #17. Faster public transportation is the train that covers the distance in 10 minutes and departs every 15 minutes from the Cais do Sodré station, along the river due west of the Praça do Comércio.

Belém, Portuguese for Bethlehem, was Lisbon's original port from which maritime explorers sailed into the unknown and returned with the fruits of their discoveries to enrich Lisbon beyond the dreams of most countries. Some of this bounty stayed in Belém. Manuel I constructed the first complete Manueline structure, the **Mosteiro dos Jerónimos** ★★★★, in thanks for Vasco da Gama's opening of the spice trade, financed by a five percent tax on the sale of all spice goods. Manuel also built a fortress in the river to protect the shipping—the **Torre de Belém** ★★. Within three blocks of these aged sights are the **Museu do Arte Popular** ★, the **Museu de Marinha** ★★ (Maritime Museum), and the **Museu Nacional dos Cochas** ★★★ (Coach Museum), each described below.

Flat, filled with parks and marinas, Belém is a treat to wander through (if you ignore the highway and train tracks). Buses #27 and #43 from the Pr. Pombal stop at the Mosteiro dos Jerónimos.

Torre de Belém ★★

Open Mon.-Sat. 10 a.m. to 6:30 p.m. (in winter to 5 p.m.) Open Sun. 10 a.m. to 2 p.m. Closed Mon. and holidays. Admission: 400$00 (250$00 in winter), Sun. free. In the river off the riverine Av. Marginal at Av. Torre de Belém. Belém Tower is a virtual icon of Lisbon. When it was constructed in 1521, the tower stood farther out in the river whose bank, after centuries of silting, has since come out to meet it. It was planned both for a river lookout and as an armed fortress to defend Portuguese shipping, paired with São Sebastião fortress across the river. It still looks suitably robust, but elegant at the same time, with its lovely porch, delicate third-story terraced windows and precious Moorish-influenced details. The inside is plainer and more Gothic in feeling, with stone spiral staircases and bare walls.

Museu de Arte Popular ★

Open Tues.-Sun. 10 a.m. to 12:30 p.m. and 2-5 p.m. Closed Mon. and holidays. Admission: 200$00.) Along the river two blocks east of the Torre de Belém (back toward town). In a building left over from the 1940 Lisbon World's Fair are displayed the arts and crafts of Portugal, arranged by region. Here is the place to acquaint oneself with the range of Portugal's folk artists and perhaps to prepare a shopping list and itinerary. Unfortunately, the building and its exhibits are not cared for. All is drab.

Mosteiro dos Jerónimos
★★★★

Open Tues.-Sat. 10 a.m. to 6:30 p.m. (in winter to 5 p.m.) Open Sun. 10 a.m. to 2 p.m. Closed Mon. and holidays. Admission to the cloisters: 400$00 (250$00 in winter). From the Museu Popular head north across the open park of the Pr. Império, which the monastery borders. Henry the Navigator had built a small monastery on this site in the 15th century, and Vasco da Gama passed a night of prayer nearby before setting out to "discover" India. When he returned, his king, Manuel I, ordered Henry's simple structure replaced by a richly endowed monastery for his own patron saint Jerónimos in thanks for the bounty flowing over the new trade route. The original plans were drawn by the French architect Diogo Boytac, a brilliant innovator, who was taken from a commission at Setúbal for the job.

Seventeen years later, after the basic lines were complete, Boytac was succeeded by João de Castilho, who brought along the Fleming João de Ruão, and the French sculptor, Nicolas Chanterene, to whom most of the decoration is due. Work was complete by 1572, in the rapid time of less than 75 years. Much later, a long extension was added west of the entrance in a style appropriate to, but without the fine taste of, the rest. By great fortune, the earthquake of 1755 caused only slight damage to the complex, so this masterpiece remains in essentially its original state. Thanks to renovations in 1994, it glistens today.

The white limestone monastery consists of a compound whose southern side, facing the Pr. Império, is the south wall of the church of Saint Mary, while the three walls of the grand cloister extending north complete the sides of a square. On the southern side, facing the park, an elegant porch to the right of the entrance inserts intricacy into an otherwise monolithic facade. João de Castilho carved this busy canopy containing statues of the four Sybils, four prophets, and four church fathers, including Saint Jerónimos, all surrounding the Virgin and child. Above the Virgin are two scenes from Saint Jeronimo's life. Below, on the central pillar, is a fine carving of Prince Henry the Navigator holding a large sword while pointing to the coat-of-arms of his native Porto.

The church entrance looms in the center of the long southern face inside an archway connecting the west wing. The carvings around the door are the pride of Nicholas Chanterene. A statue of Manuel I kneels simply but elegantly on the left side, while Saint Jermonimo stands behind. Across the door his second wife Maria, the daughter of

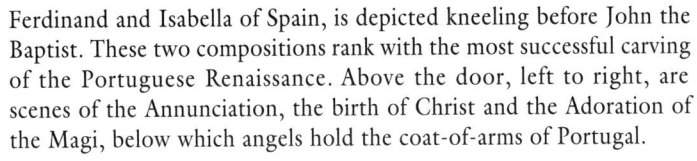

Ferdinand and Isabella of Spain, is depicted kneeling before John the Baptist. These two compositions rank with the most successful carving of the Portuguese Renaissance. Above the door, left to right, are scenes of the Annunciation, the birth of Christ and the Adoration of the Magi, below which angels hold the coat-of-arms of Portugal.

The soaring church interior is vast, with aisles rising as high as the nave. Exquisite fan vaulting is raised on paired columns whose diameters decrease for perspective as they proceed to the front of the church. Left, after the first chapel, is the tomb of Vasco de Gama borne on the back of six lions. There would be no grand church, if it were not for his pioneering voyage. The tomb opposite honors Camões, Portugal's greatest poet, though his body actually lies in an unmarked pauper's grave. The star vaulting at the transept crossing is sublime.

The end of the church consists of a royal pantheon that tells the sad story of ascendancy and riches, followed by the loss of it all, a fitting morality tale for a church.

Manuel I, the Fortunate, to whom this monastery is due, reposes in what would normally be the apse. His son and successor, João III, lies right. (Evidently one animal from India made a strong impression on the sculptor—all the tombs are borne on the backs of elephants.) Both Kings lie beside their Spanish queens, both named Maria, whose marriages would bequeath Portugal to Spain after Manuel's family ran out of descendants.

In the transept to the right lie the remains of Manuel's grandsons, allegedly including those of King Sebastião. Sebastião's early death prevented children, giving the crown to his aged uncle, Cardinal Henri. In the left transept are tombs of three of Manuel's children, including the Cardinal-King, Dom Henri, whose death after a six-month reign ended the dynasty. (See "Historical Profile: The Rise And Fall Of The House Of Avís" on page 119.)

Exit through the west entrance to enter the cloisters through the gift shop. The cloisters enclose a large space in a two-story arcade of wide arches punctuated by spires. The vaulting is fine and the sculpture incredibly rich. The galaxy of animals, vegetables and twisting ropes carved on columns and walls earn this monastery its fame and created the Manueline style. Close inspection reveals some fantastic creatures indeed.

The second story is elegant, if less exuberant. A doorway leads to the upper choir of the church, with 16th-century stalls handsomely carved from brazilwood.

Museu da Marinha ★★

Open Tues.-Sun. 10 a.m. to 5 p.m. Closed Mon. and holidays. Admission: 200$00; free on Wed. Entrance is at the west end of the Heronymite Mon-

astery. This museum consists mainly of ship models, fascinating to those willing to study them. Three anchors from Columbus' Niña stand by the entrance. Inside are models of ships from the era of the great Portuguese discoveries. Most are caravels, a Portuguese invention adopted from the Moors, and the ship that Columbus chose as well for his voyage to the New World. Without the innovation of their free lateen rigging which allowed sailing closer to the wind than stationary square sails, Africa could not have been rounded. Some of the uniforms on display are splendid in a Gilbert-and-Sullivan way.

Museu Nacional dos Coches ★★★

Open Tues.-Sun. 10 a.m. to 1 p.m. and 2:30-5:30 p.m. Closed Mon. and holidays. Admission: 400$00. R. de Belém parallels the south face of the Heronymite Monastery and leads eastward in two blocks to the museum. Housed in the indoor expanse of the former royal riding school on the grounds of the Palace of Belém (now the home of the President of Portugal) is this museum filled with nothing but amazing coaches.

True gilded fantasies are parked in long rows. It should be remembered that their function was to impress, and anyone would admit that the least of them would turn heads if it rolled past today. Favorites are the coach of José I, the king at the time of the great earthquake, the huge carriages of João V, a 17th-century French litter, and the miniature coach of Carlos I, used when he was a child, which adds pathos to the thought of his later assassination. Amid all the gilt below, don't fail to look up at the lovely ceiling frescos.

Other Sights

Museu Nacional de Arte Antiga ★★★★

Open Tues.-Sun. 10 a.m. to 1 p.m. and 2:30-5 p.m. Closed Mon. and holidays. Admission: 200$00; free Sun. morning. The museum is located along the river by the Jardim 9 de Abril at 95 R. das Janelas Verdes in the district of Lapa, which is halfway between Belém and the Praça do Comércio. A walk along the river from the Praça do Comércio would cover less than a mile and a half, although a taxi is certainly quicker. Trolley #19 or buses #27, #40, #49 or #54 pass by. This certainly is the finest museum extant of Portuguese painting, and includes much more. It is housed half in the 17th-century palace of the Count of Alvor, where Pombal lived for a while, and half in a modern addition whose west end provides the entrance.

The inside has just been remodeled, so exhibits may have been moved. Get a floorplan at the desk, and forgive us if our directions are a little off.

Inside and downstairs is the chapel of Santo Alberto, preserved from a former convent on this site. Its wooden sculpture is admirable, as are its *azulejos*. Rooms follow displaying Portuguese furniture, tapestries and carpets. Before entering the old building, opposite the entrance, ascend to the mezzanine to view a fine collection of porcelain, both from, and inspired by, the Far East. Two early 17th-century screens from Japan show the arrival of the Portuguese, the first people of European physiognomy that the insular Japanese had seen. The name for these screens comes from the Japanese word for "southern barbarian," and oversized noses show what most impressed the Japanese about these foreigners. Also on the mezzanine are collections of gold pieces and polychrome sculpture.

The second floor is devoted to Portuguese painting, including the one acknowledged masterpiece of the nation. It is a polyptych of six wood panels painted in the middle of the 15th century for the Lisbon church of Saint Vincent, since destroyed. The artist is Nuno Gonçalves, and this is his only attributable work. The painting portrays both famous Portuguese and segments of lower society, all listening to Saint Vincent who is depicted in the center of both middle panels. Important figures identified in the central panel in which Saint Vincent holds a Bible include King Afonso V kneeling at the saint's feet, his heir standing behind, and next back, alongside the saint, the mustached Prince Henry the Navigator. Kneeling on the other side is Afonso's wife in front of the sister of Ferdinand of Spain, Afonso's mother. Behind her, farthest left, is the presumed portrait of the artist. All the faces are so vibrant that one wonders where this artist could have gained a skill that ranks with the European geniuses of the period.

The great Flemish painter Jan van Eyck's early 15th century visit to Portugal influenced a century of Portuguese artists. Most notable among his artistic descendents is the 16th century painter Frei Carlos, whose *Annunciation* bears comparison with the master. In a different vein are the charming Portuguese primitives, especially an anonymous 15th-century *Ecce Homo* with a shrouded upper visage, and a *Vision of Hell* in which hell is a kitchen presided over by an Indian Satan.

Further on are rooms dedicated to the 19th century Domingos de Sequeira, a sort of Portuguese Goya—he, like Goya, lived in exile and produced wondrous drawings and etchings, in addition to oils. His paintings appeared in Paris exhibitions where he bested Delacroix and Gérricault, among others. Outstanding are his portraits, especially those of the Viscount of Santarém and his family, the young Count of Farrobo, and the artist's own children.

Past the bookstore on the ground floor of the new building, the old building begins with a superb collection of silver tableware, mainly French, from the firm of Germain. French furniture follows. Across a landing is the entrance to the museum's European masterpieces. The stars are a Dürer painting of *Saint Jerome*, which once hung in the Heronymite Monastery, and an astonishing Bosch of *The Temptations of Saint Anthony*. Saint Anthony is painted four times throughout the picture, never once looking at all the sinners demonstrating sins of excess. There is also a lovely *Virgin and Child with Saints* by Holbein the Elder, an interesting Bruegel depiction of beggars, and a fine self-portrait by Andrea del Sarto. Of the Spanish paintings, the best is Ribera's *Martyrdom of Saint Bartholomew*, although there is also a Velázquez portrait of *Maria of Austria* and a Zurbarán canvas of the *Twelve apostles*.

Museu Calouste Gulbenkian ★★★★
Open Tues.-Sun. 10 a.m. to 5 p.m. Open 2-7:30 p.m. on Wed. and Sat. in summer. Closed Mon. and holidays. Admission: 200$00; free Sun. The museum is located in Lisbon's north, about a half-mile past the end of the Parque Eduardo VII. Av. de Alcantara, which is renamed Av. António Augusto Aguiar, follows the east edge of the park and leads to the Pr. da Espanha. Turn right to the Parque de Palhava and the museum. Trolleys #24 and #27, and buses #16, #26, #31 and #56 all stop nearby. Before World War I the Armenian Calouste Gulbenkian negotiated an agreement to broker all the oil Iran sold to the West for a five percent commission. This made him one of the richest private citizens in the world. During World War II, however, Britain made him unwelcome when he refused to sever his ties with the Iranian embassy in Vichy France. When Portugal welcomed him on the rebound, he became a citizen and established a billion-dollar foundation, the largest in Europe, to aid the Portuguese arts. Upon his death in 1955, he donated his private art collection to the country.

In breadth and quality his collection was the finest remaining in private hands. Gulbenkian was a passionate collector, desiring only the best; his tastes were wide and his pockets incredibly deep. His great coup was in purchasing several works, including two Rembrandts, from the Hermitage during the late 1920s when Russia needed hard currency. Gulbenkian's bequest included funds to erect the museum, completed in 1969, designed expressly to display each part of the collection to best advantage.

What makes this collection special is that it is at once modest in size and astonishingly high in quality. Gulbenkian was not a collector who strove to complete a series, but a lover of art who purchased individual works because they captivated him. Consequently, it is a museum of stars, rather than one providing examples of the breadth of any single art genre.

Of the earliest art the Egyptian collection takes first place. The first example is an elegantly proportioned Old Kingdom alabaster chalice. A fine bronze funerary statue, a lovely wooden one of the Lady Henut-tawy, and a simple death-mask in gold follows. The Assyrian low relief is monumental. Those with an interest will find the Greek coins superb.

A highlight of the museum is its collections of Middle-Eastern carpets, Korans, ceramics and clothes. There are also refined, delicate Far Eastern porcelains and an elegant silk hanging. The European art collection begins with several jewel-like medieval ivories and illustrated medieval manuscripts, including a fine *Book of Hours*, but moves quickly to paintings. Outstanding early works are van der Weyden's *Saint Catherine*, Dirk Bouts' *Annunciation*, and a haunting *Portrait of a Young Girl* by Domenico Ghirlandaio. After a fine Hals, a Van Dyke portrait, and a Ruysdael landscape, are the two fine Rembrandt's—*Alexander* (sometimes called *Pallas Athene*), and the disturbing face of the *Portrait of an Old Man*. 18th- and 19th-century French paintings and sculpture are choice, including a Fragonard, the De La Tour pastel of *Duval de l'Epinoy*, a nice Houdin sculpture of Diana, and several Corots. French furniture ranges from elegant to ornate. An impressive display of costly silver tableware leads to rooms of English painting and later French canvases, including seldom seen canvases by Manet, Fantin-Latour (see his perfect "Still Life" with a knife overhanging a table) and Dégas, among others. Another favorite is a haunting Renoir of the recumbent "Madame Claude Monet." The exhibit ends with an overwhelming exhibit of Lalique art nouveau jewelry and glass.

Igreja da Madre de Deus, and Museu Nacional do Azulejo ★★★

The museum is open Tues.-Sat. 10 a.m. to 5 p.m. Open Sun. 10 a.m. to 2 p.m. Closed Mon. and holidays. Admission: 200$00; free on Sun. Located one block inland from the river, about 4 k west of the Praça do Comércio, at R. Madre de Deus, 4. Trolleys #3, #16, #24, #27, and buses #13, #18 and #42 stop there. This monastery was founded at the beginning of the 16th century by Donha Leonor, the widow of King João II. Here *azulejo* tiles can be seen *in situ* inside this exquisitely decorated little church, and their development is explained by displays in the museum housed in its cloisters.

Although the church (to the right of the entrance) was substantially rebuilt after the great earthquake, much of the earlier art survived inside, along with the outside Manueline west entrance. Twisted columns lining the portal support an arch in which fishnets and pelicans entwine. The fishnet was Leonor's symbol, the pelican was her husband's. Inside all seems stunningly rich. Lower walls are lined with 18th-century Dutch *azulejos*, deeper blue than the Portuguese examples. The walls above are crowded with paintings of Saint Francis, on the right, and Saint Clare, on the left. Overhead, the barrel-coffered ceiling also contains paintings, this time primitives of the life of the Virgin. The altar is gilded Baroque and holds a fine pulpit.

Steps lead down to the surviving part of the original church whose walls are lined with 16th-century *azulejos* from Seville. The main, Renaissance cloister extends off this chancel, and beyond it is a lovely Manueline cloister. The *azulejo* museum can be entered from the main cloister, but first climb to the upper gallery for more of the church. Here the chapel of Saint Anthony is tiled with 18th-century *azulejos* depicting the saint's life, above which are more early primitive paintings. Next comes the *coro alto*, the nun's choir, all in gilt with still more paintings. Finally, the sacristy is lined with Portuguese *azulejos* from the 18th century and still more 16th century primitives.

The *azulejo* museum uses both actual tiles and pictures to demonstrate the development of that art. (Pictures are necessary because the finest examples are still affixed to buildings throughout Portugal.) The Portuguese adopted the idea of decorative tiles from the Moors, perhaps from those still living in Spain or from those met in Morocco when the Portuguese came to conquer Cueta early in the 15th century. By the end of the 16th century the Portuguese were manufacturing their own. The first were predominantly blue—*azul*—hence their name. By the 17th century, the Portuguese had mastered the art and scenes, generally of outdoor life, became immensely popular. Demand remained strong until architecture changed to a simpler neo-classical style at the close of the 18th century, although subsequently it rose again.

WHERE TO STAY

Hotels in Lisbon exist in sufficient number that finding good accommodations is generally easy, except during Christmas, Easter week and June and July when reservations should be made well in advance. Although accommodations in Lisbon are among the most expensive in the country, they are not exorbitant by European or American standards, and comfortable hotels at modest prices are available.

VERY EXPENSIVE ($200+)

Hotel Da Lapa　　　　　　　　　　　　　　　Deluxe ★★★★★

R. do Pau de Bandeira (in the section called Lapa, two blocks north of the Museum of Ancient Art; take a cab). Rooms: 86, including 8 suites. ☎ *395 00 05; FAX 395 06 65; Telex 65656.* In 1993, after six years of painstaking preparation, the Hotel da Lapa opened in the quiet embassy section of Lisbon and immediately displaced the Ritz as the city's premier hotel. Rarely do we encounter a hotel at once so intimate, elegant and welcoming. The hotel, a renovated nineteenth-century *palacita* formerly owned by the Count of Valenças, has been renovated throughout under the direction of its owner, António Simões de Almeiola, with unerring good taste. Public spaces flow gently into each other to permit guests to wander, as if through a private home, and choose atmospheres suited to their mood. Every touch is perfect in the original mansion, including bedrooms and suites that are each decorated in a different style. From top floor suites the views of Lisbon and the river are spectacular. Striking views from the lower floors of the mansion and from a modern wing take in a lush tropical park below a cascading two-story waterfall. If all this were not sufficient reason to stay at the Lapa, the attentive yet never intrusive staff would be. Perfection extends to its Embaixada restaurant which serves the finest food of any hotel in Lisbon. With all this and a new full-facility health club, so far prices hit $200 only from April through June and after the middle of September. In July and August they drop to about $150.

Ritz
Deluxe ★★★★

R. Rodrigo da Fonseca, 88 (one block east of the Parque Eduardo VII). Rooms: 310. ☎ *69 20 20; FAX 69 17 83; Telex 12589 RITZ P.* The Ritz had been the best in town since a famous hotel named the Aviz closed two decades ago. In truth, since a takeover by the large Intercontinental Hotel Corporation, it coasted on its laurels, and it has always been too large to provide individual service, while its location beyond the edge of tourist interests left it out of things. But it had no serious competition for luxury before the Hotel da Lapa (discussed above) came along. The Ritz is scurrying now, as fast as a megalith can, to renovate its fading fifties decor. Modern outside, its elegance is all within, consisting of furniture and appointments. It may have the finest bathrooms in Europe. Although all of the suites are utterly elegant, many of the simple bedrooms remain ordinary, but we will see what renovation brings. A suite with a park view is well worth the additional escudos. However, ordinary bedrooms cost above $300 for a double in season.

Le Meridien Lisboa
Deluxe ★★★

R. Castiho, 149 (on the east edge of the Parque Eduardo VII). Rooms: 331. ☎ *69 09 00; FAX 69 32 31; Telex 64315.* This member of the well-regarded French chain is elegantly modern in its dress of marble and chrome, and a favorite of many business people. All rooms have lovely views of the park, but should be larger for the price which approach the Ritz's, its neighbor next door.

Lisboa Sheraton
Deluxe ★★

R. Latino Coelho, 1 (3 blocks along Av. Pereira de Melo that runs west from the southern end of the Parque Eduardo VII). Rooms: 385. ☎ *57 57 57; FAX 54 71 64; Telex 12774.* The Sheraton is the tallest building in Lisbon, so views are dramatic from the top floors. Otherwise, it provides what familiarity with the chain would lead one to expect. However, it has the audacity to outcharge the Ritz, as if to seek panache by being the highest-priced hotel in the city.

EXPENSIVE ($100-$200)

York House
R1st-class ★★★★

R. das Janelas Verdes, 32 (opposite the Museu Nacional de Arte Antiga, in Lapa). Rooms: 32, plus 2 suites. ☎ *396 25 44; FAX 397 27 93; Telex 16791.* Charming, generally an overused word in travel writing, is the perfect description of the York, and a word you'll exclaim again and again if you stay there. This *residencial* is remodeled from a 17th-century convent whose tasteful renovation included closing off the city and its noise with a high enclosing wall. All furnishings are lovely, floors are homey old wood or tile. Its location is far enough from the heart of the city for relative quiet, despite its location on a busy street, and close enough to taxi to in minutes. The best rooms are those overlooking the beautiful courtyard. Classed as a residencial, primarily because it lacks such extras as an elevator, its service is first class. Prices dip below $100 for a double through the end of April, but match the neighboring Hotel Lapa (above) in July and August. This one is very popular, so should be booked well in advance.

Veneza R2nd-class ★★

Av. da Liberdade, 189. Rooms: 38. ☎ 352 26 18; FAX 352 66 78. This 19th-century mansion has just opened as one of Lisbon's most stylish hotels. Although there is an odd contrast between elegant marble stairs in the lobby and bedrooms done in a homey green with white wicker, the former impresses and the later welcomes. This hotel combines elegance, hominess and a fine location in one intimate package.

As Janelas Verdes R1st-class ★★★

R. das Janelas Verdes, 47 (down the street from the York House, near the Museum of Ancient Art in Lapa). Rooms: 17. ☎ 396 81 43 (or 44); FAX 396 81 44; Telex 16402. Formerly this was the annex of the York House (above), now it has reopened separately owned and nicely redone. The building is a late 18th-century mansion, decorated more formally than the York to provide a stately but less charming option up the street. Bedrooms are larger, but the ones fronting the street can be noisy. For this reason and for the view, ask for a back room over the quiet patio.

Principe Real R1st-class ★★★

R. da Alegria, 53 (a few steep blocks west from the Av. da Liberdade, beside the Jardim Botanico. Rooms: 24. ☎ 346 01 16; FAX 342 21 04; Telex 44571. Each bedroom is different and tasteful, and graced with fresh flowers—this is the hotel to which the Ritz sends its overflow. The location is pastoral near a lovely park, and prices are reasonable for its style.

Avenida Palace Deluxe ★★★

R. 1 de Dezembro, 123 (halfway between the Pr. Rossio and the Pr. dos Restauradores). Rooms: 100. ☎ 346 01 54; FAX 342 22 84. This century-old hotel, most conveniently located for visiting the sights, presents crystal chandeliers, brocaded walls, curtains and handwoven carpets to suit its grand age. The staff wears tails. Bedrooms have recently been redone and are attractive, if somewhat nondescript. The only drawback is a bustling, noisy location.

Lisboa Plaza 1st-class ★★

Travessa do Salitre, 7 (halfway along the Av. da Liberdade, and a step west). Rooms: 112. ☎ 346 39 22; FAX 347 16 30; Telex 16402. The art nouveau exterior leads to restful pastels inside. Its bar comes from a more relaxed and gracious era. Bathrooms are grand and bedrooms were recently renovated for comfort, but not great style. Altogether, prices seem a bit high for the rooms, although a buffet breakfast is included. The location is convenient for walks.

Mundial 1st-class ★★
R. Dom Duarte, 4 (1 block east of the Praça do Comércio). Rooms: 147. ☎ 886 31 01; FAX 87 91 29; Telex 12308. A superior location and views of the Castelo de São Jorge from the back rooms (which are also quieter) make this a choice to consider. Bedrooms are ample, with a quietly tasteful decor, and the management is efficient. Rooms are often available here when other choices are full, not because it is a lesser option, but because few foreigners know about the hotel.

Tivoli Jardim 1st-class ★
R. Julio Cesar Machado, 7 (behind its sister the Tivoli Lisboa at Av. Liberdade 185) Rooms: 119. ☎ 53 99 71; FAX: 355 65 66; Telex 12172. Although bedrooms are small and basic, the lovely garden around this annex of the Hotel Tivoli with which it shares tennis courts and pool, make this a pleasant place to stay. Its sister, the Tivoli Lisboa, charges too much for too little to be recommended. The Jardim is quieter as well.

Altis Deluxe
R. Castilho, 11 (5 blocks along Av. da Liberdade from the Praça do Comércio and two blocks west). Rooms: 307. ☎ 52 24 96; FAX 54 86 96; Telex 13314. This is a comfortable-enough, sleek, modern hotel in a convenient location. It is affiliated with the Best Western chain. Since its prices push the expensive limits, this one should be considered only if other choices are unavailable.

MODERATE ($50-$99)

Albergaria da Senhora do Monte R1st-class ★★★
Calçada do Monte, 39 (on a hilltop just north of the São Jorge hill). Rooms: 28. ☎ 886 60 02; FAX 87 77 83. Views of the castle, city and river are perhaps the best available, and this special hotel is pleasantly decorated. Bedrooms are comfortable and all incorporate terraces. Those at the back provide the views worth coming for. While the bedrooms are not air-conditioned, they seldom need it. Admittedly, the location is not central, but the modest price saves enough for plenty of taxi rides.

Dom Manuel I 1st-class ★★★
Av. Duque d'Avila, 189 (just north of the Parque Eduardo VII). Rooms: 64. ☎ 57 61 60; FAX 57 69 85; Telex 43558. Behind a modern facade waits a nicely styled interior that make this a very good choice. It becomes even more appealing when the low price for its category is factored in. The bedrooms are tasteful, if slightly on the small side. The location is near the Gulbenkian Museum, which is a distance from the heart of the city.

Dom Carlos   2nd-class ★ ★
Av. Duque de Loule, 121 (fronting its own park two blocks east of the Pr. de Pombal). Rooms: 73, plus 17 suites. ☎ 53 90 71; FAX 352 07 28; Telex 16468. The recently remodeled Dom Carlos uses yards of glass to take advantage of a garden outside. Bedrooms are Scandinavian and wood panelled, with Portuguese touches. This is a comfortable and efficient hotel that charges a quarter of the fee of most of its neighbors.

Da Torre   2nd-class ★
R. dos Jerónimos, 8 (located beside the Mosteiro Jerónimos in Belém). Rooms: 50. ☎ 363 62 62; FAX 364 59 95. This modern hotel is furnished with some style and taste. It is endearing, and would be recommended more strongly except for the cool service. Its location is perfect for touring the Belém area; the center of town 10 k away can be reached in 15 minutes by taxi (or half an hour by public transport). The bedrooms are not air-conditioned.

Capitol   2nd-class ★
R. Eça de Queiroz, 24 (off the southeast corner of the Parque Eduardo VII). Rooms: 58. ☎ 53 68 11; FAX 352 61 65; Telex 13701. The Capitol offers the quiet of a peaceful street by a small park. Emphasis is on the bedrooms, which have a spacious feeling in part because they are sparsely furnished. Some have pleasant balconies and all are air-conditioned, but they stretch the moderate category to the limit.

Roma   2nd-class ★
Av. de Roma, 33 (near the Roma metro stop, 2 k north and 1 k east of the Parque Eduardo VII) Rooms: 265. ☎ 796 77 61; FAX 793 29 81; Telex 16586. Debits are that this hotel stands at a distance from the center of town on a noisy street and lacks intimacy. Assets are the low prices for its class, larger rooms than most, and the fact that vacancies should exist. The hotel is bright and the bedrooms are comfortable. Downtown is 15 minutes away by subway or taxi. All bedrooms are air-conditioned.

Principe   2nd-class
Av. Duque d'Avila, 301 (1 long block north of the Parque Eduardo VII). Rooms: 68. ☎ 53 61 51; FAX 53 42 14; Telex 43565. The bedrooms are roomy and the rate for children under nine is only half the listed charge. Half of the bedrooms are air-conditioned and many have balconies. The hotel is European in flavor, but otherwise nondescript.

INEXPENSIVE (UNDER $50)

Imperador   R2nd-class ★
Av. 5 de Outubro, 55 (a quarter of a mile north of the northeast corner of Parque Eduardo VII, one block west and north of the Saldanha metro stop). Rooms: 43. ☎ 352 48 84; FAX 352 65 37. Past a claustrophobic entrance wait spotless rooms comfortably decorated in muted colors.

Front rooms overlook a small garden. In truth, however, this one makes the inexpensive category only by factoring in the free breakfast.

Nazareth   R2nd-class
Av. António Agusto de Aguiar, 25 (at the northeast corner of the Parque Eduardo VII). Rooms: 32. ☎ 54 20 16; FAX 356 08 36. This one is for those who appreciate camp. It is a fourth-floor hotel with a lobby decorated as a fortress with fake vaulting on the ceiling and lots of ironwork. Not surprisingly, the bedrooms are slightly eccentric too, many with steps up or down to an adjoining bathroom.

Horizonte   R2nd-class
Av. António Agusto de Aguiar, 42 (at the northeast corner of the Parque Eduardo VII). Rooms: 52. ☎ 53 95 26; FAX 56 25 29. This *residencial* is a former apartment house fronted by an impressive stairway. Bedrooms are arranged around that stairway and very clean, despite the worn look of the lobby.

WHERE TO EAT

While only a few truly exceptional restaurants exist in Portugal, about half are situated in the capital. At these you will pay $100 for dinner for two, be treated like royalty, surrounded by elegance and savor an extraordinary meal. But fear not, there are also enough modest restaurants serving tasty dishes made from fresh ingredients for a diner to enjoy a different one every night for a year.

EXPENSIVE ($30+)

Conventual   ★★★★★
Pr. das Flores, 45 (in a little green square just west of the Bairro Alto. From R. da Escola Politecnica, which is a continuation of R. Dom Pedro V in the Bairro Alto, take a left on R. San Marcal at the Botanical Gardens, then the third right. Better still, take a cab). ☎ 60 91 96. Closed Saturday lunch, Sunday and August. Our hearts cry that this is the best restaurant in Lisbon; our wallets agree since this one charges about 30 percent less than its competition. While most elegant Lisbon restaurants earn their excellence by incorporating French recipes, Sra. Marques is a true original. Her coriander soup is sublime, monkfish with creamy herb sauce is delectable, and the sole with shellfish sauce a delight. Every dish is prepared with taste, and most succeed memorably. The restaurant is more comfortable than formal—the former convent with its old stone walls and ancient terra cotta floors has been decorated with the owner's eclectic collection of antiques. Prices hover at the bottom of the expensive range. Reservations are necessary.
Amex, Diners, MasterCard and Visa accepted.

Casa da Comida   ★★★★★
Travessa das Amoreiras, 1 (just off the P. de Amoreiras, 4 blocks west and 3 south of Parque Eduardo VII). ☎ 388 53 76. Closed Saturday lunch, Sunday and August. We wrestle mightily about whether Conventual (above) or Comida is the best restaurant in Lisbon. Let us just say they

are different, and each is a treasure. Comida adds a French touch to traditional Portuguese cuisine and serves it in a grander style than does Conventual. The restaurant is a most discrete townhouse enticing with a roaring fire in winter or a beautiful planted patio in summer. The decor is elegant, the bar inviting, and tables are decorated with style. In general the food is slightly nouveau, with the delicate portions of that genre. Special dishes include savory clam soup or a succulent cascade of shellfish. Mention the turbot with green pepper and we salivate. The extensive menu includes a number of standard dishes as well, although we confess to prefer Tágide's version of roast baby kid with herbs. Prices are high, and will easily pass $100 for a couple, but no one complains. Reservations are absolutely necessary.

Amex, Diners, MasterCard and Visa accepted.

Tágide ★★★★

Largo da Academia Nacional de Belas Artes, 18 (two blocks south of the R. Garrett in Chiado). ☎ *347 18 80. Closed Saturday night and Sunday.* The spacious windows of this former townhouse look over the port and reflect the crystal chandeliers of its elegant off-white dining room. (Request a window table.) Service is discrete, and the dishes, if anything, surpass expectations. Start with salmon pâté or cold stuffed crab. Graduate to grilled baby goat with herbs or supreme of halibut. Either the souffle with hot chocolate sauce or dessert crepes will cap a fine meal. A couple will spend about 15.000$00 with wine, which is a bargain for such exquisitely prepared food. Reservations are necessary.

Amex, Diners, MasterCard and Visa accepted.

Gambrinus ★★★

R. das Portas de Santo Antão, 25 (on a tiny square behind the east side of the Teatro Nacional a few steps north of Pr. Rossio). ☎ *32 14 66.* There is no question that this is the best seafood restaurant in Lisbon, nor that it is the most expensive restaurant in Portugal. A dinner can cost a third more than at Tágide. Fish and shellfish are invariably fresh and done to a turn as they should be at these prices. Reservations are advised.

Amex and Visa accepted.

Embaixada ★★★

R. Pau de Bandeira, 4 (in the Hotel da Lapa near the Museum of Ancient Art; take a taxi). ☎ *395 00 05.* The dining room is divided by a kind of gazebo to create intimate seating arrangements, just one example of the thought invested in this establishment. Large windows overlook a tropical garden complete with waterfall, while all Lisbon spreads beyond. The nouvelle-style food, is characterized by attention to detail and the finest ingredients. Lunch is a $25 menu which counts among the great bargains in Portugal. Dinner prices use to about $40 for an excellent five-course *menu de dégustation,* or there are fine á la carte choices.

MasterCard and Visa accepted.

Aviz ★★

R. Serpa Pinto, 12-B (around the corner (north) from R. Garret in the Chiado). ☎ 32 83 91. Closed Saturday lunch, Sunday and August. This is the most deluxe restaurant in the country. It serves very good food, but has declined recently and the service seems distracted. The restaurant, saved by its chef, is all that remains of what once was Lisbon's most deluxe hotel. Mahogany panelling, black leather, marble columns and chandeliers lend a men's-club atmosphere to the lounge. Three dining rooms are more intimate and turn-of-the-century grand. In general the dishes betray a French taste, despite being specialties of the restaurant. Vichyssoise Rothschild, for example, adds shrimp to the classic recipe. Aviz is worth a visit for the ambiance.
Amex, Diners, MasterCard and Visa accepted.

MODERATE ($15-$30)

Sua Excelencia ★★

R. do Conde, 42 (In Lapa, 1 block due north of the National Museum of Ancient Art). ☎ 60 36 14. Closed Saturday lunches, Wednesday in September, and Sunday lunches in August. This restaurant is entirely the child of its owner, Francisco Queiroz. Only a discrete awning announces it. When the doorbell is rung, the owner greets you, escorts you to a table in a colorful room with tile floor, then recites the menu of the day. Selections depend on what is fresh in the market. Sr. Queiroz speaks enough English to convey what is necessary, and one can be certain that whatever is selected will be carefully prepared. Reservations are necessary.
Amex, Diners, MasterCard and Visa accepted.

Pap'Açorda ★★

R. da Atalaya, 57 (from the church of São Roque in the Bairro Alto head west along Trav. da Queimada to take the fifth left). ☎ 346 48 11. Closed Sunday and Monday, and the first half of July and October. This restaurant, housed in an old bakery, specializes in the hearty food of the Alentejo. Naturally the favored dish is *açorda*, a delicious stew of fish, bread, and eggs seasoned with coriander. For the quality and authenticity of the food, it is a bargain. This one is very popular with locals, so reservations are necessary on weekends.
MasterCard and Visa accepted.

Comida de Santo ★

Calçada do Eng. Miquel Pais, 39 (just off the Jardim Botanico in the Bairro Alto. R. Dom Pedro V heads that way). ☎ 396 33 39. With such close ties to Brazil, Portugal would naturally support restaurants offering that cuisine, and de Santo is clearly the best. Sample any of the variety of dishes cooked in palm oil and coconut milk—some are very spicy, but others are mild. *Vatapa*, spicy shrimp, are delectable. This different and delectable dining experience all takes place in a colorful atmosphere of tropical murals. Open until 1 a.m. Reservations are advised.
Amex, Diners, MasterCard and Visa accepted.

Sancho ★

Travessa da Gloria, 14 (just off Av. de Liberdade, 1 long block north of the Pr. Restauradores). ☎ *346 97 80. Closed Sunday and holidays.* Cozy with stucco walls, fireplace, leather furniture and wood-beamed ceiling, this restaurant provides relaxed, enjoyable meals. Shellfish are specialties, and expensive, but moderately priced meat courses are offered as well. ***Amex, MasterCard and Visa accepted.***

Restaurante 33 ★

R. Alexandre Herculano, 33A (1 long block south and 2 west of Pr. Rossio at the Parque Eduardo VII). ☎ *54 60 79. Closed for Saturday lunch, and Sunday.* Although it looks English with its sedate panelling, this restaurant presents well-prepared Portuguese food, accompanied by a singer on weekends. Reservations are advised.
MasterCard and Visa accepted.

Numero Um ★

R. Dom Francisco de Malo, 44A (near the Méridien Hotel). ☎ *68 43 26. Closed for Saturday lunch and Sunday.* Here is the best steak house in Lisbon, serving platters in a cozy, pub-like atmosphere. Since Portuguese beef is disappointing, they import theirs from Brazil. Fridays Brazilian specialties are offered in addition to steaks and salads.
Amex, Diners, MasterCard and Visa accepted.

INEXPENSIVE (UNDER $15)

Bota Alta ★★

Travessa da Queimada, 35 (the street heads west from the church of São Roque in the Bairro Alto) ☎ *32 79 59. Closed Sunday.* The only problem with this place is that it is well known for tasty food and good value, so waiting in line can be expected. It is a small bistro with a smoke-stained ceiling. The *caldo verde* is delicious. Of course cod is present in many varieties, but there are also daily specials.
No reservations are taken.

Cervejaria da Trindade ★

R. Nova de Trindade, 20-B (off R. Garrett in the Chiado) ☎ *342 35 06.* The room once formed part of a convent and then a brewery, although now it is a beer hall owned by the Sagres beer company. Even if prawns are ordered, the meal should be inexpensive, filling and tasty. A tourist menu is offered for $10. Wash it down with a *mista*, a mixture of light and dark beer.

Pastelaria Bénard ★

R. Garrett, 104. ☎ *347 31 33. Closed Sunday.* This is the most fashionable of the dozen tea houses in Lisbon. Tea and cakes are the specialties, but there is a small selection of heartier foods. Best for lunch.

Xêlê Bananas ★

Pr. des Flores, 29 (from R. da Escola Politecnica, which is a continuation of R. Dom Pedro V in the Bairro Alto, take a left on R. San Marcal at the

Botanical Gardens, then the third right). ☎ 395 25 15. Closed Saturday lunch and Sunday. The pretty square opposite adds to the pleasure of the dining experience. The restaurant looks more expensive than it is, and Lisboetas know that well.

Bonjardim ★
Traversa de Santo Antão, 11 (a narrow street beside the post office building behind (east of) Pr. dos Restauradores). ☎ 342 74 24. Noted for perfectly done, roast chicken served with salad and fries, this plain-and-simple eatery is sufficiently successful to support two additional outlets on the same street. Fish soup and the pork *alentejana* aren't bad either. But don't expect atmosphere.

Great American Disaster
Pr. Marquês de Pombal, 1 (on the ground floor of the Varig building in front of the Parque Eduardo VII). ☎ 51 61 45. Here are served the best hamburgers in Lisbon, which fall short of the best in the world.

Amex, Visa and MasterCard accepted.

SHOPPING

Lisbon entices shoppers with handcrafts, not high fashion. Ceramics are lovely and reasonable, and Portuguese carpets are famous, though never cheap, as is needlework from the Azores and Madeira. Stores generally open at 9 a.m., close at noon, reopen at 2 p.m. and close at 7 p.m. Many are closed on Saturday.

Gold, by law of at least 19 karats, is reasonable by U.S. standards, as is **silver**. The Portuguese specialty is filigree work. **Sarmento**, at *R. Aurea, 251*, in the Baixa, has a distinguished century-old reputation. For quality sterling tableware visit **Joalharia Ferreira Marquês**, elegantly occupying numbers 7-9 in the Rossio.

The best and largest concentration of **antique** stores congregate along R. Dom Pedro V and its continuation, R. da Escola Politécnica, in the Bairro Alto (see direction under "Sights"). Some of the material is religious, but there are also antique ceramics and furniture. An outstanding selection of antique *azulejos* is offered by **Solar**, at #70, along with other old things.

A fascinating store for browsing is the **Centro Antiquaro do Alecrim** for drawings from old books, many handcolored. It is located at *R. do Alecrim, 48-50* (near Sant'Anna, described below). What could be more typical of Portugal than a souvenir of **cork**? **Casa das Corticas**, at *R. Escola Politecnica #4*, the continuation of R. Dom Pedro V, sells nothing else and has invented surprising, if not always serious, uses for the material.

For **ceramics** and **azulejos**, besides the fine antique ones at Solar mentioned above, see **Sant'Anna** occupying *#95-7 on R. do Alecrim*, the southern continuation of R. de San Pedro de Alcantara that leads from R. Dom Pedro V to R. Garrett. In addition to a large selection of tiles, the store also carries its own line of ceramic pieces—boxes, planters, candelabra, etc. Its only true competitor is **Fabrica Ceramica Viuva Lamego**, a fair distance away at *#25 Largo do Intendente* (by the Intendente metro stop in the north of the city). Designs here are more colorful, but less sophisticated than at Sant'Anna.

For fine bone **china**, there are several outlets of the well-known **Vista Allegra** factory. The best is at *Largo do Chiado, 18*, one block north of R. Garrett. In addition to prices that are about 20 percent less than those in the U.S. for the china, exquisite French Baccarat **crystal** is also sold at a great discount. Unfortunately, the outlets do not ship. For the well-known Portuguese crystal, Atlantis, the place to go is **Cristalissimo** at *R. Castilho, 149*, in the Meridien hotel.

The finest **embroidery** is sold in Lisbon, brought from the islands of Madeira and the Azores which remain bastions of the craft. However, cheaper copies from China make the Portuguese versions seem less of a buy. The best-known shop is **Madeira House** at *R. Augusta 131-5* in the Baixa. The selection is large, but not quite up to the quality carried at **Madeira Superbia** on *Av. Duque Loulé, 75-A* (the street that leads east from Pr. Pombal in front of the Parque Eduardo VII). The highest quality of all is carried by the prestigious **Principe Real** at *12-14 R. da Escola Politécnica* (the continuation of R. Dom Pedro V) in the Barrio Alta.

Needlepoint carpets from the village of Arraiolos are famous enough to lend their name to the style. Several stores in Lisbon sell arraiolos, but one is superior in selection, quality and honesty. People do almost as well from **Casa Quintão** on *R. Ivens, 30-4 (off R. Garrett in the Chiado)* as in the village where the rugs are made. If $2000 sounds like a lot for an eight-by-ten-feet carpet, price comparable ones in the U.S.

For **handcrafts** of great variety at inexpensive prices from all the regions of Portugal go to **Filartesanato**, which is toward Belém on the waterfront west of the Tejos bridge, *Ponte 25 de Abril*, in the Feira Internacional de Lisboa.

For an interesting shopping experience visit Lisbon's giant **shopping mall, Amoreiras** (*at Av. Duarte Pachecho, 1k due west of the Pr. Pombal;* free buses from the Pr. Pombal; open until 11 p.m.). Captivatingly post-modern outside, it is a more pedestrian mall within that contains almost 250 stores, a supermarket, 10 movie theaters and a chapel. There is everything from Vista Alegra, to Marks and Spenser, shoe shops, hair dressers and fifty restaurants. A visit will give a sense of Portuguese tastes.

Then there is the famed Lisbon **flea market**, the *Feira da Ladra* (Thieves' Market). It is held Tuesdays and Saturdays, from early morning until sunset. All the stalls are open-air and fill the Campo de Santa Clara, three blocks east of São Jorge Castle. Trolley #28 and bus #12 stop there. As with any such market, 99 percent of the goods are uninteresting, but there remains that one percent and the hope of a treasure. Diligence can uncover interesting craftswork. Bargaining is expected.

ENTERTAINMENT

The two characteristic Portuguese entertainments are bullfights and *fado*, both presented best in Lisbon.

Bullfights in Portugal are a different proposition from their Spanish counterparts. The purpose is not to kill the bull, and fighting is done with lances from horseback. The audience comes to admire the graceful movements and skills of the horse and rider as they play the bull. Since tradition dictates 18th-century dress for the participants, Portuguese bullfights are memorable spectacles. Teams arrive in carriages and emerge in embroidered vests with flourishes of tricornered plumed hats. The second half of the show consists of a group of men who try to throw the bull. Matches are held from Easter through October. In Lisbon they take place in Campo Pequeno near a metro stop. But the best events are held in the suburb of Vila Franca de Xira, which can be reached from the Santa Apolónia Station on the river west of the Alfama. Although one pays a 10 percent premium, the most convenient way to secure a ticket is from the ABEP kiosk in Pr. dos Restauradores or at *Av. da Liberdade 140*.

Fado, literally "Fate," means a deep song, a Portuguese passion comparable to flamenco in Spain—though consisting only of earthy singing, for there is no dancing involved. Readers of a certain age may remember the song "Lisboa Antiqua," which was a popularization of one *fado* tune. Performances take place in a cafe and consist of a husky-voiced singer, almost always a woman, playing plaintive songs on a guitar. Melodies betray old Middle-Eastern tonalities and tend at first to disconcert those unfamiliar with the music, though most listeners take to it increasingly as an evening progresses. Fado houses generally serve dinner until about 10 p.m., after which the show begins. Dinners are often expensive, but it is not necessary to eat in order to watch the show. One can arrive after 10 p.m. to listen, paying only a drink minimum. While after-dinner reservations are available, they are quickly exhausted. A short description of the more authentic *fado* houses—most are in the Bairro Alto—follows.

Senhor do Vinho

R. do Meio-a-Lapa, 18 *(west of the center in Lapa; best visited by taxi).* ☎ 397 74 56. *Closed Sunday and the last week in December.* Although both food and drinks are more expensive here than at most houses, the food is probably the best of all the *fado* houses and the singing tends to be the most authentic.

Amex, Diners, MasterCard and Visa accepted.

Lisboa a Noite

R. des Gaveas, 69 *(this street is the first left off Trav. da Queimada which heads west from the church of São Roque).* ☎ 346 85 57. *Closed Sunday.* The expensive food is better than most, and this time it is the owner, Fernanda da Maria, a famous *fadista*, who sings and sings very well.

Amex, Diners, and MasterCard accepted.

Mascote de Atalaia

R. da Atalaia *(from the church of São Roque in the Bairro Alto head west along Trav. da Queimada to take the fifth left.)* This is the real thing—no food, no professional entertainers, no tourists, just wine with the locals to listen to whichever *fadistas* drop in. The quality is unpredictable, but the expense is low.

DIRECTORY

ADDRESSES

U.S. Embassy • *Av. das Forcas Armadas* (☎ *726 66 00*)

Canadian Embassy • *Av. da Liberdade, 144* (☎ *347 48 92*)

American Express • *Handled by Star, Av. Sidonio Pais, 4A* (☎ *53 98 71*)

AIRPORT • Portela airport (☎ *80 20 60* for flight information) is 8 k northeast of the center of the city and handles both international and domestic flights. By taxi (about 700$00) the trip should take half an hour in traffic. Linha Verde (Green Line) buses depart from the Santa Apolona train station and make stops along Av. de Liberdade for under $2. Most airlines have offices in Pr. Marquês de Pombal, including TAP at #3-A (☎ *57 50 20*).

BUSES • The main bus depot is Rodoviária Nacional at Av. Casal Ribeiro, 18 (☎ *53 77 15*) near the Pr. Duque de Saldanha (an 8-block walk from the Pr. Pombal along Pereira de Melo). Three buses go daily to Faro in the Algarve, two *expressos* travel to Porto, and 14 leave for Coimbra.

CAR RENTALS

Avis: *Pr. dos Restauradores, 47* (☎ *56 11 76*).

Budget: *Av. Fontes Pereira de Melo, 62* (☎ *53 77 17*).

Eurocar: *Av. António Agusto de Aguiar, 24* (☎ *52 45 58*).

Hertz: *R. 5 de Outubro, 10* (☎ *53 98 16*).

CHANGING MONEY • Banks group primarily in two areas—in the Baixa, just north of the Pr. Comércio and in the Pr. Restauradores. They are open only on weekdays, close for lunch from 11:45 until 1, then close for good at 3 (service after 2:45 is chancy). Banco Pinto & Sotto Mayor in the Pr. dos Restauradores stays open until 7:30 p.m. A small *Cambio* with rates as good as a bank's at *R. do Ouro, 283*, just south of the Rossio opens on Saturday from 10-5.

CITY TOURS • **Star**, affiliated with American Express, offers half-day tours for about 4000.00, departing at 9:30 a.m. and 2:30 p.m. It is located at *Av. Sidónio Pais, 4* (☎ *53 98 71*), near the Pr. Pombal, and at *Pr. Restauradores 14* (☎ *346 25 01*). **Citirams** (☎ *560 668*), **Marcus & Harting** (☎ *346 9271*), and **Portugal Tours** (☎ *352 2902*) also provide half-day tours, most leave from the Pr. Pombal.

INFORMATION • The main office is in the Palácio da Foz on the north side of Pr. dos Restauradores (☎ *346 36 24*). Be sure to take one of the maps they offer. There is another office at the airport (open 24 hours), and one at Santa Apolónia station.

POLICE • ☎ *346 61 41*. Emergencies: ☎ *115*.

POST OFFICE AND TELEPHONES • A main post office is in the Pr. dos Restauradores, 58 (☎ *34 70 05*). Telephones are available as well.

TRAINS • Four separate train stations serve Lisbon. International trains and trains from the north use Santa Apolónia station (☎ *86 41 43*; information: ☎ *87 60 25*). The station is a 15-minute walk along the river east of Praça do Comércio. Eight *Rapidos* leave daily for the three-and-a-half hour trip to Porto, two fewer on Sunday. They also stop at Coimbra in two hours. Rossio station handles passengers from Sintra and Estremadura, the near north. It is located west of Pr. Rossio (☎ *87 60 25*) at the beginning of the Pr. Restauradores. Electric trains to the near beaches Estoril and Cascais leave from Cais do Sodré (☎ *37 01 81*) by the river just west of the Praça do Comércio. The cost is less than $1. Trains for the Algarve and south leave from Sul e Sueste in Barreiro (☎ *87 71 79*) on the south bank of the river. Tickets include the price of a ferry that leaves the bank at the Praça do Comércio.

TRAVEL AGENTS •

Star (American Express affiliate): *Pr. dos Restauradores, 14* (☎ *36 25 01*).

Viagens Rawes: *Travessa do Corpo Santo, 15* (☎ *37 0231*).

Wasteels-Expresso: *Av. António Augusto de Aguiar, 88* (☎ *57 91 80*).

EXCURSIONS

Lisbon serves as a hub for some special excursions. The longest is to **Batalha** ★★★★★, 120 k north. Batalha monastery is the premier Gothic and Manueline structure in the country, outshining even Lisbon's Mostiero dos Jerónimos. With a two-hour train ride each way the visit will consume a day, but by car other sights—such as the picturesque village of **Nazaré** ★★ and the monastery of **Alcobaça** ★★★—could be combined in one excursion. By train lovely **Óbidos** ★★, a walled medieval town, requires a change at Caçem and a trip of almost three hours each way. At less than 100 k away, travel time by car should be an hour and a half. The huge Baroque palace complex at **Mafra** ★★ is a half-day excursion including a train ride of an hour and a half each way. By car it can be combined with Portugal's version of Versailles at **Queluz** ★★★, otherwise a separate train trip. The haunting beauty of **Sintra** ★★★★ was immortalized by Byron and can be reached by frequent trains in 45 minutes. For beaches, there are elegant ones at **Cascais** ★ and **Estoril** ★, near to each other as well as to Lisbon, half an hour away. Long, uncrowded beaches surround **Setúbal** ★, 55 miles south of Lisbon, a 45-minute train ride with frequent service. All the foregoing sights are described under their own headings in the next chapter "The Environs of Lisbon."

At greater distances, requiring a hotel transfer from Lisbon, there is **Coimbra** ★★★ to the north, and **Tomar**★★, **Porto**★★★, **Guimarães**★★★ and **Braga**★★. Marvão ★★, Elvas ★, **Estremoz**★★★ and **Évora** ★★★★ to the east; and the **Algarve** beaches to the south. These sights are described in the "Northern Portugal," "Eastern Portugal," and "Algarve" chapters, respectively.

For **Cascais** and **Estoril** by car follow the river west along Av. 24 de Julho which is renamed Av. Marginal before turning into scenic N-6 for 25 k, to Estoril, another 2 k for Cascais. For **Sintra** follow the same route into Estoril where a sign directs a right turn for N6-8 to Sintra in 23 k. For **Mafra** go east at Pr. Pombal on Periera de Melo, which reaches the circle of Pr. Saldanha in three blocks. Take Av. da República north as it becomes Campo Grande with a planted center strip. After the race course on the right, follow signs right to A-8 and Torres Vedras. Stay on A-8 for 32k to exit for Malveira and another 11k west on N-117. For **Queluz** turn left at the Pr. Pombal along R. José António de Aguiar which becomes A-5, the expressway to Estoril. Take the first exit for N-117 to Sintra which becomes N-249 and brings Queluz in about 7k.

For **northern points** take the autoestrada A-1 by going east at Pr. Pombal on Periera de Melo, which reaches the circle of Pr. Saldanha in three blocks. Take Av. da República north as it becomes Campo Grande with a planted center strip. After the race course on the right, turn left on Mel. Craveiro Lopez, which bends around the airport and funnels into the autoestrada A-1 to the north. For **Óbidos** exit at Aveiras de Cima in 37 k. Take N-366 northwest toward Caldas da Rainha, 41k away, turning south at its outskirts on N-8 for the final 7 k. For **Alcobaça** follow the directions for Óbidos to Caldas da Rainha, but continue through Caldas to take N-8 north for 26 k. For **Tomar** exit A-1 at exit 7 in 80k to go west on N-243 to Entroncamento, then north on N-110 for 19 k to Tomar. For **Batalha** take exist 9 for Fátima and Batalha. Go east on pretty N-356 for a final 22k.

For destinations **south** and **east** of Lisbon take the Ponte 25 Abril by following the river west along Av. 24 de Julho to signs for the bridge at Av. de Ceuta, then north for two blocks to the circle of Largo de Alcantara, turning west to reach the ramp. Autoestrada A-2 reaches **Setúbal** in 48 k. From there, N-10 east for 35 k to Cruzamento de Pegoães joins N-4 to **Évora** in another 67 k. For the **Algarve** take N-10 from Setúbal for 21 k to Marateca to join N-5 south for 31 k to Alcácer do Sal, where the designation becomes N-120. Bear right in 18 k to continue on N-120 along the coast to the western Algarve in about 180 k. A faster route to the central Algarve is to continue on to Grandola, instead of bearing right on N-120, to take N-259 southeast, turning south on N-262 in about 20 k toward Azinheira dos Barros, and stay on the road as it becomes N-264 for a leg of 204 k.

ENVIRONS OF LISBON

Pena Palace in Sintra

Historical Profile: The Rise And Fall Of The House Of Avís

Two of the most significant events in Portugal's history left stunning memorials near Lisbon. A macabre romance, the first of these events, set a sequence in motion that erupted into the second of these events—the earliest popular revolution in Europe. This uprising ended Portugal's first royal line.

The great King Dinis capped the first Portuguese dynasty, called the Burgundian (see "Historical Profile: The Birth of Portugal" on page 157). He created or repaired a hundred castles, founded the first university, nationalized the church, improved agriculture and established the chivalric Order of Avís, in addition to composing respectable poetry. After him, it was all downhill. His son, Afonso IV, confined his attentions to sex and meddling in Spanish politics. When he threw Portugal's support behind one Castilian faction by marrying his son Pedro to the daughter of its leader, naturally the bride-to-be came to Portugal in state, accompanied by an entourage of ladies-in-waiting, including one named Inês Pires de Castro, the daughter of the Chamberlain of Castile. Young Pedro duly married his espoused, but his eyes saw only the fair Inês. It was not long before attraction blossomed into an affair that came to the King's attention. He banished Inês.

When Pedro's wife died five years later of complications following the birth of a son, Pedro summoned Inês back and sired several children with her. This infuriated his father. Historians disagree over whether the King himself hired three assassins or merely closed his eyes to someone else's intrigue, but the result, in either case, was the foul murder of Inês.

Inconsolable, Pedro took up arms against his father but lost; they remained estranged until a death-bed reconciliation. Pedro's first act on becoming king was to disinter Inês' body, dress her in regal robes, and force the nobles of the realm to kiss her skeletal hand in homage as their queen. Then he had a tomb constructed for her in the monastery of Alcobaça and commanded that his own tomb be built facing hers so she would be his first sight on the day of resurrection. So elegant and moving are these memorials that **Alcobaça** ★★★ became ever after a place of tourist pilgrimage. Pedro next sought her murderers. Finding two of them, he tore the heart from the chest of one and from the back of the other—which helped earn him the epithet "the Cruel."

However deep his affection for Inês may have been—for he never remarried—it did not prevent Pedro from enjoying other women. With one he fathered a fateful illegitimate son, João. On his majority João was given command of the religio-military Order of Avís. It was this João who would later establish the Avís dynasty.

On Pedro's death, Fernando, his son by the unloved Castilian wife, inherited the throne. Fernando was 24, handsome and impetuous, but more interested in wars than governing, which he left to a favorite courtier. The courtier arranged for the king to marry his own niece, despite the fact that she already had a husband. But her husband was no fool, for he fled to Spain, permitting King Fernando and Leonor Teles de Meneses to wed. Soon after, Juan Fernández Andeiro, a clever Spanish diplomat who had been working abroad for Portugal, returned to the court and fell in with Leonor. When she became pregnant, rumors called Andeiro the father, and Leonor blamed João, master of Avís, for instigating such vicious stories. Although the 20-year-old abbot was highly regarded at court and popular with the people, the queen chained him to rot in the castle of Évora.

King Fernando died abruptly of a strange disease that caused premature aging, leaving his heir, Beatrice, in Leonor's care. She married off Beatrice to the king of Castile, possibly influenced by her lover, the Spaniard Andeiro. Therewith, the King of Castile began claiming the title of King of Portugal, rather than that of the mere Consort of Portugal's Queen. Most of the nobles did not object, one king was much like another for them, but the prospect of Spanish control roused the Portuguese middle classes. By this time João had secured his release from prison, thanks to intercession by the English Duke of Lancaster, and came to Leonor's chambers asking for a private audience with Andeiro. When the two were alone, João stabbed him dead. Then João sent a retainer through the streets of Lisbon crying "They are killing the master." It was not the first big political lie, nor the last, but few have ever worked better. A mob gathered clamoring that João should be king, pressuring the Council of Portugal to appoint him regent.

João arrested Leonor, as soon as he assumed regency, and exiled her. At the same time, he enlisted English forces to counter the Castilian king's mobilization for war. Yet, with more than 50 towns and most of the Portuguese nobles supporting Leonor and Beatrice, the legitimate heir, the king of Castile encountered little resistance on his march to besiege Lisbon. At this dark hour, João's forces were saved by an outbreak of plague that raced through the crowded camp of the besiegers, forcing the Spanish home to regroup. With this respite, João was able to win over Portugal's populous northern area and gain the backing of the Cortes (Parliament) for his ascension to the throne. In 1385, the House of Avís crowned its first king.

Twenty-thousand Spaniards swelled by most of the Portuguese nobles, returned the next year to meet João, commanding less than half as many Portuguese plus 500 English bowmen. The armies confronted each other near Batalha, north of Lisbon. João's forces had lined a forward ditch with stakes at a place where their flanks were protected by streams. But the Spanish, confident in their numerical superiority, charged this strong defense. Within one hour they were thrown back in disarray and total defeat.

In gratitude for this great victory João vowed to build an abbey near the site of the battle. This abbey of **Batalha** ★★★★ (battle) was the first flamboyant Gothic building on the peninsula, an architectural masterpiece raised by Houget, an English architect. Therein João would be buried.

By this time João owed a great deal to John of Gaunt, Duke of Lancaster and father to the future Lancasterian line of English kings. It was John who had secured his release from prison and supported him with troops, and time to return the favor. The two joined forces to press John's claim to the throne of Castile, invading Spain. But rather than fighting, John sold his rights for cash to the monarch of Castile. João raged at what he saw as a betrayal. To reestablish the alliance, John signed the Treaty of Windsor with João in 1386 which began the longest of all European alliances—England with Portugal. He cemented the pact with the offer of any of his daughters that the bachelor king would choose. João selected the eldest, Philippa of Lancaster, a spinster over thirty.

It was a brilliant choice. Philippa had been raised in the most intellectual court of the era, one that included Geoffry Chaucer among its luminaries, to stand with the rare educated women of her time. Unlike most men, she could both read and write, and proceeded to raise her children in an intellectual atmosphere that ignited the Renaissance in Portugal. She gave birth to five sons, though the first died in infancy. The second son, Dom Duarte, was designated the *Infante* to succeed his father. Her fourth son she named Henrique, although the English-speaking world calls him Prince Henry the Navigator.

João had seized a throne only to bankrupt it with his wars; the dust settled to reveal a coinage debased to one two-thousandth of its former value. João too was spent from his exertions, but his four virile sons soon were able to help resurrect the finances. By 1415 the boys were old enough to plan an attack on the Moroccan city of Ceuta. On the eve of their departure, tragically, their mother caught the plague, but dying she urged them on. Ceuta was captured, giving Portugal its first push towards international power.

Most of the credit for the massive invasion involving over 200 ships went to Dom Henrique, who was rewarded with the dukedom of Viseu. He was already master of the religio-military Order of Christ and a rich man from his various estates, yet he set up residence at Sagres, near the furthest extremity of Europe, to dream about lands beyond those known. Dom Henrique was devout, celibate and ascetic—he drank no alcohol and owned few personal possessions. He established a kind of school for navigation, stockpiling information gathered from all the ships that put in at Sagres on their way to destinations farther north. He personally underwrote numerous voyages of exploration along the African coast, and colonized the fertile islands of Madeira and the Azores. Expeditions returned with gold to fill the royal treasury and sugar to trade for specie in Europe.

João I died in 1433 on his 77th birthday, exactly 48 years after the battle near Batalha that had secured his throne. His son Duarte I reluctantly accepted the crown, but was too sensitive for the task and died five years later mourning an abortive invasion that left one of his brothers hostage to the Moors. His heir, Afonso V, only six at the time, would reign for 43 years. In the beginning a pawn of the nobles, at the end Afonso became embroiled in the morass of Castilian politics involving Henrique the Impotent, Henrique's purported daughter Juana, and Isabella the Catholic. Afonso died in 1481, just as he had decided to retire. During the next reign, Prince Henry the Navigator, feeling death's approach, adopted Afonso's brother as his heir—from whom a king would later ensue.

Henry died in 1460. A courtier sent to examine his body three weeks later found it uncorrupted, except for the tip of his nose—a sufficient defect to prevent the possibility of sainthood. Henry was buried near his father in Batalha.

Upon ascending the throne, Afonso's son João II faced nobles grown powerful during his father's distracted reign. The Duke of Bragança, descendant of an illegitimate son of the founder of the House of Avís, controlled 50 towns and could raise an army of 13,000 men from among his retainers. João accused the duke of negotiating a secret treaty with Castile, tried and beheaded him. Then he went after Portugal's next most powerful noble, the Duke of Viseu, whose father had acquired the title through adoption by Prince Henry the Navigator. João II either killed the duke himself or ordered the deed. In either case, the duke's death left just one son remaining of five produced by Henry's adopted son, for three others had died in childhood. History would call the survivor "The Fortunate," for Manuel would become Portugal's most notable king.

King João II admitted 60,000 Jews into Portugal in 1493 after their expulsion from Spain. He charged each a tax for admittance and, for the price, permitted one year's residency. Sometime about

1483 he gave an audience to a Genoese named Christopher Columbus who proposed sailing west to China and India, but João declined to support the project. João's only son died of a fall from his horse, followed, soon after, by João's own death in 1495 after an attack of dropsy.

With no surviving heir, the throne passed to the remaining child of Prince Henry's adopted son, the king's cousin, Manuel. At 26, Manuel I was thin, green eyed and fair, with arms that dangled ape-like to his knees. He was fond of display. After restoring their former lands to the country's important nobles, Manuel called them all to the palace to form a splendid court—and be easily watched. He commissioned a spate of buildings in a new style that combined flamboyant Gothic elements with the Spanish plateresque, a style called, after him, "Manueline." Craftsmen who knew the Arabic arts incorporated the flora and fauna from newly-discovered lands in these decorations. He also revised Portuguese law, but had little use for parliamentary sessions.

Manuel married the widowed daughter of Ferdinand and Isabella of Spain. After she died in childbirth, he married another of their daughters, with whom he had ten children, but, as one condition of the marriages, Spain required that Portugal expel its Jews. Manuel appreciated the importance of these people for the economy of Portugal, so he tried to convert as many as possible so as not to lose them. His measures included seizing Jewish children from their parents to indoctrinate them in the Christian faith.

In 1495, excited and jealous about Columbus' discoveries, Manuel ordered a fleet commanded by Vasco da Gama to find India by sailing east. Bartolomeu Dias, the first explorer to round the tip of Africa, designed four ships for da Gama, two of which returned 2-1/2 years later laden with precious spices. Soon the Portuguese would found colonies in India, Madagascar, the Congo, as well as in Sumatra and Malaya—the Spice Islands. Five years later they discovered Brazil. For a time Portugal would be rich, well able to fund Manuel's passion for building, and the country would rise to the apex of power in the world.

When Manuel's heir, João III, was 14, Manuel arranged with Carlos V of Spain that the boy marry Carlo's sister. But Manuel, recently widowed for the second time, so liked the girl when he met her that he married her himself instead. Manuel died in 1521. His son João III then married a second of Carlos' sisters and sent his own sister back to wed Carlos in return. Through this merging of families, the

Spanish would one day gain access to the throne of Portugal, and confirm a Portuguese saying that from Spain comes neither good winds nor good marriages.

In 1557, soon after starting an inquisition in Portugal modeled on Spain's, João III died. He had sired ten children, but the royal family by now was so inbred that all had died before their father. Fortunately, the last managed to impregnate his wife before expiring, leaving a five-year-old named Sebastião as the next king. Next in line for the throne in this depleted family was João III's brother Henrique, a Cardinal who raised Sebastião. The young king's pleasures ran to swimming, riding, fighting with swords, and other military exercises. However, a childhood illness caused symptoms of developing impotence and peculiar behavior—including the opening of his ancestors' tombs to meditate on their bones.

Sebastião grew fixated on the idea of a holy war against the infidel. When he finally organized a ludicrously unrealistic chivalrous expedition against Morocco, it seemed almost fitting that he lose his life in the invasion.

Sebastião's death left his 60-year-old uncle, Cardinal Henrique, as the sole living member of the House of Avís. The death of this childless Cardinal in 1758, after a reign of only a few months, brought the 200-year-old royal house to an abrupt and anticlimactic end.

ENVIRONS OF LISBON

Day trips by car, bus or train from Lisbon can cover much of the variety of Portugal. Closest to Lisbon are fine, elegant beaches at **Cascais** ★ and **Estoril** ★, ten miles west. Seven miles inland from these beaches stands the forest of **Sintra** ★★★★ with three fascinating palaces. Ten miles north of Lisbon, a delicate palace abides in **Queluz** ★★★, and ten miles further waits magnificent **Mafra** ★★★, a richly Baroque monastery.

Seventy miles north of Lisbon stands the most harmonious collection of buildings in Portugal and one of the greatest examples of Gothic architecture in the world—the monastery at **Batalha** ★★★★★. West of it spreads the glorious beach of the village of **Nazaré** ★★, described as a picture-postcard, although it is difficult to spot the village today amid crowding tourists. A few kilometers away in **Alcobaça** ★★★ the sublime medieval church and monastery of Santa Maria houses elegant tombs of the lovers Inês and Pedro, the Cruel. A lovely medieval walled town rises twenty miles below Alcobaça at **Óbidos** ★★. **Setúbal** ★ sits on the sea 30 miles south of Lisbon and contains the first Manueline church, while beaches stretch nearby.

Using three days for Lisbon, eight days would cover the sights of the area.

ALCOBAÇA ★★★

Population: 5383
Area code: 062; zip code: 2460

110 k north of Lisbon. Directions from **Lisbon** *are included in the "Excursion" section of that city. From* **Coimbra** *take N-1 south for 85 k to Cruz da Legua (with pottery for sale along the streets) where N-8 goes west for 16 k. Or enter the autoroute A-1 10k south of Coimbra for 52k to exit 9 at Leiria, for N-1, and the remaining directions as above.* **Batalha** *is 8k on N-1 north of Cruz da Legua.* **Nazaré** *is 14 k northwest of Alcobaça along N-8-5.*

The reason for the existence of the town and for the tourists to swarm here is the Abbey of Santa Maria, containing the finest church in Portugal. Even the fruit trees for which the area is famed were first planted by its monks. The monastery is ancient, founded by the first king of Portugal, Afonso Henriques, to repay a vow to God for helping him capture the city of Santarém from the Moors. Work began in

1178 and finished in the first quarter of the 13th century for a cloistered order of Cistercians sent from France by Saint Bernard himself. Thus, the style of the buildings is the earliest, most monumental, and simplest Gothic, making this the finest surviving Cistercian structure anywhere.

Inside reposes a relic of one of Portugal's great romances. At the beginning of the 14th century, Dom Pedro, heir to the Portuguese throne, was betrothed to a Castilian princess. A lady-in-waiting named Inês de Castro travelled with Pedro's bride to Portugal, and the young groom fell instantly in love—not with his wife-to-be, but with the noblewoman accompanying her. Aware of his son's infatuation, Pedro's father banished Inês from the kingdom. When Dom Pedro's wife died five years later, Pedro brought Inês back to live with him, fathering two children. The King was enraged at this flouting of his command and at the fact that the children's mother was Spanish. The King sent, or at least allowed, assassins to kill Inês.

As soon as the throne came to Pedro he had two of the assassins viciously murdered, then disinterred Inês' remains, dressed her in regal robes, and ordered the nobles of the realm to kiss her skeletal hand as the reigning queen of Portugal. He buried her in high state in the Monastery of Santa Maria at Alcobaça and constructed his own tomb there, too, so his feet would face hers in order that his first sight on resurrection would be his beloved.

Mostairo de Santa Maria ★★★

Open daily 9 a.m. to 7 p.m. (to 5 p.m. in winter). Admission: 350$00 to the abbey (250$00 in winter). The church facade was greatly changed by Baroque additions in the 17th and 18th centuries, but the central portal is original, if not its statues. The limestone outside has just been cleaned to glisten whitely, which now shows clearly how dismal the facade is. To the left extends a wall hiding ranks of cells that once housed 100 monks.

The interior of the church was altered over the centuries, but desecration by the French during the nineteenth-century Peninsular War led to restoration removing later additions to reveal the pure, awesome Cistercian original—one of Portugal's most moving sights.

An unusually narrow nave accentuates the football field of length that makes this the largest church in the country. Columns are close-set and massive. Engaged pillars along the aisles are curiously truncated ten feet above the floor to gain space for choirstalls, since removed, but now providing a lovely perspective. Lighted only by the rose window of the nave and two others in the transepts, and barren of surface decoration or even side chapels, the effect is a purity that seems more modern than its venerable age.

To the left of the entrance is the Sala dos Reis containing statues—of no great artistic merit—depicting the kings of Portugal, in addition to *azulejos* portraying Afonso's victory at Santarém and the history of the monastery.

In the south transept (left) lies the 14th-century tomb of Inês de Castro resting on crouching figures, including, it is reputed, that of one of her assassins. Opposite, in the north transept, is the man who loved her, Dom Pedro. As Pedro commanded, they lie feet to feet, although with a fair distance between. Both effigies are carved of soft limestone in a florid Gothic style, but both were damaged by the French, as is apparent in the plaster reconstruction of Inês' nose. She does look beautiful, nonetheless, protected by six gentle angels surrounding her. A frieze at the top of the sarcophagus interweaves the coat of arms of Portugal with that of the de Castro family. Tomb sides depict scenes from the life of Christ. Carved on the end of the tomb's head is a crucifixion scene. Appropriately, the finest carving faces Pedro: a most realistic scene of the Last Judgement at her feet.

The effigy of Pedro looks severe, lending credence to his nickname "the Cruel." The sides of his tomb present scenes from the life of Saint Bartholomew, his patron saint, while the head-end shows Pedro's last moments. The carving at the foot is an exceptional composition of the wheel of fortune, whose details repay study. They depict events from the lives of this pair including Inês' murder. On both tombs is written *Ateão fim do mundo*—"until the end of the world."

A chapel off the south transept contains the tombs of Afonso II and III, from the 13th century, along with a strange—and mutilated—terra-cotta group surrounding St. Bernard, carved by a monk in the 17th century. Behind the high altar a charming Manueline door seems to grow vegetation as it leads to a sacristy with reliquaries emptied of their contents by some pillager or other. A door in the north aisle leads to a lovely 14th-century cloister of silence, whose upper story was added two centuries later. Arches between twisted columns are capped by roses looking out to orange trees. Here and there lie some of the statues that once graced the Cathedral portals.

The chapterhouse, entered from the north side of the cloister, is a room of round-arch doorways and windows, and graceful vaulting, although lined by distracting terra-cotta statues produced by monks in the 18th century. Stairs lead to a cavernous Gothic dormitory. From the west side of the cloister the monastery kitchen may be entered. A stream running through it was intended for washing dishes rather than, as some say, to provide the monks with fish. The colossal fireplace and chimney were tiled in the 18th century. Look up for a six story sight of the sky. Next to the kitchen is the solemn space of the refectory whose stairs, built into the end wall, lead to a fine lector's pulpit.

WHERE TO STAY

There is a comfortable, moderately priced hotel just up the hill in front of the Monastery, and a serviceable, inexpensive pension nearby.

MODERATE ($50-$99)

Santa Maria   2nd-class ★

R. Dr. Zagalo. Rooms: 30. ☎ 59 73 95; FAX 59 67 15; Telex 40143. The hotel is modern and reasonably attractive. Bedrooms are spotless, and some incorporate balconies overlooking the monastery.

INEXPENSIVE (UNDER $50)

Coracoães Unidos   P2nd-class

R. Frei António Brandão, 39 (the street leads out of the square in front of the monastery). Rooms: 16, but only 8 with baths. ☎ 421 42. The bedrooms are basic, but clean, and the management is cheerful.

WHERE TO EAT

As if heaven-sent, a hearty restaurant waits right beside the monastery.

MODERATE ($15-30)

Trindade   ★

Pr. Dom Afonso Henriques, 22. ☎ 42 397. This is not one of those restaurants near a sight that lives for tourists, but a venerable local bistro that thrives because it serves tasty, hearty food. The specialty is *açorda marisco*, a stew of shellfish and bread that is done very well here. There is also an inexpensive tourist menu.   *Visa accepted.*

DIRECTORY

TRAINS AND BUSES • The station is 5 k away in Valado dos Frades, though frequent buses transport to Alcobaça. Buses from the train station also run frequently to Nazaré.

The bus station (☎ 422 21) is on Av. Manuel da Silva Carolino, a five-minute walk to the monastery—left, then downhill and another left. Service is frequent to Batalha and Nazaré.

EXCURSIONS

The **Museu Nacional do Vinho** (☎ 422 22) stands 1 k outside of town on N-8, the road to Batalha. Guides show exhibits of the history of wine production. There is no tasting, but wine may be purchased at the end of the tour. Note that tours are generally given in Portuguese, but the guide will do his best to convey the message to English-speakers. (*Open Mon.-Fri. 9 a.m. until 12:30 p.m. and 2-5:30 p.m.; admission: free*).

BATALHA ★★★★★

Population: 7683
Area code: 044; zip code: 2440

120 k north of Lisbon. Directions from **Lisbon** are included in the "Excursion" section of that city. From **Coimbra** take N-1 south for 81 k. Or enter the auto-estrada, A-1, 10k south of Coimbra for 52k to exit 9 at Leiria. Go south from Leiria on N-1 for 11k. From **Nazaré** N-8-4 leads east through Alcobaça to Cruz da Legua (with pottery for sale along the streets) in 30 k, where N-1 north reaches Batalha in 8k more. From **Tomar** take N-113 west to Leiria in 45k, then N-1 south for 11k.

The town is aptly named by the Portuguese word for battle, for its founding was due to a fight that changed the course of history. A mighty army from Castile had invaded to contest the claims of King João I—who had usurped the Portuguese throne one year previously. (See "Historical Profile: The Rise And Fall Of The House Of Avís" on page 119.) On August 14, 1385, the Castilian army lined the plain of Aljubarrota, 12 k south of Batalha, swelled by a large body of Portuguese nobles supporting the prior royal house. The Spanish brandished 16 of the new weapons of the day—cannons. Twenty-year-old João I, with no artillery and backed by a much smaller complement of knights—although aided by citizen-soldiers and 500 Englishmen—faced this host almost twice his numbers. He vowed that if success came his way he would endow a monastery, for it seemed that only a miracle could save him. João won a resounding victory, and construction of a monastery began three years later in this valley near the site.

The first stage of construction comprised the church, founder's chapel, royal cloister and chapterhouse, finished by 1436. The first architect, Afonso Domingues, was Portuguese, but the second, Houguet, was a Norman who lent the feeling of the English Gothic, reminiscent—in those areas where perpendiculars are emphasized by pillars and spires—of Westminster Cathedral.

King João's son Dom Duarte finished the founder's chapel and added an octagonal chapel behind the apse, although it was never completed. In turn, his successor appended a second cloister named—after himself—the Afonso V Cloister. Manuel I decorated various parts in the exuberant style named for him, before turning his attention to his own Heronymite monastery outside Lisbon. His successor, João III, added dormitories and a third cloister (subsequently destroyed), before stopping work for good in 1550 to concentrate on his own building at Tomar. By then, a century and a half of building by the mightiest monarchs of Portugal had created a monastery of surpassing majesty.

Mostairo de Santa Maria da Vitoria ★★★★★
Open daily 9 a.m. to 6 p.m., (to 5 p.m. in winter). Admission: 400$00 to the abbey (250$00 in winter). A sweeping plaza sets off the square monastery. It contains a modern mounted statue of Nuno Álvares Pereira, the general at the battle of Aljubarrota. Exterior limestone, weathered to a warm ocher, culminates in a flamboyant facade of scores of small spires, but no tower or belfry. To the right is the dome of the founder's chapel; cloister walls spread left. A lovely flamboyant window surmounts the richly carved main portal filled with copies of the original statues, except for those at the top. Buttresses and lacy balustrades run in all directions providing no focus for the eye, a characteristic of this structure built by various sovereigns with different ideas.

The church interior startles with plainness, after the exuberance outside. Yet that same simplicity allows the grand sweep of the vaulting to soar unencumbered. Dappled colors from the stained glass (modern, except for Manueline glass at the end in the chancel, and above in the choir) swathe the floor, and great piers seems to anchor the ceiling from possible flight. Pass reverently by the tomb of Mateus Fernandes by the main entrance door, the architect who embellished the Capelas Imperfeitas.

To the immediate right, through a splendid doorway, is the moving **Capela do Fundador** (Founders Chapel), a square room lit by an octagonal lantern. Under delicate stone canopies beneath the lantern lies the joint tomb of the founder, João I, and his wife, Philippa of Lancaster (see "Historical Profile: The Rise And Fall Of The House Of Avís" on page 119). The king wears the insignia of the Order of the Garter, founded by Philippa's grandfather, Edward III of England. As a moving touch, he is depicted holding his wife's hand.

The rear wall contains the tombs of the exceptional sons of these parents. The one on the left holds the few remains of Dom Fernando, who had been left a hostage after an abortive attack on Tangier. Humiliation and imprisonment led to his death, probably of dysentery. His heart, cut out of his body by compatriots as it hung from the walls of Fez, was embalmed and interred here. The third tomb from the left, bearing a Gothic canopy, is that of Dom Henrique, duke of Viseu, known as Prince Henry the Navigator. His features here look quite different from those painted by Nuno Gonçalves, in his masterpiece of *Saint Vincent* in Lisbon.

The artistic highlight of the monastery is the **Claustro Real** (Royal Cloister), entered through the north wall of the church by the transept. Erected by Afonso Domingues, the first architect of Batalha, in pure, elegant Gothic style, Manuel I found it cold in feeling. He ordered his architect Mateus Fernades to add Manueline embellishments to the columns and insert tracery to half-fill the arches. Manuel had a good eye—the combination is superb, even though reconstructed today.

The **chapterhouse** is entered from the east side of the cloister. The boldness of its 60-foot expanse of unsupported vaulting amazed contemporaries. According to one story, the architect employed convicts to build it, since the dangers of its unproven construction were too great to risk the lives of honest men. Another story says the architect had to sleep beneath the vaulting for one night to convince doubters of its safety. Safe it is, for it survived the convulsions of Lisbon's 1755 earthquake. Today the room contains Portugal's Tomb of the Unknown Soldier (from WWI, for Portugal remained neutral in WWII), perpetually guarded. The east window is lovely 16th-century glass.

From the northwest corner of the Royal Cloister the adjacent **cloister of Dom Afonso V** may be entered, after a pause to inspect the Manueline **lavabo** on which carved foliage seems to grow its own vegetation. This slightly smaller cloister makes a nice contrast to its larger neighbor, for it is pure Gothic, and most elegant. Exit from its southeast corner to the outside, then round the chapterhouse to enter the **Capelas Imperfeitas**.

The chapels are entered through one of the great doorways in Portugal. Manuel's architect Mateus Fernandes covered every inch of this soaring Gothic portal with decoration. On the door columns, carved iron chains become knotted ropes, and then plants.

"Inside" (a strange term for a roofless room) the Dom Duarte's simple original design is apparent—an octagonal rotunda radiating seven chapels. He died before it was complete. Under Manuel I, Mateus Fernandes planned an octagonal roof supported by pillars, but was taken off the job before its completion, leaving stumps of the pillars, profusely carved, and a structure still unroofed. In 1533, in reaction to his father's exuberant decoration, Manuel's son added a somber balcony, but nothing more.

And so it remains, somehow more moving in its incompleteness than the finished rooms. Although intended as a pantheon for the kings who succeeded João I, the chapel contains only the tomb (mutilated by the French) of one son, and of Dom Duarte and his wife, Leonor of Aragón, opposite the entrance, along with those of a noble and an infante (prince).

WHERE TO STAY

Surprising for a town so popular with tourists, hotel choices are few, so reservations are advised.

EXPENSIVE ($100-$200)

Quinta do Fidalgo ★★★
Opposite the monastery. Rooms: 4, 1 suite. ☎ 96 114; FAX 76 74 01. Inside an unimpressive townhouse wait five special rooms, each invitingly homey, with splendid marble bathrooms. A comfortable terrace overlooks a bare garden.

Pousada do Mestre Afonso Domingues ★★
Alongside the monastery plaza. Rooms: 21. ☎ 962 60; FAX 962 60; Telex 42339. This is a low-slung modern pousada, looking like a motel. Bedrooms are comfortable, though lacking style, but prices are barely expensive. Fortunately, the soundproofing effectively muffles highway noise.

WHERE TO EAT

All the town restaurants are ordinary and touristy. The best choice is the Pousada, which serves moderately priced, if bland food with some style.

EXCURSIONS

Nazaré ★ and **Alcobaça** ★★★ are close by. See the directions from Alcobaça and descriptions in this chapter. **Leiria**, 11 k north on N-1, retains a stalwart 12th century fortress from the time of Afonso Henriques, within which a palace was added 200 years later. Leiria is also a center for ceramics. The pilgrimage site of **Fátima** ★ is 18 k east on N-336.

FÁTIMA ★

Population: 7298
Area code: 049; zip code: 2495

Fátima and Santiago de Compostella in Spain constitute the great pilgrimage sites of the peninsula, with Fátima receiving greater numbers. It must count as one of the world's great ironies that this, holiest site in the Iberian peninsula, is named for Fatima, the daughter of the founder of Islam.

On May 13, 1917, the sky suddenly brightened, causing three young children to look up to see the Virgin Mary standing in an oak tree. Their report was met with disbelief by most, but the children staunchly claimed that Mary promised to return on the same day of each ensuing month, pledging a miracle for her sixth and last appearance. Increasingly large crowds gathered on each succeeding 13th to hear Mary call for peace, a particularly appropriate message for these World War I times. On October 13, the sixth month, 70,000 people collected in a driving rainstorm. At noon the sun came out, spun in orbit and plummeted toward the earth. Then everything returned to normal, with no evidence of the rain.

The **Basilica of Fátima** stands at the end of an immense esplanade. This neoclassical church can hold 300,000 inside, but only those who are suitably attired—no shorts, no bare arms, no slacks on women—are permitted entrance. Inside, two of the three children who first saw the vision are buried. The square in front is larger than the one prefacing Rome's Saint Peter's Cathedral. The **Capelinha das Apariçoães** on the esplanade is a modern structure surrounding the site of the visitation—alas, the oak tree is no more. The **Museu-Vivo Apariçoães**, which provides a sound-and-light show of the miraculous events, stands on the park grounds. Near the park, on R. Jacinto Marto, is the **Museu de Cera de Fátima**, a wax museum that attempts, sometimes in eerie ways, to make the events real.

Note that the 12th and 13th of each month are pilgrimage times. The town fills to overflowing on those dates in May, and almost so every October.

CASCAIS ★

Population: 29,882
Area code: 01; zip code: 2750

ESTORIL ★

Population: 25,230
Area code: 01; zip code: 2765

28 k west of Lisbon. Directions from **Lisbon** *are included in the "Excursion" section of that city.*

These two towns provide the closest beaches to Lisbon. Formerly separate, a continuous community along the bay now links Cascais with its sister Estoril. Both were fishing villages that became resorts for the wealthy in the 19th century.

As the Nazis swept through Europe, royalty fled to safe Estoril (Portugal was a neutral in WW II), establishing strange courts in exile. At one time there were as many as five former kings living in small courts here and countless Princes, Counts and Dukes, taking evenings at the casino. Elegance remains, mixed with fishermen who always lived here, and a commuter population from Lisbon, making this Portugal's Riviera.

Cascais offers three fine sand beaches—crowded, but less polluted than those at Estoril, whose bay water is not the cleanest. Blue European Council flags on the beach indicate that pollution levels are satisfactory. A less-crowded beach lies west of town at Praia do Guincho. Cascais is somewhat less expensive than Estoril, more accessible and provides the better restaurants and shops. On the edge of its promontory stands a former Fort and Royal Palace, which cannot be visited because the president of Portugal still holds receptions there. The main shopping street of Cascais is R. Frederico Arouça, one block south of the train station.

Estoril is the more sophisticated of the two towns. Houses are fancier and the town hosts horse races and sailing regattas. A tropical garden park in the center is overlooked by the **Estoril Casino** (admission: 400$00, open from 3 p.m. until 3 a.m.), one of the largest and most luxurious of its kind in the world. Beaches are fine sand, but it is difficult to spot among the crowded bodies.

What is special about these resorts is that they lie minutes from Lisbon, contain fine accommodations and exude an international excitement. By the end of June they overflow with an international crowd, which is part of the attraction; at any other time both are relatively quiet and close enough to Lisbon for residence and travel to the capital, a half hour away, for sights or food.

Note: A crafts fair sets up beside Estoril's casino park evenings during July and August.

But, for better beaches, head west around the cape for Praia do Guincho ★★, around Cabo Raso, 9 k west of Cascais (buses leave from the Cascais train station). This duned beach is immense, pollution-free and relatively uncrowded. Winds are continual and sometimes strong, which makes for dramatic oceans and a strong undertow the locals take in stride. Cabo da Roca, the westernmost point of Europe, can be seen 8 k farther west. The Office of Tourism there will provide a paper certifying one's visit, and the moderately priced **Refugio da Roca** serves excellent soup.

WHERE TO STAY

Hotels come in all price ranges in these resorts, but the best values are in Cascais.

VERY EXPENSIVE ($200+)

In Cascais:

Albatroz   Deluxe ★★★★★

R. Frederico Arouça, 100 (one block south of the train station). Rooms: 40. ☎ 248 28 21; FAX 284 48 27; Telex 16052. The hotel grew around a 19th-century ducal palace belonging to the king's brother situated on a rocky crag overlooking the water, and dukes and their ilk still guest at this special place with its lovely views. Cary Grant stayed, as did Grace Kelly and Prince Rainier. Decoration is eclectic with a pleasant bower on the way to the old house and the bar. Nothing is stuffy; all is bright and comfortable. The bedrooms are by no means grand, although extremely comfortable. Views are splendid and the staff pays attention to every detail, while the dining room produces some of the best meals along the coast.

In Estoril:

Palácio   Deluxe ★★★★
R. do Parque Estoril (just east of the park). Rooms: 162. ☎ 468 04 00; FAX 468 48 67; Telex 12757. As its name and reputation says, this belle-epoque hotel is grand and elegant, even set in its own gardens, although only some of the rooms are air-conditioned. Here monarchy once stayed. The service is attentive and the staff is omnipresent. Although the cost is 20 percent less than at the Hotel Albatroz, the Albatroz is a better choice for its style, comfort and individual treatment. On the other hand, the Palácio does run its own golf course.

EXPENSIVE ($100-$200)

In Praia do Guincho:

Do Guincho   Deluxe ★★★★
Rooms: 31. ☎ 487 04 91; FAX 487 04 31; Telex 43138. This luxury hotel is incorporated into the towers of a 17th-century fortress. Bedrooms, baronial with their vaulted ceilings, are small but enchanting, and we wish we had such fine bed-linen at home. Staying here produces a wonderful sense of isolation. Views are awesome.

In Cascais:

Estalagem Senhora da Guia   1st-class ★★★
Estrado do Guincho, the coast road, 3.5 k west of Cascais. Rooms: 28. ☎ 486 92 39; FAX 486 92 27; Telex 42111. The owner of the Sagres beer brewery built this imposing villa in 1970 with no expense spared. When the heirs left, a family took it over for a hotel and remodeled it in fine taste. Each bedroom is different, but all are pleasing although not air-conditioned. Views of the coast are grand.

Cidadela   1st-class ★★
Av. 25 de Abril (the coast road). Rooms: 130. ☎ 483 29 21; FAX 486 72 26; Telex 16320. This is a modern hotel facing its own garden overlooking the sea, but the public rooms and bedrooms are huge and tastefully done. Duplex suites contain kitchenettes, dining rooms, living rooms and two or three bedrooms, each with a private bath. Suites are bargains for families or couples travelling together.

MODERATE ($50-$99)

In Cascais:

Casa da Pérgola   2nd-class ★★★
Av. Valbom, 13 (a half block southwest of the train station). Rooms: 10, only 8 with private bath. ☎ 484 00 40. Open April-October. Many will argue that these are the most wonderful accommodations in the area. The century-old private villa, smack in the center of town, hides an intimate garden patio behind a marble entrance. Elegant antiques fur-

nish the public spaces. Because this house was not built as a hotel, bedrooms are all different, but each is decorated with such taste that prettiness surrounds you.

INEXPENSIVE (UNDER $50)

In Estoril:

Smart   **R3rd-class ★**

R. José Viana, 3. Rooms: 16, some without baths. ☎ 468 21 64. The hotel is a large house, recently remodeled, with a patio garden on a street of villas. Bedrooms are clean and functional, and most have televisions, unusual for this price category.

WHERE TO EAT

Both Cascais and Estoril abound with restaurants, although most are expensive and, with the one exception below, few offer good value. However, there is an exceptional restaurant at the Guincho beach and a fine one in Cascais.

EXPENSIVE ($40+)

In Praia do Guincho:

Porto de Santa Maria   **★★★★**

Estrada do Guincho. ☎ 487 02 40. Closed Monday. This restaurant is by no means elegant, though fresh flowers at the door help. What it is is a functional place dedicated to serving the freshest seafood, which it manages as well as any restaurant in the country. For the quality, it is a true bargain and highly recommended. Always crowded, for its fame has spread, views from long glass windows over the sea set just the right tone. A huge aquarium displays the shellfish selections, priced by weight. There are several cascades of fish and shellfish, and shellfish with rice is a fabulous specialty.

Amex, Diners, MasterCard and Visa accepted.

In Cascais:

Albatroz   **★★★**

In the Hotel Albatroz at R. Frederico Arouça, 100 (one block south of the train station). ☎ 483 28 21. While the diningroom is not grand, the ocean view and the food both qualify. Start either with the wild asparagus with scrambled eggs or with a most aromatic fish soup. The three-fish medallions Mariner style is hard to better, although the cherne (rockbass) is subtle and delicious. If not in the mood for fish, the chef does a rack of lamb perfectly.

Amex, Diners, MasterCard and Visa accepted.

INEXPENSIVE (UNDER $15)

In Cascais:

Jardim dos Frangos   **★★**

On the main square of Av. Marginal. 483 06 75. ☎ 438 06 75. Unpretentious is an understatement in this case. Located beside a take-out window, the restaurant is small, crowded and, to be charitable, we'll call it undecorated. But it claims to serve *maior dos frangos*, the best roast chicken, and does not grossly exaggerate. If you like roast chicken served with hot sauce and fries, here is your place. Even with a carafe of wine and dessert it is hard to spend more than $10.

LEIRIA

See "Batalha" under "Excursions.

MAFRA ★★★

Population: 10,153
Area code: 061; zip code: 2640

40 k north of Lisbon. Directions for Mafra are included in the "Excursion" section of **Lisbon**. *If coming from* **Óbidos and north** *along N-8, turn west on N-116 at Malveira for 8 k.*

Here is Portugal's most magnificent Baroque confection. Like Batalha, it was a king's offering in return for a favor from God, even if the favor this time was more personal than military. It was commissioned by João V in thanks—after three heirless years of marriage—for the birth of his daughter. Construction began in 1717 on this palace-church-monastery complex covering ten acres. Eighteen years and two German architects later the monastery was completed—built, it is said, of Brazilian gold and diamonds.

The king wanted to overwhelm, and drained a rich treasury to do so, plunging Portugal into economic decline. Fifty thousand workers were employed at the height of the construction, not finished for 18 years. There are over 800 rooms in the complex, lighted by 4500 windows. The length of the plain dark facade exceeds 200 yards. In the center is the classic pediment and high belltowers of the basilica, from either side of which the wings of the palace stretch to terminate in bulbous domed extensions. Most of the stone inside is marble, what is not is amusing faux-stone. The left (south) wing housed the Queen and her staff, the right was for the King, and night visits entailed an appreciable, rather tiring, walk.

Mosteiro de Mafra ★★

Open Wed.-Mon. 10 a.m. to noon and 2-5 p.m. Closed Tues. Admission: 300$00, for guided tours of the palace (200$00 in winter. Entrance to the complex is through the Queen's door, the third left from the basilica The **basilica** is elegant in proportion and consists of a fine barrel-vaulted ceiling on fluted columns, culminating in a large rose-and-white cupola. All the decoration is rich marbles. In particular the ornate sacristy is virtually a museum of the stone's variety.

The **palace** may be visited only by a guided tour. When inspecting the ornate furniture keep in mind that when João VI fled to Brazil in 1807 to avoid capture by the French, he took the best furnishings from this palace with him. What we see today is his rejects or mid-nineteenth-century replacements. So little of the furniture is special, though some is interesting. The wood beds of the monks are almost elegant in their simplicity; some of the medical devices in the infirmary are funny or chilling, depending on your mood.

In the palace, note the game boards, one similar to a pinball machine. Special rooms include a trophy room in which everything is made of antlers or skins (a bit of pathos, when one remembers that the room was decorated for Carlos I who was killed by an assassin in the Pr. da Comércio in 1908); the mirrored queen's dressing room; the audience chamber with a trompe l'oeil ceiling; and an ornate throne room. Note the faux-stone walls throughout. Most dramatic is the 200 yard view down the main corridor, from one end to the other, that separated the king's from the queen's bedroom.

One room in all the complex is truly unforgettable. The marbled, almost 100 yard long, cathedral for books that is the gilded library. It can only be called awesome.

WHERE TO STAY

Albergaria Castelão 3rd-class ★

Av. 25 de Abril (opposite the palace). Rooms: 35. ☎ *81 20 50; FAX 516 98; Telex 43488.* This is a hotel of no pretensions, with comfortable bedrooms. Its price is comfortably moderate, and it serves the best meals in town, at reasonable prices.

NAZARÉ ★★

Population: 10,265
Area code: 062; zip code: 2450

123 k north of Lisbon. Directions from **Lisbon** *are included in the "Excursion" section of that city. From* **Coimbra** *and north, see the directions under* **Alcobaça**.

For decades Nazaré has been described as a picture-postcard village. Naturally, people flock to see it until their numbers almost completely obscure the picture. Once fishermen pulled their boats out of the surf by ox-teams. Crowned by long black-stocking caps on their heads, the men wore trousers so often mended that they seemed a kind of tattersall. Women wore seven petticoats of different colors under flared skirts and covered their heads with colorful scarfs above large gold earrings. But today a new harbor obviates the hauling of boats from the water, and finding a local person in traditional apparel amid the swarms of summer tourists, is difficult (other than those costumed to sell something). Still, a glorious beach remains, the high town on a precipitous bluff floats mystically, and locals are discernible in winter.

A special boat is peculiar to this one town in Europe. Possibly descended from ancient Phoenician caiques, the brightly striped boats incorporate a high prow with a pair of magical signs—most often large eyes—painted on opposite sides to ward off evil. Models are sold throughout the village, as are heavy wool cable-stitched fisherman's sweaters for reasonable prices.

In summer, Nazaré is noisy, packed to the gills and bustling. This is the one place in Portugal where hawkers and touts grab passing tourists. It is also exciting in its international flavor and spreads a crescent beach for over a mile, watched over by an incredible 360 foot bluff.

The modern town runs along the beach. Parallel alleys of whitewashed cottages at the north end house the fishermen and display clothing on omnipresent washlines. North of the beach, upon a cliff served by a cute funicular (70$00), stands the tiny original town called the **Sitio**. The reason that the populace lived upon a hill so difficult of access was to escape Algerian and Dutch raiders. Here is the attractive church of **Nossa Senhor da Nazaré**, with a vast interior covered by a wood barrel ceiling. Its transepts are lined with 18th-century Dutch *azulejos*. By repute, the statue of the Virgin inside was brought here in the fourth century from Palestinian Nazare, hence the name of this village. South of the church, at the cliff edge, is the **Ermida da Memoria**, a tiny square chapel covered floor to ceiling with *azulejos* (now mostly odds-and-end replacements). It commemorates the spot where a noble in hot pursuit of a stag watched the deer fall over the cliff, and realized that he could not prevent his own horse and self from following. However, his prayer to the Virgin of Nazaré was heard and answered. His horse miraculously stopped at the edge. The view over the new town and sea is spiritual.

WHERE TO STAY

None of the hotels in Nazaré will break a reasonable budget, but rooms are almost impossible to secure in summer. Reservations are a must during that season.

MODERATE ($50-$99)

Riba-Mar 3rd-class ★
R. Gomes Freire, 9 (on the northern end of the beach). Rooms: 23. ☎ 51

11 58; Telex 43383). Closed the last week of December. The location could not be better, opposite the beach in the most active part of town. Of course that means noise, so the choice of an ocean-view front room has to balance that defect. This hotel's decor is pleasantly eclectic. Bedrooms are small, and feel like those at an inn. Most have stall showers and no bath. The place is lively and convivial. Tasty, but inexpensive, meals are served in the rustic restaurant.

Praia 2nd-class

Av. Vieira Guimarães, 39 (opposite the market, beside the bus station). Rooms: 40. ☎ 56 14 23; FAX 56 14 36; Telex 16329. Closed December. This hotel is an unattractive six-story '60s-modern building that provides reasonably comfortable accommodations, although pushing the moderate category. A recent renovation has helped a good deal. Now it is airy and clean. A garage is available, which is a plus in the crowded summer.

Maré 2nd-class

R. Mouzinho de Albuquerque, 8 (a block behind the Riba-Mar). Rooms: 36. ☎ 56 12 26; FAX 56 17 50; Telex 15245. The modern lobby is a cozy introduction to bedrooms that are serviceable, but nothing more. They pass the moderate limit in high season.

WHERE TO EAT

The beach street is lined with moderately priced restaurants for which competition is intense and frenetic. Two of the better ones are described below, but the best food in the village is served away from the beach frenzy.

INEXPENSIVE TO MODERATE (UNDER $30)

Arte Xavega ★

Calçada do Sitio (just north of the center, on the road to the Sitio). ☎ 55 21 36. Closed Mondays and November. This most pleasant restaurant stands on a hill overlooking the sea and lower town, a pleasant contrast to the bistros in town. The menu is more adventurous than grilled fish or another grilled fish. *Arroz de marisco* is recommended.
Amex, Diners, MasterCard and Visa accepted.

Beira-Mar

Av. da República, 40 (near the Mar Bravo). ☎ 56 13 58. Open March-November. Although meat dishes are available, most clients come for the fish, served for about a third less than at the more attractive Mar Bravo. A wait for tables may be necessary at this very popular place.
Amex, Diners, MasterCard and Visa accepted.

Mar Bravo

Pr. Sousa Oliveira, 75 (at the corner of the main square, next to Riba-Mar). ☎ 55 11 80. Open in season. Special menus can keep the prices in this popular restaurant low. It is attractively white, and fun.
Amex, Diners, MasterCard and Visa accepted.

ÓBIDOS ★★

Population: 825
Area code: 062; zip code: 2510

92 k north of Lisbon. Directions from **Lisbon** *are included in the "Excursion" section of that city. From* **Coimbra** *and north, go south on A-1 to exit 9 at Leiria in 52 k. At Leiria pick up N-1 south for 16k to Cruz da Légua, where N-8 goes to Caldas da Rainha in 46k, and Óbidos in 8 k more.*

Óbidos is so quaint that it hardly seems real. This tiny walled town surrounding a proper castle has changed hardly at all since the middle ages. Originally a sea bay lapping the town hill necessitated a fortress to guard against seaborne attack. When the Moors seized the fortress they surrounded the small village grown outside the bastion with perimeter walls. After Christians reconquered Óbidos in 1148, they fitted the fortress out as a castle and several times restored the village walls—the last time being in the 16th century. By then the bay beside the town had entirely silted up, leaving the fortifications without purpose, and reducing the importance of the village. This preserved it from change. In 1228 King Dinis paused at Óbidos on his way elsewhere. His wife so admired its charm that he gave it to her as a present. By tradition Óbidos remained a fief of the reigning Queen of Portugal until 1833.

The village is so small that it takes only an hour or two to savor, but the narrow climbing streets should not be attempted by car. Park beside the main gate, the Porta da Vila, and tour the curving streets on foot.

Azulejos mark a shrine just inside the Porta da Vila. The main street of the village is the quaint R. Direita, that rises straight up to the castle. It goes past little whitewashed houses, roofed in orange tiles, with flowers on windowsills and beside doorways, to lead into the main square of the village, around a pillory and fountain.

The tree-shaded **Church of Santa Maria** ★, in the square to the right, dates to the late 17th century, although its Romanesque portal shows earlier antecedents. In 1444, ten-year-old Dom Afonso V married his eight-year-old cousin here. The walls are covered with floral *azulejos*, the ceiling is painted with arabesques, fanciful Brazilian natives, and cherubs. On the left wall is an unexpected finely-detailed renaissance tomb. To the right of the main altar are captivating 17th-century paintings by a woman from Seville, named Josefa de

Óbidos who was cloistered nearby. *(Open daily 9:30 a.m. to 12:30 p.m. and 2:30-7 p.m.; in winter to 5 p.m.)*

The **municipal museum** ★ is also located in the square, behind the church. In truth the museum is not very interesting except for one room devoted to the paintings of Josefa de Óbidos. There is an admirable quality of passion about the paintings, conveyed by diffused light. *(Open Tuesday-Sunday 9:30 a.m. to 12:30 p.m. and 2-5 p.m.; admission: 200$00.)*

R. Direita ends at the church of São Tiago, old but redone in the 18th-century, An arch beside it leads to the castle courtyard, now used for parking. To the left, steep stairs ascend the crenulated **ramparts** for a walk with nice views of the countryside. A fortunate hole in the walls looks out on one of the charming windmills of the area.

The **castle** ★ is suitably imposing. Square towers anchor its corners, the right-hand one being the main, castle keep, while round towers incongruously line the rear. In the 16th century the castle was outfitted as a palace when a Manueline door and front windows were added. Today it serves as one of Portugal's most popular pousadas. Anyone can walk inside for a look.

WHERE TO STAY

Although few visitors spend the night in Óbidos, the village contains not one, but three hotels for their consideration. Sadly, the popular pousada is disappointing.

EXPENSIVE ($100-$200)

Pousada do Castelo 1st-class ★ ★

Paço Real. Rooms: 6, plus 3 suites. ☎ *95 91 05; FAX 95 91 48; Telex 15540.* This is the most heavily booked pousada in the county. While the paucity of available rooms is part of the reason, the main source of its popularity stems unaccountably from touting by guide books and tourist brochures. Success has undone whatever chance Castelo had of being a fine hotel. After all, why should the management care, when the rooms will fill no matter what? The hotel is dingy, with narrow stone corridors lined by doors painted shed-brown. Rooms are small, cold in feeling, and not particularly comfortable. All of this is criminal, for the building truly is a medieval castle and could be made at least comfortable with a little work. It includes a truly baronial hall, suits of armor dotting the way, and windows deeply set in thick castle walls, all materials for a special hotel. To us this is the one failure of the pousada system. Still, it is an opportunity to live in a castle for a while, but only if you book months ahead. Expensive meals are served in the dining room, also baronial with its beamed ceiling, but even the meals are not the best value. However, if one is staying elsewhere, a lunch or dinner here does provide a leisurely look at the inside of the castle.

MODERATE ($50-$99)

Estalagem do Convento 2nd-class ★ ★
R. Dom João de Ornelas (just outside the town walls). Rooms: 31. ☎ 95 92 17; FAX 95 91 59; Telex 44906. Installation in a modest former convent, appropriately whitewashed with dark wood details, all make this hotel appealing. And it sparkles with cleanliness. At the same time it is too pristine and sterile to feel quite comfortable. Large antique furniture lines the corridors and inhabits some of the rooms, and the bedrooms are well designed. Good food is served in the restaurant for a very moderate price.

Albergaria Rainha Santa Isabel 3rd-class ★ ★
R. Direita. Rooms: 20. ☎ 95 91 15; FAX 95 91 15; Telex 14069. Installed in one of the old houses in the heart of the village, this attractive hotel provides a sense of the aged village atmosphere. Bedrooms are cozily furnished and there is an elevator to the upper floors.

WHERE TO EAT

The pousada is at hand for expensive dining in a medieval atmosphere, and the Hotel do Convento offers tasty food, but the best value in the village is described below.

Alcaide ★
R. Direita. ☎ 95 92 20. Closed Monday and November. The dining room is festooned with ivy and the tables are dressed with checkered cloths. Outside, a balcony overlooks an orchard. The owner is from the Azores so menu choices include unusual dishes. Everything is tasty, and prices hug the low end of the moderate scale.
Amex, Diners, MasterCard and Visa accepted.

QUELUZ ★ ★ ★

Population: 47,864
Area code: 01; zip code: 2745

Only 12 k north of **Lisbon**, directions for Queluz are included in the "Excursion" section of Lisbon. **Sintra** is 15 k west along N-249.

By a tradition going back to the mid-17th century, the second son of Portugal's king was given the use of a hunting lodge at Queluz. In 1747 the second son was Dom Pedro, who extensively rebuilt the lodge to transform it into a royal summer residence. At this first stage the edifice was too small for a proper palace, about one third the present size. Then Pedro married his niece, Maria Francisca, who had before been betrothed to France's Louis XV. She greatly admired Versailles where she had lived for a while. For her the new building had to be more grand and more French.

Starting over in 1758 under the direction of a French architect, Jean-Baptiste Robillion, the palace seen today was constructed as a sort of Portuguese Versailles, complete with formal gardens in the French manner. Included in the change was the demolition of five earlier rooms to make a suitable throne room. And the outside was painted salmon. Here then is a palace built for a queen. For, by a tortuous course Maria eventually came to the throne, and this palace was her favorite residence. When she went insane in her later years, it became her place of confinement.

Although the palace is surrounded by a modern town today, the interior and gardens spreading behind transport the visitor into a delicate Baroque age.

Palácio Real de Queluz ★★★

Open Wed.-Mon. 10 a.m. to 1 p.m. and 2-5 p.m. Admission: 400$00 for guided tour of the palace, 200$00 in winter. Formerly fronted by a grand courtyard, the exterior is reached today by something more resembling a parking lot. The low, undramatic outside fails to impress, although there is that unexpected color. The inside is another matter, as is the rear facing the garden.

While there is plenty of gilding and mirrors inside, a clear feel of French design, the overall sense is of a delicacy that does not come from the north. It would be a heresy to claim that the effect is more successful than the famous and grand French palaces of the era, so we will say no more.

The stunning Ambassadors' Hall is roofed with a fine painting of a concert in pale pastels. Although its function in later years was to receive diplomats, hence the name, it was designed originally for musical entertainments, as it looks. Lovely *azulejos* of orange trees line the corridor outside. A very French Queen's boudoir prefaces the columned bedroom of the later regent, Dona Carlota (a veritable dwarf at four feet five inches) painted with scenes from *Don Quixote*. The breakfast room, next, is charming. After a mirrored dining room with a fine Arraiolos carpet, come three rooms for princesses, elegant dressing rooms, then an imposing music room with almost-perfect acoustics.

Glass and crystal in profusion characterize the throne room, probably the most Versaille-like part of the palace. Still, this one is special because of the softening lent by green-blue touches. The chapel contains paintings by Queen Maria and her sisters. Its intense colors make it the least engaging of the rooms, although such a strong statement is understandable given its purpose.

Outside, the palace presents a very French look, impressive in its formality. The pavilion on the left (if facing the palace) is original in its pillared design. The formal gardens are serene.

WHERE TO STAY

At present no hotel entices an overnight in Queluz, not when Sintra with extraordinary accommodations, is 15 k in one direction and Lisbon is 12 in the other. This may soon change because Enatur, the pousada company, is constructing their newest hotel opposite the palace entrance scheduled to open this year. If you have reason to stay near Queluz before this is finished, there is one option at present.

MODERATE ($50-$100)

Poma e Restaurant Via Prado

In Tercena, east 4k on N-117. Rooms: 50. ☎ *437 27 45; FAX 560 81 86.* Modern and motel-like, the rooms are comfortable and clean.

WHERE TO EAT

Of course you can snack at any little restaurant in town, but you can also eat royally here, because the old kitchen of the palace now functions as a restaurant run by the pousada people.

EXPENSIVE ($40+)

Cozinha Velha ★★

Largo do Palácio, Palácio Nacional de Queluz (to the right of the palace entrance). ☎ *435 02 32.* The dining room is pleasant rather than grand, after all it was the kitchen, although some pains are taken to make it so. There is a huge fireplace, original azulejos, and a marble table groaning with food, but the decor is polished copper and the seats ladder-back chairs. You are here for the experience, more than for the cuisine which tries to be special by claiming ancient recipes, although they taste much like dishes available elsewhere. Yet all is festive and fun, not everyone can say they dined at a palace, and the vanilla soufflé is divine. *Amex, Diners, MasterCard and Visa accepted.*

SETÚBAL ★

Population: 97,762
Area code: 065; zip code: 2900

55 k north of **Lisbon***; directions are included in the "Excursion" section of Lisbon. Since the auto-estrada A-2 runs from just east of Setúbal straight to Lisbon, it is on the preferred route to the capital from either the east or south. See directions from specific individual locations in appropriate chapters.*

The industrial center and port of Setúbal makes it the third-largest city in Portugal. Although the city is not particularly attractive, neither is it as ugly as its economic functions might suggest. What makes it worth a stop is the intriguing small church of Jesus, the first Manueline building, and the fine beaches in its environs.

From **Lisbon**, **south** *and* **east**, *Setúbal is entered along Estrada da Graça which feeds into its continuation Av. Luisa Todi, with a planted center strip. In a few blocks the large park of Das Escolas appears on the right. Here parking is available.*

From the parking lot head east for one long block along Av. Luisa Todi to turn left on Av. 22 de Dezembro, which reaches the church of Jesus in about the same distance. From the bus station on Av. 5 de Outubro or the train station just east, head west along Av. 22 de Dezembro for about four blocks.

Igreja de Jesus ★★
Open Tuesday-Sunday 9 a.m. to noon and 2-5 p.m. Closed Monday and holidays. Admission: free. This hall-church was begun in the last decade of the 15th century by Boytac, the architect who originated the Manueline architectural style. He finished the church, but not the adjoining convent, because his master called him for the grander commission of the Hieronymite monastery in Belém. Given the shock of the interior even today, one can imagine how inventive the device of twisted columns would have seemed at the time. True, the columns are merely two pillars twisted into one mass, but they appear to grow down from the ceiling rather than support it from the ground, as columns had always done before. The effect is arresting, and led to the twisting, living shapes of the developed Manueline style.

A wainscotting of lovely *azulejos* from the 17th century follows both walls, and a particularly harmonious design of tiles lines the altar.

Outside is a cloister with a monastery surrounding it, now serving as the **Museu da Cidad**. On the ground floor are some nice *azulejos*. The upper floors are devoted to wonderful primitive paintings attributed to an anonymous "Master of Setúbal." Clearly influenced by the stiff figures of Van Eyke, the artist managed to convey a compassion in the faces that is his (or her) own.

WHERE TO STAY

Unless one sleeps in the fortress described below, there is no reason to spend the night in Setúbal when pleasant beach accommodations are so close (described in "Excursions" below). If castles appeal, there is a lovely one, also described below, 8 k north of Setúbal in Palmela.

EXPENSIVE ($100-$200)
Pousada de São Filipe   1st-class ★★
R. São Filipe (From Av. Luisa Todi take the second right after the Parque das Escolas. Almost immediately turn left on Estrada do Castelo de São Filipe which winds up to the pousada.) Rooms: 14. ☎ *52 38 44; Telex*

44655. The Spanish built this castle at the end of the 16th century to defend the kingdom of Portugal which they had appropriated and to cow the citizens in the city below with mighty guns. They chose a spot with a wonderful view that visitors to the pousada now enjoy. Guests stay in the former guards' quarters in bedrooms that are charmingly rustic. Getting to them requires wandering the fortress corridors, which is no chore at all. Reservations are usually necessary.

In Palmela:

Pousada do Castelo de Palmela　　　　　　　　　　**1st-class ★ ★ ★**
From Setúbal, take Av. Cinco de Outubro east from the church of Jesus. Turn left in four blocks onto Av. Portela, which becomes N-252. Just before the auto-estrada, take N-379 going west.) Rooms: 28. ☎ *235 12 26; FAX 233 04 40; Telex 42290.* This is a hotel whose grounds merit half a day's sight-seeing. It is situated in the confines of Palmela castle whose fortress dates from Afonso Henriques in the 12th century. West of the castle is the 15th-century monastery in which the pousada is lodged. A former mosque, made over into a church, in turn destroyed in the 1755 earthquake, stands in ruins in front of the castle. Around the whole are crude perimeter walls built by the Moors, surrounded by a complex 17th-century outer wall. The pousada is an example of good restoration, preserving the feel of the Renaissance monastery while providing every modern comfort. On the other hand, the bedrooms, lodged in monks' cells, are spartan, although their marvelous views are anything but.

EXCURSIONS

There are beaches south on the peninsula of Tróia, and beaches west along the Serra da Arrábida mountain range.

TRÓIA

The 8-k strip of sand and pine trees that separates the river Sado from the ocean is a highly developed beach resort, including an 18-hole Robert Trent Jones golf course. Despite the development of this peninsula, unspoiled beach remains on the ocean side and south, and moderate accommodations are available.

A car ferry leaves the commercial port of Setúbal (the Doca Comércio) every half hour in season (every hour out-of-season) for a 20-minute trip.

Aparthotel Tróia, **Rosamar** and **Magnoliamar** are three hotels forming the Torralta complex, which includes every amenity from a baby-sitting service to golf. All are apartment hotels, sleekly modern and charmless, but their prices are moderate. ☎ *442 22, for the former,* ☎ *441 51 for the latter two.*

SERRA DA ARRÁBIDA

The Arrábida mountain range lines the 40-k southern coast of the Setúbal peninsula, forming high limestone cliffs over the ocean, broken here and there by sandy coves. The scenery is dramatic.

Follow Av. Luisa Todi west to N-379-1. After about 20 k signs for **Portinho do Arrábida** *point to a steep and narrow 1 k descent. For safety it is best to leave one's car at the top, though the walk back is tiring. The bay forms a perfect curve of fine white sand embracing clear waters. Unfortunately, there are no hotels, although some private houses accept guests.*

After Portinho N-379-1 climbs north for 6 k to meet N-379 going west, 5 k of rough road leads to Santana, just past which a left turn toward the south brings Sesimbra in 2 k.

SESIMBRA

Sesimbra remains a thriving seaport, although the developers have arrived. Its lovely beaches are less spoiled, however, than comparable ones in the Algarve, and the fishermen are real. A ruined castle stands high upon the hill.

EXPENSIVE ($100-$200)

Do Mar   1st-class ★ ★

R. Combatentes do Ultamar, 10 (west of town). Rooms: 168. ☎ 223 33 26; FAX 223 38 88; Telex 13883. This is a luxury resort complex terraced down a hill. The architecture is interesting, including an aviary in the lobby. Rooms are starkly modern and comfortable, but the bathrooms could be larger. However, ocean views atone for any imperfection.

MODERATE ($50-$99)

Espadarte   3rd-class

Av. 25 de Abril. Rooms: 80. ☎ 223 31 89; Telex 14699. Some of the rooms are noisy, all are small, some are dingy and old, while others are brand-new. But the low price and a balcony overlooking the sea makes a stay worthwhile.

N-379 continues west for 12 k to Cabo Espichel, an awesomely wild and windy cape.

SINTRA ★ ★ ★ ★

Population: 20,574
Area code: 01; zip code: 2710

Sintra is located 28 k northwest of **Lisbon***; directions are included in the "Excursion" section of Lisbon. From* **Mafra** *take N-9 south for 31 k.*

The magical mountains surrounding Sintra are lush with camellias, gardenias, bougainvillea and eucalyptus in season. Byron lauded this "glorious Eden" in *Childe Harolde* and wrote his mother that it is "perhaps the most delightful (village) in Europe." There is a Black Forest quality about the mountains, which appropriately shelter a castle worthy of King Ludwig of Bavaria. All in all, Sintra is one of the highlights of Portugal. In the most dramatic setting imaginable, Sintra offers a palace, a fantasy castle and a ruined fortress of the Moors. A day would cover the sights comfortably. While tourists arrive by the bus-full, they are quickly absorbed into the vastness of surrounding nature.

Actually three Sintras wrap around the mountain. The Vila Velha clusters near the Palácio Real of Portugal's kings. To the north is the new town, called Estefania, with the bus and train station along the way, and to the south is the formerly separate town of São Pedro, which hosts a famous crafts market.

> *From* **Lisbon** *N-249 becomes the winding Estrada de Chão de Meninos, then Av. D. F. de Almeida, to end at Largo de Albuquerque. Turn left here along R. Dr. Alfredo Costa which bends right to change its name to Av. Volta do Duche, leading into the parking of the Pr. de República beside the Palácio Real. From* **Mafra** *Av. Henrique Salgado leads into the Largo de Albuquerque, from which point the Lisbon directions can be followed.*

Palácio Real ★★★★

Open daily 10 a.m. to 1 p.m. and 2-5 p.m. Admission: 400$00 for guided tour. Kings and queens favored the mountain air of Sintra for their summers since the end of the 14th century. Even before, the Moors had built a summer palace on the spot, which Dom João I tore down to build the central, and oldest part of the present palace. Additions were made over the years—including the left 16th-century wing added by Manuel I—producing a jumble of styles. It is a Gothic-Mudejar complex dominated by two clumsy conical chimneys, though individual windows and their surrounds are lovely.

Magnificent rooms inside are lined with some of the finest *azulejos* in the world and hold remarkable antique furniture. Past the **kitchen**, with its gigantic fireplaces, through the **Guest Room**, with some interesting furniture, comes, in the **Sala dos Arabes**, the first example of these *azulejos*—blue, green and white Mudejar tiles, among the oldest in the country were imported from Spain in the first decade of the 16th century.

An exterior patio leads to the exquisite **Chapel**. Its adorable frescoed walls of doves have been restored to their original look, its fine Mudejar inlaid ceiling is the marvelous original, and its patterned tiles form a carpet. After the Chinese room with an ivory pagoda donated by the Emperor of China in 1809, comes the **Sala de Afonso VI**, whose 15th-century *azulejo* floor is said to have been worn away by that king's pacing during nine years of imprisonment. A lovely muslim hanging brightens the room. Along the next corridor hangs a 16th-century Brussels tapestry of the Portuguese royal coat-of-arms, with an unusual oriental carpet below it. Then comes the wonder of the **Sala dos Brasoães** (Coats-of-Arms Room).

This space was designed for views and light, which makes the 18th-century azulejo hunting-scenes panelling the walls gleam with remarkable effect. But the purpose of the room is to display its incredible artesonado dome of the coats-of-arms of Portugal's first families. At the top is that of the Portuguese royal house, gilded and repainted to reflect the next dynasty; the arms of King Manuel's children surrounding this, then 80 more, beneath charming stags, are arranged by their importance at court. Under the dome lies quite a carpet.

Farther along comes the **Sala das Sireias** with a lovely ceiling of mermaids playing instruments, above fine azulejos from Seville. Next is the 15th-century **Sala de Pegas** (Room of the Magpies), named for the birds on the ceiling which hold a rose and the legend *Por bem* ("for the good"). Tradition had João I ordering the multiple images after being caught by his wife presenting a rose to a lady of the court and uttering "It's all for the best," a story that hardly makes sense. More likely, the magpies represent the King, and the rose represents his Queen who was indeed from the House of Lancaster.

Across the central patio the **Sala dos Cisnes** can be admired. This imposing audience hall is named for the swans embellishing the magnificent ceiling painted in the 17th-century; the woodwork is also masterly.

There are various options for the 3 k, almost-vertical climb to the Castelo dos Mouros and the Palácio da Pena atop the highest peaks in the Sintra mountains. The most pleasant journey is to walk, encouraged by the thought that the return is downhill. It will take an hour to the Castle of the Moors, another to the Pena Palace, depending on your pace. A map is available from the tourist office. Alternatively, a taxi will cost about 2000$00 for the round trip to either, including an hour's wait, or 3500$00 to both. In summer buses travel daily at 10:45 a.m., 3 p.m. and 4 p.m. for 150$00. For romantics there are horse-drawn carriages that will cost about 4000$00. By car head west (uphill) from the palace, past the post office on R. Pedroso. At the Estalagem dos Cavaleiros, now boarded up, where Byron stayed, turn left and then turn sharply

left at the next opportunity only to take an immediate right. The road twists and winds back on itself until reaching a parking place. From here a 10-minute walk remains up to the Moors' Castle. For the Palace of Pena continue to a "T," then turn right as a sign directs.

Castelo dos Mouros ★

Open Tues.-Sun. 8 a.m. to sunset. Closed Mon. Admission: free. Although called a castle, this was actually a fortress, built in the eighth or early ninth century, then captured by Christians in the 12th. It has fallen into romantic ruins, although the perimeter wall still stands with corner towers. Some restoration was attempted in the 19th-century, but given up. On a clear day there are heavenly views from atop a tower inside the walls. Also on the grounds is a Romanesque chapel dating to the 12th-century Reconquest.

Palácio Nacional da Pena ★★★

Open Tues.-Sun. 10 a.m. to 1 p.m. and 2-4:45 p.m. Closed Mon. Admission: 400$00. Queen Maria II came to the throne in 1836 and married Friedrich of Saxe Coburg-Gotha, an old titled German family of three cousins, each of whom married a queen. Cousin Leopold became King of the Belgians, cousin Albert became the consort of Queen Victoria in England and Fernando II, as the Portuguese know him, became the king of Portugal. A tinge of homesickness led him to import a German architect to build a palace at Sintra. Ferdinand had pretensions to art and worked closely on the design. What resulted was the beginning of the Victorian style, although we call it by the name of his cousin-in-law.

Outside the castle is part Moorish, part Gothic, part Baroque, tinged with Manueline—a confection of crenulations, minarets, turrets and drawbridges—a castle for the child in us all. The interior is another matter, consisting of patterns and colors jumbled on each other to create that dark, cozy, romantic cluttered look we call "Victorian."

Over the drawbridge and through a tunnel, then up a "Manueline" double stair, are remains from a Manueline monastery cloister with fine *azulejos* and a lovely alabaster altar. Then the pantry and dining room of the palace are entered to provide a foretaste of what lies in store. One special feature of this building is that the rooms actually looked lived in. Note the lace, the feathers and ornately carved furniture. This and the rooms that follow remain almost exactly as they were in 1910 when the royal family fled to exile. Their taste, however we evaluate it, is therefore evident to all.

The apartments of King Carlos include his workroom with unfinished canvases of nymphs and fauns. The bathrooms are a delight. After the chapel come bedrooms for the women, including the marvelous painted stucco of the Queen's Room, feeling Moorish. Then comes the Sewing Room, all oriental in style, and then the Private Living Room of a style unique to Ferdinand.

And so it goes, each chamber unique, each betraying the same "overdone" look that somehow works. Note the Arabian Room frescoed with trompe l'oeil mosque scenes, and the India Room, named for its furniture, with a playful Bavarian chandelier, a forerunner of the art nouveau. The multifarious ballroom furniture is a treat.

WHERE TO STAY

We sympathize with anyone who does not want to leave Sintra after a short day. Mountain nights are wonderful, the Moors' Castle is lighted, and there are a number of exceptional accommodations in the area, including the finest in Portugal.

VERY EXPENSIVE ($200+)

Palácio de Seteais Deluxe ★★★★★

Av. Bocage, 8, Seteais (1.5 k outside Sintra on N-375, which is reached by going west from the palace on R. Pedroso). Rooms: 30. ☎ *923 32 00; FAX 923 42 77; Telex 1441.* There is not a more tasteful, elegantly grand hotel in Portugal, if in the world. This one is pure romance. It feels like a French chateaux, but more lovely than any we have had the good fortune to stay at in that country. Built in the 18th century by a Dutch businessman, it was taken over by the fifth Marquis of Marialva, the Royal Chamberlain, before transformation into a hotel. Now it is run by the Tivoli Hotel Corporation in Lisbon. An appropriately long driveway leads to the palace atop a bluff overlooking miles. Most rooms face palatial formal gardens, with views to the sea on clear days. The decor is pastel, working with the warm glow of ancient floors: delicate frescos cover ceilings and walls; fine antiques grace the rooms. Everything is perfect, including the bedrooms fitted with antiques or near-enoughs. Three special bedrooms (which is almost a redundancy in this case) incorporate hand-painted murals. There is a pool and two tennis courts. For what it offers, prices are reasonable at just over $200 for a double, only $50 more for a suite. And you can knock off $100 in the winter. Other than at that time, reservations will be needed. If you cannot spend the night, go for an elegantly beautiful $30 lunch or dinner, or even for cocktails just to see the place, and you'll wish you could stay.

EXPENSIVE ($100-$200)

Quinta da Capela 2nd-class ★★★★

Estrada da Monserrate (about 2 k further along the road past the Palácio de Seteais above, past Monserrate, then look carefully for a marked turn). Rooms: 10. ☎ *929 01 70; FAX 929 34 25.* From the outside this 18th-century building looks more like a farm than a villa, but inside it is splendid, yet cozy. Two outlying cottages contain two rather ordinary bedrooms and kitchenettes. The bedrooms in the main house are more elegant by far. There is a tiny ancient chapel in the garden, a

pool and lovely views, and the young manager-caretaker is as likable a
can be. The most expensive double apartment just passes $100, bed
rooms in the old house stop short of that mark. The quinta is close
out of season, and must be reserved far in advance in season.

Quinta de São Thiago   2nd-class ★★★
Estrada de Monserrate (about 1 k further along the road past the Palácio d
Seteais above, then a marked turn along a treacherously steep and bump
road). Rooms: 14. ☎ 923 29 23. This is a lovely 16th-century vill
owned by a British and Portuguese couple who extend themselves fo
their guests. Much of the furniture is antique and there is the feel c
staying in an elegant house rather than at a hotel. A swimming poo
and a tennis court are provided, but not air conditioning. Reservation
should be made far in advance.

Tivoli Sintra   1st-class ★
Pr. da República. Rooms: 75. ☎ 923 35 05; FAX 923 15 72; Tele
42314. This hotel of modern design is an affront to its surroundings
Ignore the business-person lobby, because the bedrooms are unusu
ally large, comfortable, and the balcony views are sylvan.

MODERATE ($50-$99)

Estalagem da Raposa   4th-class ★★
R. Dr. Alfredo Costa, 3 (along the street that leads to Estefania, the nev
town, near the train station). Rooms: 8. ☎ 923 04 65. The inviting look
is that of a private house, set back from the street by a garden. Bed
rooms are comfortable and clean.

Central   3rd-class ★
Pr. da República, 35. Rooms: 14. ☎ 923 09 63. Its charm stems from its
old-fashionableness. Each bedroom is furnished with whatever was
available, but the location is good and prices are low.

INEXPENSIVE (UNDER $50)

Casa Adelaide   R3rd-class★
Av. Guilherme Gomes Fernandes, 11 (just before R. Dr. Alfredo Costa
bends left, turn right into Largo Virgilio Horta, then left again past the
police station). Rooms: 10. ☎ 923 08 73. The rooms are homey and
some provide views.

WHERE TO EAT

For ambiance to spare and the best food in the area, reserve at the Mon
serrat restaurant of the **Palácio de Seteais Hotel.** Good food in pleasant
surroundings is served at Galeria Real. The moderately priced food in the
restaurant of the **Tivoli Sintra** is decent, certainly better than the dining
room would lead you to expect.

EXPENSIVE ($40+)

Restaurant Monserrat   ★★★
In the Palácio de Seteais hotel, Av. Bocage, 8, Seteais (1.5 k outside Sintra

on N-375, which is reached by going west from the palace on R. Pedroso). ☎ 923 32 00. A lovelier dinner area would be hard to imagine, including fantastic views over the countryside. The food is elevated to match its surroundings, and four course set meals can be had for about $30. Ok, maybe the romance of the setting affected our taste buds, but it probably will do the same to yours. Eating here is an experience that is not to be missed.   *Amex, Diners, MasterCard and Visa accepted.*

MODERATE ($15-30)

Galeria Real ★
R. Tude de Sousa (on the main street in São Pedro). ☎ 923 16 61. Closed Monday evening. This is a pretty, second-floor restaurant located in a warren of antique shops. The ceiling is hand-painted beams, the floors tiled, and flowers decorate each table. Codfish souffle is the delicious specialty. Otherwise the menu is not adventuresome.
Amex, Diners, MasterCard and Visa accepted.

INEXPENSIVE (UNDER $20)

Alcobaça ★
R. da Padarias, 7 (the street runs uphill from the tourist office, just west of the Palácio Real). ☎ 923 16 51. Closed Wednesday and December. This is an eminently local place that serves standard Portuguese dishes at very fair prices. If the cooking wasn't good, it wouldn't be so crowded.   *No credit cards accepted.*

SHOPPING

A large crafts fair is held in the township of São Pedro on the second and fourth Sunday of the month, providing examples of all the local arts. If you miss the fair, samplings of local crafts are on sale at **Central Bazaar** next to the Hotel Central in the Pr. da República in front of the palace.

DIRECTORY

INFORMATION • Located at the south end of the Pr. da República (☎ *923 11 57*).

TRAINS AND BUSES • The train station is on Av. Dr. Miguel Bombarda (☎ *923 26 05*), halfway between the Vila Velha and the new town of Estefania. Trains serve Lisbon every 15 minutes, stopping at Queluz. Trains connect with Óbidos, but connections elsewhere are difficult.

The bus station is across the street from the train station and is best for surrounding towns.

POST OFFICE AND TELEPHONES • Located across from the Office of Tourism (☎ *923 11 57*).

POLICE • Located in Largo Dr. Virgilio Horta, which is to the left of R. Dr. Alfredo Costa that connects the Vila Velha with Estefania (☎ *923 34 00*). For emergencies: ☎ *115*.

EXCURSIONS

Sintra is readily combined with **Mafra**, 20 k north or with **Queluz**, 20 k east. Descriptions are contained in this chapter under those respective headings. For Mafra, follow the directions at the beginning of the Sintra entry in reverse. For Queluz see the directions in the "Excursion" section of the Lisbon chapter.

A pleasant excursion for those interested in wine is to the remarkable vineyards of **Colares**, 6 k west of Sintra. What makes its wines special is that vine roots are buried deep in sand which protected them from the phylloxera blight that struck Europe in 1865. All other vines in Europe succumbed and had to be grafted to American roots that were immune to the blight. Today only a Colares red is made from true European grapes. The *Adega Regional de Colares* promotes these wines and may be visited. Purchases are possible.

Moorish Castle above the forests of Sintra

NORTHERN PORTUGAL

The stairs to Bom Jesus near Braga

Historical Profile: The Birth of Portugal

We expect a country to be naturally defined by water and mountain borders, so the Iberian Peninsula looks as though it should be counted a single country. Portugal's northern border meanders through minor mountains to leave a chunk of Spain laying atop Portugal. Although the Atlantic marks a natural end west and south, the long eastern border haphazardly follows one river for a while, before drifting to the next.

What are the reasons for the existence of such an erratic border, or any border at all? A difference in language does not explain the separation, for the division of Portugal from Spain was what caused the diversity of the languages, rather than the other way around. The Portuguese attribute their independence to a national hero, Afonso Henriques, who dared to proclaim himself a king. But Portugal's boundaries remained stable for centuries after his death, despite continual wars with Spain. The answer seems to be that, rather than any crucial event or person, Portugal owes its nationhood to a series of battles going the right way at the right time over a span of centuries.

This is not to say that every difference between Spain and Portugal is the effect rather than the cause of their being separate countries. The historic stock from which the Portuguese descend differs slightly from Spain's. During the 16th and 17th centuries Portugal's commercial concerns lay in Africa and the Far East while Spain focused on the Americas to the west. And Portugal's long alliance with England was one factor keeping the nations apart. But history's accidents were also essential, for in the beginning Spain and Portugal were joined.

When Romans came to the peninsula in the second century B.C., they found a mixture of people already there—those known as Celtiberians. As was the Roman style, they set out to conquer and colonize them. One tribe they called Lusitanians, who inhabited the area that would later become Portugal, proved to be formidable opponents. Led by a hero named Virianthus who, despite inferior numbers, regularly out-generalled all Roman troops sent against him, the Lusitanians could not be beaten. In desperation, the Romans bribed three of Virianthus' lieutenants to assassinate him, then the leaderless Lusitanians were subdued, followed, a few decades later by the other tribes in the peninsula.

The Romans quickly organized all of Iberia into smaller provinces, for administrative reasons, many of which soon developed the separate identities they would bear ever after. One province, Lusitania, corresponded to the northern half of Portugal. Its major city, Olissipo, would become Lisbon.

By the third century A.D., Rome's declining control opened her empire to "barbarians." German tribes crossed the far borders and migrated down to the peninsula—a tribe called the Vandals took the south, Alans the east coast, and Swabians seized the area of Lusitania, which they found congenial in soil and climate to their native corner of Germany. When fiercer Visigoths followed two centuries later, they conquered all the peninsula except the territory of the Swabians, thus leaving a partially different population stock for Portugal than for Spain.

But the Visigoths did not control the peninsula for long. In 711, Islamic Moors chased them to the northern extremity of the peninsula. The Moors, like the Romans, then established a number of provinces, naming Portugal *al Garbi*, "the West," from which comes the modern name Algarve for Portugal's southern coast.

Reconquest by Christians slowly won the peninsula back, mostly under the leadership of Castilian kings. Alfonso VI crossed what would later be a border to free Lisbon in 1070, and reestablished a bishopric at Braga to the north. His success so frightened the Moors, however, that they called for help from brethren in Morocco, who chased Alfonso VI back to where he had come. Alfonso now was outmanned, and called on France for assistance.

In 1095, the son-in-law of the King of France arrived with reinforcements, including his cousin, Henri of Burgundy. After some military success, Alfonso VI gave Henri his illegitimate daughter Teresa as a reward for his service. Her dowry included the title of Count of Portucale, the northern part of later-day Portugal. It was named for the Roman town of *Portus Cale*. Much later the town's name would be shortened and made more Portuguese-sounding as "Porto," but "Portucale," later transmogrified into "Portugal," remained the term for the original Christian area and for all that its people would conquer from the Moors, which is to say, in time, the whole of Portugal.

Henri established his court at Guimarães, in the extreme north, near the ancient bishopric of Braga. To encourage the economy he set aside a street for foreign merchants, and rebuilt the cathedrals of Braga and Porto nearby. With wife Teresa's help, he also produced a son they named Afonso Henriques.

Henri died in 1112, when his son Afonso Henriques was five, leaving his wife to act as regent for the young count. But when the king of Castile called on his nobles to pay obligatory feudal homage for their territories, Teresa refused. Eventually the king compelled her homage by force. She had taken a lover and given birth to another child by that time, estranging herself from her son, who claimed that his mother's oath was not his. Slowly, Afonso Henriques began grabbing the reins of government, leading, by his early twenties, to war with his mother. When Afonso defeated her army, she fled north into the Spanish territory of Galicia, chased by Afonso and his troops. This incursion into his territory was too much for the king of Castile, who attacked Afonso Henriques, defeated him, and forced the homage this vassal had so long withheld.

Then another Muslim sect from Morocco crossed the straits and conquered their brothers in the peninsula. They turned their avaricious attention on the king of Castile, giving him more trouble than he could handle. Afonso Henriques had some success against one detachment of these Moors who entered his territory in 1139. Feeling powerful, he started calling himself "king of Portugal."

Of course, the king of Castile did not agree, but he was too occupied with the Moors to do anything about the matter. In 1179, Afonso Henriques gained the pope's recognition of his title in return for a small annual tribute of gold. From this time forth, except for one interlude 400 years later, Portugal remained independent of Spain.

Afonso Henriques is described as fair complexioned, bearded and a giant of a man—as founders are wont to be imagined. He married Mafalda, the daughter of the count of Savoy. Originally, his territories comprised a little less than the northern half of modern Portugal, but he set out to expand them by conquering the southern lands still held by the Moors.

In 1140, with the aid of Crusaders on their way to the Holy Land, he besieged Lisbon but retired when the defenders paid him off. In 1177, he enlisted English, Normans, Flemings and Germans on their way to the Second Crusade to attack Lisbon again. Witnesses claimed the city held 150,000 men, women and children behind strongly fortified defenses. The city stood firm against the attackers' catapults, which delivered up to 5000 missiles during one ten-hour period; the walls resisted their rams and fortified ladders. For 17 weeks of siege, the city held out before capitulating on October 23, 1147.

After this success, Afonso Henriques continued the conquest south, at one point controlling all but the southernmost quarter of the country. But the Moors fought back, first retaking, then losing land, as fortunes on both sides changed. Afonso Henriques also tried to carry conquest north into the Spanish territory of Galicia, where he was not only defeated but suffered a broken leg when a town portcullis fell on him, and endured the ignominy of capture by the king of Castile. He gained his freedom by paying a ransom, but the injury ended his wars. He died in 1185, at nearly 80, after 57 years on the throne, and left his son Sancho I a kingdom.

Sancho continued the effort to conquer southern Portugal, gaining the major city of Silves in 1189 with help from yet another itinerant army of Crusaders. But the Moors retook the city two years later. Sancho died in 1211 at age 57. His son Afonso II, the Fat, concerned about the great power of the church, began investigating ecclesiastical abuses. The Pope's response was to excommunicate him. After a reign of only 12 years, Afonso died of leprosy, leaving a 12 year-old heir.

That boy, Sancho II, remained under the thumb of advisors who encouraged him to marry the widow of an Andalusian captain. This frightened many Portuguese who feared Spanish influence at the court. With the backing of the nobles, his uncle Afonso petitioned the Pope to declare the marriage illegal. The Pope ordered Sancho to abandon his wife and accused him of a catalogue of crimes it would seem impossible for one so young to have accomplished. Nonetheless, when Sancho refused to leave his wife, the Pope designated uncle Afonso as king in his stead. To make certain that no heir could be bred, Afonso III (as he was now titled) captured his nephew's wife, married her himself, then chased Sancho to Castile. With the Church's backing, Afonso III was able to complete the conquest of the south, once and for all. He convened the first Cortes which included representatives of towns, the nascent middle class, in addition to nobles and clergy.

His son Dinis I succeeded to the throne when Afonso III died in 1277. The new king was known as *Rei Lavrador*, "the Farmer King," for his interest in agriculture. To increase production, he decreed that anyone who raised crops for ten years on the same land be given title to it, which turned former serfs into land-owning citizens. He also founded the first Portuguese university, originally in Lisbon, then moved to Coimbra when the rowdiness of the students caused complaints from Lisbon's citizenry. He had time to compose poetry and to marry Isabella, the daughter of the king of Aragón. In her time she was considered saintly, partly for her acceptance of Dinis' philandering, and was later canonized. In 1325 Dinis died after a golden reign of 46 years.

Dinis I was the star of the house founded by Afonso Henrique, called the Burgundian line after the homeland of its founder. With Dinis' successor, Afonso IV, the end would begin.

NORTHERN PORTUGAL

Portugal's one arterial highway, the A-1 autoestrada, makes northward travel from Lisbon fast and easy, speeding past an array of worthy sights. The highway ends at Braga, about 50 miles below the Spanish border. This chapter covers those northern sights, beginning above Leiria, 80 miles north of Lisbon, although including Tomar which, though south of Tomar, is an equal distance from Lisbon. (Sights between Lisbon and Leiria are covered in the previous chapter the "Environs of Lisbon.")

But travelling east of Lisbon, like going crosstown in Manhattan, is a more difficult matter than north-south commuting. Although the longest eastward journey is no more than 130 miles, clogged roads make slower going, so that, once you arrive, it makes sense to visit surrounding sights rather than work your way back again later. The next chapter, "Eastern Portugal," arranges these sights in one package.

The present chapter draws a line, roughly down the center of Portugal, to encompass what is most conveniently visited as offshoots from the autoestrada whizzing up the west coast. The distance from Lisbon to Viana do Castelo, near the extreme northern border, is 225 miles, less than the distance from New York City to Washington. This chapter will not take you more than 50 miles east of the autoestrada, with the exception of a trip to Bragança, 100 miles from the coast. Thus, the area covered by this chapter is not excessively large, and we concentrate on sights of interest to average travellers, relegating more specialized locales to excursion sections.

Tomar ★★★, 100 miles northeast of Lisbon, preserves the mysteries of a 12th-century church of the Knights Templar, embellished by splendid Manueline and Renaissance additions. In the same area, in the middle of the Tagus River, waits the most romantic castle in Portugal, **Almourol** ★★. **Coimbra** ★★★ with a grand site and Medieval university lies just 125 miles directly north of Lisbon, and serves as a center for pleasant excursions. There are beaches nearby at **Figueira da Foz** ★ and at **Aveiro** ★★, and ceramics shopping in **Coindixa**, with the best Roman ruins in the country on its outskirts at **Conimbriga** ★. **Viseu** ★★, 60 miles northeast of Coimbra, is the perfect Portuguese town, containing the features that most do, but more attractively. It also offers an art museum displaying two little-known but superior Portuguese painters from the Renaissance.

NORTHERN PORTUGAL

Porto ★★★ is a mere 120 k north of Coimbra, even less from Viseu. It retains the character of its 19th-century port wine exporting industry. About 50 k north stands **Braga** ★★, a town of Baroque splendors, within 100 k of the northern border. Nearby, in **Guimarães** ★★★, is the castle in which the first king of Portugal was born thus earning this town the title of birthplace of the country. Its bonus is an imposingly medieval palace. Near the eastern border with Spain, 250 k due east of Porto, reposes the mountain town of **Bragança** ★★ in blissful isolation, which bred Portugal's last ruling dynasty.

ALMOUROL CASTLE ★★

See "Tomar excursions."

AVEIRO ★★

Population: 29,646
Area code: 034; zip code: 3800

From **Lisbon** A-1 runs north for 243 k to the "North Aveiro" exit, then a leg of 12 k on the Aveiro expressway. Thus, Aveiro can serve as a stopover on the way to Porto and north. From **Coimbra** A-1 can be joined for a 74 k run north to the Aveiro exit, then a jag west for 12 k. From **Porto** A-1 runs south for 46 k to the Aveiro exit and a turn west for 12 k. From **Guarda**, to the east, N-16 heads north then west for 68 k to **Viseu**, then continues west for 70 k to cross the autoestrada for a final leg of 12 k.

Parking should be available along the Canal Central and its extension, the Canal do Cojo, in the city center.

Aveiro stands beside a huge lagoon extending north for 45 k and west for 10 k beside the ocean. It is an unusual city with the flavor of a dutch burgh and situated near good beaches. Its canals are plied by high bow, flat bottomed, punted boats, not dissimilar to gondolas—except for brightly painted bow emblems and the fact that they serve not as water-taxis, but as seaweed collectors.

Aveiro has had its ups and downs. Until the end of the 16th century it thrived as a port for cod fishing. In the 17th century, however, a storm shut Aveiro's lagoon from the sea so it quickly silted up, leading to two centuries of economic depression for the city. Because of the loss of its port and the malarial marshes that formed after the silting, Aveiro's population declined by two thirds. Then, in 1808, the sandbar was breached by engineers, making Aveiro a port again. Today the city lives off fish, plentiful salt from the huge lagoon for the salted cod of Portugal, and seaweed for fertilizer.

Aveiro's main interest for tourists will be her beaches, but it is an attractive town as well with pleasant sights. Boats quietly ply the water (which can, however, emit a smell on summer days). Attractive mansions line the **Canal Central**; the **Convent of Jesus** ★ contains a pretty church and museum of worthwhile paintings; and a boat tour of the **ria** ★★ (lagoon) is a pleasant outing with local color to see. The **Vista Alegre** factory bustles 7 k south near Ilhavo on N-109. Although the secrets of the manufacturing process are guarded, there is a museum showing the development of this ware from clumsy beginnings, and, of course, a shop selling the finished product.

The sights of Aveiro are central and compact. All roads converge on the main square of town, the Pr. Humberto Delgado, which is actually a wide bridge over the Canal Central. West of this bridge the canal is lined with eccentric buildings. Here too is the **tourist office** which provides information about boat trips through the lagoon. Just east of the bridge, on the same side as the tourist office, is a run-down, yet wonderful, art deco house. Branching off, further east, runs the wide shaded main avenue of town, Dr. Lourenço Paixinho, lined with stores. The city **train station** festooned with charming azulejos, waits eight pleasant blocks along this avenue. Along the way, look for the headquarters of the local Communist Party on the south side of Paixinho, set back from the street, with azulejos of St. Anthony.

The 16th-century church of **Misericordia** flanks the east side of Pr. República, a short block south of Delgado. With a nice doorway and *azulejos* facade, it faces an elegant 17th-century **Town Hall** opposite. Two blocks west runs a large, pleasant municipal park with an eccentric building overlooking a wood bridge over the pond. By following Rua da Grande Guerra south past the church front, the second left leads to the **Convent of Jesus** housing a surprisingly good regional museum that stands opposite the Cathedral, separated by a fine Gothic cruizeiro (pillory).

Convento de Jesús and Museu de Aveiro ★★

Open Tues.-Sun. 10 a.m. to 12:30 p.m. and 2-5 p.m. Closed Mon. Admission: 350$00. The convent and its church were built in the 15th century but decorated in the early 18th. The church interior contains some of the finest Baroque gilded work in Portugal, finding its apex in the vaulted front chancel.

At the end of the 15th century the city received Donha Joana, the young sister of King João II. She was a celebrated beauty who had captivated Louis XI of France and almost married Richard III of England, but had decided to give up this world to enter a convent in Aveiro. She devoted the last 18 years of her life to sewing hair shirts, and was beatified for it. Scenes from the life of Saint Joana line the church walls. The choir contains the memorable tomb of this saint, one that required 12 years to manufacture as the intricacy of the polychrome marble mosaic demonstrates. Despite its complexity, it manages to be moving.

Installed in the cloisters and former convent, in rooms of great interest for their azulejos and painted ceilings, is a museum containing a mixed lot of sculpture, polychromed wood, crucifixes, furniture and Vista Alegre porcelain. Best are the primitive paintings, including a 15th-century portrait of Saint Joana which some attribute to the great Nuno Gonçalves. The survey of Baroque gilt is stunning.

The closest beach is **Praia de Barra**, on the sandbank 13 k due west. Proximity to Aveiro makes it crowded, while other beaches remain secluded. 26 k further south along N-109 and then a 5 k run west on N-334 brings **Praia de Mira**, a most attractive beach livened by stilted houses. Here fishing boats are still hauled by teams of oxen, as they once were in more famous Nazaré. Northern beaches require circling the lagoon on N-109 to Estareja in 20 k, then turning west on N-109-5 to bridge over to **Torreira**, which is an attractive, upscale little resort bordering a fine beach. In fact one beach or another runs 13 k beside pine forests to **São Jacinto** beach, opposite Aveiro. São Jacinto beach stretches long and flat, like our Jersey shore, although the town is rather rundown. It can only be reached by road through this circle through Torreira, or by an Aveiro ferry.

WHERE TO STAY

For those moving quickly onward, a hotel in town is probably best, and Aveiro offers a number of good values, although value also characterizes the beach hotels. Unless otherwise indicated, the establishments below are in the city of Aveiro.

EXPENSIVE ($100-$200)

In Águeda 24 k southeast:

Palácio de Águeda 1st-class ★★★★

Scenic N230 heads east from Aveiro before angling southerly along the Vouga river to Águeda in 22 k. Take N1 south for 2 k to Quinta da Borralha. Rooms: 41, plus 7 suites. ☎ 60 19 77; FAX 60 19 76; Telex 37823. Lying behind a wall and gate that suggests a ranch in the countryside, this hotel is situated in an unattractive industrial city, and not in the best part of town. But behind the gate, glistening white with delicate yellow trim, stands a veritable mansion, a former manor house of the Counts of Borralha. Substantially renovated by a Frenchman with perfect taste and deep pockets, the Águeda is as lovely as any hotel in the country. Interior colors are oranges and browns, and Islamic motifs characterize many of the public rooms, for the owner spends part of his year there. Formal gardens stretch behind. Bedrooms are large, elegant, and their bathrooms are grand. All facilities are available, and the setting is restful behind its wall. Live like a noble for a night, at a price that barely crests the expensive. The only thing that prevents us from going all out and awarding a fifth star is the management, which, although very willing and agreeable (you will be enchanted by the young women in their "school-girl" uniforms at the desk), is not up to truly first-class service. In most cases, however, this should not distract from a pleasant night in a truly memorable hotel.

On the sandspit between Torreira and São Jacinto:

Pousada da Ria　　　　　　　　　　　　　2nd-class ★ ★ ★
Bico do Muranzel. Rooms: 19. ☎ *483 32; FAX 483 33; Telex 37061.* Water on three sides adds drama to this modern building, whose plentiful windows make the most of its setting on the still lagoon. An inside-outside papyrus and goldfish pool adds a nice touch to the light and airy interior, while views of seaweed harvesting boats plying the lagoon provide restful days in rooms that are comfortable but of no great style. Tennis is available too, at this heavily booked pousada.

MODERATE ($50-$99)

Paloma Blanca　　　　　　　　　　　　　R1st-class ★ ★ ★ ★
Rua Luís Gomes de Carvalho, 23 (near the east end of Av. Dr. Lourenço Peixinho, close to the train station). Rooms: 50. ☎ *38 19 92; FAX 38 18 44; Telex 37353.* Simply put, the Paloma Blanca is an almost perfect little hotel. The house is a former Moorish-style mansion surrounding a tropical garden, which most rooms overlook. The interior is replete with rich deco panelling in the reception and bar. Tasteful antiques, including old machines, fill the nooks and crannies. Bedrooms are large, comfortable, include semi-antiques and are decorated with exceptional style. This may be the cleanest hotel in the country, and adds an extra bonus with free underground parking. Don't tell the owner his prices are too low.

In Torreira:

Estalagem Riabela　　　　　　　　　　　　2nd-class ★ ★
About 1 k north of the pousada. Rooms: 35. ☎ *481 37; FAX 481 47; Telex 37243.* Views of the lagoon, plus tennis and restful scenery at a truly modest price make this a pleasant hotel.

In Aveiro:

Imperial　　　　　　　　　　　　　　　　　1st-class ★
Rua Dr. Nascimento Leita (on the square beside the Convento de Jesus).

Rooms: 107. ☎ 221 41; FAX 241 48; Telex 3794. This is an unexceptional modern structure, but the bedrooms are comfortable. The lagoon and convent gardens lie outside the window. It is affiliated with the Best Western chain.

INEXPENSIVE (UNDER $50)

Arcadi 3rd-class ★

Rua Viana do Castelo, 4 (on the north edge of Pr. Humberto Delgado over the canal, just north of the Pr. da República). Rooms: 49. ☎ *230 01; FAX 218 86; Telex 37460.* The location is central and the hotel has been modernized recently. It occupies the 2nd-4th floors of an attractive building, but the bedrooms are a dreary tan and noise can be a problem. Still, they are serviceable and include TVs.

WHERE TO EAT

Restaurant choices in Aveiro are not numerous, but those that exist are authentic, and one stands out.

MODERATE ($15-$30)

Centenario ★★

Largo do Mercado, 9 (opposite the covered market, a third of the way along Av. Dr. Lourenço Peixinho, then a right down Pereira da Silva and down the steps right again). ☎ *227 98. Closed Tuesday, and the first two weeks of May.* Although its prices hover at the bottom of the moderate level, this restaurant, with its modern paneled dining room, looks like more. A must to begin is *Sopa do Mar*. Fish and meat are equally good, so order any of the specials with confidence.

MasterCard and Visa accepted.

DIRECTORY

INFORMATION • *Located in the main square of Pr. da República beside the bank of Fonsecas & Burany.* (☎ *236 80*).

TRAINS AND BUSES • *Both trains and buses are served by the station at the east end of Av. Dr. Lourenço Peixinho* (☎ *244 85*). Service is frequent to Lisbon, Coimbra and Porto.

SHOPPING • The Vista Alegre factory, museum and store are planted in the company town of Vista Alegre a mile south of the town of Ilhavo, 7 k south of Aveiro by N-109. The factory does not allow tours without special arrangements, but a fine little museum of the development of this ware is open Tuesday through Friday from 9 a.m. until noon and from 2 p.m. until 4:30. The adjoining store, open weekdays from 9 a.m. until 6 p.m., offers a fine selection including pieces not seen elsewhere. It charges about the same prices as other outlets in Portugal, although about 20 percent less than in the U.S. (*Lugar da Vista Alegre, 3830 Ilhavo;* ☎ *034 32 23 65.*)

NORTHERN PORTUGAL

BOM JESUS

See Braga excursions.

BRAGA ★★

Population: 64,113
Area code: 053; zip code: 4700

Braga is north of **Porto** *by A-1 for 51 k. From Vigo in* **Spanish Galicia** *take A-9 south for 32 k to Tui on the border, then N-13 in Portugal south for 68 k to Viana do Castelo. From there N-113 merges with N-103 for a 47 k run to Braga.*

Verdant hills and a fertile valley brought inhabitants to Braga far back in prehistoric times. When the Romans arrived, they nominated Braga as the capital both of northern Portugal and present-day Galicia in Spain. Through most of its history, however, Braga was better known for its religious fervor than for political status.

When Swabian polytheists conquered Portugal they were converted to Christianity through synods at Braga, and made the city both a bishopric and their capital. Later, after conquest by the Moors and reconquest by the Christians, the Pope resolved a power struggle between the bishop of Braga and his counterpart in Santiago de Compostela in Braga's favor, designating Braga as the seat for all of Spain and Portugal—"Primate of the Spains." Primacy did not last, however, going early to Toledo in Spain and to Lisbon in Portugal by the 18th century. Yet Braga remains the most devout and conservative city in Portugal.

In the 18th century, perhaps to make up for the loss of ecclesiastic power, two successive bishops undertook a reconstruction of the city and its numerous churches—all in the Baroque style. Wide avenues were cut, gardens planted, and fountains were placed all around. The reconstruction of the churches is to be deplored—most lost their aesthetic interest—but the city does present a handsome face as a result of its renewal. Here the religious side of the Portuguese is plain to see, with churches on every corner. The city provides enough to merit half a day's exploring, and sights in the environs will fill the remainder.

From **Porto** *the traffic interchange of Pr. do Condestavel is soon reached. Bear right along Av. da imaculada Conceicão for five blocks until reaching the wide Av. de la Liberdade for a left turn. The avenue ends at Pr. da República,* *with a park to its right. A parking lot lies beside Av. Central, the appropriately named road through the park's center.*

At Rua do Souto, which forms the south border of the park, turn east for a block to the chapel of **N. S. de Penha de França** on the south side of the street. It retains nice *azulejos*. Proceeding east along Rua do Souto, after crossing the wide Av. de la Liberdade, the **Torre de Menagem** stands on the right side. This tower formed part of a 14th-century fortress that once guarded the medieval city walls.

The first street angling left, Rua San Marco, leads past the **Casa da Gelosia** on its left, for an opportunity to admire rare remaining examples of *mashrabiyas*, latticed Moorish-style windows to let women look out without being seen. Across the next intersection stands a very Baroque **Igreja Santa Cruz**. Turn left through the Largo Carlos Amarante for two short blocks to look at the *azulejos* facing the **Casa do Raio** at the corner on the right.

Return to Santa Cruz church, bearing left to take the first right past **Capela dos Coimbras** with a Manueline tower. Rua do Souto is regained by a short walk north. Across the street is the imposing former **Episcopal Palace** with components from the 14th, 17th and 18th centuries. Now it's a superb library which includes a document confirming Afonso I as Portugal's first king. The courtyard is worth entering for a look at an ornate yet graceful fountain of castles, cherubs and spouting waters. West of the Archbishop's palace stands the fine 18th-century **Camara Municipal** (City Hall), with the **Museu Casa dos Biscainhos** behind it, and south is the large complex of the **Cathedral**.

WHAT TO SEE AND DO

Cathedral ★★

Open daily 8:30 a.m. to 6:30 (in winter closes an hour earlier and for lunch from 12:30 to 1:30 p.m.). The treasury is closed Mon. Admission: 200$00, for a guided tour in Portuguese to the pendant chapels and treasury. Entrance to the Cathedral is through a courtyard on the north side, a right turn through the cloister and a final left turn. Although this is Portugal's oldest cathedral, built in the 11th-12th centuries, later additions and decoration hide most of the original structure. In the dark interior, a simple nave fights the distraction of 18th-century gilt in the chapels. At the front of the Cathedral the chancel vaulting and altar are intricate and focus on a 14th-century Virgin. A chapel to the right incorporates a polychrome altar carved to represent a painting by Rubens. The chapel to the left of the chancel is lined with fine 18th-century *azulejos*. At the rear of the Cathedral stands a Manueline baptismal font and, opposite, a chapel contains the bronze 15th-century tomb of a prince named Dom Afonso.

Exiting the Cathedral into the cloisters again, the entrance to the treasury opens immediately left. Although the works inside are poorly displayed and ill-conserved, genuine treasures lurk. The plain iron cross, called the Cruzeiro do Brazil, was carried with Pedro Alvares Cabral when he discovered Brazil. There are curiosities, such as brain cases—one containing the sixth-century grey matter of the first bishop—and platform shoes for a very short bishop. But included are an astonishing number of beautiful early crosses and coffers, from the 10th through the 12th century.

The *coro alto* is entered from the treasury and features inlaid choir seats and two incredibly ornate 18th-century organs.

Saint Catherine's chapel at the north end of the cloisters holds votive offerings of body parts. The King's Chapel, with elegant Gothic vaulting, is entered from the east side of the cloister. The tombs of Henri of Burgundy and his wife Teresa of Castile, the parents of Afonso I, the first king of Portugal, are 16th-century. The legs of Henri's effigy have been partly amputated, apparently to allow it to fit into a smaller space elsewhere at one time. Also on view is the gruesome mummy of Bishop Lourenço Vicente. After blessing the troops before the battle of Aljubarrota in 1385, he entered the fray himself and received a slash on his cheek in the melee. The scar is faithfully reproduced on his effigy.

At the east end of the courtyard wait two more Gothic chapels. The first depicts the life of Saint Gerald, the first archbishop of Braga, in lovely 18th-century *azulejos*. On the left side is the entrance to the Chapel of Glory, a marvelous 14th-century structure covered in Mudejar decoration and fine frescos. The charming tomb of Bishop Pereira, who built the chapel, lies in the center.

Museu Biscainhos ★

Open Tues.-Sun. 10 a.m. to 12:30 and 2-5:30 p.m. Closed Mon. and holidays. Admission: 200$00. The house in which this museum is lodged dates from the middle of the 17th century and was the grand mansion of the Biscainhos family for two centuries. The rooms and furniture inside reflect the refinements of noble life. Groundfloor exhibits display finds from Roman excavations three blocks south of the casa (one may observe the ongoing excavation there for free). A passage leads past stables to lovely gardens in the rear. Here is buried a horse, shot by the mansion's last owner, which had belonged to a commoner the owner's daughter married against his wishes. After shooting the steed in anger, the owner walked away from his lovely house forever.

IN THE OUTSKIRTS

Bom Jesus ★★★

Buses marked "02 Bom Jesus" leave frequently for the 6 k trip to Bom Jesus from Largo Carlos Amarante, at whose corner stands the aforementioned church of Santa Cruz. By car turn left at the end of the wide Av. da Liberdade onto Av. João XXI. Watch for a sign about 1 k outside of town for a right turn to Bom Jesus, a further 5 k. For the stairs, look for an archway over the road, and pull over there to look up, for that is where the fancy part begins. It is not often that one journeys just to see flights of stairs, but these are among the most extraordinary stairs ever constructed. They are not merely a means of climbing, but penitent stairs to remove sin by hard exercise.

The lower flights were built in the first quarter of the 18th century, the upper flights were added 50 years later, all during the height of the Baroque style. The view up shows how surpassingly elegant architecture can be, for the otherwise busy double flights of the second tier form repetitive patterns of complex harmony. Although the first three flights seem ordinary at first, details gradually emerge that make them special. One notices that the banister's end at the bottom whips around pillars. A fountain stands at the beginning of the remarkable second tier, heralding others along the way. From this point a double stair crisscrosses at every landing, ornamented with statues of Old Testament figures and small obelisks.

The final stage is flanked by chapels to the three virtues. While the church on top is not sufficient reason for the climb, the countryside views and formal gardens certainly are.

Citânia de Briteiros ★

Frequent city buses marked "Ruães" stop at Briteiros. They leave from near the church of São Vicente on the street of that name, which is a continuation of Av. de Liberdade. Occasional buses depart from Bom Jesus, above. By car, from Bom Jesus go east along N-103-5 for 9 k to Sobreposta, at which N-309 goes south for the final 4.5 k. Briteiros is a rare excavated site of the pre-Roman Celtiberians, a people about whom little is known. The town thrived from the third century B.C. through the first century of the Christian era, representing the last bastion of the Celtiberian's against the Romans. It is a large site, serenely situated on a hill, surrounded by remains of an extensive town wall. Over 100 dwellings are known and indicated by a few courses of their walls, but several conical houses with thatched roofs have been reconstructed to show what the rest would have looked like. The dry stonework is evocative. A visit is a must for those interested in archaeology, and pleasant for anyone who enjoys sylvan excursions.

WHERE TO STAY

Those visiting Braga have the option of sleeping at one of two memorable pousadas located 22 k to the southwest in Guimarães. Braga itself offers nothing as splendid, but does provide values in low-cost accommodations. In addition, there are two interesting hotels nearby in Bom Jesus—although providing nothing whatsoever to do at night except eat.

MODERATE ($50-$99)

In Bom Jesus:

Do Elevador   1st-class ★★

Rooms: 25. ☎ 67 66 11; FAX 67 66 79; Telex 33401. The public rooms are shabby now, although the bedrooms remain comfortable. What makes this hotel special are incredible views that by themselves make a stay a pleasure, but to add a final incentive, good, moderately priced, genuine Portuguese meals are also provided on a dining terrace overlooking miles of Portugal.

Do Parque   1st-class ★

Rooms: 49. ☎ 67 66 79; FAX 67 66 79; Telex 33401. The building is a 19th-century mansion converted to a hotel by the same people who own Do Elevator. The decor here tries for the worst sort of Portuguese elegance with red upholstery. While this hotel doesn't offer the countryside views of its sister, it substitutes a nice garden in their place.

In Braga:

Carandá   2nd-class ★★

Av. da Liberdade, 96. Rooms: 100. ☎ 61 45 00; FAX 61 45 50. This brand-new and tasteful hotel charges unexpectedly low prices. Bathrooms are modern, the bedrooms are air-conditioned, and there are fine views of the city.

Turismo Dom Pedro   1st-class ★

Praceta João XXI (at the south end of Av. da Liberdade). Rooms: 132. ☎ 61 22 00; FAX 61 22 11; Telex 32136. This is the big hotel in town, modern and impersonal, but also spotless and with balconies overlooking a park. It's a good value, for its rates barely climb into the moderate category.

WHERE TO EAT

As with its hotels, Braga restaurants are not fancy, but good values.

MODERATE ($15-$30)

O Inácio   ★★

Campo das Hortas, 4 (this small park is a few steps south of the Museu Casa Biscainhos, discussed above). ☎ 61 32 25. Closed Tuesday and from the middle of April through the middle of September. Rough stone walls and hand-hewn beams lend O Inácio the rustic look of an old tavern, although the food is prepared with greater care than the image suggests. Daily specials can be recommended; and the wine selection is choice, which generally demonstrates a proprietor's concern for his clients' dining experience.

Amex, Diners, MasterCard and Visa accepted.

INEXPENSIVE (UNDER $15)

Abade de Priscos ★★
Pr. Mousinho de Albuquerque, 7 (a garden square one block due north of the parking lot). ☎ 766 50. This small, intimate, family-run restaurant serves good food that is remarkably low-priced for its quality.

DIRECTORY

INFORMATION • Located at the corner of Av. da Liberdade and Rua do Souto, by the park (☎ 225 50).

TRAINS AND BUSES • Located at Largo da Estacão (☎ 221 66), four blocks due west of the Cathedral. Take Rua Dom Diogo Sousa west, continuing as it is renamed Rua Andrade Corvo. Connections are frequent to most cities, but require a change of trains at Nine. The bus station is located in Central de Camionagem (☎ 234 33), which is reached by going north from Av. da Liberdade for about four blocks. Service to Porto and Guimarães is frequent, but less so destinations at greater distances.

POLICE • Campo de São Tiago (☎ 719 50), which is at the end of Rua do Anjo that runs southwest from the church of Santa Cruz.

EXCURSIONS

Barcelos ★ for crafts, **Bravães** ★★ for an extraordinary Romanesque church, **Guimarães** ★★★ for an atmospheric medieval walled town and **Viana do Castelo** ★ for beaches—all summon the tourist to travel a few miles from Braga. Guimarães is described under its own heading in this chapter.

BARCELOS ★

Population: 4031
Area code: 053; zip code: 4750

Barcelos lies 22 k west of Braga on N-103.

Barcelos is an attractive village famous for two things: a huge market-day that takes place every Thursday, and naive, brightly painted pottery in the shape of fantastic figures.

The market is held in the huge main square, the Campo da República. On Thursday mornings the acreage fills with thousands of people, as many selling as buying. Then, as noon passes, the crowd melts away. The range of offerings is vast—from pottery, sewn-work, pillows, painted ox yokes, and old and new clothing to rugs, furniture and even live animals.

The symbol of Barcelos pottery has its origin in the Middle Ages. A passing pilgrim accused of theft was brought before a judge in the midst of a meal. To corroborate his innocence, the pilgrim called upon the judge's lunch—a roasted rooster—to crow. It purportedly did, giving rise to the over-cute rooster trademark of Barcelos potters, displayed throughout Portugal. (Incidentally, this same tradition exists in Spain, which does make one wonder about the truth of the tale.) More interesting work is done, however, by a few fine artisans in the village who craft amusing figures, often with animal heads. The **Tourist Office** in one of the towers of the village wall on Rua Duques de Bragança doubles as a crafts center with a large selection, but smaller shops dot the village as well.

BRAVÃES ★★
Population: 653

Scenic N-101 goes north to Ponte da Barca in 33 k. From there N-203 goes west to Bravães in 5 k.

The little church of São Salvador makes a trip to this tiny community worthwhile. The church is unadulterated Romanesque from the 12th, or possibly even the 11th century. While Romanesque churches seldom incorporate carvings on their portals—or, at most, some simple lamb-of-God scene—for some reason this one church is a riot of charming primitive art, including figures of bulls and monkeys. Even the south portal is carved—with griffins and the Holy Lamb. In the dark interior reside more naive carvings on capitals that frame windows, and there are rare original murals. This church should be a national treasure included on most tourists' itineraries. Instead, being located in a village of no particular note, it remains lonely and desolate. *(If closed, apply at the cafe across the plaza.)*

VIANA DO CASTELO ★★
Population: 15,336
Area code: 058; zip code: 4900

N-103 west reaches Viana in 47 k.

This elegant resort town is situated on the north bank of the River Lima estuary at the foot of green hills. Viana owes its appearance to the fact that it achieved prosperity exactly at the height of King Manuel's reign, so affluent citizens built their mansions in the Manueline style. Then prosperity drained away, so the 16th-century mansions were never replaced by more up-to-date styles.

The central **Praça da República**, with surrounding mansions and center fountain, is one of the loveliest squares in Portugal. Three blocks west, along Rua Manuel Espregueira, stands a fine 18th-century palace, which, since it's now the municipal museum, may be toured. (Open Tues.-Sun. 9:30 a.m. to noon and 2-5 p.m.; closed Mon.; admission: 100$00.)

The beach along the river is gravelly, but a ferry from the port goes to an island off-shore and the attractive **Praia do Cabedelo**. In addition, there are pristine beaches a short car-ride north.

WHERE TO STAY

As with most resorts, the hotel-escudo does not go as far as elsewhere.

EXPENSIVE ($100-$200)

On Monte Santa Luzia, 6 k north of town:

Pousada Santa Luzia ★★★
Estrada Santa Luzia. Rooms: 55. ☎ *82 88 89; FAX 82 88 92.* Surrounded by green, high on a bluff, overlooking Viana and the sea, stands the modernista white building. Done in art deco inside for a change from the ordinary hotel decor, the bedrooms are commodious and fairly priced.

MODERATE ($50-$99)

Viana Sol 1st-class ★
Largo Vasco da Gama (near the river, three blocks southwest of the Pr. da República). Rooms: 65. ☎ *82 89 95; FAX 82 89 97; Telex 32790.* The hotel's attraction is that it provides a full range of facilities at moderate prices. Bedrooms are spare but pleasant.

INEXPENSIVE (UNDER $50)

Viana-Mar R2nd-class ★
Av. dos Combatentes da Grande Guerra, 215 (one block west of the Pr. da República). Rooms: 36. ☎ *82 89 62; FAX 82 98 62.* This comfortable little hotel offers good value for the money.

WHERE TO EAT

Viana is no mecca for the gourmet, but the recommendation below stands out.

MODERATE ($15-$30)

Os 3 Potes ★★
Beco dos Fornos, 7 (just off the east side of the Pr. da República). ☎ *82 99 28. Closed Monday.* Installed in the 16th-century public bakery, the remodeled restaurant retains a rustic feel, lightened by delicate touches. The food is surprisingly good for the modest price, and simple *caldo verde* is delicious. However, on summer weekends folk dancing can be a trifle touristy. *MasterCard and Visa accepted*

BRAGANÇA ★★★

Population: 14,662
Area code: 073; zip code: 5300

From **Braga** *N-103 goes east presenting lovely lake views to Chaves in 127 k. From here a slower-going, ill-repaired, N-103 continues for the final 96 k of mountain scenery. From* **Porto** *the autoestrada A-4 speeds east to Amarante, where a slow-going N-15 twists directly to Bragança in 250 k. From* **Viseu** *N-2 goes north to Villa Real in 108 k, then the scenic but twisty N-15 going east reaches Bragança in 160 k more. From* **Coimbra** *and south one has the option of going to Porto and following the directions above from there, or of going to Viseu and following its directions. The latter route is slower, but more scenic. From* **Guarda** *take N-16 north to Celorico da Beira in 22 k, then N-102 north to Macedo de Cavaleiros in 172 k. Just north of that town N-15 goes northwest to Bragança in a final 41 k. From Spanish* **Zamora** *(which is 62 k north of Salamanca) N-122 goes west to the border where it changes its designation to N-218 for a trip of 114 k.*

By **train** *from Porto the trip takes eight hours, for the train does not average as much as 20 m.p.h., but the views are awesome and the carriages are turn-of-the-century wooden ones (with primitive restrooms) to enchant railway buffs.* **Buses** *are faster by a factor of two.*

Bragança is tucked into the northeast corner of Portugal, a good 200 k from any area of interest to tourists. It lies in the heart of the province called Trás-os-montes, "behind the mountains" and indeed it is behind in many senses. The area is poor—because rolling hills keep farms small and unprofitable—and isolated politically and socially from the rest of Portugal by its mountain barrier. The inhabitants live in a different time from ours, and the reason for visiting is to view this older way of life. Farmhouses throughout the countryside are hand-built of stone, with slate, tile or thatched roofs, and nestle into bucolic hillsides covered in grass and scrub. Slate or granite cribs hold wheat away from rodents, but with crosses on their ends to make them seem like cemetery vaults. Wood-wheeled carts—pulled by lyre-horned oxen and driven by bearded men—will often be seen.

The town of Bragança is known for the imposing walls of its citadel, its ancient **keep** ★, its early medieval **town hall** ★, and its importance for Portuguese history. In the 17th century when the Spanish controlled Portugal, the duke of Bragança was the most powerful man in the country. He led the opposition against this foreign domination, and, after defeating the Spanish, became King João II. His was to be the last dynasty in Portugal, enduring until the revolution of 1910.

Bragança stands at an elevation of half a mile, but is still overlooked by an amphitheater of hills. All roads converge on the Cathedral square, with parking below the citadel high upon its hill. (Parking is also available beside the citadel entrance.) Given the insistent draw of the medieval citadel above, the 16th-century Cathedral need detain no one, apart from a glance at its azulejos inside. Head up toward the ramparts along Rua do Conselheiro Abilio Beça to reach the **Museu do Abade de Baçal**.

Museu do Abade de Baçal ★
Open Tuesday-Sunday 10 a.m. to 12:30 p.m. and 2-5 p.m. Closed Monday and holidays. Admission: 200$00. This house is a former 16th-century bishop's palace remodeled two centuries later. Two bishop's litters are displayed on the ground floor among archaeological pieces, including in the garden, two strange, crudely carved rocks called *berrões*. Generally just over a yard long, and usually depicting either boars or bulls, several hundred of these carvings have been discovered in the countryside of Trás-os-montes province. Their function —and the culture and dates of the carvers—is unknown. Certainly they are pre-Christian, in purpose if not date.

Several second-floor ceilings of the palace are notable, including one carved with fruit. Rooms display ecclesiastical paraphernalia—some elegant, some curious—as well as paintings—some nice work by Abel Salazar, from this century—and ethnographic pieces—including a scold's bridle with a tongue depressor to silence the offender.

Continuing up toward the citadel, the first church passed on the right is **São Vicente** ★, in which Pedro the Cruel claimed to have married his mistress Inês de Castro. (See "Historical Profile: The Birth of Portugal" on page 157.) The present 17th-century facade covers a much older structure. Inside is a fantastic three-dimensional Christ from the 19th century flying across the ceiling. (*It should be noted that churches in Bragança are not easy to get into. Luck will find them open, otherwise all that can be done is to ask anyone who passes.*)

Just before the citadel, to the left, is **São Bento** ★ with a nice Renaissance portal. The nave is a wooden barrel-vault covered in Renaissance trompe l'oeil, while the chancel is sheltered by a fine Mudejar ceiling.

The crenulated walls around the citadel are of indeterminate age but appear to be 15th-century renovations of earlier fortifications. It so, they are in remarkable repair. The **castle** ★★ consists mainly of a tall square keep with turrets and towers surrounding. It was built by Dom Sancho I in 1187 and reinforced in the 15th century. There is a drawbridge, a dungeon and tiny doorways leading to unexpected rooms and corridors. The so-called Torre de Princesa actually held a queen captive—Donha Leonor, the wife of Dom Jaime—who was suspected of infidelity. The keep now serves as a military museum.

To the left of the castle is **Santa Maria** with another painted nave ceiling. Beside it is a unique pentagonal structure, the **Domus Municipalis** ★. It is the oldest surviving town hall in Portugal, if not in the world, dating to the 12th century. The orange tile roof is incongruously bright, and the building has often been restored, but it retains its original plan of a single large chamber. Clearly its function was not to house officials, but to serve as a meeting hall for general discussion of municipal affairs. Below the hall is a large cistern for supplying water to the citadel during times of siege.

WHERE TO STAY

There are few hotels in Bragança. Although there are also few tourists, those who come generally stay the night, making room availability uncertain. It is best to reserve before arrival.

MODERATE ($50-$99)

Pousada de São Bartolomeu   1st-class ★★
Estrada de Turismo (0.5 k southwest, above the citadel). Rooms: 16. ☎ *224 93; FAX 234 53; Telex 22613.* This pousada was built in the late 1950s and retains the feel of that era, but its best feature is a perfect view of the citadel. Craft pieces from the region are used for decoration. The bedrooms are wood with cork ceilings for soundproofing. It is a peaceful place, with balconies for meditative views.

Bragança   2nd-class ★
Av. Dr. Francisco de Sá Carneiro. Rooms: 42. ☎ *225 79.* This modern hotel primarily serves businesspeople, but its location is central and the bedrooms are comfortable, with some providing views of the citadel. Altogether, it's a reasonable choice if the pousada is full.

INEXPENSIVE (UNDER $50)

São Roque   R2nd-class ★
Rua da Estacada, 26-7 7th-8th floors. Rooms: 36. ☎ *234 81; FAX 269 37.* Most of the rooms look out to the citadel and are decorated pleasantly, for a price that approaches a steal.

Albergaria Santa Isabel   R1st-class
Rua Alexandre Herculano, 67. Rooms: 14. ☎ *224 27; FAX 269 37.* Despite a jolly blue-and-white-tiled facade, the hotel seems sad inside.

Perhaps because it has seen better days. The São Roque above, under the same management, is a much better buy.

WHERE TO EAT

No one travels to Bragança to dine.

MODERATE ($15-$30)

Lá em Casa
Rua Marquês de Pombal. ☎ 221 11. Closed Monday. Rustic bare stone walls and crockery decoration lend a homey feel. The cooking is more adventurous than at the competition.

Plantório
Estrada Cantarias. ☎ 224 26. This large modern place offers fine views of the citadel and is popular with local businesspeople. The food is tasty, if unexciting, but the wine list contains bargains.

BRAVÃES

See Braga excursions.

BUÇACO FOREST

See Luso under Coimbra excursions.

COIMBRA ★★★

Population: 79,799
Area code: 039; zip code: 3000

From **Lisbon** *the autoestrada A-1 can be taken north for 180 k to the Coimbra exit, then a 5 k jag into town. From* **Batalha** *take N-1 north for 11 k to Leiria, where N-113 goes to the autoestrada A-1 in 5 k. The Coimbra exit is 62 k north. From* **Porto** *the autoestrada A-1 runs south to exit #9 in 92 k. Here a short extension east brings the city.*

Frequent **trains** *from Lisbon reach Coimbra-B station in 2 hours, from which another train goes to the downtown Coimbra-A station. From Porto the trip consumes less than 2 hours.* **Buses** *take almost a third longer.*

Coimbra, Portugal's third largest city, tumbles down a steep riverbank by the gently flowing Mondego river. The city is situated midway between Lisbon and Porto, making it a convenient stop along the way. To encourage visits, the city offers a fine museum—the **Museu Machado de Castro ★★**—and regal **university quarter ★★★**, plus mansions, monasteries and churches, including the most imposing **Romanesque church ★★** in the country.

Portugal's most extensive Roman remains stand nearby at **Conimbriga** ★, while the enchanted forest of **Buçaco** ★★ and a vast beach at **Figueira da Foz** ★★ both lie less than an hour away. All this makes Coimbra popular with tourists, but it is large enough to absorb them gracefully.

Although Coimbra has been occupied since Roman times, in its earliest days it was an insignificant appendage of nearby Conimbriga, the administrative seat of a Roman province. But when repeated sackings— first by barbarian Swabians, then by Moors—caused Conimbriga to be abandoned in the ninth century, many of its remaining citizens fled to Coimbra, making it a kind of descendant of the abandoned Roman town. Even Coimbra's name is probably a corruption of "Conimbriga." When he assumed his crown in 1139, Afonso I, Portugal's first king, chose Coimbra—then the largest city in Christian hands— as his capital. It remained the seat of the government for two centuries, breeding the first six kings after Afonso, until the court moved permanently to Lisbon in 1255. Portugal's original university was established in Coimbra in 1308. Later it, too, moved to Lisbon, but complaints about boisterous students returned it to Coimbra again, where it remains to dominate the town both literally, high on the hill, and figuratively, as the major institution in the city.

The city divides into three parts. Above the east bank stands the university quarter—the Velha Alta, site of the medieval city; at its feet lies the Baixa, or lower town; and, lastly, on the west bank of the river sprawls the newer town, which retains some old monasteries and churches that originally stood outside the medieval city. We divide our discussion of the sights into those on the Velha Alta hill, which include most of what is noteworthy, and those located elsewhere. We suggest starting with the university, as walking downhill is always easier.

> *Parking is a problem in Coimbra. Two options exist. From* **Lisbon** *Coimbra is entered on the east bank of the river. The road runs to the Ponte Santa Clara which crosses to the west bank. Turn left along Av. Emidio Navarro, with a divided center on which parking may be possible. If full, continue to the plaza in front of the train station, where the avenue ends. Turn right there through the Largo das Ameias, then take the first left along Av. Fernão de Magalhães. Parking is often available in two blocks in a large square on the right. From* **Porto**, *by continuing straight, one travels along Av. Fernão de Magalhães. After passing through the large*

plaza of Largo do Arnado, bear right to continue on Av. Magalhães, and parking should be available in the large park on the left in three blocks. If full, continue along Av. Magalhães for two more blocks where it ends at the Largo das Ameias. Turn right, then take the next left along Av. Emidio Navarro, where parking often is available in the center divider.

WHAT TO SEE AND DO

VELHA ALTA AND THE UNIVERSITY

Climb or taxi up this hill, then walk down. Begin at the Porta Ferrea of the Velha Universidade (Old University). Ask the taxi to stop in the Pr. Dom Dinis, then turn west between two colleges.

Velha Universidade ★★★

Opening times of buildings are different and change with the University year, and some require small admission charges, but the hours from 10 a.m. to noon and 2-5 p.m. will generally find everything open. During its first two centuries, the university passed between Coimbra and Lisbon, but settled here in 1537 under orders from King João III.

Before that time, only degrees for priests were conferred and the caliber of the education was mediocre by any standard. Dom João, determined to raise the quality, first donated his Coimbra palace to house the university magnificently, then hired Andre de Resende from the University of Paris to whip the faculty into shape. In his inaugural address the new rector accused the faculty of gross ignorance and sloth. Continuing his quest for excellence, the king offered impressive stipends to attract scholars of international repute, including Erasmus. Although that renowned scholar declined, other fine academicians accepted, lifting the University's caliber of instruction. A school of Liberal Arts was established, expanding the student population beyond prospective clergy, and soon after a college of law was inaugurated, followed by a college of pharmacy.

By the end of the 16th century, about 1500 students, mostly non-cleric, were in residence and the reputation of the university ranked with the very best in Europe. Although the institution was to suffer ups and downs over the following centuries—at times even selling degrees for a fee—today, with an enrollment of almost 15,000 students, it stands again as the premier Portuguese institute of higher learning. Famous residents have included Luis Vas de Camões, Portugal's greatest poet, Saint Anthony of Padua, and Dr. António Salazar, who served as a professor of economics before becoming Portugal's dictator. Today some students still wear the traditional uniform of black capes with ribbons on the sleeve to indicate their college. Light blue indicates science; darker blue, Liberal Arts; violet, pharmacy; yellow, medicine; and red, law. Students in their final year sport wider ribbons than underclassmen.

This is the only university in the world housed in a king's palace, the part entered through the 17th century Porta Ferrea (Iron Gate). Here the grey Patio das Escolas presents the most interesting buildings of the university. As it's used as a parking lot, the effect of the plaza's size and perspective is diminished today. In the center stands a statue of João III, who donated his palace. Naturally, the palace was much altered for the purpose.

To the left is São Pedro College, a 16th-century addition, in which the royal family stayed when visiting the university and where college rectors live today. To the right, facing the open end of the "patio," an imposing gallery, the Via Latina, is appended to the front of the original palace. Called the "Latin Way" because only Latin could be spoken here in earlier times, stairs ascend to the gallery, inside of which, a door to the left marked "reitoria" leads into the Sala dos Capelos. Before remodeling this was the throne room of the palace. Portraits of the kings of the first two dynasties look down on the university ceremonies that take place here today. Overhead hovers a most remarkable painted ceiling. To the left of this hall is the sumptuous Sala do Exame Privado hung with portraits of former rectors below a brilliant ceiling. It is hard to imagine focusing on an exam in such a room.

Returning to the courtyard and continuing counterclockwise leads to the clumsy clock tower in the corner. It summoned students to their classes and earned one frequently rung bell the name "The Goat." Continuing, a part of the former palace is passed, at whose approximate center is a fine Manueline portal leading into a corridor on whose left is the University Chapel. Tickets for admission to the chapel and the library (further along) are available in the bookstore down this corridor.

The chapel ceiling is painted, *azulejos* line its walls, but its most impressive feature is an 18th-century organ, a fantasy of gilded wood. Over all, the chapel is a complex of bright pattern on pattern.

Outside, and further along, waits the Baroque entrance to the library. (If the door is closed, ring the bell.) It was a gift from King João V in 1724, whose coat-of-arms is blazoned over the door. There is no library in the world that can compare with its always ornate, sometimes elegant, finely crafted Baroque decoration that covers every surface. It simply must be seen. At the library's end glowers a portrait of its royal donor encased in the most ornate frame imaginable. All three rooms are awesome, making one wonder how readers surrounded by such visual stimulation could concentrate.

Proceed back through the Porta Ferrea, through its plaza, then left (north) along Rua de Miranda which passes between several colleges of the university to open up into the large Largo da Feira, down a flight of stairs. Nestled between university buildings on the north side of the square is the **Se Nova** (New Cathedral). To the left of the square is the former **bishop's palace** and the church of **São João de Almedina**, both built in the 12th century, although the bishop's palace was modified in the 16th. Today the palace houses the excellent **Museu Machado de Castro**. Note the **Moorish tower** by the entrance.

Museu Machado de Castro ★★

Open Tues.-Sun. 10 a.m. to 12:30 p.m. and 2-5 p.m. Closed Mon. Admission: 200$00. Largo Dr. José Rodrigues. This museum displays the best collection of native sculpture in the country, and some fine paintings and objets d'art in a building that adds its own interest.

The collection begins to the right side of the entry courtyard with early sculpture. A Visigoth angel hovers charmingly. A mounted knight resting a mace on his shoulder is outstanding both as a composition and as a rare secular work from the Gothic era, besides being adorable. More 15th-century work follows, of which an assemblage of three knights in mail at the Sepulcher, and a pregnant Virgin by Master Pero stand out.

In the 16th century Coimbra became the artistic center of Portugal by enticing Nicolas Chanterene, Jean de Rouen (Ruão) and Philippe Houdart (Hodart) from France. Here they were joined by the Portuguese Castilho brothers—João and Diogo. Their sophisticated work betrays a strong Italian influence, and is of the highest quality. Among other things, what attracted them to Coimbra was easily worked fine white limestone from nearby Ança. They initiated Renaissance sculpture in Portugal and are responsible for most of the fine Manueline carving throughout the country. The museum displays an admirable assemblage of their work. See Chanterene's *Virgin Reading*, Rouen's *Entombment*, and Houdart's *Paschal Feast*. By the 17th century, wood replaced stone as the medium of choice and, with a few exceptions the quality of sculpture declined.

The ceilings on the second floor deserve as much attention as the exhibits. A representative display of Coimbra pottery shows its development from the 17th century on. The best paintings are in two rooms devoted to Renaissance religious works by Portuguese and Flemish artists. Quentin Matsys is always interesting, and, on the Portuguese side, there are compelling works by the Master of Sardoba (or his school), the Master of Santa Clara, and three sensitive paintings by Josefa de Óbidos.

The basement is formed of the remains of an eerie Roman cryptoporticus, a two-story platform (the lower story of which is closed) which once elevated a Roman forum that stood on this site. Today Roman and Visigothic artifacts are displayed in the nooks and crannies of this eerie structure.

Walk around the river end of the museum along Rua de Borges Carneiro which winds in a block to the Old Cathedral.

Sé Velha ★★

Open daily 9:30 a.m. to 12:30 p.m. and 2-7 p.m. Admission: 50$00 to the cloister. Largo de Sé Velha. This church was erected when Coimbra first became the capital of Portugal in the 12th century. That the town did not yet feel safe from the Moors is evidenced by the fortress facade of the church, complete with merlons on top. Overall it's the most imposing Romanesque church in the country. The main facade (west) is pure Romanesque, the later north portal is one of the first constructed in a Renaissance style, and the apse includes a rare and lovely Romanesque gallery.

The interior is awesome. Here the second and third kings of Portugal were anointed. The fine Gothic retable of the Assumption of the Virgin rising above the four Evangelists was carved by two Flemings. Its surrounding foliage contains charming figures, including a pig playing the bagpipe. The chapel in the south transept (to the right) holds a semicircular retable by a member of the Coimbra school, and the chapel of São Pedro to the left, lined by nice *azulejos*, presents a crumbling retable of the life of Saint Peter by Jean de Rouen.

Cloisters lie through the first door in the south aisle, and up. These are very early, 13th-century Gothic, although the bays are filled with tracery as would become the style two centuries later. In the first chapel on the left stands a fine font carved by Jean de Rouen. The chapterhouse holds the tomb of Dom Sisnando, the first Christian governor of Coimbra after its reconquest. There are indications that he was of Moorish blood.

Descend the stairs of Escades de Quebra-Costas opposite the Cathedral front, and take an immediate right along the narrow Rua de Sobre-Ripas to reach two mansions standing across from each other. On the left side of the lane is the 16th-century **Casa Sub-Ripas**, privately owned, with a Manueline doorway; on the right side is the **Casa do Arco**. In a few steps further, the lane passes beneath an arch to reach the **Torre do Anto**, remaining from the old city walls. Today it houses the Coimbra Regional Handcraft Center, an extensive display of local crafts. As it is an artists' cooperative, the pieces are for sale as well as for looking. Return to the beginning of the lane again to head down across the little square for a right turn through the **Almedina gate**, surmounted by a tower. This gate is 12th century, part of the medieval city walls, and still bearing the Moorish name of "The City." After angling left, a cross street is reached. Turn right onto the main shopping street of Coimbra, Rua Visconde da Luz, to reach the open Pr. 8 de Maio in a few blocks and the **Mosteiro de Santa Cruz**, in a building half of which now is occupied by the town hall. This is the lower town (Baixa). Behind the Mosteiro, east, is a fine open Pr. do Comércio surrounded by townhouses and shops. São Tiago from the 12th century, in the northwest corner, has a nice timber ceiling.

ADDITIONAL SIGHTS

Mosteiro de Santa Cruz ★★

Open daily from 9 a.m. to noon and from 2 p.m. to 6:30 p.m. Admission 100$00 to the sacristy and cloister; Pr. 8 de Maio. The original monastery, built in 1131 before Portugal had a king, preceded even the Old Cathedral. Portugal's first two monarchs—Dom Afonso I and his son Dom Sancho I—were buried here. However, the church needed major renovations by the beginning of the 16th century, and the result of that rebuilding is what one sees today. As the burial place for the first kings, this church held a special place in royal hearts, so, although small, it is richly endowed with art. It was in this church that King Pedro forced the courtiers of Portugal to kiss the skeletal hand of his deceased love Inês.

The present church facade was designed by Diogo de Castilho and decorated with statuary by Jean de Rouen and Nicholas Chanterene. These three were the shining lights of a special assembly of artists who gathered in Coimbra early in the 16th century and were responsible for much that is wonderful in Manueline art. Sadly, the stone has weathered badly, and what remains is spoiled by an 18th-century doorway, so it is difficult to appreciate what should have been a seminal piece of architecture.

Fortunately, there is no problem with deterioration inside. A Manueline ceiling covers a nave lined with *azulejos*. The octagonal pulpit is an extraordinary piece of carving, probably by Nicholas Chanterene. On either side of the altar lie the tombs of Kings Afonso I, the first King of Portugal, and his son, Sancho I, left and right, respectively. Originally, they had been buried in the courtyard in front of the church, but were disinterred and installed in these tombs early in the 16th century. It is thought that Diogo de Castilho designed the anachronistic Gothic tombs and that Chanterene did the carving.

Left of the altar is the entrance to the sacristy. Some of the paintings are worth attention, but the period furniture is more interesting. The cloister is unusually simple Manueline, with bas relief for the most part instead of the usual high relief. Stairs lead up to the *coro alto* which contains choir stalls carved and gilded along the top. The work is superior.

ACROSS THE RIVER

The ruins of **Santa Clara-a-Velha** ★ stand less than half a mile across the river. Cross on the Ponte Santa Clara and continue past the left turn to Lisbon for the next left onto a lane. Here are atmospheric ruins of a

14th-century Gothic church, destroyed by the floods of the river Mondego and time. Half buried in silt, the skeleton manages to convey greater age than the church of the Santa Cruz monastery, which is actually two centuries older.

Just west of the ruins is the **Portugal dos Pequenitos** park. It presents child-sized models of all of Portugal's famous monuments, plus exotic buildings from former colonies. Adults feel like Gulliver; children enjoy it almost as much. (Open daily 9 a.m. to 7 p.m., or 5 p.m. in winter; admission: 200$00 for adults, 50$00 for children.)

WHERE TO STAY

Hotels in this city are not the best. Perhaps its sizable student population has something to do with the situation, but the fact is that the best hotels attain only the second-class category, and they aren't numerous. More pleasant options are available at the lovely Palácio Águeda, in Águeda, 43 k north off N-1 (see the description in "Where to Stay" in the Aveiro section of this chapter), or at a most unusual hotel in the nearby Buçaco forest, or in the new pousada in Condeixa, 10 k south, or at hotels at the resort of Figueira da Foz 50 k west, all described below.

EXPENSIVE ($100-$200)

Tivoli Coimbra   1st-class ★★

R. João Machado, 4 (the street is six blocks north of the Pr. 8 de Maio along R. de Sofia). Rooms: 90. ☎ 269 34; Telex 52 240; FAX 268 27. Built in 1990, the hotel looks like countless others, sleek, clean, and without character. Accommodations are exactly what you would expect.

MODERATE ($50-$99)

Astória   2nd-class ★★★

Av. Emidio Navarro, 21 (on the avenue that parallels the river, just north of the bridge). Rooms: 64. ☎ 220 55; FAX 220 57; Telex 42859. This 1920s hotel with the froufrou of the era to lend individuality and interest is in fine repair and holds comfortable bedrooms. It has the most character of any Coimbra hotel.

Dom Luís   2nd-class ★

Quinta da Verzea (on N-1 to Lisbon, 2.5 k south of town). Rooms: 104. ☎ 44 15 10; FAX 81 31 96; Telex 52426. This is the newest hotel and more stylish, if less swank, than the Tivoli. It's outside the city, however, but offers views.

Oslo   2nd-class

Av. Fernão de Magalhães, 25 (near the Coimbra-A train station). Rooms: 30. ☎ 290 71; FAX 206 14. The Oslo is a pleasant enough place, but with the cold feeling of Scandinavian decor and too much noise. Rooms at the back are preferred for this reason.

Bragança   **2nd-class**

Largo das Ameias, 10 (the square in front of the Coimbra-A train station). Rooms: 83. ☎ 221 71; FAX 361 35; Telex 52609. The Bragança is a modern box of no charm, but could serve for a night and is reasonably priced.

INEXPENSIVE (UNDER $50)

Domus   **R3rd-class** ★

Rua Adelino Veiga, 62 (1 block north and 1 east of the beginning of Av. Fernão de Magalhães). Rooms: 20. ☎ 285 84. The second-floor hotel provides large, clean, erratically decorated bedrooms that are true bargains.

Almedina   **R2nd-class**

Av. Fernão de Magalhães, 203 (four blocks north of the Coimbra-A train station). Rooms: 43. ☎ 291 61. Functional, clean and very inexpensive—all of which makes us wish there were more character about the place.

WHERE TO EAT

Chanfana, goat stewed in red wine, and *leitao*, suckling pig, are specialties of the area. City restaurants provide good value for the money, but not memorable food. Zé Manuel and Pedro dos Leitôes, see below, are exceptions. And if you are willing to travel 29 k west to Montemor-o-velho, we can promise an exceptional dining experience.

EXPENSIVE ($40+)

In Montemor-o-velho:

Ramalhão   ★★★★

R. Tenente Valadim, 24 (Montemor is 29 k west of Coimbra, just off N-111, the road to Figueira da Foz). ☎ 68 9435. Closed Sunday night, Monday and October. Here is one of the great restaurant finds in Portugal, and it is appropriately difficult to ferret out. Take a right off the Montemor main square. About a hundred yards along this road, with the backs of houses on the right side, look very closely for a tiny, dimly lit sign on one rear fence. (There is a more visible entrance on Tenete Valadim, but it is difficult to drive up this street or park when you arrive). Inside the restaurant is as cozy as can be and always full, because those in the know return again and again. They realize that this place serves the most elevated authentic Portuguese cooking. The food is by no means fancy, sauces are seldom employed, but the combinations are those the Portuguese developed over the ages. Many will find the dishes somewhat dry and too lightly seasoned, but everyone will discover some new tastes. You can look past the bar, from some seats, into the small kitchen to spot the two venerable women who produce the meals. They instill absolute confidence. Dishes change daily, so it makes little sense to go with any special dish in mind. Put

INEXPENSIVE (UNDER $15)

Zé Manuel ★★★
Beco do Forno, 12 (a little street behind the Hotel Astória). ☎ 237 90. Don't be put off by the unassuming entrance, or even by the less assuming inside, with walls plastered in notes and papers, plain wood furniture set around, and an open kitchen in view. The customers come for the food, not the decor, and the upstairs is a bit nicer. The *sopa da pedra* is hearty and the *açorda de mariscos* as good as it gets, but almost any dish will please.

Pedro dos Leitões ★★
On N-1 in the village of Mealhada, 21 k north of Coimbra. ☎ 220 62. This little village is the roast suckling pig center for the country. Restaurants line the road, all announcing *leitao assado*. This particular large establishment is generally mobbed for lunch. It roasts the little critters over glowing coals, pricing the pig by weight, so you can satisfy either a large or small appetite. *Visa accepted.*

Trovador ★
Largo da Sé Velha, 17 (by the north face of the Old Cathedral). ☎ 254 75. *Closed Monday.* The atmosphere is inviting rather than elegant, although the waiters sport bow ties. The food is quite good, especially the *chanfana*. Fado is performed late on weekends.

O Alfredo ★
Av. João das Regras, 32 (just across the Ponte Santa Clara). ☎ 44 15 22. Tasty seafood is served in a simple setting, along with well-prepared meat dishes.

Dom Pedro
Av. Emidio Navarro, 58. (Along the river, south of the bridge). ☎ 291 08. *Closed Monday and holidays.* With a splashing fountain in the center, the restaurant tries hard for style. The food is pleasant enough, but betrays the same lack of good taste that the decor exhibits.
Diners, MasterCard and Visa accepted.

DIRECTORY

SHOPPING • Coimbra is known for pottery, producing a faience brightly decorated with animals and birds. The best place to view the selection, and perhaps to buy, is at the **Artensanato da Região de Coimbra** in the Torre de Anto at Rua de Sub-Ripas, 45 (discussed above). A good shop for modern copies of elegant 16th-to 18th-century patterns is **Jorge Mendes** at *Pr. do Comércio*, 9 (at the foot of the Almedina gate). Or, travel to Condeixa, see below, for more such and the factories.

INFORMATION • Located in *Largo da Portagem*, which is beside the Ponte Santa Clara, the office can provide a helpful map (☎ 238 86).

TRAINS AND BUSES • A shuttle connects the downtown Coimbra-A station at Largo das Amenias, upriver from the bridge (☎ *349 98*), with the Coimbra-B station outside of town. Trains beyond the surrounding area all leave from Coimbra-B. Lisbon, Porto and Figueira da Foz are well-served, and five trains go to Viseu daily. A high-speed train, the Alpha, reaches Lisbon in 2-1/2 hours, but requires advance reservations.

Buses leave from *Av. Fernão de Magalhães*, about ten blocks north of Coimbra-A train station (☎ *270 81*). Service is not as frequent to large cities as the train, but better for smaller ones.

POLICE • Located on *Rua Olimpio Nicolau Rui Fernades* (☎ *220 22*).

EXCURSIONS

Extensive Roman ruins lie at **Conimbriga** ★★ outside Condeixa, only 15 k southwest. The lovely **forest of Buçaco** ★ at Luso, with sylvan walks, holds a most interesting hotel, a former royal retreat. **Figueira da Foz** ★ is a resort with vast beaches and a casino, 45 k west. Further afield, but within a 100 k radius are **Tomar** ★★★, **Aveiro** ★★ and **Viseu** ★★★, each described under separate headings in this chapter, along with magnificent **Batalha** ★★★★★, described in the "Environs of Lisbon" chapter.

CONDEIXA ★

Population: 1697
Area code: 039; zip code: 3150

From **Coimbra** *cross the Ponte Sta.Clara to the west bank of the Mondego and take the first left to N-1 and signs for Lisbon. In 10 k comes a sign at a traffic light for a left turn to Condeixa. A sign at the first true right directs to Conimbriga in 2 k, or angle leftish for the pousada in less than 1 k. From* **north** *or* **south**, *exit 11 of the autoestrada is for Condeixa (13 k south of Coimbra), then 1 k east to N-1 for 3 k south to the traffic light and sign.*

The Avic Mondego bus leaves opposite the hotel Astoria on weekdays at 9:05 a.m., on weekends at 9:35 a.m. The return from Conimbriga leaves at 12:55 p.m. on weekdays, but not until 6 p.m. on weekends. More frequent service leaves from the Coimbra bus station to and from Condeixa-Nova, which is a walkable 2 k from the ruins.

Condeixa is a small town that seems larger because it borders the busy old main north-south artery, N-1, and because of the ceramics factories there. The term "factory" may create a wrong impression. These are centers that produce pottery shapes and bake the final glaze, but the real work, the painting, is a cottage-industry done in the homes of numerous artisans. Coindixa is the place to find the greatest variety and best prices for all the copies of antique ceramic patterns sold around the country. That, and visiting the Roman ruins are all the town offers, but it is a pleasant place to do both.

Conimbriga ★★

Open daily 10 a.m. to 1 p.m. and 2-8 p.m.; until 6 p.m. in winter. The museum opens at 10 a.m. and closes at 6 p.m.; closed Mon. in winter. Admission: 300$00 (200$00 in winter).

A sign in the Condeixa town square, one block after the turn off N-1, directs to a 2 k run on N-347 at which point a sign on the right points to the ruins.

Originally, Conimbriga lay on the main road between the two large Roman centers of Braccaria (modern Braga) and Olissipo (now Lisbon), and prospered from passing traders and the good farmland surrounding it. The city was founded in the first century, or a little before, but artifacts dug from the site show that Celts preceded the Romans by as much as 900 years. The city's heyday came in the third century A.D. when huge villas were constructed, the largest in the Roman world. By the end of that century, fear of barbarians caused a defensive wall to be built around the town that consumed parts of these splendid villas for building material. By the fifth century the town had fallen to the Swabians and was gradually abandoned thereafter. This exodus accounts for the preservation of the remains, for there has been no construction on the site since. Excavation began almost 100 years ago, although so far only about one-third of the site has been dug and the most important city monuments have just recently been made available to the public.

Start in the museum, whose maps, maquettes and artifacts provide some orientation and a sense of what will be seen. The entrance to the ruins passes the **House of the Fountains** ★ on the right, named for the unusually large pond in the center with provisions for water jets. Fine mosaics cover the floors, including hunting scenes and a chariot drawn by four horses. Through the city gates and to the right is the **House of Cantaber**, one of the largest homes known from the Roman world. There are several pools and, at the rear, private baths, a great luxury in this era of public bathing. The path continues to the city forum, donated by the emperor Flavian. Other remains are difficult to decipher, but lovely mosaics reward the explorer.

WHERE TO STAY

There is only one place worth considering, but a very good choice.

MODERATE ($50-$99)

Pousada de Sta. Cristina ★★★★

Condeixa-a-nova 3150 (keep left at the main square in Condeixa, after the turn off of N-1, for about 1 k). Rooms: 45. ☎ *94 40 25; FAX 94 30 97.* This is the newest of Portugal's pousadas, housed in a former mansion and decorated with molding and furniture saved both from the original mansion and from a house of the same owner in Lisbon that burned. Remodeling produced a lovely light–and–airy effect that is saved from any coldness by the older touches. Altogether this is among the most pleasant and comfortable of the pousadas, and especially graced by a young, attentive and enthusiastic management. Neither the pool nor tennis court were completed when we were there, but should be when you arrive.

DIRECTORY

SHOPPING • Condeixa is the outlet for all the charming blue-and-white and polychrome ceramics seen throughout Portugal that copy 17th- and 18th-century pieces. Most factories are located in the Zona Industrial, which is the first left after the Condeixa main square. Another factory is located immediately left after the turn from N-1 at the light for Condeixa. These factories are not set up to sell to retail customers, but they will wrap and ship. The issue is what you will find for sale, for most of what is on hand is ear-marked for orders. Alternatively, take N-347, the road to Conimbriga, as a sign in the square directs. After about 1 k there will be a sign for two Artessanados, one on the left, another on the right. Both display a good selection, much of which they have painted themselves. At these shops and at the factories the lack of a common language should present no difficulty.

LUSO ★

Population: 864
Area code: 031; zip code: 3050

From **Lisbon** *take A-1 north two exits past Coimbra to Mealhada for 199 k. Head east for Luso on N-234 for 7 k. Signs direct to the forest entrance. From* **Porto** *take the A-1 south for 84 k to the Mealhada exist and follow the directions above. From* **Coimbra** *follow the river road, Av. Emidio Navarro, to take a right through the plaza, Largo das Ameias, in front of the train station. Turn left at its end onto Av. Fernão de Magalhães which connects with N-1 going north to Porto. At Mealhada, the suckling pig capital, in 21 k turn east onto N-234 which reaches Luso in 7 k*

Five buses daily stop at Buçaco on their way to Viseu. The last bus from Buçaco leaves at 6:45 p.m.

Buçaco Forest ★

Follow signs to the forest entrance. Buçaco National Forest crowns a peak of the Serra do Buçaco. Something is enchanted about its lovely waterways interspersed with palms, its ancient trees and vales of ferns. Monks thought so, and chose the forest for their solitary contemplations as early as the sixth century. Popes thought so, and from far away Italy forbade women to enter the forest, while decreeing excommunication to anyone damaging a tree. Kings thought so, and supported royal hunting lodges on its grounds for centuries, before erecting a final royal retreat in 1910. There is nothing to do except walk—cars aren't allowed—and little to observe except nature, which, if the season is right, will overpower with mimosas, camellias, magnolias, hydrangeas, and lilies-of-the-valley.

True, there is the odd little chapel to come upon unexpectedly, and also, smack in the center, a gingerbread confection of a former royal palace, designed by an Italian who had worked on theater sets. It seems the king wanted a Manueline building three centuries after the style had become passé, so he was given a stage set. This fantasy of Renaissance times is a truly strange place to wander through and spend a day in, which one can. It now serves as a hotel for 60 guests who reserve months in advance.

The tourable forest, landscaped to suggest nature, extends only about half a mile by a quarter of a mile wide, although there are some steep hills. Several walking trails are laid out, the best entered off the far side of the Palácio Hotel past a small 17th century monastery where a sign points to the "Fonta Fria." This "fountain," more a series of pools and cascades, leads down to a lake, then through a fern valley. All is still, dark, and ferny as the trail leads past almost 700 different species of trees. Here and there are remains of stone hermit huts, just large enough to lie in.

Palace Hotel do Buçaco   1st-class ★ ★ ★

Foresta do Buçaco. Rooms: 62. ☎ *(031) 93 01 01; FAX 936 09; Telex 93450.* The forest's enchantment seems to have affected the travel writers who stay at this hotel, for they are unanimous in their praise. Viewed more soberly, the hotel is really quite eerie, with overtones of *The Shining.* Of course its effect depends very much on the person, but one thing we feel confident about is that no one would consider the food very good or the service gracious. The bedrooms are a mixed lot that vary enormously in size. Some are impressive, but most feel like an institution, and an old one at that. With all our complaints it must be acknowledged that this is a most unusual hotel, for former royal residences do not accept most of us commoners as guests. Some of the decoration is remarkable, and the setting is quiet and sylvan. Expensive at the 20.000$00 level, fixed–price meals are more moderate in cost. We can only hope that the new management may correct some of the problems we found.

FIGUEIRA DA FOZ ★

Population: 13,397
Area code: 033; zip code: 3080

Follow Coimbra's river road, Av. Emidio Navarro, to take a right through the plaza in front of the train station, Largo das Ameias. Turn left at its end onto Av. Fernão de Magalhães which connects with N-1 going north to Porto. In just a kilometer or two look for the turn onto N-111 west which reaches Figeira in 45 k. About halfway, the romantic ruins of the **castle of Montemor-o-Velho** *are passed.*

Figueira da Foz is one of the most popular resorts in Portugal, but mainly with the Portuguese and Spanish, rather than we non-Iberians who have yet to make its discovery. Its appeal is a huge two-mile-long beach. There is little to do but walk, swim and bask, although the village is prosperous and attractive, and a **casino** housed in a former palace opens in the afternoon. At the northern end of the beach, two miles away, reposes the almost unspoiled fishing village of **Buarcos ★**.

WHERE TO STAY

Catering mainly to Portuguese, prices at these hotels have not yet risen to international levels.

EXPENSIVE ($100-$200)

Grande Hotel da Figueira 1st-class ★
Av. 25 de Abril (on the promenade by the beach). Rooms: 91. ☎ *221 46; FAX 224 20; Telex 53086.* This is the fanciest hotel in town, all 50's glass and marble, but a bit antiseptic in feel. Still, the bedrooms are comfortable, some have lovely sea views, and prices are barely expensive.

MODERATE ($50-$99)

Aparthotel Atlântico 2nd-class ★
Av. 25 de Abril (near the Grande Hotel). Apartments: 70. ☎ *240 45; FAX 224 20.* Although the architecture is undistinguished, this high-rise presents lovely views over the ocean. Each apartment includes a sitting room and kitchenette—all at a very fair price.

INEXPENSIVE (UNDER $50)

Nicola R1st-class
Rua Bernardo Lopes, 36 (the street leading from the river past the casino). Rooms: 24. ☎ *223 59.* Although showing signs of wear, the hotel is clean and its bedrooms will serve.

WHERE TO EAT

Grilled seafood is the thing to eat, and there are several moderately priced places to enjoy it.

MODERATE ($15-$30)

Tubarão ★
Av. 25 de Abril (on the promenade, at the southern end). ☎ 234 45. Plain, almost without decoration, the restaurant impresses as being all business, and the business is grilling fish.

Tamargueira ★
Estrada do Cabo Mondeo (outside of Buarcos, 3 k north). ☎ 225 14. Fishing implements announce what this rustic restaurant serves. The terrace with ocean views is most pleasant, and the grilled fish is fresh, but soups are good as well.

CONIMBRIGA

See "Coimbra" under "Excursions."

FIGUEIRA DA FAZ

See "Coimbra" under "Excursions."

GUIMARÃES ★★★

Population: 22,092
Area code: 053; zip code: 4800

See the directions to Braga. Guimarães is 22 k southeast of Braga along N-101.

Guimarães is Portugal's birthplace. Henri, second son of the Duke of Burgundy, came to Spain to help Alfonso VI battle the Moors and received the king's illegitimate daughter as a reward. When Henri and Teresa married in 1095 they were given the County of Portucale, as northern Portugal was then known, for a wedding present. At the time Guimarães was not even a village—only the site of a monastery—but the newlyweds took one of the monastery towers, fit it out as a noble's residence, and settled in. In that tower of Mumadona monastery, their son Afonso was born in about 1110. After his father's death, he declared his territory independent from Spain and assumed the title of King of Portugal.

Today Guimarães thrives on weaving, cutlery manufacturing and tanning. Handwork still is practiced in the form of ox yokes, embroidery, and linen damask. Industrial Guimarães surrounds the older sights, leaving the center attractive with squares, gardens and monuments. Parking is where one finds it, but should be available at the Paço dos Duques on the green hillside below the castle.

*From **Braga** Rua de São Gonçalo funnels into Rua de Gil Vicente, which bends left after passing the post office and receives the name Av. Henrique Delgado. Either the first or second right thereafter will lead to the castle.*

WHAT TO SEE AND DO

Castelo ★★
Open daily 10 a.m. to 12:30 p.m. and 2-5 p.m. Admission: free. First built in the 10th century, this castle is not only among the oldest but among the most imposing in the country as well. Old walls of indeterminate great age surround a castle consisting of a massive keep amid seven towers of various heights. Each are topped by triangular merlons that make the whole look fierce. The original tower was remodeled in the 11th century to serve as a palace in which Afonso I, the first king of Portugal, was born. Additions over the centuries greatly expanded that original; then the whole became a prison early in the 19th century. Soon after, the complex was abandoned and used as a quarry for public buildings throughout Guimarães. Prime Minister Salazar decided that this was one of the most historic buildings in the nation and, in 1940—recapturing as many of its stones as could be found—set about restoring it.

With so much alteration, it is no longer clear which tower was the original—the one in which the first king was born—or even if that tower still exists. Regardless, the monolithic complex is suitably awesome for a national monument, and its walls provide fine views.

Just outside the castle walls is the Romanesque chapel of **São Miguel** from the 12th century. Inside, a font from an earlier church is said to be the one used to christen Afonso. Below the grassy hill is the grey, fortress-like Palace of the Dukes of Bragança.

Paço dos Duques de Bragança ★★
Open daily 10 a.m. to 5:30 p.m. Admission: 300$00 for a guided tour, 200$00 in winter. In about 1420 Don Afonso, an illegitimate son of the first king of the Avís line, constructed this huge manor house for himself and his wife. Later he would be named the first duke of the Bragança dynasty that would grow powerful and rule Portugal one day. The duke decided to build a new palace because the castle on the hill was not modern enough for his needs. Four buildings, each with a corner tower, form a cloister in the center. The style is that of the late Gothic in Burgundy, since the duke employed a French architect. The large number of brick chimneys (39) was unusual and remains a striking feature, showing how important the comfort of heat was for owners.

The palace was abandoned in the 17th century and suffered horribly until Prime Minister Salazar ordered its repair in 1940, at the same time that the castle was receiving similar treatment. In the case of the palace, because Salazar intended to live in it, renovation—rather than restoration—was performed. The present structure, therefore, provides an interesting study of the difference between fixing the old without depriving it of its look of age, and making the old perfect again. Today the building functions as a museum displaying the noble life-style of some indeterminate century, for there are pieces inside from the 14th through the 19th centuries, in a building without the nicks and wear of its age.

Despite complaints about its renovation, the palace provides a good idea of what a late medieval palace would have been like. Still, it is the furnishings that are of primary interest—from Aubusson and Gobelins tapestries, to antique Persian carpets, Chinese porcelain, and 17th-century Portuguese furniture. In addition, the ceilings in the dining hall and banquet hall are restored wonders. Three still lifes by Josepha de Obidos should be sought out.

Proceed downhill by taking the first left, **Rua Santa Maria**, *which passes the front of the Convent do Carmo. Many houses are from the 14th and 15th century. A square is soon passed with the former* **convento de Santa Clara**, *now the town hall. Continuing, the Largo de São Tiago is reached, at the end of which stands the 16th-century* **Paços do Concelho**, *a former town hall. Past it the Largo de Oliveira* ★ *opens up, impressively medieval, at whose east side, next to the pousada, is the church and convent of* **Our Lady of the Olive Tree**.

Nossa Senhora da Oliveira ★

Museum open Tues.-Sun. 10 a.m. to 12:30 p.m. and 2-5 p.m. Closed Mon. Admission: 200$00, free on Sun. This convent is the descendant of the original 10th-century monastery that Henri of Burgundy and his wife found occupying this site. As its name indicates, the founding had something to do with an olive tree. Legend has it that, in the 7th century, Visigothic nobles approached the shepherd Wamba in his fields to beg him to be their king. By way of refusal, he thrust his staff into the ground and vowed that he would not accept unless his olive staff flowered. It did and he did. In the 10th century a monastery commemorating the miracle was constructed on this spot.

An unusual 14th-century Gothic canopy covering a cross prefaces the church, to commemorate a 14th century victory over the Moors. The church facade is of the same era, although its tower is 16th-century Manueline. The church interior is older, 12th century, but redecorated in this century and of little interest. What is interesting are the Romanesque cloisters whose second floor serves as a fine museum.

Called the Museu Alberto Sampaio, it can be entered just south of the church.

An astonishing collection of rich ecclesiastical plates are displayed. Also on view is a tunic that João I, the first king of the House of Avís, wore in the battle of Aljubarrota where he defeated Portuguese nobles and their Spanish allies to secure his throne. The most amazing work on display, however, is a 14th-century gilt triptych altarpiece donated by João after that battle. One story claims that he captured it from the Spanish, another contends that he commissioned it afterwards. Whatever its origins, it is a masterpiece displaying the Nativity in the center panel, the Annunciation and presentation at the temple on the left panel, and the adoration of the Magi and shepherds on the right. Elsewhere, chalices, monstranses and elegant crosses all fight for attention.

A grand vista at the end of the square leads down (southeast) to the church of **Santos Passos**, *majestic from a distance, although of little interest inside. Walk toward it to take the second right along the Alameda da Liberdade gardens for one block to the church of São Francisco to the left.*

São Francisco ★
Open Tues.-Sun. 10 a.m. to 12:30 p.m. and 2-5 p.m. Closed Mon. Admission: free. Of the original 15th-century church only the main portal and apse remain, the rest being 17th century. One cannot fail to notice the tile-covered mansion next door that seems to announce that the reason to enter the church is for sublime blue-and-white Delft *azulejos* lining the chancel walls.

For those interested in archaeology a walk to the **Martin Sarmento Museum** *is in order. Continue to the west end of the Alameda gardens, where the* **Office of Tourism** *is found. Turn right to walk through the plaza, continuing north along Rua Paio Galvão, which passes more garden to reach the Gothic* **São Domingos** *in one block on the left, with the museum installed in its cloisters.*

Museu Martins Sarmento
Open Tuesday-Sunday 10 a.m. to noon and 2-5 p.m. Closed Mon. Admission: 200$00. Named for the archaeologist who excavated Citânia de Briteiros (see "Braga" under "Excursions"), this museum displays the smaller objects found there and elsewhere in the area. Included are two headless statues of Celtiberian warriors holding round shields, and—most dramatic of all—the Colossus of Pedralva, all ten feet of him. Some of the smaller bronze pieces are surprising, such as dolphins and a hermaphrodite figure.

WHERE TO STAY

For moderate and inexpensive accommodations, Braga is a better bet than Guimarães. However, the most majestic of all of Portugal's pousadas is installed in Guimarães' outskirts, and another, comfortable pousada resides in the lovely Largo da Oliveira in town.

EXPENSIVE ($100-$200)

Pousada Santa Marinha da Costa　　　　　　　**Deluxe ★★★★★**
Estrada de Penha (on a hill 2.5 k east, directed by abundant signs). Rooms: 50. ☎ *51 44 53; FAX 51 44 59; Telex 32686.* Do not judge this one by its whitewashed exterior suggesting a huge factory. Actually, it is a former convent, founded in the 12th century but completely restored in the 18th. Inside it is grand, but even more impressive is its elegant taste. In fact it would be difficult to decide whether this or Rainha Santa Isabel in Estremoz is the most elegant of the pousadas, but no question at all that this one is the most imposing. The fortunate will stay at both. Hallways are grand enough to ride horses through, as happened in olden days, and tiled with luscious azulejos. You will never suspect that a terrible fire in 1951 destroyed much of the grand corridor, so skillfully has it been reconstructed. Bedrooms are formed from the original monks' cells, which you would not suspect for they are grand today. Some include canopied beds, far from a monk's original equipment. As this is the flagship of the entire pousada chain, the service is always on its efficient toes. Even the meals in a grand hall are a treat. The only true surprise comes with the bill—the price of a room barely crosses the expensive line.

Pousada Santa Maria da Oliveira　　　　　　　**1st-class ★★★**
Rua Santa Maria. Rooms: 16. ☎ *51 41 57; FAX 51 42 04; Telex 32875.* If two pousadas served the same town one would hope for a difference in what each offered. This one is for city mice. It is constructed from a block of old townhouses, now joined by interior corridors, so it has the feel of an old village inn. There is nothing grand about the accommodations, some warmth, but little personality.

MODERATE ($50-$99)

Fundador Dom Pedro　　　　　　　　　　　　　**1st-class**
Av. Don Afonso Henriques, 740 (due south of the Tourist Office, at the end of the Alameda gardens). Rooms: 63. ☎ *51 37 81; FAX 51 37 86; Telex 32866.* If both pousadas are full, this is a perfectly comfortable option, although modern—in fact the only high-rise in town—and lacking atmosphere.

If needed, the similar, but first-class, **Hotel de Guimarães** is next door to the Dom Pedro with 72 more rooms.

WHERE TO EAT

Of the two pousadas, the food is more exciting at Pousada da Oliveira where meals are moderate in cost, although its dining room cannot offer the grandeur of its more elegant sister pousada.

EXCURSIONS

A pleasant two-stop outing is possible for those interested in lace and a stroll through a pretty town. Take Rua Dona Constanca de Noranha, the road that follows the southern edge of the castle park, which leads to N-101 toward Amarante. In 7.5 k comes **Trofa** where, on a nice day, all the women will be tatting on their doorsteps. Feel free to inspect their wares. A command of Portuguese is unnecessary; the will to communicate finds a way.

In 25k more, the town of **Amarante** ★ is entered. It lies pretty-as-a-picture in the mountains along the clear Tamega River. The newer houses are 18th century. Wooden balconies overhang the river which is spanned by a fine massive bridge from 1790. There is a 16th-century convent and church, if some sight-seeing objective is necessary, just across the bridge. The most pleasant course is to walk and stop frequently to look around.

LEIRIA

See "Batalha" under "Excursions" in the "Lisbon" chapter.

PENEDA-GERÊS NATIONAL PARK ★★

> From **Braga** the scenic N-103 leads east for 28 k to Cerdeirinhas, 1 k past which N-304 heads north into the park and the spa of Caldas do Gerês. From elsewhere follow directions to Braga, then those above.

This is Portugal's largest national park, covering 175,000 acres in a horseshoe that comprises in each arm the two mountain ranges of Peneda and Gerês. Highest peaks attain about 5000 feet and spill precipitously down to rushing valley streams.

Since the landscape is elevated and carved from granite, it is covered in pines, ancient oaks, firs, ferns and heather, although wildflowers burst forth in the spring. The vegetation is as dense as the soil permits because of the highest rainfall in the country. Fauna include stags, golden eagles, wild horses, boar and goats. Several lakes have been formed by modern dams, but more common are racing streams, for the water rides over impenetrable granite.

Cars may be driven through the park. Of course there are abundant opportunities for walks, but no official trails. You will instead follow the paths worn down by humans and their animals for centuries.

Peneda-Gerês Park ★★

The best tour begins along N-304 at the Saúde entrance, just north of Cerdeirinhas. It winds downhill, passing the Pousada São Benito high on its hill to the left in about 2k. The first bridge over the Cávado passes a village submerged by the rising waters of the nearby dam. Then comes an intersection at which N-308-1 to the right for Gerês should be taken.

A second bridge is crossed that leads into the park proper. The road follows the lake and then a rushing stream to the pleasant spa of Caldas do Gerês in a narrow scenic valley. Here a base can be made for further explorations and a map for drives and walks secured from the office of tourism.

From Gerês there is the choice of continuing on through the nature preserve and past a section of Roman road, or of taking a more spectacular, although rough road, west. For the later backtrack for 1 k from Gerês to take a forest track on the right toward Lamas. After 3k comes the Fragra Negra Fountain, where a hike up the stairs is rewarded by a glorious view. The track runs on through forest and rocky outcrops, before descending, soon after a crossroad, to São João do Campo, then on to the Vilarinho das Furas Dam.

WHERE TO STAY

Caldas do Gerês is the most convenient village with lodgings, but there is also a pousada just outside of the park.

MODERATE ($50-$99)

Pousada de São Bento ★★

North of Cerdeirinhas on N-304, well signed. Rooms: 29. ☎ *(053)64 71 90; FAX (053) 64 78 67.* Appropriately rustic like its mountain setting, this is a pousada that provides simple comforts with a view that is anything but. Unfortunately the view is only provided from the lounge, for the bedrooms have small shuttered windows.

In Gerês:

Hotel do Parque 3rd-class ★

Av. Manuel Francisco do Costa. Rooms: 60. ☎ *(053) 67 65 48; Telex: 32217.* The decor is a little faded, but one doesn't expect luxury in the mountains. For extras it offers a pool.

Hotel das Termas 3rd-class

Av. Manuel Francisco do Costa. Rooms: 31. ☎ *(053) 39 11 43; Telex: 32217.* This one costs a few escudos more than the preceding for about the same offering, minus the pool.

PORTO ★★★

Population: 335,916
Area code: 02; zip code: 4000

From **Lisbon** the autoestrada A-1 speeds to Porto in 314 k. From **Coimbra** a drive north on N-1 of 9 k allows a connection to the autoestrada A-1 for the final 131 k. From **Évora** take N-114 northwest to Montemor-o-Novo in 30 k, where N-4 goes west to Cruzamento de Pegões in 37 k. There N-10 goes northwest to Vila Franca de Xiro, where the autoestrada A-1 is picked up for a speedy 314 k. From the **Algarve** follow directions to Lisbon, but to skirt the city, at Maratecs take N-10 north, instead of N-10 west to Setubal. Continue past Cruzamento de Pegões in 14 k toward Villa Franca de Xira in a further 49 k, where A-1 is picked up and the remaining Lisbon directions may be followed. From **Braga** take N-14 south which reaches the autoestrada A-4 in about 10 k. The remaining trip is 54 k. From **Viseu** take N-16 due west for 65 k to the autoestrada A-1, which goes north to Porto in a further 46 k. From **Tomar** get to Coimbra and follow directions from there.

Train service is frequent from most parts of the country, although most trains end in the Campanha station, which is a distance from the center of the city. Change there for a five-minute ride to the Estacão São Bento in the heart of town. A Lisbon express train takes about three hours, twice the time from Coimbra. Buses almost double those times, although they are as convenient as trains from nearer departures, such as Braga and Viseu. At four-and-a-half hours, the bus beats the train handily from Guarda.

Of course, a plane is fastest. Pedras Rubras airport is 14 k south of the city. A taxi costs from the airport less than 3000$00. Alternatively, the #56 bus takes about 45 minutes to reach Pr. de Lisbōa, one block west of Av. dos Aliados, and costs less than $1.

A Roman settlement originally occupied the south bank of the wide mouth of the Douro River. The north bank served as its port. Gradually, another town grew around the port. The two towns were respectively called Cale and Portus (The Port) by the Romans. By the 10th century, after the Moors had been chased south of the

Douro, the northern territory then in Christian hands combined the two Roman names to call itself Portucale. Thus, too, the fiefdom inherited by Afonso I and over which he styled himself king, was designated by that name. Since Christian reconquest of the rest of the country involved adding more and more territory to this original area, the name came to designate the entire country, and was later transmuted into "Portugal."

The present city of Porto (known to the English as, Oporto, confusing the Portuguese *O Porto* "the port") occupies the site of the Roman town of Portus, sprawling down the long, steep north bank of the Douro, 6 k from the sea. With almost a million people in the extended agglomeration, it is easily the second largest city in Portugal and the one most single-mindedly devoted to commerce.

Porto has a long history of independence. In the 13th century its citizens disputed the right of the king to impose tariffs on their shipping. In response, the king established a royal city on the opposite bank, now called Villa Nova de Gaia, and wrangled an agreement that a third of the shipping—upon which he was allowed to impose taxes—would depart from his city. Much later, when Lisbon fell meekly to Napoleon in 1808, Porto held out, setting up a junta to rule in the king's place when the court fled to exile in Brazil. A year later, Napoleon's General Soult captured Porto, but the English under Wellesley, later the Duke of Wellington, regained it four months later. In 1820, Porto's citizens rebelled against the occupying English to adopt the first liberal constitution in Portugal. Eight years later, when Miguel I returned from two decades of pleasant exile in Brazil to reign as an absolute monarch, the city revolted again—siding with Miguel's brother Pedro IV in his successful fight for the crown. Finally, in 1890 Porto began the antimonarchist republican rebellion that bore final fruit in Lisbon in 1910, when the last monarch was expelled.

Portugal in general, but Porto in particular, also has a long history of close ties with England. In the 17th century, France closed its borders to imports of English clothing, and in response Charles II forbade the importation of French wines, leaving English thirsts unslaked. The English began sending their cloth to Portugal, trading for wine from Porto. This arrangement was formalized in the Methuen Treaty of 1703, which stipulated that the two countries would remain perpetual friends. Soon Englishmen came to Porto, bought up inland vineyards along the Douro, and formed shipping companies for the wine that floated down the river to Porto. Whether to prevent spoilage or to satisfy the English palate for sweet drink, a method was developed for adding grape brandy to the wine to stop its fermentation while half of the grape sugar still remained. It produced a sweet, fortified wine of as much as 30 percent alcohol that is called after its place of embarkation, *port*. To earn the name, wine originally had to age in Villa Nova de Gaia, across the river from Porto. Famous port houses, such as Sandeman, still maintain "lodges" (warehouses) there today, although aging now is permitted anywhere along the Douro littoral.

Porto today presents the face of a 19th-century commercial port—full of granite-trimmed buildings, few more than three stories high. The heart of the city is the wide, grass-lined, Av. dos Aliados, which runs five blocks inland from, and perpendicular to, the river.

All of the sights lie south of this landmark. The **Cathedral** ★★, with a fine altar, stands two blocks directly south; the church of **San Francisco** ★★, the non-plus-ultra of the Baroque, a block from the river to the southeast beside the **Palácio da Bolsa** ★, containing one impressive hall in the style of the Moors. Lining the river in front of San Francisco is the **Cais (quay) de Ribeira**, the oldest and most picturesque quarter. Across the river in Villa Nova de Gaia stretches a row of **port lodges** ★ for free tours and tastings. Upriver from the lodges stands the architecturally interesting **Convento de Nossa Senhora da Serra do Pilar**. All told, there is less to see in Porto than its size might suggest, but the ambiance of the city is different from any other in Portugal and the sights merit a day's stay.

> *One-way streets complicate entry into the city. Centralized parking is available at the north end of the Av. dos Aliados, north of the imposing town hall, on either side of the grand church of Trinidade.*

> *From **Lisbon** and **south** on the autoestrada A-1 the Ponte da Arrabida is crossed leading to a cloverleaf on the north bank. Exit here, following signs for "Centro" by heading east along Rua do Campo Alegre. When the street ends at a "T," take Rua de Julio Dinis right. R. Dinis ends at the garden of the Crystal Palace; turn left along Rua do Dom Manuel II. After passing the 18th-century Carranças Palace, the road ends at a "T." From here the going is trickier to describe than to follow, for one-way streets offer few choices. Go right on Rua Alberto Aires de Gouvela for one block, turn left on Rua da Restauracão, which soon follows the edge of the garden of João Chagas past the rear of a uni-*

versity complex. At the east side of the university buildings is the Pr. de Lisbōa whose southern edge is followed on *Rua dos Clericos*, which in two blocks lets into the Pr. de Liberdade with a fountain in the center. Turn left along *Rua dos Almada*—with the garden in the center—for 5 blocks, passing the city hall to reaching the large church of Trinidade. Parking is available both to the right and to the left of the church.

From **N-1** the course is simpler. Ponte de Dom Luis I is crossed to reach Av. Vimara Peres, which changes its name after passing the Cathedral on the left to Av. de Dom Afonso Henrigues. Then it passes the São Bento train station and ends at the Pr. de Liberdade. Go north along *Rua do Almada*—with the garden in the center—for five blocks, past the city hall to the front of the large church of Trinidade. Parking is available both to the right and to the left of that church.

From **Braga**, the **north** and the **airport** the simplest course is to turn left on N-12, the Estrada Circunvalacão, at a large traffic circle. Take the first exit to the right onto *Rua do Amial* which changes its name successively to *Rua do Vale Formoso*, *Rua de Antero de Quental* and *Rua de Lapa*, before entering the large Pr. da República. Turn left at its end, then right at its corner to pass a church before taking a soft left. This ends in a "T." Go right on *Rua de Camões* to find parking to the right side, opposite the Trinidade church.

If parked beside the Trinidade church, walk downhill past the neo-Renaissance city hall (to the right of which is the **Office of Tourism**) for three blocks along the gardens in the center of Rua do Almada. At the end of the gardens is the Pr. da Liberdade, an animated plaza with a center statue of Pedro IV, who Porto fought for against his more reactionary brother. Turn right at the southeast corner to enter the Pr. de Almeida Garrett, where the train station of **São Bento** is left. Extensive blue azulejos *inside show scenes from Portuguese history. Continue south along Av. de Dom Afonso Henriques to turn right in one long block at the intersection with Rua Saraiva de Carvalho. Here, atop its *knoll, is the Cathedral, with a medieval pillar in front symbolizing church authority on which the children play.*

WHAT TO SEE AND DO

Cathedral ★
Open daily 9 a.m. to 12:30 p.m. and 2-5:30 p.m. Admission: 50$00 to the cloisters. Of the 12th-century Romanesque fortress church in which João I married Philippa of Lancaster in 1387, little can be seen, since so many decorative additions now cover it over. The central window of the facade is lovely Romanesque, but the portal is Baroque. Baroque is the dominant decorative theme of the interior, yet the space is simpler Romanesque.

A treasure graces the Chapel of the Holy Sacrament in the north (left) transept. A retable and altar front of chased silver from the 17th century is a marvel of mannered figures that seem to move in the dim light. A door at the end of the south transept (right side) leads to a solemn 14th-century cloister whose upper tier was wrapped in charming *azulejos* in the 17th century.

Toward the river in the Cathedral plaza is a fine 18th-century **Old Bishop's Palace**, *now an office building. A lane behind the apse of the Cathedral leads to R. Dom Hugo and the 18th century building at number 32 that serves as the* **Museu Guerra Junqueiro** *for interesting decorative arts (open Tues. through Sat. from 10 a.m. until 12:30 and from 2 p.m. until 5; on Sun. from 2 p.m. until 5:30; admission 100$00).*

A lane leading left just before that museum leads downhill to cross the access road to the Ponte de Dom Luis I for the church of **Santa Clara**, *covered inside in 18th-century carved gilt. The ceiling is elegant. Remains of the old* **city walls** *stand behind the church.*

If the above sights do not appeal, descend the western flank of the Cathedral hill through the quaint and dirty Old Town to emerge into sunlight again at Av. Mousinho de Sovveira. It goes south for about one block to the Pr. Infante Dom Henrique, at the rear of the church of **São Francisco**. Adjacent to the north side of the church is the **Palácio da Bolsa**.

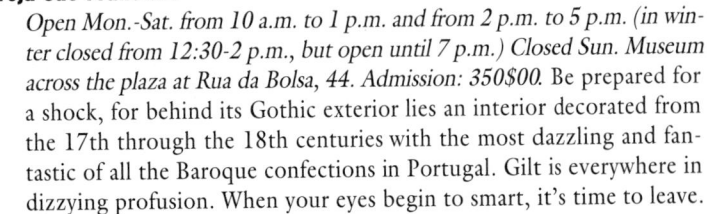

Igreja São Francisco ★★
Open Mon.-Sat. from 10 a.m. to 1 p.m. and from 2 p.m. to 5 p.m. (in winter closed from 12:30-2 p.m., but open until 7 p.m.) Closed Sun. Museum across the plaza at Rua da Bolsa, 44. Admission: 350$00. Be prepared for a shock, for behind its Gothic exterior lies an interior decorated from the 17th through the 18th centuries with the most dazzling and fantastic of all the Baroque confections in Portugal. Gilt is everywhere in dizzying profusion. When your eyes begin to smart, it's time to leave.

The tour of the nearby museum starts in eerie catacombs, whose gloom is the perfect contrast to the gilt next door. You walk on what seem to be doors that house the last remains of a reputed 30,000 mortals. Afterwards, there is a museum of mixed oddities, then the rich Sala de Sessões presided over by a painted bishop who seems to be eyeing your warm body avidly.

Palácio da Bolsa ★

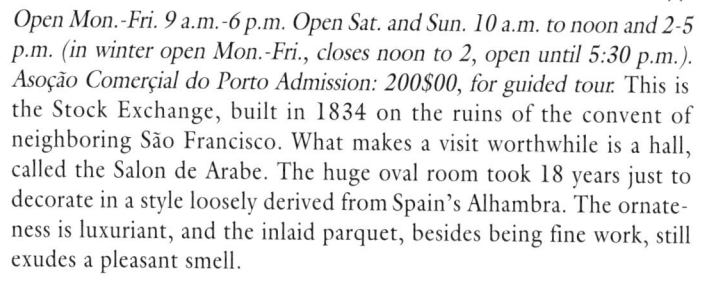

Open Mon.-Fri. 9 a.m.-6 p.m. Open Sat. and Sun. 10 a.m. to noon and 2-5 p.m. (in winter open Mon.-Fri., closes noon to 2, open until 5:30 p.m.). Asoção Comerçial do Porto Admission: 200$00, for guided tour. This is the Stock Exchange, built in 1834 on the ruins of the convent of neighboring São Francisco. What makes a visit worthwhile is a hall, called the Salon de Arabe. The huge oval room took 18 years just to decorate in a style loosely derived from Spain's Alhambra. The ornateness is luxuriant, and the inlaid parquet, besides being fine work, still exudes a pleasant smell.

Past the west end of the Bolsa a right then an immediate left brings the Largo São João Novo, named after the church there. Opposite the church is the **Museu de Etnografia i Historia**. *Exhibits are a mishmash of 19th-century and early 20th-century curiosities and folk pieces that are generally interesting. (Open Tues.-Sat. 10am to noon and 2-5 p.m. Closed Sun., Mon., and holidays. Admission: free.)*

Returning to the Pr. Infante Dom Henrique at the rear of the church of São Francisco, descend Rua da Alfandega that leaves its southeast corner. On the right the house where Henry the Navigator was purportedly born, now hosting art exhibits, is passed. Further downhill and right at Rua da Reboleira is the **Center of Traditional Arts and Crafts**, for a look or a purchase. Down to the river and upstream (east) is the area called **Ribeira**, a lively district full of restaurants.

Vila Nova de Gaia ★

This is the name for the area across the river where port wine is warehoused in what the trade calls "lodges." They line the bank opposite the center of Porto, all clearly marked by neon company signs. One can walk or taxi—taxis are entitled to a surcharge for crossing the river—across the lower level of the Ponte de Dom Luis I. (Buses #57 and #91 also make the trip.) Do not fail to notice the lovely **Maria Pia railway bridge** upstream (east), designed by Gustave Eiffel of the Paris tower fame, and the newer **Arrabida road bridge** downstream, crossing in a single span measuring 1000 feet.

All the lodges offer free guided tours and samples. All are open on weekdays from either 9 a.m. or 10 p.m. to noon and from 2-5 p.m. A few, such as Sandeman and Real Vinicola, are open on Saturday as well. Note that three such tours bring most people to the edge of intoxication. A few of the better ones are:

Sandeman *Largo Miguel Bombarda, 2.* ☎ *30 40 81.*

Ferreira *Av. Diogo Leite, 70.* ☎ *30 08 66.*

Real Vinicola *Rua Azevedo Magalhães, 314.* ☎ *30 54 62.*

Calem *Av. Diogo Leite, 2.* ☎ *39 40 41.*

WHERE TO STAY

Porto recently added a spate of luxury hotels to remedy a lack at that level, although all charge very high prices. With the exception of the truly elegant infante de Sagres, they are gleaming modern hotels that, in our opinion, are not worth their lofty rates. Better values exist in Porto's moderately priced lodgings.

EXPENSIVE ($100-$200)

Infante de Sagres Deluxe ★★★★★
Pr. Dona Filipa de Lencastre, 62 (one block west of Av. do Almada, about half way along). Rooms: 74. ☎ *201 90 31; FAX 31 49 37; Telex 26880.* The Infante is one of the great hotels of Europe and, unquestionably the most luxurious in Porto. Although built in the 1950s with a perfectly ordinary exterior, no cost was spared inside to make it as grand and lovely as could be. It is richly Victorian in style, replete with elegant paneling, crystal chandeliers, velvet wallpaper, and wrought iron work. We would nominate its Dona Filipa restaurant as the most elegant in the country, and for once the lighting is subdued. Bedrooms are truly spacious, with marble bathrooms, although their vaguely directoire decor is not up to the exalted standards of the public spaces. Our one complaint is that water from the shower spills onto the floor. But what is truly outstanding is the service, for there are as many people providing assistance as spending the night. The guest-list of this hotel includes the royal, great and famous. Anywhere else in Europe a hotel of this caliber would cost three times its less than $200 per double price.

Le Méridien Porto Deluxe ★★★★
Av. da Boavista, 1466 (about 2 k west of the center). Rooms: 232. ☎ *600 19 13; FAX 600 20 31; Telex 27301.* Every service is efficiently provided by this modern hotel that lives up to the fine reputation of the Méridien chain. However, its size precludes the impeccable service of the Infante above, it charges more, and it's a 10-minute taxi ride from the sights.

Dom Henrique 1st-class ★★★
Rua Guedes de Azevedo, 179 (1 block east of the Trinidade train station which is just north of the Trinidade church at the top of the Rua do Almada). Rooms: 112. ☎ *200 57 55; FAX 201 94 51; Telex 22554.* This too, is a modern hotel with all services, as opulent as the preceding

But it's close enough to the sights to walk and charges at the bottom, rather than at the top, of the expensive range. Some rooms have fine views over the city.

Porto Sheraton   Deluxe ★★
Av. da Boavista, 1269 (across the street from the Méridien). Rooms: 253. ☎ 606 88 22; FAX 609 14 67; Telex 22723. Newer even than its neighbor the Méridien, the Sheraton provides an expected modern look and services. For those pining for home it might be a good choice, although it charges more than the Infante.

MODERATE ($50-$99)

Albergaria Miradouro   R1st-class ★★
Rua da Alegria, 598 (3 blocks east and 2 north of the Trinidade train station, which is just north of the Trinidade church at the top of the Rua do Almada). Rooms: 30. ☎ 57 07 17; FAX 57 02 06. This 13-story modern building in a quiet neighborhood offers dramatic views of the city and the river traffic for a modest price. The decor is tasteful and the walk to sights is downhill. Its Portucale restaurant is one of the best in the city.

Albergaria São João   2nd-class ★★
Rua do Bonjardim, 120 (although one-way in the wrong direction, Rua de Fernandes goes east from the Trinidade church to reach the hotel in 4 blocks). Rooms: 43. ☎ 208 02 61; FAX 32 04 46. This hotel occupies the top floor of a modern building, yet it is cozy with antiques and a fireplace. The bedrooms are large and intelligently laid out so that each includes a sitting area. The location is most convenient.

Castor   2nd-class ★
Rua das Doze Casas, 17 (a half block north and a short turn west from the Miradoro above). Rooms: 63. ☎ 57 00 14; FAX 56 60 76; Telex 22793. This is a tasteful, contemporary and quiet hotel, with comfortable bedrooms that could, however, be larger. Walking to the sights is feasible.

Grand Hotel do Porto   2nd-class ★
Rua de Santa Catarina, 197 (Rua do Dr. Magalhães Lemos runs east from the middle of Rua do Almada. A left turn onto Santa Catarina in 2 blocks brings the hotel.) Rooms: 100. ☎ 200 81 76; FAX 31 10 61; Telex 22553. "Grand" is stretching it, but the hotel tries with a marble lobby and crystal chandeliers. The bedrooms are surprisingly bright and comfortable, and the location is good.

INEXPENSIVE (UNDER $50)

Rex   R1st-class ★★★
Pr. da República, 117 (this major plaza is 1 block west of the Trinidade train station). Rooms: 21. ☎ 200 45 48; FAX 38 38 82; Telex 20899. This converted townhouse overlooks a gardened, serene square. The house is a neoclassic charmer with marble staircase, paneled wood and

intricate stucco ceilings. Really, it *is* inexpensive, despite its more luxurious look. The bedrooms are lovely, with painted stucco ceilings and larger than alternatives at this low price.

Albergaria Girassol R1st-class

Rua do da Bandeira, 133 (1 block east of the southern end of Rua do Almada). Rooms: 18. ☎ 200 18 91. The hotel occupies the top floor of a building and provides large bedrooms with dressing rooms for modest prices. It's a long walk upstairs past rather dingy walls, but the location is most convenient.

Peninsular 3rd-class

Rua do da Bandeira, 21 (a few steps north of the São Bento train station). Rooms: 50 (a few lack private baths). ☎ 200 30 12; FAX 38 49 84. The neon sign out front does not bode well, but the bedrooms are more pleasant than that introduction. The location is prime. A dramatic central skylight, shows what the new owner can do. Now there stained glass in the dining room and more comfortable bedrooms. We await further word.

WHERE TO EAT

What can one say about the food in a city most famous for tripe? If one likes tripe stewed with spicy sausage and white beans (*tripas a moda do Porto*) obviously one can say a good deal. On the whole, the food is hearty rather than gourmet—as in *bacalhau a Gomes*, a casserole of cod, onion and potatoes, or *caldeirada*, a fish stew in tomatoes and onion. Almost any restaurant along the Ribeira will do a good job on such dishes—and at moderate cost—but they will do better with simple grilled fish. Wash it all down with a *vinho verde*.

EXPENSIVE ($40+)

Portucale ★★★

Rua da Alegria, 598 (in the same building as the Albergaria Miradouro, blocks east and 2 north of the Trinidade train station, which is just north of the Trinidade church at the top of the Rua do Almada). ☎ 57 07 17. The dramatic view alone would make this place special, but it also serves the best food in the city. The dining room is pleasantly decorated with modern hangings, and the tables are attractively dressed with good linens, silver, china and flowers. Despite the stunning views, an intimate feeling is maintained. Both *tipas á moda do Porto* (in casserole with white beans, bacon, chicken and sausage) and *cabrito a serrano* (kid stewed in red wine) are cooked nowhere better. Reservations are advised. *Amex, Diners, MasterCard and Visa accepted*

A Porta Nobre ★★★

Largo do São Francisco, 133 (at the western end of the Ribera, opposite São Francisco). ☎ 38 49 42. This granite river house from the turn of the last century has just been lovingly renovated to serve elegant meals. There are two dining rooms, one blue the other bright yellow on each of two floors with large windows overlooking the Douro. Th

chef is Swiss-trained to present classical French food. A choice wine list is offered, the presentation is elegant, and the food is quality.
Amex, Diners, MasterCard and Visa accepted.

MODERATE ($15-$30)

Mesa Antiga ★★

Rua de Santo Ildefonso, 208 (Leave the southeast corner of Pr. da Liberdade at the southern end of Av. do Almada on Rua de do da Bandeira. In one block, round the church to enter Rua de Santo Ildefonso for one block). ☎ 200 64 32. *Closed Saturday and the first two weeks of October.* Old wood and blue-and-white *azulejos* create the proper cozy atmosphere for food that is prepared with care. This is a family-run place, where the main work is done in an improbably small kitchen. Try the tripe, or sole in delectable green sauce, or any daily special. Reservations are advised. *MasterCard and Visa accepted.*

Aquário Marisqueiro ★

Rua Rodrigues Sampaio, 179 (a step or two east of the Pr. do General H. Delgado, which fronts the city hall). ☎ 200 22 31. *Closed Sunday and holidays.* This is fish heaven. Clams are good, as is shellfish *açorda*—a bread thickened stew—and sole done any which way. Reservations are required. *MasterCard and Visa accepted.*

O Escondidinho

Rua de Passos Manuel, 144 (2 blocks east of the middle of Av. do Almada). ☎ 200 10 79. *Closed Sunday.* The place exudes an old club atmosphere with its blackened beams, fireplace and antique ceramics on the walls. The waiters are informal, although they know their business and recite the day's specials, which, unfortunately, range from very good to bland. A steak is always a good choice, as are charcoaled sardines. Reservations are advised. *Amex, Diners, MasterCard and Visa accepted.*

INEXPENSIVE (UNDER $15)

Chez Lapin ★★

Cais da Ribeira, 42. ☎ 264 18. Let us get the bad part out of the way first. This restaurant is so tiny as to be claustrophobic, the decor is happenstance, and it is noisy. However, the reason for the noise is that it is always full, for the food is quite good, and the claustrophobia soon disappears in the convivial atmosphere. Fish are the thing here, fresh and grilled perfectly. An equally minuscule upstairs is a bit quieter.

Taverna de Bebobos ★★

Cais da Ribeira, 25. ☎ 31 35 65. *Closed Sunday and March.* This restaurant is well over 100 years old, granite, woodbeamed and small, which contributes to the coziness and makes reservations imperative. The upstairs is more intimate. The cuisine is typical Portuguese, done as well as at all but a few much more costly restaurants. Grilled sardines are perfectly done, and the *caldeirada* (fish stew) is delicious. Because

of its small size reservations are strongly recommended.
No credit cards are accepted.

Standard Bar ★
Rua Infante Dom Henrique, 43 *(the street on the south edge of São Franicisco).* ☎ *239 04. Closed Sunday.* This is another small, crowded place that serves only a few dishes, but at very low prices. The cod *açorda* (in bread stew) is quite good.

DIRECTORY

AIRPORT • Pedras Rubras international airport is 16 k north of the city (☎ *948 21 44*). A taxi will cost under 2.000$00. Buses #44 and #56 connect with the central Pr. do Lisbōa. The main TAP office is at Pr. Mouzinho de Albuquerque, 105 in the Boavista rotunda (☎ *69 98 41*), which is a mile east of the Pr. da República at the top of the Av. do Almada.

INFORMATION • *Located at Rua Clube dos Fenianos, 25* (☎ *31 27 40*) on the west side of the city hall. Lots of advice is available about port tastings, boat trips up the Douro and vineyard tours.

POLICE • The main station (☎ *268 21*) is located on Rua Alexandre Herculano, which runs southeast of the Estacão de São Bento.

POST OFFICE AND TELEPHONES • The main post office (☎ *38 02 51*) is on the east side of Pr. do General H. Delgado by the city hall. Telephones are available until 11 p.m.

Shopping • Shopping is fun in Porto because one sees unusual products and the good shops are concentrated. Better stores center on the streets leading off Pr. da Liberdade, at the south end of Av. dos Aliados. Good streets are R. dos Clérigos, going west of the square, R. da Sa Bandeira, going northeast, and the parallel R. de Sta Catarina. The latter two host numerous shoe shops.

For all-in-one shopping there is a large mall called Centro Comércial de Brasileiraon Av. da Boavisto parallel to the river, northwest of the center.

Of course port wine is on sale all over town, but more fun to buy after touring the lodge itself, see above.

A small flea market can be found almost every day in front of the Cathedral square.

TRAINS AND BUSES • Three separate train stations are located in Porto. Local trains, such as those to Guimarães, embark from the Trinidade station north of the city hall. Most other trains depart from the inconvenient Estacão Campanhã (☎ *56 41 41*), at the east edge of the city. There is, for example, a 3-1/2-hour express to Lisbon. The station can easily be reached by a five-minute connection from the central Bento station a few steps southeast of Pr. da Liberdade at the southern end of Av. do Almeda. Service is very good to almost anywhere in Portugal.

There also are three separate bus depots. The main one is Garagem Atlantico (☎ *200 69 54*) on Rua Alexandre Herculano at Rua Alexandre Herculano, 366 which is west of the Estação de São Bento. It serves most of the country and handles the national RN lines. Another depot, Estação de Camionagem, is used for shorter trips. It is located at Pr. do Dona Felipa de Lencastre (☎ *200 61 21*), which is one block east of the Av. do Almada, by the Infantes hotel. The third depot is little used.

EXCURSIONS

The most peaceful Porto excursion is a *cruise* up the Douro river—and the most ideal cruise is to Pinhão with an overnight in Regua. Including all meals for two days and sleeping accommodations, the trip costs about 20.000$00 per person. This and shorter trips are conducted by Endouro at *Muro dos Balhoeiros, 104* (☎ *32 42 36*). Or, for those with less money or time, there are cruises of the river bridges offered by Cruzeiro das Tres Pontes. Boats depart hourly from a dock in Villa Nova de Gaia, behind the Ferreira port lodge. Service runs from May through Oct.; between 10 a.m. and 6 p.m., except Sun.

Porto is 50 k from the fine beach and canals of **Aveiro**, and 65 more from elegant **Viseu** with its museum. **Braga** with Baroque churches is 70 k north, and **Guimarães**, Portugal's birthplace, is 24 k southwest of it. All are described under separate headings in this chapter. There is also the pottery town of **Barcelos** and lovely **Amarante**, both described under Braga "Excursions."

One special excursion of about 60 miles from Porto is to visit the lovely manor house of Mateus, so familiar from the wine bottles of that name. Incidently, the Solar (as it is called) has no connection with the wine makers who simply pay for the right to include its picture on their bottles.

MATEUS ★

Population: 1865
Area code: 059; zip code: 5000

From downtown **Porto** *the simplest route is to take R. do Dr. Magalhães Lemos going east from a block north of the Pr. da Liberdade. It soon changes its name to R. do Passos Manuel, before entering a square at which one should continue in the same direction, now on R. de Mornado Mateus. Turn left at the next square to take the first right onto Av. de Ferão de Magalhães going north. The avenue feeds into the main Estrada da Circunvalação around Porto. Go left (west) to the first exit onto A-3 toward Braga. But take the first exit onto A-4 toward Amarante and Vila Real. In 62* k at Amarante, join N-15 to Vila Real in 36 k. Go 1 k on N-15 past Vila Real to a sign for a right turn to Mateus.

Solar de Mateus ★★

Open 9 a.m. until 1 p.m. and from 2 p.m. until 5 p.m. in summer only. Admission: 600$00 for a guided tour. This stands as the most elegant of all the Baroque manor houses in Portugal, perhaps because it was designed by an Italian. Suitably prefaced by a grand cedar-lined lawn, the house facade seems magical. A grand double staircase under a family escutcheon forms the center, whose deep recess emphasizes the sweep of wings on either side. Although somewhat busy, this style of whitewash facade with details picked out in granite epitomizes the Portuguese national style.

The house is still inhabited by the family who owns it, although not in summer, of course, which is beach time. As a result only certain parts are included on the tour. Left of the front is a fine Baroque chapel. Inside the main building is a grand hall with an extraordinary carved wood ceiling, almost matched by another in the main salon. Some of the furniture is attractive, and there is a small museum with pieces we wouldn't mind owning at all. After the tour, wander through one of the most beautiful gardens in the country.

TOMAR ★★★

Population: 14,821
Area code: 049; zip code: 2300

From **Lisbon** *take the autoestrada A-1 north to exit 7 at Entrncamento 80k, 1k east of which N-110 goes north to Tomar in 19 k. From* **Coimbra** *take A-1 south for 70 k to the Leiria exit, where N-113 is jointed going southeast through Fátima to Tomar in 40k. From* **Batalha** *take N-1 north for 11 k to Leiria and follow the preceding directions. From* **Marvão** *get back to N-246 and go west to Alpalhão for 25 k where N-118 continues west for 67 k to Rossio. There N-3 goes west to Villa Nova da Barquinha in 29 k. Two k west N-110 goes north to Tomar in 19 k.*

Trains *run often enough from Lisbon and take two hours, including a change at Santarém. It takes almost as long from closer Coimbra. The bus is slower by almost an hour from Lisbon.*

Tomar, a quaint town of cobblestone streets, straddles the river Nabão. Its quaintness, however, is not what draws tourists. In woods above the town, a church consecrated to secret rites was embellished ver the centuries by some of the greatest architecture in Portugal. And, nearby, on an island in the center of the Tagus river, reposes the 12th-century castle of Almourol peering above its wooded slope, the most romantic castle in Portugal.

When Jerusalem was captured in 1119 during the Second Crusade, a group of French knights created the Order of Knights Templar for the purposes of defending the Holy Sepulcher to the death, and of protecting pilgrims in Palestine. Despite such vows, Jerusalem was soon lost, but the order continued, now as a military arm of the Catholic Church. Within a century 20,000 members could be counted, who manned 9000 castles throughout Europe, and most European banking lay in its firm grasp. Kings begged contributions from the order for their wars and tread carefully in its presence, lest they antagonize such immense power. The order answered to no authority below the pope. Individual members, subject only to the Master of the order, strode the streets of Europe in white tunics blazoned with a red Maltese cross, afraid of no one up to and including the rank of king. Their rites were shrouded in deep mystery, known to no outsider.

In 1128 the Knights Templar were given land to erect a castle in Portugal by Dona Teresa, the mother of the first king of Portugal. Their contribution to her son Alfonso's military success against the Moors was substantial. In 1147 the order traded their original land for acreage at Tomar and there built a castle on a hill, completed in 1160. A church followed two years later; then all was surrounded by fortress walls. By the 14th century, however, the power of the order had become too threatening to people in high places. Phillip V of France arrested the Master of the Knights Templar in 1307 and executed him. Pope Clement V decreed the disbanding of the order five years later.

But a sympathetic King Dinis resurrected it in Portugal in 1320 by creating a similar organization with a new name—the Order of Christ. Later, Prince Henry the Navigator, as a third royal son, was given charge of this order in lieu of a throne. Its Maltese cross glowed fiery red on the sails Henry sent searching for undiscovered worlds. Prince Henry added to the Templar church at Tomar; Manuel I supplied a nave done in the Manueline style—including the most ornate, most photographed window in the country; and João III changed the order into a monastic brotherhood to which he contributed cells for the monks and a solemn neoclassical cloister. Additions were made over the course of five centuries, but none disturbed the lines of the 12th-century octagonal Templar church.

This church and its later embellishments are what bring the visitor to Tomar.

> The Convent of Christ reposes atop a wooded park on the west bank of the Nabão. Rua Serpa Pinto crosses the Ponte Velha and leads to the main square, Pr. da República. Here the 15th-century church of **São João Babtista** has an imposing later Manueline tower and a most elegant door. Parallel to R. Pinto, and three blocks south (left), Av. Dr. Candido Madureira climbs to the Sete Montes park, after passing the **Office of Tourism**. The road through the forest zigzags up to the 12th-century walls of the precinct to pass through a gate beside which stands the keep of the original castle. To the right are ruins of the palace built by Prince Henry. Parking is available.

Convento de Cristo ★★★

Open daily 9:30 a.m. to 12:30 p.m. and 2-6 p.m. (closes at 5 p.m. in winter). Admission: 300$00; 200$00 in winter. The complete monastery is a confusion of buildings, because it is formed of additions that spanned five centuries. All the additions were constrained by the desire to be close to, but not impinge on, the original Templar church. This goal is illustrated by the strange angle of the cloister walls protruding to the right of the entrance stairs, and in the constricted entrance to the church. The present entrance was added in the 16th century, designed by a Spaniard in his splendid Plateresque style. It is worth a moment's study of the exuberant, yet mannered, contained Plateresque to compare it later with the riotous Manueline style of Portugal. A plaque marks the original entrance.

The present entrance leads into the nave with the original octagonal Templar church, known as the *Charola*, to the right. Although many authorities claim the Charola was modeled on the Holy Sepulcher in Jerusalem, its polygonal shape and cupola match the Islamic Dome of the Rock more than any Christian prototype. Eight painted piers support a two-story octagon with an altar in the center. Coats of arms may be discerned painted on the cupola above. Except for a few paintings, some choir stalls and a number of 16th-century polychrome statues of saints leaning against the piers, little decoration survived the damage wrought by the occupying French in the 19th century. Enough remains to give some sense of the original look, but not of its intended functions.

Some say the knights attended services on horseback, while others claim that this was a place for vigils by novice knights. There are stories telling how the orientation of the building and details of its design provide secret messages about the location of buried treasures. But for most people the pleasure of seeing an unusual architectural design from the hoary early Middle Ages suffices without rationales.

The nave was added on early in the 16th century to form a more typical church, although its construction required breaking through the west wall of the Charola. Exuberant Manueline decoration makes the hall airy, in contrast with the more intimate charola. A doorway to the north leads to the Cloistro do Cemitario, named for two 16th-century tombs laying within—one being that of Baltasar de Faria, the first Inquisitor-General of Portugal. The cloister was built by Prince Henry the Navigator and later covered with *azulejos*.

On its right, after an alcove with more lovely azulejos, is another of the seven cloisters of the monastery—the Cloistro da Lavagem, containing tanks for water. On its left is the sacristy with a small museum.

A portal from the south side of the nave lets out to the splendid two-story Cloistro Principal, added by João III in the middle of the 16th century. Its Renaissance neoclassicism derives, as its unadorned sweeping arch and columns suggest, from the Italian Palladio. At each corner a grand spiral stair leads up to the terrace of the adjoining Santa Barbara cloister for a view of the window that epitomizes the extreme of Manueline ornateness.

This window is actually the central window at the end of the church nave viewed from outside. It was carved in 1510, although the identity of the artist is unknown. At the bottom a bust of a sea captain sprouts roots of a cork tree that rises through seaweed, coral and pieces of chain up masts framing the window sides. Above are symbols of Manuel I—a shield and a cross between two spheres. "Cables" run from the window to two turrets, one wrapped in chain (left), the other by a buckle. If the latter is seen as a garter, then the turrets might represent the orders of the Golden Fleece and of the Garter, respectively. Many pieces have been broken and lost, which only make us wonder how it would look entire.

The remainder of the convent is used as a hospital by the military and is presently off limits to tourists.

WHERE TO STAY

Tomar provides perfectly acceptable hotels, but another option is the Pousada de São Pedro, Estalgem de Lago Azul or the Estalagem Vale da Ursa, all on sylvan lakes nearby.

MODERATE ($50-$99)

On the river Zêzere:

Estalgem Lago Azul   **R1st-class ★★**

Casstanheira, 2240 Ferreira do Zêzere (From Tomar head north on N-110 toward Venda Nova and Pintado. In 7 k, after Pintado, turn right on N-238 toward Aguas Belas, looking for a right turn in 9 k onto N-348 to Ferreira do Zêzere. Continue on N-348 through the town for about 11, the last of which provide lovely views from a bumpy road.) Rooms: 20. ☎ 36 1 45; FAX 36 16 64. This hotel shows clear signs of wear and seems dark but it is all air-conditioned and has an attractive pool. What it offers as lovely a lake view as anyone could want, and peace and quiet. If yo stick to the fish, the restaurant will please. A sight-seeing boat stop by for river cruises.

In Castelo do Bode:

Pousada de São Pedro 2nd-class ★ ★
Castelo de Bode (take N-110 south for 7 k, then N-358 east for a final 7 k Rooms: 15. ☎ 38 11 75; Telex 42392. The building was erected in th 1950s to house engineers constructing the Castelo de Bode dam Today it is a pousada that offers quiet and the best view of the dam Although why someone would want to contemplate a dam when th lake above is so lovely seems a little strange. The structure is not par ticularly imposing and its high tension lines rather spoil what scener there is. On the other hand, the hotel has just been remodeled, afte a terrible fire in 1991, to very comfortable standards and is a pleasan place to spend a night. Even better is the annex, a largish house 10 feet from the Pousada. It is tastefully decorated, the prices are 20% les than in the main hotel and the views take in the attractive pousad rather than the unattractive dam. The pousada restaurant produce quite good food.

Near Cernache do Bonjardim:

Estalagem Vale da Ursa R1st-class ★ ★
On N-238, 10 k southwest of Cernache do Bonjardim (Take N-238 north west of Tomar for 30 k to the Zêzere river.) Rooms: 12. ☎ 995 11; FA 995 94. Now here is a hotel that provides calming lake views, along with quiet, tennis and fishing. However, the public spaces and bed rooms are dated and showing signs of wear. They are, as the British say "a little off." Time spent on the terrace overlooking the reservoir will make you forget about almost any concern, however. Fresh fish in the restaurant can be sublime.

In Tomar:

Dos Templários 1st-class ★
Largo Candido dos Reis, 1 (beside the public garden). Rooms: 84. ☎ 32 17 30; FAX 32 21 91; Telex 14434. The best feature of this hotel is its views of the convent on its hill. Otherwise, it provides the service expected of its category and ordinary bedrooms, but, considering it moderate prices, there is no reason to complain.

Residencial Trovador R1st-class
Rua Dr. Joaquim Ribeiro (near the bus station). Rooms: 30. ☎ 32 25 67 FAX 32 21 94. This hotel is pleasant enough and the service is friendly but it lies outside the center of the old town and lacks the views of the Templários, which makes it the second choice.

INEXPENSIVE (UNDER $50)

Residencial União   R2nd-class ★

Rua Serpa Pinto, 91 (near the Pr. da República). Rooms: 21. ☎ 31 28 31. Airy, tastefully decorated rooms all incorporate sparkling bathrooms. In the most expensive high season, they are a bargain; out of season—at 20 percent less—they can only be called a steal.

Pensão Luanda   R2nd-class ★

Av. Marquês de Tomar, 13-15 (across the public gardens). Rooms: 14. ☎ 31 29 29. The location offers attractive views and the hotel itself is modern, clean and hospitable. Prices are very modest.

WHERE TO EAT

With two exceptions, restaurants in Tomar specialize in blandness. The best choice is located 2 k outside of town.

MODERATE ($15-$30)

Chico Elias   ★★

Algarvias (take N-349-3 west toward Torres Novas for about 2 k. The restaurant is announced by no sign, so one must look for a grey farmhouse with a green door on the right side of the road.) ☎ 310 67. Closed Tuesday. The decor is utterly rustic, but the cooking is inventive and tasteful. Among the delectable entrees are cod with pork, rabbit stewed in a gourd, and a stew of snails, sausage and ham. Reservations are essential.

Chez Nous   ★

Rua Dr. Joaquim Jacinto, 31 (between the two river bridges). ☎ 31 47 43. Closed Tuesdays. Unlike the other restaurants in town that strive for blandness, the French taste of the owner irrepressibly infuses his food. There are interesting beef dishes, and cod combinations even the Portuguese never thought of.

EXCURSIONS

Fátima ★ of the miracles lies on the way to **Batalha** ★★★★★ and its incredible monastery, a trip of 50 k. Both are described in the Environs of Lisbon chapter under "Batalha." The charming fortified hilltop town of **Marvão** ★★★, described under its own heading in the Eastern Portugal chapter, is 130 k east. Directions are included in the beginning of the Tomar section.

The most romantic Tomar excursion is to the castle of **Almourol** ★★, which sits atop a wooded isle in the middle of the Tejo river. It seems the stuff of fairy tales.

Drive south from Tomar on N-110 for 19k to turn east on N-3, after Atalaia. In about 5 k comes Tancos, on the Tejo, after which a sign in about 2 k directs a right turn down to the river.

Castelo Almourol ★

The tiny island in the wide, quiet Tagus is improbably densely wooded, so its castle flies above the trees. It is an archtypical medieval fortress, straight from all our imaginations—ten golden-hued stone towers that anchor walls surrounding a massive square keep. Because the island is a hill, castle parts stand at different elevations to lend the false perspective of a larger structure. Early in the morning, when mist envelopes the river, the castle floats in a dream.

A Roman fortress first crowned the site before the Knights Templar—as part of a strategy of recapturing land from the Moors and then raising defensive castles to retain it—built the present castle in 1171. In little more than a century the Moors had been driven so far south that this castle lost its defensive purpose and was abandoned. Abandoned it remains, although an appropriately weathered boatman is pleased to motor visitors either out to the castle or around it for a nominal fee.

VIANA DO CASTELO

See "Braga" under "Excursions."

VISEU ★★★

Population: 21,454
Area code: 032; zip code: 3500

From **Lisbon** *A-1 runs north for 243 k to the exit for Aveiro and Viseu. IP-5 east leads to Viseu in 67 k, with a final 2 k on N-2 as signs direct. From* **Porto** *take the autoestrada A-1 south for 46 k to the exit for Aveiro and IP-5, which goes east to Viseu in 67 k, with a final 2 k on N-2 as signs direct. From* **Coimbra** *take A-1 north for 60k to the exit for Aveiro and Viseu where IP-5 goes east for a final 67 k, then 2 k on N-2 as signs direct. From* **Guarda** *take IP-5 which begins north then turns west for 68 k.*

Trains *from Lisbon and Coimbra require changes and take 5 hours and 1-1/2 hours respectively. From Porto the trip consumes just under four hours. Buses travel in about the same amount of time.*

Viseu is a peaceful, attractive city that serves as the capital of the Dão wine region. In many ways it is a typical Portuguese town, but the typical features seem more enchanting in Viseu. There are the usual stands of 16th-century houses, a large cathedral and cathedral square. But the 16th-century houses, untypically, are arranged on wide streets to show them to fine effect; the Cathedral is grand; and its square is expansive and surrounded by especially imposing buildings. While every town in Portugal seems to display a pretty whitewashed baroque church with details picked out by contrasting stone, Viseu's Misericordia church presents the loveliest face of them all.

Unique to Viseu were the two Renaissance artists who lived and worked here, combining forces to decorate the Cathedral. Today their production is enshrined in a fine museum. Gaspar Vaz joined Vasco Fernandes in the early part of the 16th century, to decorate the Viseu Cathedral altar. Led by these masters, a school of painting known as the Viseu School assembled the finest Portuguese paintings of the era. In particular, the later works of Vasco Fernandes excel in sensitive portraiture and vibrant color. To the Portuguese he is known simply as "O Grão Vasco," the Grand Vasco.

> *From* **Lisbon**, **north** *and* **west** *N-2 becomes Av. Emidio Navarro as the Pavia river is crossed. Turn right just after the first plaza along Av. Cap. Silva Pereira, which reaches the major intersection of Largo de Santa Cristina in three blocks. A left turn would lead to parking in two blocks, but parking is often available in the more interesting main plaza, Pr. da República (a.k.a. Pr. Rossio) by taking a soft right on R. Formosa for two blocks. From* **Guarda** *N-16 becomes Rua 5 de Outubro in the town and goes straight to the major intersection of Largo de Santa Cristina. Here a sharp left would lead to parking in two blocks, but parking is often available in the more interesting main plaza, Pr. da República (a.k.a. Pr. Rossio), by continuing straight for two blocks.*

The splendid Cathedral square, Adro da Sé, stands on the highest part of the town, anchoring the convoluted streets of the old town that rise to meet it. Two blocks below, the tree-lined, small park of the Pr. da República faces the townhall and incorporates the very Baroque **São Francisco** with fine azulejos inside. From the northwest corner of this plaza, R. Nunes de Carvalho climbs to meet the Cathedral, passing through a remaining gate in the original town wall just before disgorging in the Cathedral square.

This square is an open plateau overlooking the town. On its east side stands the grey Cathedral; beside it, on the north, is the former Bishop's palace, now the **Grão Vasco Museum**; and on the west is the lovely **Misericordia church**. Once this was the loveliest square in the country, anchored at both ends by picturesque churches of different eras and styles, now it is a parking lot. Look above the cars or blot them out with your hand to see what the plaza could have been.

WHAT TO SEE AND DO

Cathedral ★★

Open daily 9 a.m. to noon and 2-7 p.m. The treasury closes at 5 p.m. Admission: 100$00, to the treasury. Little that is visible remains from the 12th-century original, remodeled, as was the case with so many churches in Europe, in the 16th and 17th centuries and then redecorated in the 18th. Twin towers outside remain from that original church, but topped by 18th-century crowns. The 17th-century facade seems an afterthought, as bored looking Evangelists march around the portal. Yet, a surprisingly elegant space waits inside.

Although the aisles were removed in the 16th century, original, massive, early Gothic columns remain, and overhead, the ceiling was redone with graceful ribs in the form of ropes knotted at intervals. Keystones present the coats of arms of the first bishop, Alfonso V, and of King João II. The barrel ceiling above the altar was painted in the 17th century, and a century later the original altar retable by Vasco and others was removed to the Grão Vasco museum in favor of the present Baroque confection.

Azulejos line the north transept (left) leading to a sacristy, roofed by charmingly painted wood, and to stairs up to the high choir. The stalls are lovingly carved into fanciful animals. From here the upper level of a fine Renaissance cloister may be entered.

Before descending to the ground floor, a visit to the chapterhouse and the Cathedral treasury is worthwhile. Among miscellany, the treasury contains two lovely 13th-century Limoge coffers and a 12th-century Bible. The experience will be heightened if the guide is the sacristan, who delights in performing slights of hand. The ground floor of the cloisters blends neoclassical arches on Ionic columns with 18th-century *azulejos* on the walls. The chapel of Our Lady of Mercy has a fine retable in low relief of the Descent from the Cross. Note the elegant Gothic doorway that leads back to the Cathedral.

Museu Grão Vasco ★★

Open Tuesday-Sunday 9:30 a.m. to 12:30 p.m. and 2-5 p.m. Closed Mon. Admission: 200$00, free on Sunday. In this former bishop's palace fine carvings are displayed on the ground floor along with a collection of Virgins of lesser interest, ceramics, Arraiolos carpets, and a small group of interesting early paintings. The second floor is devoted to furniture and ecclesiastic plate, with a few nice watercolors by the 19th-century painter Alberto de Sousa. But it is the third floor for which the museum is proudly named. Here are the paintings of Vasco Fernandes, the Grand Vasco, who spent his last 30 years in Viseu creating his finest work.

In room one hangs part of the former retable of the Cathedral. The work is by several hands as the lower figures reveal. *Saint Peter* on his throne and the *Martyrdom of Saint Sebastian*, with a background reminiscent of Holland, show a fine aptitude for the painter's art, although whether these were painted by Vasco Fernandes or by Gaspar Vaz remains in dispute. Room two is entirely devoted to the Grand Vasco, and the *Crucifixion* in luminous reds and yellows is memorable. Room three contains two masterworks by Gaspar Vaz: a triptych of the Last Supper and *Christ in the House of Martha*. Room four presents a fine series of 14 panels from the Cathedral retable depicting the life of Christ. Note Balthasar in the *Adoration of the Magi* panel depicted as an Indian from newly discovered Brazil.

Igreja de Misericordia ★

Although the interior is of slight interest, the exterior, completed in 1775, presents—silhouetted against the open sky—the Portuguese Baroque church par excellence. Elegant stone window-surrounds echo the curves of the central roofcomb. The towers are stately and the balcony above the door is a fine touch. This example makes it evident that an earlier gap between ecclesiastic and secular architecture has narrowed. For without its small cross and towers, this facade could well front a grand mansion.

Stairs at the rear of the Cathedral, by the south end of the apse, lead down to **Rua Direita**, *a pedestrian walk lined with fine 18th-century houses. In two short blocks the street intersects with another. Turn back left along* **Rua dos Andrades** *to traverse three short blocks of 16th-century houses, some corbelled, interspersed with crafts' shops. Rua Direita continues right from this meeting and soon arrives at Rua Formosa, a right turn on which leads back to the Pr. da República.*

WHERE TO STAY

Except for festival times, hotels in Viseu are adequate to the demand. None are grand, but all offer good value for low prices. The following are close enough to inexpensive that none lesser need be considered.

MODERATE ($50-$99)

Grão Vasco   1st-class ★

Rua Gaspar Barreiros (on a park half a block south of the Pr. da República). Rooms: 100. ☎ *42 35 11; FAX 270 47; Telex 53608.* This low, modern building frames a swimming pool and a pleasant park. Bedrooms are somewhat larger than most, although not the most tasteful. A pleasant grassy area surrounds a pool.

Moinho de Vento   R2nd-class ★

Rua Paulo Emilio, 13 (2 blocks then a short right along Rua de M. Bombarda, which leaves the southwest corner of Pr. da República). Rooms: 30. ☎ *42 41 16; FAX 42 96 62; Telex 52698.* Although lacking a pool and garden, the Moinho is otherwise as good a choice as the preceding. Bedrooms are more modern but not quite as large, although comfortable and available at an engaging price.

INEXPENSIVE (-$50)

Avenida — R3rd-class ★

Av. Alberto Sampaio, 1 (a few steps west of the south end of the Pr. da República). Rooms: 40. ☎ 42 34 32; FAX 267 43; Telex 52522. This hotel has just been renovated, which may change the rating. Now there is a dramatic two-story skylight brightening the interior, and the bedrooms have been cleanly redone. Aesthetically, these now are the most attractive accommodations in Viseu, although lacking some of the services of others.

WHERE TO EAT

Cooking in Viseu is more adventurous than in similar towns. Moderately priced treats await anyone dining at the following choices. Of course, one should have a bottle or a carafe of Dão to wash down the meal.

MODERATE ($15-$30)

O Cortiço ★

Rua Augusto Hilário, 43 (a few steps southeast of the statue of Dom Duarte below the Cathedral square). ☎ 42 38 53. Rustic with granite walls, this restaurant serves the most authentic cuisine in town. The service could be more gracious, but the wine-fed rabbit and the veal with rice are delicious. *Amex, MasterCard and Visa accepted*

Trave Negra ★

Rua dos Loureiros, 40 (three blocks down the hill northeast from the Cathedral on the corner of Av. Emidio Navarro where N-2 leads into town). ☎ 261 38. This candle- and lantern-lit place serves well-considered food with elegant touches. Reservations are recommended.
Amex, Diners, MasterCard and Visa accepted.

INEXPENSIVE (UNDER $15)

Cacimbo ★

Rua Alexandre Herculano, 95 (One block east of the Pr. da República, R Herculano runs south). ☎ 228 94. Come here for the roast suckling pig in the window.

DIRECTORY

- **INFORMATION** • Located on Av. Gulbenkian (go south from the Pr. República until a right fork which leads to the tourist office). ☎ 279 94.

- **TRAINS AND BUSES** • Train service to Viseu was discontinued in 1990. The bus station is located on Av. Dr. António José de Almeida, about five blocks north of the Pr. República (☎ 41 23 37). From Lisbon (via Leiria) the express bus takes about 5 hours, or 3 hours from Coimbra.

Service is about twice per day. Less frequent are buses from Porto, that arrive in just under 3 hours. Service to Guarda is frequent and takes under 2 hours.

EXCURSIONS

Viseu is centrally situated for many other sights of interest. There's the fortified hill towns of **Guarda** and its environs 68 k to the east, **Aveiro** for beaches an equal distance to the west, the medieval university of **Coimbra** 65 k west and 74 k south, **Porto** 65 k west and 46 k north, with Baroque **Braga** 54 k beyond that. Except for Guarda which is treated in the Eastern Portugal chapter, all are described under their own headings in this chapter.

EASTERN PORTUGAL

Roman Temple in Évora

Historical Profile: The End of the Monarchy and its Aftermath

When the last survivor of the house of Avís died in 1580, the only direct claim to the crown belonged to Felipe II of Spain, who bribed and lobbied his way to the palace. For the next 60 years the Spanish ruled Portugal. Initially, her kings respected Portuguese institutions and left governing to the native Portuguese, but they increased their control as time passed, fostering growing resentment. What followed was more a soap opera than academic history.

The most powerful Portuguese noble of the time was the Duke of Bragança, the overlord of a third of a million people. Fearing that he might serve as a rallying point for rebellions, the Spanish tried to seduce him with power, even granting him permission to raise troops to preserve civil order. Of course it was not long before the Duke using the distraction of a civil war in Spain, turned these troops against the Spanish. He conquered Portugal in a matter of days and crowned himself João IV in 1640. Portugal's long, last dynasty had begun.

A number of Portuguese nobles still believed, however, that their fortunes lay with Spain and resettled across the border. The commander of the Portuguese colony of Ceuta in Morocco handed control to Spain, which has kept it ever since. By 1656, after inconclusive battles and vain attempts at diplomacy, João died, still seeking international recognition for his monarchy. His son Afonso VI was crowned king at age 13. Some childhood disease had partially paralyzed Afonso's left arm and leg, and slowed his speech and understanding. When he married the daughter of the Duke of Savoy, he celebrated by eating alone in bed while his bride entertained the guests. To no great surprise, she soon departed for a convent to petition the Pope for an annulment.

Circumstances were not conducive, to say the least, to producing an heir. Afonso was forced to resign in favor of his normal brother Pedro who, after the annulment of Afonso's marriage, wed his brother's wife himself and took control of the state.

In time Pedro's son João V came to the throne, a well-educated, shy young man. He married Maria Ana, a daughter of the Archduke of Austria. When three years had passed with no heir, João promised God that he would build a magnificent monastery if his wife were delivered of a child. After his wish was fulfilled, João constructed the sumptuous monastery-palace of Mafra. He also built hospitals and fountains, founded libraries, and created Portugal's Royal Academy of History, before dying in 1750.

João was succeeded by José I, as indolent a king as ever reigned. He spent his days playing cards, listening to opera, or taking outings to Belém estuary. At 8 p.m. he would return to his Lisbon palace, but not present himself for affairs of state until 11 p.m. Work for him consisted of signing papers, for he left governing to a virtual dictator—Sebastião José de Carvalloe e Melo, Count of Oeiras and Marquis of Pombal, nicknamed "the Pasha."

Despite his titles, Pombal descended from a mere cavalry officer, but had used an uncle in the government and marriage above his station to achieve the post of prime minister by the time he was 31. He claimed expertise in economics, a sorely needed science in a country bankrupt from the long effort to free itself from Spain. Pombal found inspiration in England's capitalist system, and tried to impose a similar economy on Portugal. His country, however, lacked both England's traditions and its significant middle class, so he was able to create only the semblance, not the substance of an English economy. A company he founded to control the Brazilian trade modeled on Britain's East India Company, for example, went quickly bankrupt.

Pombal's power, so strong that he ruled as a virtual dictator for a quarter of a century, stemmed from his fortitude after the great earthquake in Lisbon in 1755. The heart of the city was leveled. For nine months the king and court lived in tents, immobilized by an awareness of the magnitude of the destruction and daunted by the difficulty of resurrecting it. Pombal stepped forward to rebuild the capital, earning the king's undying admiration.

Empowered, Pombal set out to increase his control over the mighty nobles. An attempted assassination of the King gave Pombal his opportunity to harass them. Although the actual culprits were probably relatives of a woman the king had seduced, Pombal suspended the normal rules of justice for this case he called "regicide" while his investigators and police interrogated one lord after another. At the inquiry's end, the mighty had been cowed and a score had lost their heads.

Now almost all offices of power, both in the government and the church, were held by a relative or henchman of Pombal. Pombal reorganized the educational system to teach Portuguese instead of Latin grammar for the first time. He established a Royal Board of Censorship which proscribed the writings of Hobbes, Locke, Voltaire, and any others who intimated that a king's power might be less than absolute.

When King José I died in 1777, his daughter, as regent, called Pombal to audience and summarily fired him. Five years later, under indictment for, but as yet unconvicted of embezzlement, Pombal died. If Portugal verged on bankruptcy before Pombal, it reached destitution after. Pay for civil servants fell months in arrears; the royal bulls, horses, and mules were sold to raise cash; and worse was to come.

Revolution in France had elevated Napoleon to Emperor. At war with England, he pressured Portugal to renounce all treaties with her ancient ally. When Portugal agreed only to neutrality, Napoleon invaded, frightening the royal family and court to dash aboard 15 ships for Brazil. There they set up a monarchy in exile.

England did not forsake her ally, sending 16,000 troops for Portugal's defense under Sir Arthur Wellesly. They defeated the French who retreated to safety in Spain. A second time the French invaded Portugal, but now Wellesly chased them back into Spain where he routed them at Talavera. Wellesly was rewarded for his victory with the title of Viscount, later Duke, of Wellington. When the French attempted one more time, in 1810, to take Portugal, Wellington's troops met them in the stately forest of Bucaço and sent them home for good.

The Peninsular War had ended, but Portugal's monarch remained abroad enjoying the congenial climate of Brazil. A regency tried to rule in his place with English assistance, but the liberalism sweeping Europe by now had infected Portugal. Soon a new kind of Parliament assembled based on proportional representation rather than old inherited titles. Its members invited the king to return, but only with the status of a constitutional monarch, rather than an absolute king.

King João VI returned in 1821 after a 13-year sojourn abroad, leaving his eldest son, Dom Pedro, as regent in Brazil. João formally accepted the new constitution, but his Spanish wife and second son, Don Miguel, remained unrepentant absolutists. When the King left Lisbon to quash a revolution they fomented in Sintra, the frightened Parliament, without its monarch in attendance, dissolved itself. João VI died in 1826 after granting Brazil its independence.

The son who had remained in Brazil thus became Pedro II, the Emperor of Brazil, and simultaneously Pedro IV, the King of Portugal. Pedro preferred his life in Rio de Janeiro, so ceded his Portuguese crown to his brother Don Miguel, the absolutist. There was one condition to the deal—Miguel had to marry Pedro's daughter, Maria. Miguel duly took over the government in 1828, but neglected to marry his niece, enraging Pedro. To protect Maria's inheritance, Pedro abdicated his Brazilian crown to come to fight for Portugal's. Miguel besieged him when he landed in Porto, but Pedro broke through and rushed to Lisbon. By 1834, with help from the English and Spanish, Pedro IV was again the King of Portugal. In the three months left of his life, he restored the republican constitution and, following the lead of other European countries, confiscated the vast lands belonging to the Church.

Maria II was 15 when her father died, no age to control the powerful forces of liberalism, anarchy, and radicalism rampaging through Portugal and the rest of Europe. She endured strife and continual threats of revolt until her death in 1853, which preceded the death of her son and heir Pedro V by only 8 years. Pedro's brother Luis I, however, managed a reign of 28 years until 1889. He was blessed with an able prime minister, Fontes, who worked economic miracles by building roads and railroads, laying a telephone cable to Brazil, and, at the same time, significantly reducing the national debt.

The reign of Luis' son Carlos I was abruptly curtailed, along with his life and the life of his heir, by assassins' bullets in 1908. Antimonarchical republicanism was in the air—Carlo's second son, Manuel II, would be the last king. Though republicans had little success in taking over the Parliament through elections, they managed to infiltrate the ranks of the navy, and, in 1910, warships bombarded the palace outside Lisbon. Manuel fled to England and a republic was proclaimed.

The republican rebels of 1910 were idealists opposed to all that the monarchy represented. They regarded religion as a superstition, yet maintained an unfailing faith in the worth of individuals. They removed saints' days as official holidays and opened new universities for education at a nominal fee. They also allowed just one political party, their own, in elections they invariably won.

When problems began to surface, as they must for any form of government, republican ideals became lost in simpler, more violent solutions. After a minor incursion by advocates of the deposed King, the government arrested hundreds while severely limiting freedoms of the press and speech. Bayonets became the normal tools for ending workers' strikes. Whenever the Parliament became intransigent, governments were created during vacation adjournments. So governments came and went with the seasons—four in 1919, seven in 1920, and five in 1921—while the *escudo* fell to one-twentieth of its prerevolutionary value. For idealistic reasons, Portugal entered World War I on the side of the Allies. Afterwards, she had to stand in line with those on the losing side to beg the League of Nations for financial assistance.

To say the least, democracy was not working and everyone knew it. In 1925 three attempted army coups failed; then, in 1926, one succeeded. Gomes da Costa, a general in the Great War, formed a new government, assigning Dr. António de Oliveira Salazar, a professor of economics at Coimbra University, to the all-important post of Finance Minister. Salazar had resisted earlier offers of government posts and demanded extraordinary powers to buy his acceptance of this one, including veto power over any proposed government expenditure. In office, Salazar turned annual deficits into surpluses and reduced the long-term debt, earning reverence for his financial legerdemain. By 1932 he was named President of the Council, or Prime Minister.

Ironically, the last king of Portugal died on the day Salazar accepted his post in the government that he would come to rule as a dictator. Salazar was a strange man, so private that little is known of his personal life. Perhaps asexual, he never married. His sister looked after his house.

Salazar's first act as prime minister was to produce a new constitution. According to his model government, the Parliament consisted of two houses—an assembly elected by direct suffrage plus a "corporate chamber" in which representation was based on economic power. Consistent with the tenets of fascism, businesses were organized into federations, workers into unions, and professionals into orders, each represented by parliament delegates. But only one party existed, Salazar's National Union (UN). Salazar created the PIDE, secret police, to maintain order. Twenty-thousand informers crowded its ranks before long.

During the Spanish Civil War, Salazar's sympathies lay with Franco, and he provided supplies, although he committed no troops. In World War II, he maintained neutrality against pressure from both sides for more partisan commitment. He sold essential ores to Hitler but allowed Allied ships to put into Portuguese ports. After the war, he constructed three dams to electrify Portugal and a quarter of Spain as well, and used some of the water for irrigation. However, by the 1960s his economic miracle no longer was effective. Portugal had fallen badly into debt again, while her colonies in Africa posed equally severe problems.

Portugal still controlled Africa's Guinea, Mozambique, and Angola, the residue of her explorations in the 16th century. Angola alone covered half a million square miles with a population almost as large as Portugal's. But countries all over Africa had begun crying for independence and, one by one, received it. Only Portugal decided to fight to retain her colonies, committing 50,000 troops to Africa, where, as a foretaste of the United States' experience in Vietnam, they fought guerrillas they could not catch. The undertaking was expensive, the conscription it necessitated was unpopular, and the effort in no way stopped the inevitability of the independence movement.

In 1968 Salazar suffered a stroke, causing brain damage from which he never recovered. He was replaced by Dr. Marcelo Caetano, a founding member of Salazar's party. Salazar himself did not die until 1970, still believing he controlled the government because no one had the courage to tell him otherwise. Caetano called for elections the next year, the first in which women voted, but for slates that still comprised only candidates acceptable to the ruling party. As combat in Africa continued, unrest in the universities and among junior officers in the army increased.

On April 24, 1974 the citizens of Lisbon woke to find their streets filled with flower-bedecked tanks. This bloodless "flower Revolution" exiled the government to Brazil and elevated General Spinola, a hero of the war in Guinea, to the presidency of a leftist government. As a military man, Spinola appreciated that force could not hold Portugal's colonies. He granted independence to them all in 1975.

Spinola named Avelino Gonçalves, a Marxist, as his Minister of Labor, in an effort to represent the political spectrum in his government. Gonçalves used his position to manipulate appointments in the government-controlled media until none but communists ran this powerful resource. From this base Gonçalves was able to raise himself to the position of president of the Council (prime minister), forcing Spinola to resign. Then Gonçalves purged the military and universities—telling students they could fire any professors they disliked, which the students happily did. It was again a time of economic crisis as 700,000 refugees from former African colonies flooded into Portugal, 300,000 to Lisbon alone.

By the time of its 1975 elections, Portugal had grown intensely politicized, as if making up instantly for centuries of deprivation. Posters on every available wall covered other posters to a measurable depth. On election eve, one could walk any street in the country and stay informed—every radio and television was tuned to the results. The communists were soundly defeated by socialists, but Gonçalves refused to step down. Risings began in the north, and farmers from the south marched on Lisbon, threatening a food blockade. In 1976 the military removed Gonçalves.

One of the army officers who had organized this putsch became president. He chose as his prime minister a longtime socialist—Mario Soares. Numerous changes in governments have

taken place since 1976 by normal democratic process, without arm
uprisings or civil disturbances. It may be that Portugal at last ha
found democracy. Over the years, Soares has been voted out of offic
and then voted back in. Presently he serves as the President of the re
public, with a government that represents about the same values a
our own Republican party.

EASTERN PORTUGAL

This chapter covers two areas, both east of Lisbon. One comprises the heartland of Portugal, called the Alentejo, the other the Estrella mountains. The two regions could hardly be more different, sharing only an eastern location.

The Alentejo (from *alem Tejo*, "beyond the Tejo" River) is a flat plain, occupying one third of Portugal. It bakes in summer and chills in the winter. The horizon stretches wide in clear air over land growing wheat, olives and the famed cork oaks of the country (recognized by naked strips on tree-trunks). Farms are huge, deriving from great Roman latifúndias, and the population sparse (only one Portuguese in twelve) clustered in widely separated towns. The people are poor in general—one can still see men in sheepskin capes and women in traditional black felt hats. Food ranges from pork (the region is famed for pigs feed on flavorful acorns), as in *porco à Alentejana*, to garlic soup, as in *açorda à Alentejana*. Wines from the area are high in alcohol content and rich in taste.

In contrast to the flat plains of the Alentejo, a series of mountain peaks forms the Serra da Estrela, "Mountains of the Stars." Views can be astonishing, as can the hairpin curves of the roads. This mountain wall on Portugal's eastern border became a fortress armed with redouts in the Middle Ages. Many of these forts remain, for the romantic in us, along with the mountain scenery. Here habitations are happenstance, and the food tends toward fresh trout and delicious *serra* cheeses.

Although the Alentejo is a huge expanse, the sights of interest concentrate around Estremoz, with most of the most entertaining forming a circle not wider than 50 miles. In the Estrela, fortresses circle Guarda for about 25 miles. Thus, each of the two areas lends itself to settling in one spot to tour its surroundings for two days or three.

In the Alentejo, lovely **Évora** ★★★★ stands two thirds of the way across the width of the country, about two hours from the capital. It is an elegant town, with a day's pleasant sights for savoring. Nearby is **Estremoz** ★★ with one of the most beautiful pousadas in the country. There are wonderful accommodations at the Hotel Convento de São Paulo in **Redondo**, close by, and special accommodations in Évora too, if a step below the exalted levels of those two mentioned first. **Elvas** ★★, with extensive 18th-century fortifications, stands 22 miles west of Estremoz, and **Marvão** ★★★, with lovely medieval walls, lies less than 30 miles north. **Arraiolos**, for rugs, and **Borba**, for antiques, both provide shopping interest in the area.

Little **Guarda** ★★ in the Serra da Estrela sits 160 miles north above Estremoz, serving as the center for a concentration of atmospheric hilltop villages fortified in the Middle Ages.

ARRAIOLOS

Population: 3567
Area code: 068; zip code: 7350

*Arraiolos is 22 k north of **Évora** by N-114-4, which becomes N370. From **Estremoz** it is 43 k west along N-4.*

For over two centuries this village has been in the business of making carpets. Portuguese exploration of the east brought an awareness of Indian and Persian carpets, which soon became the rage in upper-class Portuguese households. By the middle of the 17th-century homegrown copies were being produced in the area around Arraiolos. Fashions changed in time to favor more formal Aubusson styles from France, and Arraiolos kept pace.

Today the carpets are still produced by the same techniques used two centuries ago. Rather than woven, as are oriental carpets, women in Arraiolos embroider with wool in gros point on a linen canvas. Styles and colors cover a wide range, in fact, almost any design or color scheme can be custom-made. Being entirely created by hand, these carpets are not cheap—costs run about $120 per square yard. What they are is future heirlooms since they easily stand up to a century of wear, retain their colors, being naturally died wool, and do not burn.

Rua Dr. Manuel Pinto, the main street of Arraiolos, consists of little more than shops selling "tapetes." A cooperative at the corner of the main square carries a large selection where prices should be less, although they generally turn out to be about the same as those charged by the retail shops. Other than at this cooperative, some gentle bargaining may pay off in savings.

If you tire of shopping, Arraiolos provides a lovely 14th-century **castle** perched on the highest ground, for exploring. Also, just south of the town hall in the main square stands **Misericórdia** with elegant azulejos inside.

BORBA

Population: 4652
Area code: 066; zip code: 7350

EASTERN PORTUGAL 237

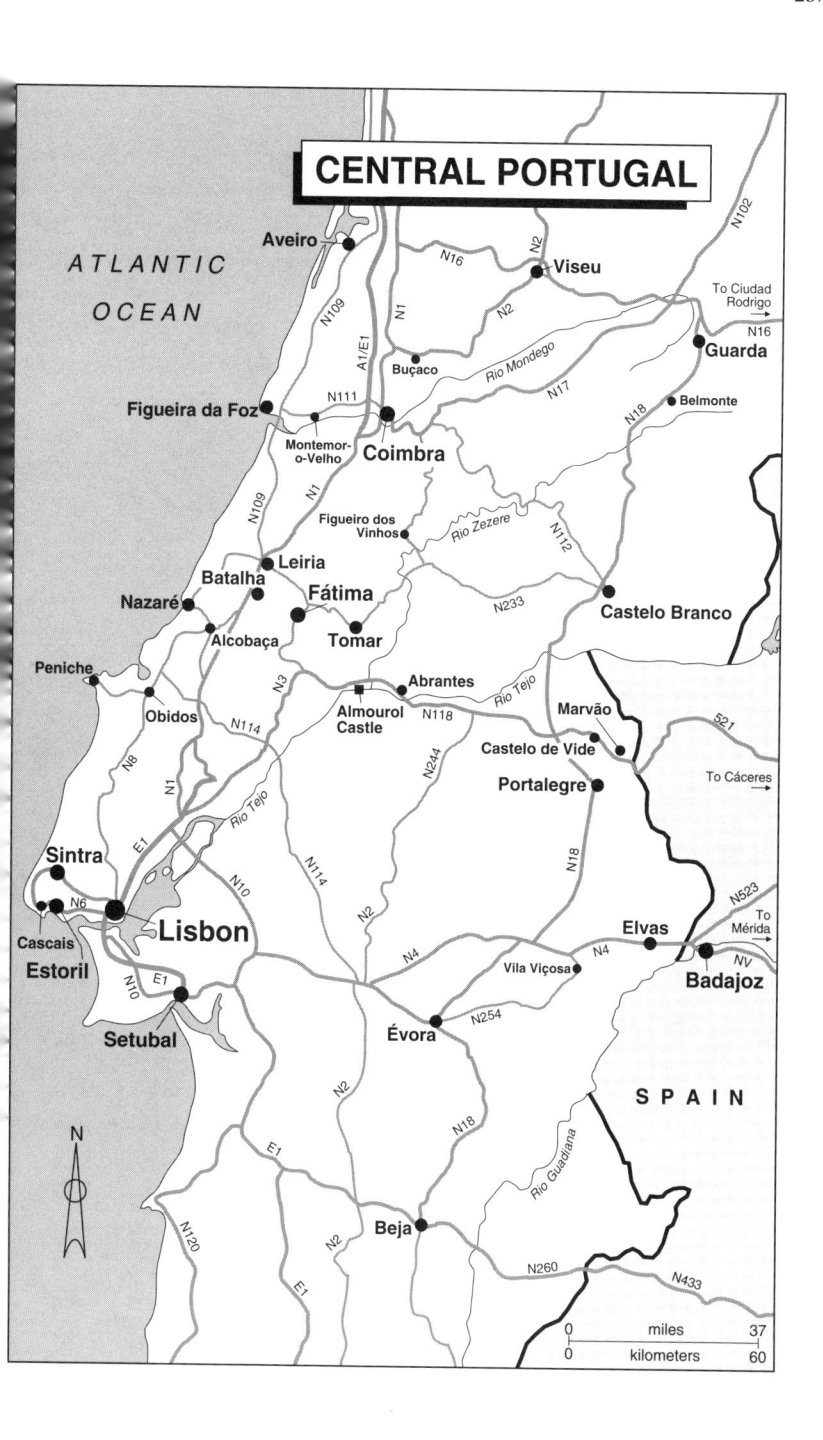

Borba is 11 k east of **Estremoz** *along N-4, or 28 k west of* **Elvas**, *by the same road. From* **Évora** *go 46 k by N-18 to Estremoz, then 11 k east on N-4.*

Borba is famed in Portugal for fine marble quarried from nearby mountains. You will seldom see so much of the calcite in such a small town. But for us, Borba stands for antiques. This quaint little town devotes three blocks of its main street to store after store—we once counted 20. Note, these are not the high-priced fancy shops that the word antique may bring to mind, but those dusty second-hand places where costs range from a few dollars to a few thousand, and the fun is in the exploring.

If you need some excuse to come for browsing, the main square, Pr. do Cinco de Outubro, is bordered by an 18th-century **town hall** and the pleasant 16th-century church of **São Bartolmeu** known for its azulejos. In the town center, at the junction of the road to Vila Viçosa, stands a little park with a fine marble (what else) fountain in the center.

CASTELO BRANCO

See Marvão excursions.

CASTELO DE VIDE

See Marvão excursions.

ELVAS ★★

Population: 13,507
Area code: 068; zip code: 7350

Situated beside the Spanish border, Elvas is just 22 k west of Spanish **Badajoz** *along the Spain's N-V and Portugal's N-4. Spain's* **Mérida** *lies just 66 k further east along N-V. From* **Évora** *take N-18 northeast to Estremoz in 46 k, then turn east on N-4 for an additional 43 k. From* **Lisbon** *head south past Setubal on the autoestrada A-2 for 50 k. Join N-10 going east for 21 k to meet N-10 north toward Cruzamento de Pegões for 14 k, just after Águas de Moura. Turn east on N-4 at Cruzamento for 37 k to Montemor-o-Novo, to continue on N-4 for the remaining 111 k. From* **north of Lisbon** *follow Lisbon directions until reaching A-1. Exit A-1 at villa Franca de Xira, 35 k north of Lisbon, for N-10 going 49 k to Cruzamento de Pegões. There N-4 goes east to Elvas in 148 k. From* **south of Lisbon** *follow directions to Évora, then the directions above. From* **Guarda** *follow directions to* **Estremoz**, *in 270 k, then head east along N-4 for 40 k.*

By **train** *Elvas is just over five hours from Lisbon. Connections can be made from Marvão, but the trip takes more than three hours. There is an express bus from Lisbon that beats the train. A bus from Évora takes under two hours.*

Standing by the Spanish border, Elvas' traditional business has been to defend Portugal against invasion. Its fortifications are not, as so often seen in Portugal, quaint relics of romantic struggles against Moors, but serious 17th-century ramparts that found good use during a siege as recently as the 19th century. Given the continual threat of attack, naturally the town of Elvas huddled within its fortified walls, which meant that houses had to be small and streets narrow to amble in quaint ways.

Because Elvas was regained from the Moors a century later than Lisbon, Moorish relics are more in evidence. The occasional gateway or tower whose elegance catches the eye is surely a Moorish structure.

For its imposing fortifications Elvas is worth a visit. Cobbled streets and tiny houses add atmosphere, but Elvas is not so full of monuments as to detain a visitor for long. After an hour or two wandering, most people are happy to have come, but have seen enough to leave satisfied.

WHAT TO SEE AND DO

There are nice views of Elvas' imposing **aqueduct** ★ to the west as the town is approached. It took almost a century to build. Not completed until the early 17th century, the aqueduct runs for five miles, 100 feet high in places, forming an elegant, if somewhat chunky, line of arches and tiers that still carry water to the city.

The old town is entered through a gate in the south rampart wall a few blocks uphill after passing the pousada. Inside, Rua de Olivença leads up to the main square, the **Praça da República**, paved in geometric shapes. The former **town hall**, from the 16th century, stands on the near side housing the **tourist office**, and the squat **Cathedral** (or such was its employ until the bishop left in 1882) stands opposite (north). The Cathedral exterior looks like a castle, the interior is an impressive space with azulejos lining the walls.

A small street beside the right side of the Cathedral leads behind it into the pretty **Largo Santa Clara** surrounded by attractive houses. In the center of the triangular-shaped square a **pillory** dangling iron hooks stands as a reminder of times when punishment was public.

On the near (south) side of the square rises the octagonal-shaped churc[h] of **Nossa Senhora da Consolação** ★★. It was built in the 16th centu[ry] during the Manueline era to duplicate the shape of an earlier Templ[ar] church that stood on the same site or nearby. Inside, it is a glory of color[ed] azulejos, which line the walls and even the cupola supported by gilded ma[r]ble columns.

At the north end of the square a **Moorish gate** beneath a logia is flank[ed] by twin towers. Passing through this gate, ascend to the Largo [da] Alcaçova, then bear left, then right at the "T" to walk the lovely little R[ua] das Beatas to the **castle**.

Castle

Open Fri.-Wed. 9:30 a.m. to 12:30 and 2:30-7 p.m.; closes at 5:30 p.m. [in] winter. Closed Thurs. Original construction was Moorish, but the ca[s]tle was reworked from the 14th through the 16th centuries. A wa[lk] along the top of the ramparts provides fine views of the countrysid[e]. The old governor's residence displays a reconstructed kitchen a[nd] bedroom.

For a different route back to the Olivença gate, follow the walls left fro[m] the castle.

A drive around the fortifications shows them to their best effect, inclu[d]ing another fortress just southeast. This **Forte de Santa Luzia** is star-shape[d] to force attackers into cross-fire between the rays.

WHERE TO STAY

Elvas is short on hotels, but there are elegant accommodations in Évor[a,] a special hotel outside Redondo, and a regal pousada in Extremoz, all d[e]scribed in this chapter.

MODERATE ($50-$99)

Pousada do Santa Luzia   1st-class ★★

Av. de Badajoz (at the end of N-4, as it enters the town). Rooms: 16. ☎ [62] 21 94; FAX 62 21 27; Telex 12469. This white-tiled, villa-like hot[el] from the 1940s recently became a pousada after failing as a priva[te] enterprise. The first floor is all spacious public rooms looking out [on] a fountained courtyard. Upstairs and annex bedrooms are decorate[d] colorfully and pleasingly. Not the most elegant pousada, it entice[s] with a relaxed feeling.

Dom Luis   2nd-class

Av. de Badajoz (at the end of N-4, as it enters the town). Rooms: 9[0.] ☎ 62 27 56; FAX 62 07 33; Telex 42473. This modern hotel is showin[g] signs of wear, but it still offers comfortable bedrooms and more ame[n]ities than its prices would suggest.

INEXPENSIVE (UNDER $50)

Estalgem Don Sancho II   R1st-class

Pr. da República, 20 (the main square within the walls). Rooms: 26. ☎ [62]

26 86; FAX 62 47 17. This is a friendly hotel, located in the heart of town, offering bedrooms that, although small, are cozy and attractively furnished with near-antiques. Meals served in the appealing downstairs restaurant are the best bargains in town.

WHERE TO EAT

For bargain dining, try the Estalgem Don Sancho II, mentioned above. For more expensive, but still moderately priced meals, see the selections below.

MODERATE ($15-$30)

Pousada de Santa Luzia ★

Av. de Badajoz (at the end of N-4, as it enters the town). ☎ 62 21 94. The pousada bills itself as offering the best cooking in Europe. While this is a laughable exaggeration, the cuisine rises above the average pousada. *Ensopado de borregoi*, garlicky mutton, green pepper and bread stew, and shellfish stew are good specialties. Would that the dining room were more attractive. *Major credit cards accepted.*

Dom Quixote ★

On N-4 3 k east of town. ☎ 62 20 14. Here you will find the citizens of Elvas dining, not at the pousada. This restaurant specializes in fish, served in a bright, convivial dining-room. *Major credit cards accepted.*

DIRECTORY

INFORMATION • Located in the Pr. da República (☎ 62 22 36).

TRAINS AND BUSES • The train station is two miles north of the city in Fonainhas (☎ 628 16). Buses from there drop you in the Pr. da República. Trains from Lisbon take five hours, cost about $6. and depart four times per day. One train per day come from Badajoz in Spain, one hour away.

The bus station is located in the Pr. da República (☎ 628 74). Five buses arrive from Lisbon daily, after a four hour ride, for a lower fare than the train. Three buses travel from Évora on an hour-and-a-half trip for about 500$00.

ESTREMOZ ★★

Population: 7869
Area code: 068; zip code: 7100

From **Lisbon** head south past Setubal on the autoestrada A-2 for 50 k. Join N-10 going east for 21 k to meet N-10 north toward Cruzamento de Pegões for 14 k, being careful to angle left as signs direct just after Águas de Moura. At Cruzamento, turn east on N-4 for 37 k to Montemor-o-Novo. A few k outside that town N-4 bears northeast to Estremoz in 68 k. From the **Algarve** take N-264 north *from Albufeira for 70 k to Ourique, outside of which N-123 heads east, then feeds into N-391 going north toward Beja just before Castro Verde. Circle Beja in 60 k. to take N-18 north for 78 k to Évora. From there take N-18 north for 46 k. From* **Guarda** *take N-18 south past Castelo Branco, Portalegre and Estremoz for 289 k. From* **north of Lisbon** *follow directions to Lisbon but exit A-1 at villa Franca, 35 k north of Lisbon, for N-10 going to Cruzamento de Pegões in 49 k. There N-4 goes east to Montamor-o-Novo in 37 k, from which N-114 reaches Évora in 30 k more.*

From **Évora** *follow the Estrada de Circunvalacão northward to turn left on N-18, passing Evoramonte (discussed in the Évora "Excursions") to reach Estremoz in 46 k.*

Estremoz, surrounded by 17th-century ramparts, is famous for two things. It produces unglazed jars of eccentric shapes, and boasts a fine medieval palace, now Portugal's most regal pousada.

Through the town walls the sandy expanse of the main square, Rossio, is reached for parking. Here a large regional fair, mostly for food, is held every Saturday, though some stalls remain through the week. The south side of the square consists of the **town hall**, formerly a convent from the end of the seventeenth century. On the east, #62b, stands a small regional **museum** displaying Alentejo scenes in miniatures carved by senior citizens, and curiosities (open Tues through Sun. from 10 a.m. until 1 p.m. and from 3 p.m. until 5 p.m. for tours; admission: 50$00).

Head past the **pillory** at the north end of the Rossio to follow the alley on the right uphill. The old town is entered through 17th-century fortifications. Keep heading up to the castle past pretty white-washed houses that are Manueline or older.

All that remains of the original castle is its rectangular **keep** bristling with battlements at the top. Three kings worked on it, finished by King Dinis in 1258. An octagonal room on the third floor is lined with fine windows, and the platform on the tower roof provides extensive views. (If closed ask at the pousada.) King Dinis later constructed a **palace** beside the keep for his lovely wife Isabel of Spain who became a saint. She died in what is today called the audience chamber. An explosion at the end of the 17th century wrecked most of the palace, although it was restored in the next century, and finally transformed into a luxurious pousada. Plain on the outside, it is grand within. Anyone can wander through. It is a treat.

The castle square contains the attractive 16th-century church of **Sant Maria** (seldom open) with some nice paintings. Beside it is the former **Audience Hall** of the original palace where Queen (Saint) Isabel died, with fine azulejos illustrating events from her life (open Tues. through Sun. 9 a.m. until noon and from 2 p.m. until 6 p.m. for tours; apply at the Municipal Museum on the south side of the square).

Although the town's eccentric water jars are curiosities, more charming examples of ceramic work in the form of naive little figures and animals are also produced here and are sold around town.

WHERE TO STAY

Estremoz presents as difficult a hotel choice as any you will ever face. The most regal pousada sits at the top of the town, and an incredible old monastery converted into a superior hotel lies in its own forest outside of Redondo, about 15 k away. See the description of the Hotel Convento de São Paulo under the "Redondo" section of Évora excursions. For the regal pousada read on.

EXPENSIVE ($100-$200)

Pousada da Reinha Santa Isabel 1st-class ★★★★★
Largo Dom Dinis. Rooms: 23. ☎ *226 18; FAX 239 82; Telex 43885.* Save up for this one (it costs a bit over $100 for a double) and reserve months in advance. It's your chance to walk where kings walked and sleep, if not in the same room, at least in the same building where they dreamed. A saint also spent time here, and the king granted Vasco da Gama an audience but did not invite him to stay the night. Antiques abound amid velvets and marble; the entrance hall impresses; the marble stair is regal and the corridors are elegant. Most rooms include canopied beds and the views that royalty came to see. Of course it's expensive, but the experience and the unobtrusive pampering make it well worth every escudo.

DIRECTORY

INFORMATION • Located in the Largo da República, 26, just off the Rossio (☎ *22 538*).

TRAINS AND BUSES • There is no train service. The bus station is located in the Rossio (☎ *22 282*). Six buses travel the one hour route from Évora for just over $2. An express bus from Lisbon takes about 3 hours. Service is available to and from Arraiolos and Elvas as well.

EXCURSIONS

Arraiolos for carpets, **Redondo** for ceramics and **Borba** for antiques are nearby. **Évora** is 30 miles distant with **Évoramonte** passed on the way. All are described under separate headings in this chapter, except for Évoramonte which is discussed as an excursion from Évora. A special outing from Estremoz is tiny Vila Viçosa, just 17 k east, with something for everyone.

VILA VIÇOSA ★

Population: 4282

Head east from Estremoz along N-4, with fine views of the town, for 11 k. Turn off to Borba and signs for Vila Viçosa 6 k southeast.

Buses connect with Estremoz and Évora.

It seems incongruous that this little town of orchards, flowers and whitewashed houses should contain a huge palace, a splendid convent and a fortress. The explanation is that it was the seat of the Duke of Bragança, the most powerful family in Portugal during the years of Spanish occupation (see "Historical Profile: The Birth of Portugal" on page 157). Here the Duke and his family lived in the highest style. Then the Duke became King in 1640 and left Vila Viçosa for the capital, which ended the festivities for this little town.

Entering from Borba you pass the huge square called the Terreiro do Paço (Terrace of the Palace), fronting the long, multi-windowed facade of the Ducal Palace.

Paço Ducal ★

Open Tues.-Sat. 9:30 a.m. to 1 p.m. and 2-6 p.m. Closes an hour earlier in winter. Admission: 400$00 for a guided tour. The museums of coaches and of armor costs 100$00 more. Entrance in the center. Understand that when the eighth Duke left for Lisbon to be crowned King, he took most of the good stuff with him. The palace is still owned by the Bragança family who have restocked it as best they could, but they aren't kings any more. The highlights of the palace are the rooms rather than what inhabits them.

The palace was built from the 16th through the 17th centuries in an Italian Renaissance style. It includes a main, public wing whose walls are covered with azulejos and whose ceilings are delicately frescoed, and another wing for the family that contains more intimate articles, including paintings done by the penultimate King Carlo, who was assassinated in Lisbon.

The **Convento das Chagas** which houses the bodies of the Bragança Duchesses amid fine azulejos occupies the south side of the square. Opposite the palace is the **Mosteiro dos Agostinhos** full of white marble tombs for all the Dukes, set off by rococo gilt. Back a little way along the Borba road stands the whimsical **gate** to the former royal forest. This often-pictured Manueline depiction of stone knots is one of the last surviving parts of a wall that kept the deer inside the hunting area.

Continuing past the Paço, the Av. Duque de Bragança climbs to the old town and its **castle**. This is a stout citadel raised in the 13th century and strengthened in the 17th. Inside is a collection of picturesque houses and churches.

ÉVORA ★★★★

Population: 35,117
Area code: 066; zip code: 7000

From **Lisbon** *head south past Setubal on the autoestrada A-2 for 50 k. Join N-10 going east for 21 k to meet N-10 north toward Cruzamento de Pegões for 14 k, being careful to angle left as signs direct just after Águas de Moura. At Cruzamento, turn east on N-4 for 37 k to Montemor-o-Novo. A few k outside that town N-114 bears southeast to Évora in 30 k. From the* **Algarve** *take N-264 north from Albufeira for 70 k to Ourique, outside of which N-123 heads east, then feeds into N-391 going north toward Beja just before Castro Verde. Circle Beja in 60 k. to take N-18 north for the final 78 k. From* **Guarda** *take N-18 south past Castelo Branco, Portalegre and Estremoz for 289 k. From* **north of Lisbon** *follow directions to Lisbon but exit A-1 at villa Franca, 35 k north of Lisbon, for N-10 going to Cruzamento de Pegões in 49 k. There N-4 goes east to Mon-*

> tamor-o-Novo in 37 k, from which N-114 reaches Évora in 30 k more.
>
> Direct **trains** from Lisbon depart four times daily and take about three hours. Trains from Faro, in the Algarve, consume just under six hours (costing less than 1000$00). All told the bus is better, with expresses from Lisbon taking only two-and-a-half hours. From Elvas there are two daily departures and the trip takes under two hours.

Évora is a special town. It is a kind of Portuguese Florence—with bright houses topped by red-orange roofs—as well as a Portuguese Seville—gloriously flowered. UNESCO declared the town a world treasure.

Évora thrived during Roman times and was designated a *municipium*, giving it the right to coin money. Later, the Moors conquered it and held on for 450 years. It was liberated in 1166 by an outlaw knight named Geraldo Sem-Pavor (Gerald, the Fearless), whose reputation in Portugal is similar to El Cid's in Spain. To storm the town he impaled lances in the walls for his troops to climb like stairs. Once in Portuguese hands, the royalty found Évora more congenial than Lisbon, and spent as much time in residence as their duties permitted. During this period—from the 14th through the 16th centuries—Évora flourished as Portugal's Athens, a city filled with palaces, churches and art. But when the Avís dynasty died out in 1579 and the Spanish took over Portugal, Évora became a forgotten city consigned to preserving relics from its time of glory.

All the sights lie within the walls of the old city, and most are concentrated at the very center. They comprise monuments marking every era of greatness—from a Roman temple to 16th-century mansions. At least a day is required to savor them properly.

Anyone arriving during the last week in June will find Évora at its most festive. This is the fair of São João which includes folk dancing, and stalls selling food or local crafts.

> *Parking is generally possible in the Pr. do Giraldo. If full, there are spaces in two blocks along Rua Nova, which runs east from the northern end of the plaza.*
>
> *Arrivals from* **Lisbon** *reach the city walls, but are prevented by one-way streets from proceeding further east. Turn left along the Estrada da Circunvalação for a quarter of a mile to turn right through the next entrance into*

the walls. Inside, the street first is called Rua Candido dos Reis, then Rua João de Deus, then it enters the Pr. do Giraldo for parking. From the **Algarve and south** turn left onto Rua A. J. D. Almeida at a large intersection one block before reaching the city walls. It leads to a traffic circle in two blocks; take the left hand road, Estrada do Circunvalacão past gardens to turn right through the walls along Rua da República, which arrives in five blocks at the Pr. do Giraldo for parking. From **Guarda**, **Estremoz** and **northern** areas turn right at the city walls along Estrada da Circunvalacão, through the aqueduct and then left at the next entrance through the walls. Inside the walls the street is first called Rua Candido dos Reis, then Rua João de Deus, before entering the Pr. do Giraldo for parking.

If no parking is found here, turn left at the end of the plaza for four short blocks then right along R. de Santa Clara. After three tiny blocks turn right again and take the next left (R. de São Domingos to parking around the Pr. Joaquim António de Aguiar.)

Start at the **Pr. do Giraldo**, the elongated main square almost exctly in the center of the walled town. A fine 16th-century fountain lays in the center. Interesting houses and arcades surround the quare, now lined with cafés but formerly the site for immolating vicms of the Inquisition. The **Office of Tourism** is located near the iddle of the west side of the plaza. On the east side, a low arcade overs the sidewalk. About half way along, Rua 5 de Outubro leads phill past attractive crafts shops to open wide in the Largo Marquês e Marialva. Adjoining the cathedral on its left side is the **Museu de vora**. While further left one cannot help but notice a Roman temle.

WHAT TO SEE AND DO

athedral ★★★
Open Tues.-Sun. 9 a.m. to noon and 2-5 p.m. Closed Mon. and holidays. Admission: 150$00. The cathedral was begun late in the 12th century and finished by the middle of the 13th in the earliest Gothic style. With a few exceptions, it retains its original design. The monolithic facade flanked by square towers presents a fortress face, broken by the deeply recessed porch of the entrance. Each side of the entrance is lined by a 14th-century series of the Apostles, most of whom seem to have the same face, but the animals are delightful.

The interior is disconcerting because its stone blocks are picked out with bright mortar, producing a checkerboard effect that fights with the solidity that should be conveyed. Still, the lantern above the transept crossing is elegant, and the fine rose windows lighting the transepts are originals. Not so the retable. The old one is now displayed in the Museu de Évora; what presently overlooks the altar is an 18th-century work in marble, quite out of keeping with the style of the cathedral. At the end of the north transept a carved portal with marble head is attributed to Chanterene.

After buying tickets near the main entrance, a fine Gothic cloister may be entered from the south transept. The heaviness of the cloister reflects an early Gothic aesthetic, although lightened by circles of Moorish open tracery. Statues of evangelists stand in each corner. At the southeast corner a chapel contains the moving sepulcher of the founding bishop of the cathedral, his head held gently by angels. All the carving in this chapel merits appreciation.

The glory of the treasury, housed in the tower beside the west entrance, is a 13th-century French ivory statue of the Virgin that opens to show events from her life (an odd wooden replacement-head sits on her shoulders). In addition to the usual sacerdotal vestments and ecclesiastical plate there is an impressive cross in gilded, enameled silver studded with over 1000 precious and semi-precious stones.

Museu de Évora   ★★

Open Tues.-Sun. 10 a.m. to 12:30 p.m. and 2-5 p.m. Closed Sun. and holidays. Admission: 200$00. The museum is housed in the grand former bishop's palace from the 17th century. Sculpture is displayed chronologically on the ground floor. A fragment of Roman bas-relief of a vestal virgin's lower half is notable for the subtle depiction of diaphanous dress. There are some fine medieval tombs and outstanding Renaissance carving by Nicolau Chanterene, especially the effigy of Bishop Afonso. Displayed on the second floor is a good collection of Portuguese primitive painting. The main attraction is in room two—a colorful 13-picture series of the life of the Virgin from the late 15th century, the original retable of the cathedral. It is Flemish work by the look, although Italian buildings serve as backgrounds.

Proceeding northward past the museum, enter another large plaza, the Largo Conde de villa-Flor. In its center, framed by the open plaza, is a **Roman Temple**. *A part of the 16th-century building at the northwest corner of the largo belonged to Vasco da Gama before his appointment as Viceroy of India. Later the building housed the first Office of the Inquisition in Portugal. To the west is the* **Convento dos Lóios** *beside the* **Igreja de São João Evangelista**, *and beyond it, north, is the* **Palace of the Dukes of Cadaval** *beside a garden affording views of the countryside over remains of the Roman town walls.*

Templo de Diana ★

This lovely second-century temple in the ornate Corinthian style, is called Diana's temple, although there is no evidence proving who was worshipped in it. Its base remains along with 14 of the original 18 granite columns sandwiched by marble capitals and bases.

The temple owes its fine state of preservation to continued use through the centuries, so its stones were not carted away for building material. During one period, it served as a fortress; at another, as the municipal slaughterhouse.

Paço dos Duques de Cadaval ★

Open Tues.-Sun. 10 a.m. to noon and 2-6 p.m. Closed Mon. Admission: 150$00, for a ticket good for São João Evangelista as well. The palace was built in the 14th century by João I, and incorporated a turret from the medieval city walls as its northern tower. Later, he presented it to the ancestors of the Cadavals whose descendants substantially remodeled the facade in the 17th century. Two kings—João III and João V—lived inside, but the palace today is still owned by the Cadaval family, who also possess the Church of Saint John the Evangelist adjoining. A museum displays a gallery of the dukes, along with two fine Flemish bronze plaques.

Igreja de São João Evangelista ★★★

Same hours as the Paço dos Duques de Cadaval above. This tiny church contains some of the finest **azulejos** in Portugal. After the 1755 earthquake, it was extensively remodeled, for it had been erected 200 years before by Rodrigo de Melo, the Count of Olivença. The flamboyant Gothic entry remains from the original. Inside, the nave is lined with chapels forming a pantheon of the Melo family. But it is the amazing *azulejos* that captivate. They are by the greatest artist in the medium, Antonio Oliveira Bernardes, at the height of his powers in 1711. Note the *trompe l'oeil azulejo* window! The sacristy holds some unexceptional paintings, but also one of a Pope, whose eyes not only follow the viewer, but whose feet seem to as well.

The convent of São João now is a most elegant pousada whose former chapterhouse door ranks with the great portals in Portugal. Next to the cloisters of São João stands a large library from 1805 connected by an arch to the bishop's palace. Pass under the arch and turn left to face a **Manueline mansion** *with a mashrabiya balcony (for looking out without being seen). Continue past a tower next to the* **Paláco do Condes de Bastos**, *originally a Moorish palace, although the facade is 15th century. Parts of first-century Roman town walls are visible.*

Returning to the rear of the cathedral and passing around the apse, continue south along the charming Rua do Cenáculo. In one block take the right arm of the "T," Rua da Freina de Baixo, which leads in a short block to the **mansion of Garcia de Resende** on the left side. The Manueline decoration of the second-floor windows is worth a look. Turn right to pass between two towers of the Medieval town wall into the picturesque **Largo das Portas de Moura**. An elegantly simple Renaissance fountain plays in the center of the square and a number of fine houses border it. Especially grand is the 16th-century **Corovil mansion** at the southern end, with twin arcades and horseshoe arches.

Return toward the two towers, turning left just before reaching them to travel two blocks along Rua Misericordia, past the rococo **Igreja da Misericordia**, into the small Largo de Alvaro Velho. At its southwest end, steps lead down the picturesquely arched **Travessa da Caraça** to enter the Largo de Graca with a **Renaissance church** of the same name. Its facade is done in Italian classical style, topped by four rising atlantes. Leaving the largo by its west end opposite the church, turn left for a few feet along Rua da República to take the first right into the Pr. 28 de Maio, dominated by **Igreja de São Francisco**.

Igeja de São Francisco ★★

Open Mon.-Sat. 9am to 1 p.m. and 2:30-6 p.m. Open Sun. 10 a.m. t 11:30 a.m. and 2:30-6 p.m. Admission: 25$00. The grandiose entry por tico is formed of rounded, pointed and horseshoe arches, which abou covers the genre. Inside, the aisleless nave is dizzyingly high. As is th case with the Cathedral, the stones are picked out by white morta the peculiarity of this town. Except for the altar—with two galleries t either side— the church is relatively free of decoration which lets th architecture speak well.

But what everyone remembers about this church is not elegance bu its gruesome chapterhouse, entered from the left of the altar. Here th bones of perhaps 5000 dead have been collected as a reminder of wha awaits us all. The sign at the entrance translates: "We bones who ar here await your bones."

Opposite the church is the misleadingly named **Museu de Artesanato**, for it is actually a store. At the lower end of the square a public garden is bordered on the south by part of the imposing 17th-century town walls. A bandstand in the park presents summer concerts beside ruins of one royal palace and a copy of part of another. The Pr. do Giraldo, from which we began, is two blocks due north of the church of São Francisco, along Rua da República passing behind it.

WHERE TO STAY

Évora has long been in the tourist business and can usually accommodate as many visitors as wish to spend the night. Establishments, however, are all rather small; no 100-room hotels exist. There is an exceptional pousada in town, and one of the most wonderful pousadas in the country is 46 k away in Estremoz. See Redondo under "Excursions" for yet another incredible hotel in this area.

EXPENSIVE ($100-$200)

Pousada dos Lóios 1st-class ★★★
Largo Conde de villa Flor (beside the Cathedral). Rooms: 32. ☎ *240 51; Telex 43288.* Installed in a 16th-century convent, the elegance of its surroundings make this a special pousada. Rooms envelope a lovely two-story cloister, used for dining in the summer. One of the great doorways in the world, a Gothic-Moorish fantasy, leads to the former chapterhouse. However, all the beauty of this pousada is exhausted in its public rooms, the bedrooms are another matter. They are small, with doorways only a child could walk through upright, and furnished in a forgettable style. Still, to say that the location is convenient to the sights is an understatement. It is one. Would that the management cared more.

MODERATE ($50-$99)

Riviera R1st-class ★★
Rua 5 de Outubro, 49 (the street that leads east from Pr. do Giraldo). Rooms: 22. ☎ *233 04; FAX 204 67.* This hotel, a former townhouse, enjoys an ideal location near the sights on a street lined with nice shops. It could be more tastefully decorated but is otherwise a fine choice.

Planicie 2nd-class ★★
Largo Álvaro Velho, 40 (1 block south from Pr. do Giraldo along Rua da República, and 2 short blocks east along Rua M. Bombarda). Rooms: 33. ☎ *240 26; FAX 298 80; Telex 13500.* The exterior is attractively Renaissance-looking, and the location is good—in a lovely square, near the sights. The interior is not up to the promise of the exterior, however. Public rooms are coldly marbled and the bedrooms are spare, although some provide views. The hotel is affiliated with the Best-Western chain.

Albergaria Vitória R1st-class ★
Rua Diana de Lis (1 block south the Estrada Circunvalação, at the southwest corner of the old town). Rooms: 48. ☎ *271 74; FAX 298 80; Telex 44875.* This is a modern hotel of no architectural character, but it offers comfortable rooms and balconies for views of the lovely town. Although located outside the old town, this problem is solved with a car or taxi ride.

Evorahotel 2nd-class ★

Quinta do Cruzeiro (on N-114, the Lisbon road, less than 3 k before Évora). Rooms: 114. ☎ 73 48 00; FAX 73 48 06. In a pinch this spanking new hotel with lots of room will serve well. Rooms are large, indeed contain a small cooking area. The decor is acceptable and there is a pleasant pool.

INEXPENSIVE (UNDER $50)

O Eborense R2nd-class ★★★

Largo da Misericordia, 1 (1 block south from Pr. do Giraldo along Rua da República and 2 short blocks east along Rua M. Bombarda). Rooms: 29. ☎ 220 31. This delightful little hotel is installed in a 16th-century townhouse on a pleasant square near the sights. The decor is eccentric but fun. Bedrooms are clean, newly decorated and reasonably comfortable but without luxuries.

Policarpo R3rd-class ★

Rua da Freiria de Baixo, 16 (beside the Miseracordia church, 1 block south of the Cathedral, near the two towers of the Largo das Portas de Moura). Rooms: 16. ☎ 224 24. This is a former nobleman's house that functions today as a bare-bones hotel. It is atmospheric, dark, and far from spic-and-span, but those with a sense of adventure who enjoy out-of-the-ordinary places will love it. So, too, will those trying to save money. Bedrooms are large, but the decor varies from pleasant to atrocious.

Santa Clara 2nd-class

Travessa da Milheira, 19 (2 blocks west from the Pr. do Giraldo along Rua Serpa Pinto, and 1 short block north). Rooms: 51. ☎ 241 41; Telex 43768. This is a simple hotel that offers the necessities at reasonable prices.

WHERE TO EAT

Nothing in Évora draws the gourmet. While tasty meals are available for modest prices, there is little variety—all the restaurants try for old tavern looks and serve similar dishes.

MODERATE ($15-$30)

Fialho ★

Travessa das Mascarenhas, 14 (north of the Pr. do Giraldo for about 5 blocks to the Pr. J. A. de Aguiar, from which this little lane goes north). ☎ 230 79. Closed Monday, the first three weeks of September, and from the last week of December until after New Years. The restaurant has the look of an old tavern with crockery hanging from the walls. The food is traditional Portuguese, and, while not exceptional, it is tasty and authentic. We prefer the lamb to the pork dishes. Reservations are recommended. *Amex, Diners, MasterCard and Visa accepted.*

Guião

Rua da República, 81 (1 block south of the Pr. do Giraldo). ☎ 224 27.

Closed Monday and from the middle of November to the middle of December. As with most restaurants in Évora, this one is decorated as an old tavern, although somewhat more tastefully than others. The food is traditional Alentejo, which means that pork with clams is one specialty, and the meals are filling.

Amex, Diners, MasterCard and Visa accepted.

Cozinha de Santo Humberto

Rua da Moeda, 39 (this street leaves the west side of Pr. do Giraldo). ☎ *242 51. Closed Thursday, and November.* The building dates from several centuries ago, and anything old the owner could find is hung on the walls. Flowered tables and comfortable seating are pluses, although the food could be better.

Amex, Diners, MasterCard and Visa accepted.

DIRECTORY

INFORMATION • Located in the Pr. do Giraldo (☎ *226 71*). This is a most pleasant office with a staff that speaks English.

TRAINS AND BUSES • The train station (☎ *221 25*) is located half a mile to the southeast of town along a continuation of Rua da República.

The bus station (☎ *221 21*) is near the church of São Francisco on Rua da República.

POLICE • Located just east of the north end of Pr. do Giraldo (☎ *220 22*).

EXCURSIONS

Marvão ★★★, pretty as a medieval postcard, lies northeast along N-18 for 105 k to Portalegre, then 16 k further north on N-359. **Elvas** ★★, only 89 k northeast, is similar in its medieval-Moorish character to Évora. The medieval town of **Estremoz** ★★ offers a lovely castle made into one of the most elegant pousadas in the country, pleasant houses and local pottery. Attractions even nearer at hand include the embroidered carpet-making village of **Arraiolos**, and the antique shops of **Borba**. All are described under their own headings in this chapter, with direction to Évora that can be followed in reverse from Évora.

Also near are the fortified town and Gothic castle of **Evoramonte** ★, and the similar, but more evocative fortified village of **Monsaraz** ★. For ceramics and an exceptional hotel, read on about **Redondo**. These three are described below.

Note also, that this area has the highest concentrations of mystic Celtic dolmans—tombs built of massive boulders—and menhirs—circular places of worship formed by rock rings—in the country. They may be seen in their splendid isolation in the countryside. The Tourist Office provides a map of locations.

EVORAMONTE ★

Population: 935

> Follow **Évora**'s Estrada de Circunvalacão northward to turn left on N-18, toward Estremoz. Evoramonte lies north about 33 k along N-18. Signs for "Castelo d'Evoramonte" in the modern village point to a steep road up to the castle.

Tiny Evoramonte's moment in history came in 1834 when King Pedro IV and his younger, more absolutist, brother Miguel duked it out for the Portuguese crown a few miles away. After winning, Pedro signed a treaty with his brother in a house in Evoramonte that still commemorates the event with a plaque.

The village castle and massive walls were built long before, in the 14th century, on Moorish and Roman foundations. As with many such castles, renovation occurred in the 16th century, but, unlike most, the renovation did not significantly change the style from the massive Gothic original. What is startling about this castle, however, is the vanilla color of a preservative covering its walls. Otherwise, it is a fine castle with four cylindrical towers that offer breathtaking views.

MONSARAZ ★

Population: 1290

> Follow the Estrada de Circunvalacão southward around Évora to turn right on N-18 going south toward Beha. In about 15 k N-256 bears east for 35 k, where a sign just before the Guadiana river directs a 4 k turn left to Monsaraz.

About two kilometers after turning onto the road to Monsaraz, look left to see a prehistoric megalith about 12 feet high surrounded by smaller stones away from the road. It conveys some of the feel of Stonehedge. Who raised it is a subject of controversy, but, whoever it was, did a lot of other building in this area.

Beginning in the 13th century, almost all towns near the Spanish border were fortified for defense. Monsaraz was no different. But when fortification ceased to be important, Monsaraz had nothing else to offer, so it has stayed the way it always was—today for our enjoyment. The village consists of just four cobblestone streets, lined with houses that are small and individual as only very old houses of the same general style can be. Many bear arms of the owners and most retain their outside stair—a style dating from the 16th-17th centuries.

Its ruined castle was rebuilt in the 13th century and given an outer massive perimeter wall in the 17th. Later, a small bullring was added inside. Few places in the world so preserve the atmosphere of a Renaissance village.

REDONDO ★

Population: 3596
Area code: 066; zip code: 7170

From **Évora** *go east on N-254 for 34 k. From* **Estremoz** *go south on the scenic N-381 for 27 k.*

While the 16th-century church of Nossa Senhora da Anunciação in a pretty square is worth a look, this typical alentejo town is more often visited for its crafts. Conveniently located within less than twenty miles of both Évora and Estremoz, Redondo produces painted wood furniture and some good artisan ceramics. There are small stores spread around the town selling these wares. A folk festival springs up on the first weekend in August.

The other reason for passing through Redondo is to visit one of Portugal's most unusual hotels, 10 k north of the town on N-381.

EXPENSIVE ($100-$200)

Hotel Convento de São Paulo   1st-class ★ ★ ★ ★ ★

Aldeia da Serra, Redondo 7170 (15 k on N-381 from Estremoz, or 10 k north of Redondo are signs for the hotel). Rooms: 21. ☎ *999 100; FAX 999 104.* When your car arrives at an iron gate it is electronically opened to let you drive along a private road to a veritable ancient monastery. The monastery originated in the 14th century, although what survives is mainly from the 16th. After it was seized from the monks by the government about a hundred years ago, it was bought by the family of Henrique Leotte Tavares, the present owner. Only in the late 1980s, however, was permission granted to make a luxury hotel out of the structure. No money has been spared to restore its faded glory yet provide all the luxury anyone could ask for. There are tennis courts and a pool, vast gardens and about five square miles of private forest for walks. The hotel interior is enchanting, and includes a lovely cloister in the center, but it is the 50,000 azulejos covering its corridors that astonish. The dining room is the cavernous original in which the monks ate, still covered with frescos that are damaged but serene. Here we have had some of our best meals in Portugal, served by the most attentive staff. We drool every time we think of the tomato soup.

EVORAMONTE

See "Évora" under "Excursions."

FLOR DE ROSA

See "Marvão" under "Excursions."

GUARDA ★

Population: 14,803
Area code: 071; zip code: 6300

From **Lisbon** take the autoestrada A-1 north for 180 k to the **Coimbra** exit. The fastest, but less scenic route, is to go north on N-1 from Coimbra for 7 k to pick up IP-3 to Viseu in 87 k. From **Viseu** take IP-5 east for 68 k. More scenic, if you have the time, is to take a 5 k jag from the A-1 into Coimbra. Follow the river along Av. F. de Magalhães, then Av. E. Navarro to signs for N-17 and Guarda. N-117 heads southeast for a bit before turning northeast. The road is scenic, but slow going, for 138 k to Celorico da Beira. On the outskirts of that town, IP-5 east completes the final 22 k to Guarda. From **Porto** take either the autoestrada or N-1 south to Albergens-a-Velha in 46 k. There take IP-5 east to Guarda in a further 133 k. From **Évora** N-18 leads northeast to Estemoz in 46 k and continues through Portalegre and Castelo Branco to reach Guarda in a total of 289 k. From **Tomar** go south on N-110 to the outskirts of Entroncamento to pick up N-118 going east. In 76 k it reaches Alpalhão where N-18 leads to Guarda in 160 k more. From the **Algarve** either the directions from Lisbon or from Évora may be followed, with the former being quicker and the latter more scenic. In either case it is a distance of about 450 k. Guarda is a straight drive from Spanish **Salamanca** along N-620 which changes its designation at the Portuguese border to N-16. The distance is 157 k.

Trains leave from Lisbon four times a day for a trip of 6-1/2-8 hours, depending on the train. The trip is 3 hours from Coimbra.

At two-thirds of a mile above sea level Guarda is the highest town in Portugal, so it's cool in summer but freezing in winter. The reason for its name (Guard) is evident from this summit. Since fortification in the 12th century, Guarda's job has been to guard against Spanish invasions, for it is only 60 k from a border that once moved to and fro. Guarda forms one component of an incredible string of 20 similarly fortified crests within a 50-k radius that, in medieval times, formed a sort of Maginot Line. Granite-grey Guarda is not the most attractive of these towns, but it offers the best accommodations in the area so it serves as a base for the fortress tours described under "Excursions."

Guarda's principle square, **Largo Luis de Camões**, is surrounded by 16th- through 18th-century houses and contains the town **Cathedral**.

Cathedral ★

Construction on the Cathedral began at the end of the 14th century, under the direction of the architect of Batalha cathedral, which explains its flying buttresses, clerestory and spires. Work dragged on for a century and a half, by which time Boytec, the Manueline architect, arrived to add his gargoyles and twisting columns. After an exterior constricted by two octagonal towers, the inside seems vast, although it has little lightness about it. The limestone retable in high relief is attributed to Jean de Rouen. Whether or not the attribution is correct, the work lacks the life that characterizes most of his work.

Remains of the **castle** look down upon the plaza. Little of the original stands except for the massive tower donjon. Downhill and to the north (right), beside the town walls, stands the **church of Misericordia** with a most elegant 17th-century baroque facade. It faces across to one of the original town gates, the **Torre dos Ferreiros**.

WHERE TO STAY

Although only two hotels are worth consideration, between them they contain 150 bedrooms which should easily satisfy the demand. But if you would like the peace of a mountaintop chalet, there is a rustic pousada in the mountains nearby.

MODERATE ($50-$99)

In Manteigas, 49 k west:

Pousada São Lourenço ★★★

Manteigas 6260, on the road to Gouveia (Turn from N-18 toward Manteigas on N-232 at Belmonte, 20 k south of Guarda. The road winds and climbs about 35 k to the hotel. Having once driven from the other direction, from N-17 through Gouveia, we wouldn't do it again.). Rooms: 20. ☎ *(075) 98 24 50; FAX (075) 98 24 53; Telex 53992.* Perched at an elevation almost a mile high, this pousada is appropriately rustic, has a

cozy fire when it's cold and provides views for 50 miles. The bed
rooms are functional enough, and the management is gracious.

De Turismo   1st-class ★

Av. Coronel Orlindo de Carvalho (at the end of the town gardens). Room
105. ☎ 21 22 05; FAX 21 22 04; Telex 53760. The look of an in
invites you into comfortable bedrooms. The hotel is efficient in
quiet way that breeds confidence, and it has been recently redone
although a feeling of mustiness still can be detected.

Filipe   R1st-class ★

Rua Vasco da Gama, 9 (in the square with Misericordia Church). Room
45. ☎ 21 26 58; FAX 21 64 02; Telex 53746. At prices one third les
than de Turismo, bedrooms here are certainly adequate and reason
ably comfortable.

WHERE TO EAT

Both of the Guarda hotels above serve quite good food. The dining
room of the Felipe is the more attractive of the two, and serves more inter
esting dishes.

EXCURSIONS

Attractive **Viseu** ★★ lies 68 k west along the speedy IP-5
Coimbra ★★★ with its ancient university is an hour and a half furthe
along. **Évora** ★★★★ and **Porto** ★★ can be reached in a half-day. Al
are described under their own headings in the Northern Portugal chapter
except Évora, which is described in the present chapter.

But the reason for the trip to Guarda is the score of fortresses in the
countryside around it. Note that there is no requirement that all 20 mus
be seen. A sameness grows about them because all repose in tiny town
perched on hilltops, and all date from the same medieval era. Nonetheless
some have features that distinguish them, so the whole group would con
stitute an instructive two-day excursion. A car is the only way to reach
every one. We divide our description into a larger group of fortresses locat
ed, for the most part, south of Guarda, and a smaller group located to the
north. Of the two tours, the southern one covers the more interestin
sights.

THE SOUTHERN FORTS

South on N-18 brings **Belmonte** in 22 k, just off that main road.

Belmonte   ★★

The pretty Belmonte square is full of attractively restored mansions
but the monolithic granite **fortress** above exerts a pull. King Dini
erected it in the 13th century and it looks so right that it seems a
movie set. (Open daily 9 a.m. to noon and 1-5 p.m.; admission
100$00.) Here Pedro Alvares Cabral, the discoverer of Brazil wa
born. The coat-of-arms of the Cabral family is blazoned on the
gate—two goats for *cabra*, which means goat. The church of **São Tiago**

stands beside the keep. Its simple interior (with some faint frescos) contains the Cabrals' tombs.

Two k north of Belmonte along N-18, a dirt road to the right toward Comeal da Torre shortly brings **Torre Centum Cellas**, a curious Roman tower. The three-story square tower is constructed of granite without mortar and dates at least to Roman times. Its function is debated, but its abundant windows argue against a fortress or watchtower.

Continue south from Belmonte on N-345 toward Caria in 11 k. There take N-18-3 toward Carvalha and past for 9k where a sign directs left for a final 7 k to Sortelha on its hill.

Sortelha ★

All in granite and surrounded by boulders of the same material, the town huddles inside 13th-century fortified walls. Most of the houses are empty, as is the imposing castle, artfully fitted into the living stone. The scene is memorable.

An excursion further south to the boulder bestrewn village of Monsanto is possible. If interested, return to N-18-3 to go east to Terreiro das Bruxas in 7 k. N-233 south leads through Penamacor (with a 16th-century fortress) in 22 k, after which N-232 goes to Medelim in 23 k, where a left turn onto N-239 reaches to Monsanto in 7 k more.

Monsanto ★★

Mammoth boulders seem to perch precariously on the steep side of the hill to which Monsanto clings. Boulders fill the town too, and its houses—constructed of the same granite material—seem almost to be boulders themselves. A castle was built here in the 12th century, but the top was blown off by an explosion in the 19th. Today it is a romantic ruin of granite walls and stairs, covered in lichen. The view seems to extend forever.

Otherwise, continue to N-18-3 from Sortelha to go east to Terreiro das Bruxas in 7 k. Continue east, now on N-233 for 13 k to Sagubal.

Sabugal ★

This time the castle is a bit later—14th century. It is also quite complete since it has been restored. The five sides of the keep are unusual, and the ensemble of fortifications forms a pretty picture. (If it's closed, apply at the town hall.)

Continuing north on N-324, the highway IP-5 is met in 56 k crossing to Spain. A right turn here would pass **Castelo Mendo** *with some castle ruins in a few k on the left just before crossing the Rio Coa, and* **Castelo Bom**, *with one tower of its castle remaining.*

But continue north on N-332 for 9 k more to take a right for 9 k on N-340 to find Almeida.

Almeida ★

This peaceful village displays formidable 18th-century fortifications in the form of a six-pointed star. This style is named Vauban, after its originator, who is said to have worked on Almeida. Monolithic in design, the walls force attackers to concentrate where they become easy targets for fire from walls on two sides. Almeida's fortifications are double: should one wall be breached, another could still be defended. In spite of the cleverness of the construction, the fort was stormed—once by the Spanish and later by the French. Some attractive mansions dot the town within the fortifications.

THE NORTHERN FORTS

From Guarda take N-18 north for 5 k to join IP-5 east for one exit to N-221 northeast for 48 k to Castelo Rodrigo. Or, from Almeida continue north on N-332 which meets N-221 in about 17 k at Castelo Rodrigo.

Castelo Rodrigo

Do not be misled by the quiet and intimacy of this little village within fortified walls—its early citizens had passion. In the 16th century, when the lord of their castle helped Felipe II of Spain acquire the Portuguese crown, the populace set fire to his castle. So today it is a ruin, with a bit of romance about it.

Take N-222 north through Figueira to pass Almendra for 21 k to joint N-222 for 4 k more to Castelo Melhor.

Castelo Melhor

The little village clings to the side of a rocky peak below a fine medieval wall steadied by strong round towers. Alas, the castle inside is gone, replaced by grass.

Continue on N-222 as it descends and bends to meet the highway N-102. Take the highway south (left) for about 21 k to the village of Marialva, about 1 k to the right.

Marialva ★

The old walls above the modern village gird the ghost town of an earlier village. The castle and walls date to the beginning of the 13th century. The old village seems to have been abandoned for at least two centuries. An absolute time-warp is contained within the walls. There are remains of the castle keep, a tower wall, a church with a Manueline doorway, a 15th-century pillory and various aged houses, all empty.

Continue south along N-102 for 22 k to turn right on N-226 for Tancoso in 4 k.

Trancoso ★

In the 13th century King Dinis strengthened the original ninth-century walls and built a castle inside. Here he married his 12-year-old bride, Isabel of Castile, who later became a saint. As a wedding present Dom Dinis gave the village to his bride. Although it still retains some 16th-century houses, the walls at the northern end with their castle and squat keep are more interesting. (If it's closed, apply at the town hall.

Continue south along N-102 to Celorico da Beira in 13 k. Here N-16 can be taken east back to Guarda in 22 k. For the insatiable, there is castle donjon standing in busy Celorico da Beira before the turn.

MARVÃO ★★★

Population: 309
Area code: 045; zip code: 7330

From **Lisbon** go north along the autoestrada for 112 k to exit 7 for Entroncamento. Follow signs for Entroncamento and N-3 east. Continue on N-3 east for 40 k to little Rossio where N-118 is picked up. In 59 k Alpalhão is reached. Take N-246 east to Castelo de Vide in 14 k. There N-246-1 goes southeast to Portagem in 9 k for a turn north on N-359 for 4 k. From **Évora** take N-18 north, through **Estremoz**, for 105 k to Portalegre. Outside that city N-359 twists through mountains to Portagem in 17 k. Marvão is 4k further north on N-359. From **Coimbra** get to exit 7 for Entroncamento on the autoestrada A-1, 112 k south of Coimbra. From there the Lisbon directions apply.

Train service is infrequent, although connections can be made from Lisbon, Elvas and Portalegre to Beira, then a 10 k bus ride.

Portugal possesses a surplus of fairy tale hilltop villages surrounded by medieval walls commanded by ancient castles. Excursions from Guarda in this chapter cover ten such sites, and an equal number more could have been added. However, everyone agrees that Marvão is the most charming of the lot—the one to see, if seeing just one. Marvão exudes a calming atmosphere and shows prettiness at every hand, but there is not much to see in the tiny village butted against the eastern border with Spain. Sufficient variety in nearby excursions, however, justifies a stay overnight.

Since we are accustomed to villages nestling in valleys, the initial sight of Marvão is surprising—perched atop a steep hill with houses seeming to strain to reach even higher. The reason, of course, was for defense. The village castle was raised at the close of the 13th century and surrounded by curtain walls. A second wall was added to envelope the whole in the 17th century.

From the access road—that circles all arrivals around the peak—the village seems utterly impregnable. And so it has proven to be. Dazzlingly whitewashed houses, sporting orange tile roofs, cling to the walls. Hardly any are newer than the 17th century, so a walk through the cobbled street to the castle is hardly different today than it would have been three centuries ago, save for the odd TV aerial and telephone wire.

Rua do Espirito Sant leads to the castle, past handsome wrought-iron balconies. Four successive fortified gates must be passed to reach the fortress, which essentially consists of one massive keep. On a clear day the view from the walls is as fine as any in the country—looking east one sees Spain, a mere five miles away. Next to the castle stands a white chapel that serves both the **Office of Tourism** and the **Museu Municipal**, whose most interesting exhibits are mannequins in local costumes. (Open daily 9 a.m. to 12:30 p.m. and 2-5:30 p.m. Admission: 200$00.) The Office of Tourism maintains a list of inexpensive bed-and-breakfast rooms or even small houses rented by the locals.

WHERE TO STAY

Other than bed-and-breakfast rooms, there are only two hotels. Both are fine choices, but heavily booked.

MODERATE ($50-$99)

Pousada de Santa Maria 2nd-class ★★★
Rua 24 de Janeiro, 7. Rooms: 29. ☎ 932 01; FAX 934 40; Telex 42360. Three old town houses were joined to create this pousada. Its comfortable decor and spectacular views make this one of the nicer places to stay in Portugal. There is no attempt at elegance or grandeur, just cozy relaxation, including wood fires when there is a chill in the air.

INEXPENSIVE (UNDER $50)

Estalagem Dom Dinis R2nd-class ★
Rua Dr. Matos Magalhães. Rooms: 8. ☎ 932 36. This is a quiet, inviting place, with comfortably solid furnishings. A cheerful reception sets just the right tone.

WHERE TO EAT

While the food is somewhat better at Dom Dinis, the views from the relaxing Pousada dining room so enhance the experience that it must be the first choice. Prices are moderate.

EXCURSIONS

Past **Portalegre**, famed for tapestry, is the intriguing Knights' Templar monastery of **Flor de Rosa** ★, an outing of 36 k each way. **Castelo de Vide** ★, with a spa and ancient Jewish quarter, is only 12 k to the west, and a further 83 k would bring **Castelo Branco**, its lovely Bishop's palace and gardens, plus remarkable embroidered bedspreads.

PORTALEGRE

Population: 15,876
Area code: 045; zip code: 7300

Take N-359 southwest for 21 k. The road leads into Largo A. J. Lourinho. The tapestry workshop is one short block south and another east.

The city first acquired renown in the 16th century for sewing exquisitely detailed tapestries. A century later silk brought real prosperity and led to a clutch of fine 18th-century houses. But the tapestry work—still using woolen thread—continued and is still produced today in a workshop in an old monastery. A tour takes the visitor through all the steps, from making a slide of a work to be copied, to projecting it on graph paper (indicating the color of each stitch), to viewing actual pieces being sewn. None can be purchased, since all work is by commission, but nothing except the cost (roughly $4000 per square meter) stands in the way of ordering a piece for yourself. (Open for tours except Sun. 9:30-11:30 a.m. and 2:30-5:30 p.m.)

FLOR DE ROSA ★

Population 394

After 2 k from Portalegre on N-18 toward Alpalhão, take N-119 west for 34 k to Crato. There take N-245 north for 3 k.

The present town is so small as to be overwhelmed by the massive fortified monastery in its midst. The monastery is surrounded by a crenulated wall, and its buildings resemble small forts. Knights Templar of Malta constructed the monastery in the middle of the 14th century. On the right stands an elegantly simple church with a most impressive nave. Its small cloister is lovely. This is a favorite spot for those who take the small trouble to come here, and one generally has the complex all to oneself.

CASTELO DE VIDE ★

Population: 2558
Area code: 045; zip code: 7320

From Marvão regain the highway N-246, south of the village. Go west for 11 k.

Standing even higher than Marvão, Castelo de Vide presents a similar picture of whitewashed houses. The main square, **Praça Don Pedro V**, is ringed with 17th-century buildings and an 18th-century mansion. Beside the church of Santa Maria in the square, a sign shows the way up to the castle. To the right is the **Judiaria**, the ancient Jewish quarter.

The Judiaria is a jumble of small houses, many with two entrances, one for business, the other for family. Houses are small and crowded together because an ordinance decreed that Jews had to live separately from Christians, and locked inside their quarter each night.

Uncharacteristically, the **castle** lies inside its own walls outside those of the village. Its keep suffered damage from an explosion, but the 12th-century tower that leads to it is of interest. A 17th-century **church** on the site contains nice *azulejos*. Downhill from the Judiaria is a picturesque square, the **Fonte da Vila**, whose fountain waters are reputed to possess curative value and certainly taste sweet.

CASTELO BRANCO ★

Population: 24,287
Area code: 072; zip code: 6000

From Marvão continue past Castelo da Vide on N-246 for 25 k to Alpalhão. There N-118 continues in the same direction for 15 k to join IP-6 going north for 65 k.

Head straight through the city along Av. 1 de Maio which feeds into Rua de Se. Rua de Se bends left, then changes its name to Campo da Patria, as it climbs to the gardens of the former Bishop's palace.

The **gardens** of the former Episcopal Palace are a formal fantasy of clipped ornamental hedges, pools and unexpected statues. (*Open daily from 9 a.m. until 6 p.m.; admission: 100$00.*) To the left is the Episcopal Palace itself, with the **Museu Tavares Provença** installed inside (*Mon-Sat. from 10 a.m. until 12:30 and from 2 p.m. until 5:30; admission: 150$00*). Its most interesting exhibits are a series of *colchas*, embroidered bedspreads, for which this town has been famous since the 16th century. They are linen, embroidered with brightly colored figures in large-stitched silk thread. Originally, young women made them for their trousseaux. At the workshop, adjacent to the museum, pieces may be bought or commissioned.

MONSANTO

See "Guarda" under "Excursions."

MONSARAZ

See "Évora" under "Excursions."

REDONDO ★

See "Évora" under "Excursions."

THE ALGARVE

The beach at Praia da Rocha

Historical Profile: When Portugal Ruled the World

The name Algarve derives from the Arabic *al Garb*, which means "the west." It was the place where the Moors made their last stand in Portugal, retaining possession from the 8th until the middle of the 13th century. The orange, lemon, and almond trees covering the landscape; the water-wheels for irrigation; and the whitewashed houses with their cool interior patios are all the legacy of the Moors. Sadly, the 1755 Lisbon earthquake destroyed all but a few of the Moor's actual buildings, even in the distant Algarve.

By the 14th century, the Christian Portuguese had conquered the southern Muslims. Early in the next century, this territory had been consolidated with the north to create the first unified country in Europe. Now the burning question was what to do with national power, for it was a force no one yet knew how to employ.

Conquest was the first project. In 1415 King João I and his four sons sailed an armada of 240 ships across the narrow arm of the Atlantic between the Algarve and coastal Ceuta in Morocco to invade. It was a smashing success. The prime mover of the expedition, Prince Henry, who would later earn the name "the Navigator," received a long list of titles for his reward which brought control over vast acreage and, thus, huge wealth.

A first success naturally led to thoughts of another. In 1437, preparations were complete for a second invasion, this time of the major city of Tangiers. What transpired was a military disaster that could hardly have been worse. Worst of all, one of Henry's brothers, left behind as a hostage, languished until he died in prison. So much for conquest.

By this time, Prince Henry had embarked on a different course to prosperity. His idea was to gain wealth, not through conquest, but as the by-product of exploration. Henry was a strange man of ascetic tastes who, despite his wealth and power, took up residence in barren Sagres, the western end of the Algarve. He lived here because this windswept cape is the southwestern-most piece of Europe and, according to the ancients, the edge of the world. Here he could dream about lands unknown. More practically, he could interview sailors pausing on their way to cities further north to pick their brains about the sea.

Either at Sagres or perhaps at the better port of Lagos Henry established a sort of college of the sea, where students studied ship design along with the nascent science of navigation. At this early time, sailors feared losing sight of land because landmarks were their only guides to position. True, ships plied the Mediterranean and the European coast, but seldom the deep Atlantic where location could only be guessed at and offshore winds blew steadily against their voyages.

Henry financed his first expedition to waters off the coast of Morocco. Three of the four ships returned with nothing to report except the disappearance of one vessel. That ship, seemingly lost when blown away by a gale, later returned to Sagres with news of the first Portuguese discovery. An uninhabited island had been spied about

400 miles southwest of Sagres which the sailors named Porto Santo. Henry sent ships to colonize and develop this new resource, although difficulties arose after the rapidly proliferating progeny of a pet rabbit devoured all that was green on the island.

When sailors reported dense clouds hovering ominously on the horizon southwest of Porto Santo, Henry persuaded two retainers to investigate. They sailed into the cloud to emerge in the beautiful bay of a densely forested island they named Madeira, for the Portuguese word for wood. This was no mere dot in the sea but a volcanic hulk of almost 300 square miles. At first, the island's timber repaid the cost of the explorations many times over, then a fire broke out that burned for seven years to destroy the lush forests forever. Yet, ashes from the conflagration fertilized the soil to produce abundant crops, especially the rewarding cash-crop of sugarcane.

Four years later, in 1427, Henry financed the bravest voyage of the time, a sail straight west into the vast Atlantic. The risk was rewarded when the first of the volcanic string of mid-Atlantic Azores was sighted. Henry spent ten years organizing the colonization and development of these lush lands, including the importing of a settlement of Flemings, since the tiny population of Portugal provided few people to spare.

It must be noted that Henry was no pure scientist in conducting these ventures. In return for his financial support he demanded a full quarter, and sometimes half, of any profits realized. However, his greed was not personal—he remained simple in his tastes and style of living to the end—rather it was for the financing of still more ventures into the unknown.

As unknown as the Atlantic Ocean was, the continent of Africa formed an equally huge blank. But Africa was a prize because Europe craved herbs and spices from the east that passed overland through assorted middle-men via north Africa, adding many times to their costs. There were rumors of gold in Africa, and the enticement of people to convert to the "true" religion. All of which made the "dark" continent burn in Henry's brain.

Henry sent expedition after expedition down Africa's coast hoping for gold, for natives to convert, and, eventually, for the rounding of the continent to sail directly to the valuable spices. Huge obstacles, however, stood in the way. The first was Cape Bojador, at a thousand miles south of Europe the limit of known Africa. It took 20 years to finally round the cape, years without any of the returns Henry sought. But, once the cape was passed, all Africa lay open to exploration, if only the coast could be sailed. This was a problem, however, because traveling further south meant sailing against the wind, which sailboats cannot do.

Henry's college now came to the rescue. Designers adopted an old North African sailing vessel into a new model. It was a fat little ship, about 60 feet long, called a caravel. Its innovation, at least for Europe, was sails of triangular shape on movable spars, hence more maneuverable than the rigid square version. With such sails a ship could beat closer to the wind than anything the Europeans had known before.

Henry still had 26 years left to his life which he spent urging his captains further south. By his death the Portuguese had gained 2000 miles down Africa to Sierra Leone. The great western bulge of Africa had been rounded, leading some to believe that by travelling a little further they would be able to turn north to sail for the Spice Islands. Little did they know that they were not yet half way to Africa's tip. But fortresses to secure the territory had been built, a little gold found, some natives converted, and an inevitable impetus created that would eventually push the Portuguese the rest of the way.

At the same time, under Henry, a trade in human lives developed in which natives were captured or bought for sale as slaves in Portugal. Even with this blood-revenue Henry's countless ventures had exhausted his resources, leaving him in debt. In November of 1460, Prince Henry the Navigator died of fever in his palace in Sagres.

The Portuguese, of course, did not devote their energies only to exploration. After Henry's death, the next King had designs on Spain. He married the daughter of Castile's King, hoping to unite the two countries when her father died. After the death of the King of Castile, however, rumors spread that the King's new wife was illegitimate so the heir should be the Castilian king's half-sister. It took a war to decide the issue between the monarch of Portugal along with his Spanish wife, against forces siding with a young Castilian princess named Isabella who had married a prince from Arágon named Ferdinand. Needless to say, Portugal lost the war.

The succeeding king turned again to exploration. João II, called by Machiavelli "the perfect prince" for his complex and secret maneuvers, in 1487 underwrote the cost of three ships captained by Bartolomeu Dias. Dias was determined to round Africa. The voyage was a nightmare of contrary winds that forced the fleet to hole up in ports for days, then came unexpected cold as they fared south and, finally, a storm that blew them who-knew-where for two weeks.

After the winds calmed, Dias set course east, but sighted no land. He finally turned north out of desperation and landed 200 miles past the tip of Africa. They had rounded the continent. Since his sailors had no stomach left for storms, Dias returned to Portugal, this time sighting the cape he named *Boa Esperancia* (Good Hope). Three months after departing all three ships returned to Lisbon.

They arrived at precisely the moment to change the course of history. The young Christopher Columbus had adopted Portugal as his new country and applied to its king for support to sail west to China. King João II had put him off to consider the idea, but just as Columbus returned for a final decision, Dias sailed into port. The king now had no use for a second route to China, if his own sailor had opened one already. Columbus, rejected, went to Spain for funding. The rest is, as they say, history.

The Portuguese took five years to digest Dias' reports and plan the next stage to the Indies. Then, on March 6, 1493, Columbus sailed into Lisbon on his way back to Spain, reporting that he had just returned from those same Indies by a westward sail. Suddenly, the Portuguese faced competition.

Both Portugal and Spain rushed diplomats to the Papal Court in Rome, each claiming the rights to every new land that should be discovered and to a monopoly on trade in the Indies. A treaty between the two exploring powers was signed the next year giving Portugal all lands east of a longitude that divided South America in half lengthwise, all of Africa that the Portuguese had or would discover, and the Far East through most of China. Spain's sphere of control was east of a latitude that gave it North, Central and the western half of South America, along with easternmost China and Japan. Not that anyone knew at the time that the American continents existed, nor did either party to the agreement bother to ask the millions living in those areas what they thought of the deal.

Soon after signing the treaty, João II died after the short reign of 14 years. As soon as the next king, a 26-year-old aptly named Manuel "the Fortunate," consolidated his throne, he ordered that a fleet be fitted out to confirm by possession what the treaty specified in theory. The plan was to sail around Africa then all the way east to the Indies. By 1497 four stout ships under Vasco da Gama left Lisbon, tacked down the coast of Africa, rounded the Cape of Good Hope and landed for provisions at the furthest point Dias had reached. A half year after setting out, the flotilla reached Mozambique, only a quarter of the way up the east coast of Africa.

Their luck improved when they took on a native of India as a pilot who directed them straight across the Indian Ocean to his country. It was a leg of less than a month, even with island stops for provisions. After a voyage of ten months they had indeed reached India and, two years after embarking from Lisbon, they returned laden with spices.

King Manuel was thrilled with his profit of 60 times his investment. Eager for more, he commanded that his shipyards build a fleet of 13 ships to carry 1500 men on the next trip. This armada sailed south in 1500 under the command of a giant of a man named Pedro Alvares Cabral. Concerned about the difficulties others had encountered in rounding the Cape of Good Hope, Cabral decided to swing far west to catch winds that would blow him right by. After a month of this westward sail, however, land was unexpectedly sighted. The fleet anchored to investigate, traded with the natives, and left a delegation of former convicts to convert the inhabitants. Cabral then continued to India, not realizing that what seemed to be an island was in fact Brazil.

An expedition the next year to explore the western land that Cabral had found carried a Florentine named Amerigo Vespucci. Vespucci, a geography buff, realized that the "island" was in fact a continent. Later, a volume of supposed letters by Vespucci describing the events of this voyage became a best-seller in Europe. In one edition, a printer added *Americus*, the Latinization of Vespucci's first name, to title the map in his volume, and thus did the continent get its name.

By 1510 Portugal had received the port of Goa in India as an enclave for trade; by 1518 it had seized Ceylon; by 1557 a trading post had been established at Macão in China. Portugal now controlled all the European trade in eastern spices, making it the richest country on the continent. In addition, she had claim to two-thirds of Africa and to the entire country of Brazil, which occupies more than a quarter of South America.

But, with a population of only about a million and a half, Portugal was too small to retain for long what larger, more powerful countries envied. One by one, her possessions fell away either to stronger countries or to native independence movements. Portugal's riches and glory shined brightly, but not long.

THE ALGARVE

With clear summer skies, breezes to make a 90-degree sun pleasant, and 200 k of transparent water lining white-sand beaches, the popularity of the Algarve seems inevitable. And popular it is—especially among the English and the Germans—but its celebrity is recent. In 1960, the entire area held accommodations for about 10,000 visitors; today hotel capacity passes a quarter of a million and private accommodations double that number. Yet enough beaches exist to cradle so many bodies comfortably. The peculiar herding instincts of our species dictates that some towns will crowd with us, while others, equally or even more appealing, will remain relatively deserted. In sum, the crowd situation in the Algarve is not intolerable, especially considering that by whatever standard beaches are assessed, these are the best in Europe.

Development has added some of the world's premier golf courses, luxury accommodations, and fine restaurants. The Algarve can be expensive at such places, but enough bargains exist to make Algarve beaches potentially the best values in Europe.

But there always seems to be some problem with anything good in this world. The difficulty with the Algarve is that too many people want to come at the same time—July and August. For these two months the bed-capacity of the area strains. Reservations are imperative then, and must be made long in advance—by the end of January, the most desirable rooms will already be booked. True, a few places will have vacancies, and we will tell you about them, but to guarantee the trip you desire it is better to reserve well in advance. Failing that, check our descriptions of hotels that may have vacancies and reserve at one of them. Unfortunately, they tend to be expensive places. If such do not match your budget, the next best bet is to make reservations as soon as you can at second- and third-class hotels, for they tend not to be so well known.

The good news is that the sun shines strongly in May and remains warm into October; reservations are not even necessary before or after July and August (although June picks up tempo), and beaches become tranquil.

The Algarve separates into three geographic areas. From Faro to the Spanish border on the east the land is low, dunes form lagoons along the sea. A ribbon of sandbars just off the mainland calms the water and serves as a vast beach. The eastern resorts are Faro, Olhão and Tavira.

The center, from Faro west to Lagos, is lined by sandstone cliff that open to modest bays and harbors. Besides Lagos, these beaches comprise Praia do Rocha, Almação de Pêra, Albufeira, Vilamoura, Quarteira, and Vale do Lobo.

From Lagos to the western end of the Algarve at Cabo de São Vicente, high granite cliffs break into grottoes and wild rock formations, cut by small coves that are exceptionally scenic. Resorts include Sagres, Salema, and Praia de Luz, going from west to west.

We add a fourth area, the southwestern coastline—which technically is counted as part of the Alentejo, rather than the Algarve. A beach is a beach, so it seems sensible to include all the southern beaches, rather than give in to government divisions. These southwestern beaches generally remain undeveloped, which is good news and bad. Good, for the absence of crowding, and bad, for the lack of facilities. They face the wide sweep of the Atlantic Ocean which cut soft rock into picturesque coves embraced by cliffs. These beaches include Porto Covo, Vila Nova de Milfontes, Almograve and Odeceixe.

Only the center—from Faro to Lagos—sees excessive crowds. Secluded beaches exist both east of Faro and west of Lagos, with Tavira on the east and Sagres on the west excelling. Whether crowded or not, the sand is fine and white all along the coast. Temperatures are the highest in Portugal. Vegetation is lush, and the ocean is clean.

The resorts and villages of the Algarve are each unique. Since they form a line along the coast, the most convenient presentation is geographic rather than alphabetic. We cover the resorts starting from Sagres, the westernmost, then work our way east, leaving the beaches of the southwestern Alentejo to their own section at the end.

West of Albufeira the major road is the dual-laned N-125 that clogs in summer and runs inland, but connects with the resorts by feeder roads. From Albufeira, roughly the center of the Algarve, east to Spain the autoestrada IP-1 speeds traffic conveniently. Although trains run parallel to the coast, for the most part they chug inland stopping only at a handful of coastal towns. Local buses serve every village, but often with frequent, time-consuming stops.

From **Lisbon** *autoestrada A-2 reaches* **Setubal** *in 50 k. From there N-10 east for 21 k reaches Marateca to join N-5 south for 31 k to Alcaçer do Sal to change its designation to N-120. For the more scenic route, bear right in 18 k to continue on N-120 along the coast to the western Algarve in about 180 k. A faster route is to continue to Grândola and*

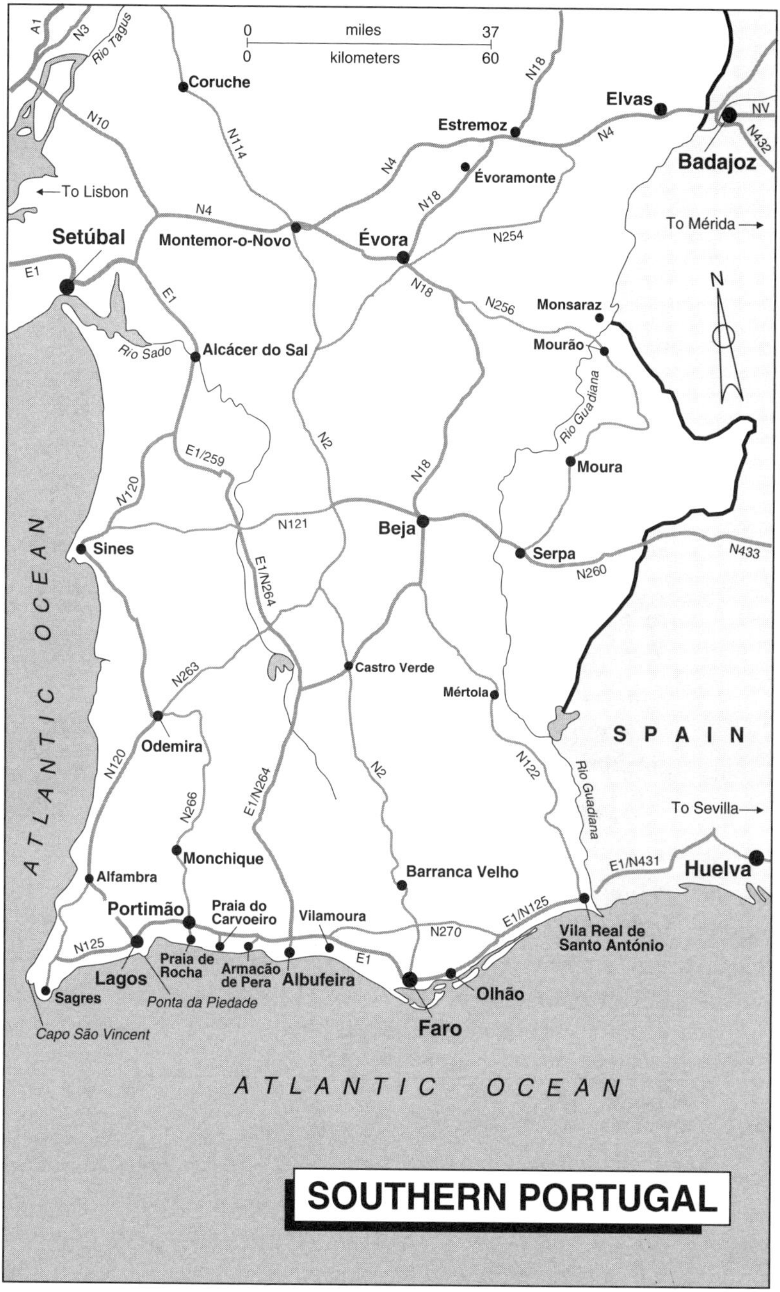

0 miles 37
0 kilometers 60
A1
N3
Rio Tagus
Coruche
N10
N114
To Lisbon
Estremoz
N18
Elvas
N4
NV
Badajoz
N432
Évoramonte
N18
N4
Setúbal
Montemor-o-Novo
Évora
N254
To Mérida
E1
N18
N256
Monsaraz
N
Rio Sado
Alcácer do Sal
Mourão
Rio Guadiana
N2
Moura
E1/259
N120
N18
N121
Beja
Sines
Serpa
N433
N260
E1/N264
ATLANTIC OCEAN
Castro Verde
N263
Mértola
SPAIN
Odemira
N120
N122
Rio Guadiana
N2
N266
E1/N264
To Sevilla
Monchique
E1/N431
Huelva
Alfambra
Barranca Velho
E1/N125
Portimão
Praia do Carvoeiro
Vilamoura
N270
Vila Real de Santo António
N125
Praia de Rocha
Armacão de Pera
Albufeira
E1
Lagos
Sagres
Ponta da Piedade
Olhão
Faro
Capo São Vincent
ATLANTIC OCEAN
SOUTHERN PORTUGAL

take N-259 southeast, turning south onto N-262 in about 20 k toward Azinheira dos Barros. Stay on the road as it becomes N-264 for a leg of 204 k. The trip of 272 k takes less than 5 hours except in busy summer, and ends near Albufeira, roughly the center of the Algarve. The recommended route, however, is to Évora to see some of Portugal's finest sights, spend the night, and travel on. Directions to Évora are included in the "Excursion" section of "Lisbon"; the leg from Évora to the Algarve is described below. From **north of Lisbon**, skirt Lisbon by turning east onto N-10 just before Vila Franca de Xira (a crafts center for brass, rugs, and objects made of horn), 35 k before the capital. In 49 k N-10 reaches Cruzamento de Pegões where attention is required in order to remain on N-10 for a southern swing of 14 k to Marateca, from which the Lisbon directions apply. From **Évora** N-18 heads southeast toward Beja, 78 k away. Continue south along N-122 which changes its designation three times—to N391, then to N-123—in the 60 k to Ourique. A final leg on N-264 ends near Albufeira after 79 k. From **Spain** the shortest drive is from Ayamonte, which is a direct 159 k from Seville. A bridge now crosses the Guadiana River to Vila Real de Santo Antonio at the eastern extreme of the Algarve. From north of Andalusia follow directions to Évora, then the directions above.

Daily **flights** of 40 minutes connect Lisbon with Faro. The train from Lisbon to Faro takes about 7 hours, with the bus taking as long and being only slightly cheaper. Special "Alta Qualidade" buses streak to Albufeira in 4-1/2 hours. Express buses take 5 hours, and cost more than the train that does the same trip in 4 hours.

SAGRES ★★

Population: 2032
Area code: 082; zip code: 8650

West of **Lagos** N-125 deteriorates, as fewer tourists and towns result in less upkeep. In 23 k from Lagos, Vila do Bispo is reached; N-125 ends and N-268 is picked up turning south for a final 10 k to Sagres.

Sagres is the only true town on the Sagres Peninsula, a land—as the sparse vegetation indicates—of constant wind. Here Prince

Henry the Navigator resided, whose energies and finances fueled the Portuguese exploration of the world. Living at the southwestern-most tip of Europe, Prince Henry came as close to participating in those discoveries as his duties allowed.

The present village of Sagres on the sheltered east side of a small promontory is newer, consisting of but three streets paralleling the water. It is popular with fishermen, backpackers and nature lovers. The village is spreading and dusty, rather like a frontier town, but the three peninsulas—one east, one south and Capo São Vincente to the west—are lovely. Scenic coves around the town provide beach shelter from the wind.

Prince Henry lived about 5 k west of the village on the naked extremity of Cabo Vicente. Today as then, the cape is desolate, and awesome for it. Sir Francis Drake destroyed Henry's monastery in a raid just before the time of the Spanish Armada and burned his great maritime library. Today, nothing but the land is as Henry knew it. A 16th-century fortress has been partly reconstructed, inside of which stands a 14th-century sailors' chapel. A compass marked on the grounds dates from after Henry's time. Close to the cliff edge a lighthouse presents awesome views of waves whipped into froth by wind and rocks.

While the town beaches are serviceable, there is a quieter one in Praia do Martinhal reached by leaving town on N-268 toward Vila do Bispo. Turn right at a sign in 2 k. A truly spectacular beach lies beyond Vila do Bispo, by continuing on N-268. In the little town a sign to the "praia" directs a left turn that becomes a bumpy road circling steep hills for three k on the way to a string of three scenic beaches. The first beach, called Castelejo, starts from a precipitous headland at its south end and stretches to craggy offshore rocks on the north. The sand is long and fine. There, Restaurant Castelejo serves mouthwateringly fresh fish. The road continues to a second and third beach, neither so large or lovely as the first, but useful if crowds push you on. Since these beaches line the western Atlantic, they tend to receive breezes even when other Algarve beaches swelter airlessly.

If these beaches are not isolated enough, try Praia da Bordeira with a Big Sur magnificence. Long rolling waves crash against sand dunes, and there is nothing around. In fact the beach is so deep it looks like the desert. It is reached over a bumpy dirt road after a turn from N-268 at "Carrapateira", 13 k north of Vila do Bispo. There is a decent restaurant just before Citio da Rio.

WHERE TO STAY

Accommodations are easier to come by here than elsewhere along the coast.

EXPENSIVE ($100–$200)

Pousada do Infante 1st-class ★★★
Ponta da Atalaia (halfway between the harbor and Mareta beach, well signed). Rooms: 23. ☎ *642 22; FAX 642 25; Telex 57491.* This new pousada is styled as a monastery gleaming white atop a small promontory just outside of town. It is quite imposing. The location is prime—beach lies below, a pool and terrace above present the ocean stretching infinitely. Bedrooms are comfortable, with the same glorious views, but antiseptic in feeling. A tennis court and riding stables adjoin. As far as comfort goes, there are no complaints and the view is as good as a view ever gets. Still, there is a coldness about the place. More warmth is to be found in some of the moderate choices below.

MODERATE ($50–$99)

Residêncial Dom Henrique R2nd-class ★★★
Sítio da Mareta (in a cul de sac off the Pr. República, on the cliff above Mareta beach). Rooms: 28. ☎ *641 33.* Here the ocean is your backyard, for this is the closest hotel to Mareta beach. The views match those of the pousada at a third of its price. This hotel is the proverbial "charmer," even to a funky bar in the garden and an aviary next door for soothing bird sounds. The hotel is a large, quaint house with guest rooms to rent. Every one is comfortable and the more expensive ones provide ocean and beach views. Demand one. The management is very accommodating.

Motel Os Gambozinos 3rd-class ★★
At the Praia do Martinhal, 3.5 k northeast, off N-125 at the sign for "Martinhal". Rooms: 17. ☎ *643 18.* If the idea of a secluded hotel above a cozy deserted beach appeals, here it is. The hotel is shaped as a long bungalow, and run by a Dutch couple with the cleanliness one would expect of such proprietors. Rooms are simple and white, but charmingly decorated with little frescos. Good taste is evident. A walk through the garden leads down to the beach, so that you feel in the country while staying at the seashore. Note, at these low prices air conditioning is not supplied. The restaurant below the hotel is good enough for a visit even if staying elsewhere.

Aparthotel Navigator A2nd-class ★★
R. Infante D. Henrique (next to the pousada). Rooms: 56. ☎ *643 54; FAX 643 60; Telex 57179.* This new tall, white structure looks grand from the outside, but more modest within. All its rooms are apartments with sitting rooms and include cooking facilities, which is a fine idea for a resort. While the decor is rather drab, the price is remarkably low for what it buys. Rooms numbered from 11 through 17 on each floor own the best views.

aleeira   2nd-class ★

On the cliff above the village. Rooms: 118. ☎ 642 12; FAX 644 25; Telex 75467. The views overlooking the beach and port are lovely, but the bedrooms are less so. Some are small and most have linoleum floors. There is a dramatic pool and a tennis court, however, and prices are comfortably moderate which makes this a reasonable choice.

WHERE TO EAT

Sagres village is full of inexpensive and moderately priced restaurants. or food that is a cut above, one has to travel 5 k to Cabo São Vicente.

MODERATE ($15-$30)

ortaleza do Beliche   ★

5 k along the road to Cabo Vicente (at the traffic circle in Sagres, take the road to Beliche). ☎ 641 34. This establishment is run by the ENATUR pousada system and offers four rooms for sleeping, but primarily serves as a restaurant. It is installed in a tiny fort, hence the name, that can only be described as cute. The decoration used to be a rather phoney Henry-the-Navigator in theme, but the restaurant was being renovated when we last stopped. After renovation, food and the view should continue to be good but we will check.

Major credit cards accepted.

Tasca

In the little Sagres port. ☎ 641 77. This is the most popular restaurant in town, but not with us. It is a barn of a building decorated with wine bottles imbedded in patterns in cement walls. Tables are heavy wood. It is better to dine on the large terrace outside. All indications make this seem like a place where the fish should be fresh and the cooking authentic. In fact, while the fish is fresh enough, it is cooked with no great care, a lack of seriousness that extends to the wait-people too rushed to care either. If meals had cost half what they do, we would feel twice as charitable.

DIRECTORY

INFORMATION • Located in the Pr. de Liberdade (☎ 641 20).

SHOPPING • Hipperceràmica Paraíso in Raposeira, which is 3 k east of ila do Bispo on N-125, is a barn of a place on the highway that sells the heapest **pottery** in the country. While some pieces can be ghastly, prices re amazing for attractive plain planters and serving dishes.

For reasonably priced hand-woven **sweaters**, go to the fort on Capo São 'incente where mobile stands generally display their wares.

Bikes and **mopeds** can be rented either at the GULP gas station on the ircle entering town or at the kiosk called "do Papa" on the main street ito town.

SALEMA ★

Population: 1232
Area code: 082; zip code: 8650

From Sagres take N-268 for 10 k to Vila do Bispo where N-125 is picked up going east toward Lagos. In 6 k, just past Fiqueira a sign to Praia da Salema indicates a right turn and a 3 k drive. From Lagos take N-125 for 15 k to pass Budens where a sign indicates a left turn and a 3 k drive to Praia da Salema.

The village of Salema consists of just a few stores, houses and hotels that cluster near a nice beach. While there are more spectacular shores along the coast, for some reason this one draws a crowd of British. In fact, British is the language most heard here. It is a jolly town, where families holiday, but with nothing much to do except sun and swim.

WHERE TO STAY

Although only the British seem to know about this little community they do their best to fill all the rooms, so accommodations are not easy to come by.

MODERATE ($50-$99)

Estalagem Infante do Mar   E1st-class ★★

Praia da Salema (17k. east, above the village of Salema). Rooms: 1 ☎ 651 37; FAX 574 51. This hotel is rustic and bright. The bedrooms are spotless and comfortable, though modest in size, and all present fine sea views from their balconies. The bathrooms could be larger but parking is easy. While it is a hike to the beach, the view from your room repays the sacrifice.

Residêncial Salema   R2nd-class ★

R. 28 de Janeiro (one block up from the beach). Rooms: 32. ☎ 653 28 FAX 553 29. This modern monolith offers no surprises. It is spare clean and boxy. For some reason, it is aligned sideways to the beach so the rooms do not provide as much view as they could. Air conditioning is a bonus for the low prices.

WHERE TO EAT

A number of small restaurants dot the village, but our favorite is the one on the beach.

INEXPENSIVE (under $15)

Atlântico   ★★

On the beach. This is the simplest of restaurants where only simple food is provided on either a veranda or within a small interior. How ever, the freshest of fish with french fries and a salad costs a pittance. The fish will melt in your mouth and leave the aroma of wood smoke. If fresh fish is your desire, this is your place. Those who are contrary can order a hamburger and fries. Even the pudim Molotov is good.

PRAIA DA LUZ ★★

Population: 1013
Area code: 082; zip code: 8600

From **Sagres** *take N-268 for 10 k to Vila do Bispo where N-125 is picked up going east toward Lagos. In 16 k, at Espiche, a sign to Praia da Luz indicates a right turn and a 3 k drive. From Lagos take N-125 for 15 k to pass Budens where a sign indicates a left turn and a 2k drive to Praia da Luz. From* **Lagos***, take N-125 west for 6 k to the other side of Espiche where a sign indicates a left of 2 k to Praia da Luz.*

Although the homes are the typical Algarvean white, they are fewer and larger here. This beach community is cosmopolitan, affluent and hip. There are boutique shops, cute restaurants, nightclubs and very expensive cars. Development appeared only recently by and for the British, who come for the long stretch of beach scenically lined by barren hills.

WHERE TO STAY

There is really only one hotel in the village, but that one is a huge complex separated into four locations. The original section, which earns the "club" part of the hotel name, is a tennis center serious about the sport and teaching of it. The complex is large enough that it often has a room or two free even when other resorts are overflowing.

MODERATE ($50-$99)

The Ocean Club 1st-class ★★
Praia da Luz 8600, Lagos. Rooms: 250. ☎ *78 94 72; FAX 78 97 63.* All of the complexes are elegant designs and lushly gardened. The rooms are large for the price, clean white, and have sea views. Your choice is between the club, the garden and the waterside village, near the beach. Rooms come in many varieties, from studios, which are quite inexpensive, to apartments with cooking facilities. Only the two and three bedroom apartments pass the moderate price category. Note: a five-day minimum stay is sometimes imposed.

WHERE TO EAT

A number of attractive small restaurants have opened in the village. We like an old standby overlooking the water.

MODERATE ($15–$30)

O Poço

Av. dos Pescadores (on the ocean road and one block west of the center the village). ☎ 78 91 89. The dining room is on the second floor the ocean can spread out before you. It is somewhat dark and a litt worn, but the owners are serious about food. The menu is varied, b fish is best. *Major credit cards accepte*

LAGOS ★★

Population: 10,054
Area code: 082; zip code: 8600

From **Sagres** take N-268 for 10 k to Vila do Bispo where N-125 is picked up going east toward Lagos for 24 k. From **Portimão** Lagos is 17 k on N-125. From **Faro** take N-2 north to the autoestrada in 11 k, then west on IP-1 to the end near Albufeira in 33 k. Here N-125 goes to Lagos in another 45 k.

Lagos is the gateway to the western Algarve. Although small b most measures, it is the second largest of the coastal resorts, and live ly and cosmopolitan. It conveys the bright and busy feeling of a Riv iera-type resort.

Somehow Lagos is able to perform the miracle of absorbing tou ists while remaining itself throughout the summer invasion. Havin one of the widest bays on the coast helps. Sheltered by promontorie both east and west, the town lines the estuary of the river Bensafrir to command a huge bay. It attracts tourists with its gorgeous Don Ana beach whose stone pillars in the water are so often photo graphed that for most people this beach represents the Algarve Nearby are sea grottos where the light turns the water neon green.

The problem with Lagos is that there are no truly exceptional ac commodations. For this reason Praia da Luz might be a better bet An 8 k ride by car, taxi or bus would bring you all that Lagos offers

It was from Lagos that King Sebastião set out in 1578 to conque Morocco. (See "Historical Profile: The Rise And Fall Of The Hous Of Avís" on page 119.) This romantic who dreamed of God an chivalry died in battle, as he surely would have wished, but neglecte to leave any heirs. His death created a vacuum that let the Spanish seize Portugal, and the Portuguese have longed for their chivalrou king ever since. A modern statue of Dom Sebastião in the mai square enhances his myth by presenting the young king in the guis of a spaceman.

Although razed along with so many other Portuguese towns by the 1755 earthquake, Lagos preserves a quantity of 18th-century houses built immediately afterwards. The old part of town, just inland from the ancient **fort** with drawbridge at the river mouth, contains many. The Pr. da República opens up at the north end of the riverine corniche. Under the arches of the **customs house** bordering the square, slave auctions were held until the 19th century, one of the sorriest aspects of the Portuguese explorations. No sign marks these events.

One block west from the Pr. da República is the chapel of **Santo António**, with a wood facade and an interior that is a gilded rococo gem. Note the trompe l'oiel barrel ceiling, and the elegant polychrome altar that survived the quake. Adjoining stands the **Museu Municipal**, displaying an eccentric collection that ranges from Roman mosaics to mutant animals preserved in jars. There is, as they say, something for everyone. (*Open Tues.-Sun. from 9 a.m. to 12:30 and 2-5 p.m.; closed Holidays; admission: 200$00.*)

Parallel to the river, one block inland, runs a lively pedestrian mall of shops and outdoor cafes that begins at the Pr. Gil Eanes.

As to beaches, **Praia de Dona Ana** is a fantasy of rocks carved into wild shapes by the sea and mysterious grottoes washed by green waters. It lies 2 k due south. Here the **Ponta da Piedade** (Point of Piety) presents stunning views. To walk, follow the river road, Av. dos Descobrimentos, west to its end at the fort where a sign points to Praia de Pinhão. At Praia de Pinhão beach paths lead to Praia Dona Ana, after a total walk of 30 minutes. Alternatively, motorboats from the port take sightseers to explore the grottoes. The **Office of Tourism** just behind the main square of Pr. Gil Eanes at Largo Marquês de Pombal has details. For a wide stretch of sand there is Meia Praia—all 4 k of it—to the east of Lagos, across the bay. Although extensive, this beach is backed by railroad tracks and a line of depressing shanties.

WHERE TO STAY

The option to stay in town rather than on the beach is a viable one, for the town is lively.

EXPENSIVE ($100-200)

De Lagos   Deluxe ★★

Rua Nova da Aldeia (on a hill near the bus station, opposite the port). Rooms: 317. ☎ *76 99 67; FAX 76 99 20; Telex 57477.* This luxury complex sprawls over a hilltop and is a peculiar hotel you will either love or be puzzled by. The lobby is an arena where tour groups mill. The rest of the hotel combines inside hallways like village streets with rooms reached by outside passageways. The idea, we think, is to provide an outdoor feeling. Bedrooms are comfortable, but with faded 60s decor, and provide views either of the town, the pool, or the lush courtyard. Don't expect any warmth from the staff, although they do automatically enroll guests in the Duna Beach Club that the hotel owns on Meia Praia beach. A jitney regularly makes the five-minute trip from the hotel. Golf is available.

At Praia Dona Ana:

Golfinho   Deluxe

Praia Dona Ana, 8600 Lagos. Rooms: 262. ☎ 76 99 00; FAX 76 99 99. For a hotel of this class overlooking such a lovely view, the Golfinho could hardly be more disappointing. It is greatly in need of renovation, but deals mainly with tour groups who seem not to care. At half the price, the nearby Sol e Praia below is more than twice the value.

MODERATE ($50-99)

Marazul   R3rd-class ★★

Rua 25 de Abril 20, 13 (one block south of the Pr. Marquês de Pombal). Rooms: 18. ☎ 76 91 43; FAX 76 99 60; Telex 58760. Closed from the last week in November to the end of December. Attractive, centrally located, and immaculate, this is a pleasant place to stay. It's on the second floor and the floors are marble. Furniture is attractive wicker. Back rooms have water views and quiet, but all rooms are moderately priced, and as clean as can be. Not air-conditioned.

At Praia Dona Ana:

Casa de S. Gonçalo de Lagos   R1st-class ★★

Rua Cândido dos Reis, 73 (in the heart of the old town). Rooms: 13. ☎ 76 21 71; Telex 57411. The layout is somewhat unconventional in this old house, as is the decor, but all is decorated with style and the roof terrace is sylvan. If it were not for the noise of revellers from the bars nearby, this hotel would be more strongly recommended. Avoid street-level rooms for that reason.

Sol e Praia   2nd-class ★

Praia Dona Ana, 8600 Lagos. Rooms: 56. ☎ 76 20 26; FAX 76 02 47. Closer to the beach than the more expensive Golfinho, the rooms are basic but with pleasant balconies. The management is warm.

São Cristovão   2nd-class ★

Rossio de São João (on the main intersection at the edge of town). Rooms: 80. ☎ 76 30 51; Telex 56417. This modern hotel is well run and offers comfortable bedrooms at a very fair rate. The problem is its location, both because of the traffic and the distance from the beach.

Lagosmar   R2nd-class ★

Rua Dr. Faria e Silva, 13 (just north of the Pr. Marquês de Pombal). Rooms: 45. ☎ 76 37 22; FAX 76 73 24. In the same area as the Marazul and with more rooms, if smaller, this is a perfectly adequate and squeaky clean second choice.

Meia Praia   2nd-class
On the beach of Meia Praia, 2 k east. Rooms: 66. ☎ *76 20 01; Telex 57489. Closed from November through the middle of April.* This is a hotel that has seen better days on a quiet part of a beach backed by railroad tracks and shanties. It is all just a bit depressing. There are gardens for relaxing, however, and a feeling of isolation. Two tennis courts are provided in addition to a pool. The bedrooms could be more attractive, but those with sea views are decorated by the planet's best decorator.

WHERE TO EAT

Inexpensive restaurants congregate along Ruas Lopes and Sociro da Costa, stretching north of the museum.

EXPENSIVE ($50+)

Alpendre ★
Rua António Barbosa Viana, 17 (1 block west of the Pr. Marquês de Pombal). ☎ *76 27 05. Open in season only.* This is the most celebrated restaurant in town, once praised by *Gourmet* magazine. We do not know why. Although the restaurant is a fine one, such praise is excessive—restaurants that flambé everything prize effect above subtle flavors. The dining room is attractive, but a sort of Musak intrudes on the mood. Reservations are necessary.

Amex, Diners, and MasterCard accepted.

MODERATE ($15-$30)

Dom Sebastião ★
Rua 25 de Abril 20-2 (in the mall 1 block south of the Pr. Gil Eanes). ☎ *76 27 95. Closed Sunday off season and from the middle to the end of December.* This restaurant enjoys great popularity because it serves good Portuguese food. Specialties include shellfish, which can run up the bill. The wine list is superb. The dining room has the feel of an old, comfortable inn in dark wood and offers fine value for the price.

Amex, Diners, and MasterCard accepted.

Dom Henrique ★
Rua 25 de Abril 75, (3 blocks south of the Pr. Gil Eanes). ☎ *76 35 63. Closed Sunday off season and from the middle to the end of December.* This is the most attractive of the taverns along the mall, all cozy wood and inviting. Prices are low for the quality. Try the shrimp omelet.

Amex, Diners, and MasterCard accepted.

Os Arcos
R. 25 de Abril, 30 (two blocks south of the Pr. Gil Eanes). ☎ *76 32 10. Closed Sunday off season and from the middle to the end of December.*

Attractive and busy it is, but the food is a rung below the preceding.
Amex, Diners, and MasterCard accepted.

INEXPENSIVE (UNDER $15)

Hasan's Doner Kebab ★

Rua Silva Lopes, 27 (at the south end of the mall). ☎ 76 46 82. This is a hole-in-the-wall, primarily for take-out of falafel, shwarma and donerkebob. Everything is tasty and inexpensive.

ALVOR ★

Population: 1365
Area code: 082; zip code: 8500

From **Lagos** *head east along N-125 for 14 k until a sign past Figueira points to the feeder road south for 6 k more. From* **Portimão** *Alvor is reached in 6 k by taking Estrada de Alvor that cuts through the center of town. From* **Albufeira** *go west on N-125 past Portimão for 35 k. Look for the sign to turn left for the last 6 k.*

Although midway between the two very international resorts of Lagos and Portimão, tiny Alvor has managed to retain its Portuguese character. It still is a fishing village dressed all in white, only today it is overlooked by characterless, giant high-rise hotels.

Igreja Matriz, from the 16th century presents a lovely face in the form of an intricate Manueline doorway, although inside, except for some attractive azulejos on the right replicating windows, little is memorable.

The beach is expansive and long, which is what brought all the big hotels. Unfortunately, there are no wonderful accommodations for enjoying the quaint charm of the town and its ample beach to the fullest.

WHERE TO STAY

As indicated, the hotel situation is drab in the main. There are plenty of rooms in high-rises on the hill outside of town, but they deal mainly with tour groups and are as impersonal as hotels can be. The better choice would be the Prainha complex, outside of town, or the moderate selection below.

EXPENSIVE ($100-200)

Praihha Club Hotel Deluxe ★ ★

Praia dos Três Irmãos, Apartado 25, 8500 Portimão (above the spectacular beach of Três Irmãos 2 k east of Alvor). Rooms: 300. ☎ 763 458 677; FAX 459 569. There is no more dramatic beach in the Algarve and this elegant complex sits on 86 well developed acres above it. This is a hotel that will sell you a room in addition to renting one, for it is a condo complex that rents available units for the night. So bright white on the outside that it hurts the eyes, accommodations inside are more restful and very well designed.

Alvor Praia — Deluxe ★★
Praia dos Três Irmãos, 8500 Portimão (above the spectacular beach of Três Irmãos 2 k east of Alvor). Rooms: 217. ☎ *458 900; FAX 458 999.* Right on the beach, this hotel provides everything you desire except character. All services are available from saunas to golf and entertainment. Only 160 of the rooms have sea views. Prices are on the high side even of expensive.

Delfim Hotel — 1st-class ★
Praia dos Três Irmãos, 8500 Portimão (on the road into Alvor from N-125). Rooms: 312. ☎ *458 901; FAX 458 970.* The plain high-rise does what it can to maximize a special setting above a gorgeous beach. But the management is so busy with package tours that they have little time for individuals.

MODERATE ($50-99)

Aparthotel Alvor Jardim — 2nd-class ★★
Sitio de São Pedro (just before Alvor). Rooms: 28. ☎ *763 458 022; FAX 458 024.* This is among the very few hotels in this convivial town that feels friendly. All the rooms are apartments, which means that they incorporate cooking facilities, although they range from one room, to a separate bedroom, to two separate bedrooms. They are priced by size, but all are good values. The rooms are simple and contain minimal furniture, but they glisten. The town is four blocks away and the beach is reached in about a ten minute walk.

WHERE TO EAT

Two little authentic restaurants have been in business beside the Alvor quay since before the tourists came. **Os Pescadores**, all white with blue doors, and **Aba Abuja**, small with dark wood, can be counted on for fish that just wiggled their last at inexpensive prices.

PORTIMÃO/PRAIA DA ROCHA ★

Area code: 082; zip code: 8500

*N-125, coming from **Albufeira**, leads to Portimão in 30 k. It is 17 k **east** of Lagos on that same road. Praia da Rocha lies at the end of a 2 k feeder road to the coast.*

Praia da Rocha is the beach for the city of Portimão, a grey, sardine-canning town with nothing but fresh sardines to attract the visitor. Its beach is quite another matter. It is flat, golden, long, spotted with the eccentric boulders that gave it its name, and backed by varicolored cliffs at either end. This beach will not, however, be a personal discovery, as the high rises forming a solid line obscuring the cliffs will prove. It is only the first of a series of beaches that stretch to Lagos 18 k away. West along Av. Tomas Cabreira comes Praia do Vau in 3 k, then Praia dos Três Irmãos in 4.5 k and Praia d Alvor in 5 k, followed, after a deviation inland, by Meia Praia in 14 k All are long and lovely and attract an upscale crowd to their expensive hotels.

To be blunt, development has ruined Praia da Rocha, which once was the jewel of the Algarve. Today it is a mile long strip of shops restaurants and hotels lining a road beside the beach. Naturally, the beach is covered with all the bodies that inhabit those numerous hotels. In Praia da Rocha's case, forget natural beauty and think Miami Beach.

WHERE TO STAY

This popular resort offers accommodations in all ranges. We wish w liked the town more because it offers some wonderful hotels.

VERY EXPENSIVE ($200+)

Algarve 1st-class ★ ★

Av. Tomás Cabreira (on the main drag at about the middle of the beach Rooms: 220. ☎ *41 50 01; FAX 41 59 99; Telex 57347.* The Algarve is modern luxury hotel perched so close to the beach that its terrace i cantilevered over it. Decoration is glittery and every service is available. The rooms are handsome and the lobby is impressive, but noth ing is wonderful enough to merit the prices, not when there are fou more interesting hotels in town all substantially lower in cost.

Hotel Apartamento Oriental 1st-class ★ ★ ★ ★

Av. Tomás Cabreira (just east from the Algarve on the main drag). Room. 85. ☎ *413 000; FAX 412 413; Telex 58788.* We would spend for thi one because it is fun. The hotel is built on the site of the old casino and the city fathers decreed that any building replacing that landmar would have to copy its style. That is why the outside is Moroccan. Th reason for the five-story atrium inside is just the whim of opulence Everything sparkles of the finest materials. As opposed to the mor expensive Algarve, in the Oriental you get not a room, but a smal suite with cooking facilities, and for less. Like the Algarve, it is literall on the beach with great ocean views. Garden apartments line the side

EXPENSIVE ($100-200)

Bela Vista 1st-class ★ ★ ★

Av. Tomás Cabreira (toward the west end of the beach). Rooms: 14 ☎ *240 55; FAX 41 53 69; Telex 57386.* This hotel is a century-ol former summer mansion that has been a hotel for half a century. Thu it owns the seasoned atmosphere that no modern hotel can buy Enough grandeur remains to make an adventure of investigating th art nouveau rooms and azulejoed halls. And, it is right on the beach with a relaxing terrace. You feel like a rich person here, even though it doesn't cost a fortune. Bedrooms all are different in style and price, but if the only availabilities are in the annex, go elsewhere. The management is friendly.

úpiter   **1st-class ★**

Av. Tomás Cabreira (across the street from the Bela Vista). Rooms: 180. ☎ 41 50 41; FAX 41 53 19; Telex 57346. At half the cost of the Algarve hotel nearby, this hotel is about half as good. Bedrooms are nothing special, and the service is about what is expected for the category. Since it is not on the beach side of the street, the sea views are over hotels. Affiliated with the Best-Western chain.

MODERATE ($50-99)

Albergaria Vila Lido   **A1st-class ★ ★ ★ ★**

Av. Tomás Cabreira (at its extreme east end, by the fort). Rooms: 10. ☎ 241 27; FAX 242 46. Closed from the middle of December to the middle of January. Twenty years ago this villa where the Kennedys once stayed was lovingly restored to perfection by the sweet family that runs it. You'll feel you're staying in a home you wish you owned. It isn't grand, but every detail is perfect, and you can order the best suite, a huge room with an imposing terrace, while remaining in the moderate-price category. We call that a steal.

Avenida Praia   **2nd-class ★**

Av. Tomás Cabreira (toward its west end). Rooms: 61. ☎ 41 77 40; FAX 41 77 42; Telex 56448. The views are about the same from this comfortable hotel as from others charging several as times much.

INEXPENSIVE (-$50)

Residential Toca   **R2nd-class ★ ★**

R. Engenheiro Francisco Bivar (take a left at the Avenida Praia, then a second left). Rooms: 14. ☎ 240 35. Open from April through October. At these prices you don't get a sea view. But you get as clean (or cleaner) accommodations as at the finest hotels and it's only a block walk to the beach. The management is friendly, daughter Monica speaks English and there are always fresh flowers, thanks to Mom. You'll like it, we guarantee.

Residencial Solar Penguin   **R2nd-class ★ ★**

Av. Tomás Cabreira (in a tiny park at the extreme west end of the beach). Rooms:14. ☎ 243 08. You will tell your friends about this one. Its location is prime—on the beach atop a small cliff for fabulous views. The building is over 100 years old, first owned by a Scot who liked penguins (hence the name), now owned by an expatriate English woman named Dorothy Bolter who has been there for, shall we say, a while. The place oozes with the character of better days it has seen. Of course there are cleaner places, and hotels with more services, but

none run by Dorothy. Last summer a bar out front played loud musi
We hope it doesn't return.

WHERE TO EAT

The best food is served in a clutch of inexpensive seafood restauran
that congregate by the river bridge. Next best are the chinese restauran
that seem to follow the British.

ARMAÇÃO de PÊRA ★★

Population: 2894
Area code: 082; zip code: 8365

>From **Portimão** *take N-125 east for 14 k to Porches, where a right turn for 3 k comes to a fork, the left tine of which goes to Senhora da Rocha chapel in 1k more, the right to Armação in 3 k. The turn-off at Porches is 17 k more distant from* **Lagos**, *and 15 k west from* **Albufeira**, *after gaining N-125.*

Halfway between the major cities of Portimão and Albufeir crowded with people, little, upwardly mobile Armação reposes owning the longest beach in the Algarve. Indeed, all things consid ered, this might be the best beach anywhere along the coast. Eve better, outside the village two luxury resorts hide unnoticed by mos of the world. You will consider Armação a great discovery (althoug the presence of resort complexes does suggest that someone mus have found it before).

Alone on a headland 3 k west of the village (actually, it is not en tirely alone, since it is next to the large Hotel Viking) **Nossa Senhor da Rocha** chapel on a thin promontory seems poised to jump int the sea. Its interior is covered in azulejos and votive offerings o boats. Below it is one of a score of undersea **caves** in which the wate glows iridescently. Here the beach is at its scenic best. Boats can b hired near the chapel to tour these caves, or from Armação's easter beach by the sign for "Balneários sanitarios."

The village of Armação is white, full of monolithic hotels an pleasant, but it provides little to do except beach activities. Actio awaits less than 10 miles away, however, in sophisticated Albufeira All told, the best choice would be the lush quiet of one of two hid den luxury compounds 2 1-2 k to the west. Here the beach is inti mate and scenically surrounded by rocks and cliffs. Althoug technically open to the public, these beaches are virtually private do mains of the hotel guests.

WHERE TO STAY

This is not an area for those with faint pocketbooks. Accommodations are expensive at best.

VERY EXPENSIVE ($200+)

Vila Vita Parc   Deluxe ★★★★
Alporchinhos, 8365 Armação de Pêra (2 1/2 k west of Armação then down a lane directed by a sign). Rooms: 194, including villas and suites. ☎ *31 53 41; FAX 31 53 33.* This is the Algarve's newest and possibly most spectacular resort complex. It is a private compound that provides every service: five restaurants, seven bars, four pools, health club, medical facilities, nine-hole golf course, five tennis courts, and all water sports. The beach is divine. Intensely white buildings dot lush green gardens surrounding pools and fountains. Everything is designed to impress, and, in truth, it does. Incidently, the rooms are soft and lovely. For all this the Vita charges over $200 for a double, and the price is not out of line. However, it is having trouble filling its rooms and offers numerous deals for stays of two nights or more to bring the price way down. It is often possible to get last-minute reservations.

EXPENSIVE ($200+)

Vilalara   Deluxe ★★★★★
Alporchinhos, 8365 Armação de Pêra (2 1/2 k west of Armação then down a lane directed by a sign). Rooms: 130, including and suites. ☎ *31 49 10; FAX 31 49 56; Telex 57460 NELSON P.* This is the original luxury compound built 20 years ago that the Vila Vita Parc across the road tried to copy and outdo. The two are an interesting study. The Vita is larger with a few more facilities, but tries in every way to impress with size and opulence. The Vilalara is more distinguished, hiding its treasures rather than shouting about them. Most impressive are the lush tropical gardens landscaping the grounds. The layout is brilliant in that you never feel part of a large hotel complex, rather you seem alone in a still garden. Seldom do you see other guests, never a crowd. The buildings are adobe in style in an earth tone. Bedrooms are soft in color and huge. The luxury restaurant serves excellent food, and the private beach, although small, is spectacularly scenic. A feature of the hotel is the special sea water treatment called Thalassotherapy. If you don't know what this is, you haven't been reading your *Town and Country*. It is possible to find last-minute reservations.

Hotel Viking   Deluxe ★★
Praia Senhora da Rocha, 8365 Armação de Pêra (3 k west of Armação). Rooms: 184. ☎ *31 48 76; FAX 31 48 52; Telex 57492 ALVIK P.* Huge, modern and popular with a German crowd, the Viking's best feature is its location jutting out over the lovely Senhora da Rocha beaches. The rooms are not very attractive and the area around the hotel is dusty and desolate, but there are those beaches and sea views.

Hotel Garbe   1st-class ★★

Av. Marginal (actually on the beach). Rooms: 140. ☎ 31 51 87; FAX 31 50 87; Telex 58590 GARBE P. This modern monolith is somewhat more attractive than others and boasts of a prime location on the beach. The rooms are very plain, but the views are anything but.

Hotel do Levante   1st-class ★

Sítio das Quintas (at the western end of the beach). Rooms:41. ☎ 31 49 00; FAX 31 49 99; Telex 57478 ALVIK P. Attractively situated above the beach cliffs just outside town, the best feature of the hotel, beside its location, is a small formal garden. Also, it is not a high-rise for a change. Rooms, however are smaller than they should be and a little dingy. The service could be delivered with more warmth. And don't look over the fence at the unsightly trailer park.

MODERATE ($50-99)

Hotel Algar   2nd-class ★

Av. Beira Mar (across the street from the beach). Rooms: 47 apartments ☎ 31 47 10; FAX 31 49 56. This hotel is not grand but it is new and clean and includes cooking facilities in rooms that could be larger. The price is about right and the beach is close.

WHERE TO EAT

The best restaurant in the area is the expensive one at the Vilalara hotel described above. In town the best choice is Santola, although we enjoy Flor do Campo almost as much.

MODERATE ($15-$30)

Santola   ★

Largo da Fortaleza (in the old town, near the beach). ☎ 31 23 32. This place is a cut above the usual Algarve fish restaurant. It is a venerable institution that has survived because it knows to cook fresh food simply and well.   *Visa and MasterCard accepted.*

INEXPENSIVE (under $15)

A Flor do Campo

Estrada Nacional 125, Alcantarilha (on the right side of N-125, if heading to Albufeira). ☎ 31 49 64. This is a large hall of a place with no ambiance, but friendly service and delicious grilled chicken.

DIRECTORY

INFORMATION • Located on Av. Marginal beside the beach (☎ 31 21 45).

SHOPPING • Casa Algarve with a and large selection of ceramics at very reasonable prices is on N-125 east of Porches.

ALBUFEIRA ★

Population: 17,218
Area code: 089; zip code: 8200

From **Armação** *go east on n-123 for 14k to turn right at the sign for 4 k more. Albufeira is 34 k from* **Portimão** *east on N-125 and 17 k more from* **Lagos***. It is 44 k from* **Faro** *by the autoestrada IP-1.*

Take the crowds away and this would be the perfect Algarve town. Fishermen's houses cling together along cobblestone alleys on a cliff overlooking a working beach lined with brightly colored skiffs. The town gleams and seems smaller and more manageable than its actual size. One of its beaches is connected by a tunnel carved from rock to another beach backed by contorted cliffs facing a transparent sea. But, Albufeira is the most popular of all Algarve resorts, especially with the tour packagers, so one cannot eliminate crowds.

It is hard to find space on the town beaches in summer, which is a pity. The beaches are scenic, the town is attractive and includes abundant restaurants and shops. Adding interest, there is an old town at the top of the modern city that is a maze of interesting buildings.

WHERE TO STAY

Packagers consume most of the hotel space, making accommodations difficult to find.

VERY EXPENSIVE ($200+)

Vila Joya   **E1st-class ★★★★★**
Praia da Gale, Apartado 120, 8200 Albufeira (head west along the coast for 6 1/2 k to Praia da Gale, near the Salgados Praia golf course). Rooms: 16. ☎ *59 17 95; FAX 59 12 01. Closed from the middle of January to the middle of February and from the second week in November to the middle of December.* We hesitate even mentioning this place for two reasons. One, it is our favorite hotel in the Algarve, and, two, it is so small and heavily booked that it is almost impossible to get rooms anyway. If interested, try half a year or more ahead. What makes this hotel so special is the utter good taste of the German owner. He and his wife have thought of every comfort a guest might require and some he wouldn't have thought of. Of course, the rooms are generously large, all have terraces, there is a garden spilling down to the beach and you would be happy to live in the bathrooms. To top it all off, the chef is the best on the coast, bar none. Note, they do not accept credit cards!

Sheraton Algarve   **Deluxe ★★★**
Praia da Falésia, Apartado 644, 8200 Albufeira (located above Falésia beach, 10 k east of Albufeira). Rooms: 215. ☎ *50 19 99; FAX 50 19 50; Telex 56288.* This is a most attractive, inviting Sheraton, above a lovely beach less crowded than those in town, that functions as a resort. Beside water sports, there are tennis courts and an attractive

9-hole golf course. Rooms are ample but a little too obviously decorator-designed.

Montechoro ### Deluxe ★
Av. Dr. Francisco Sá Carneiro (3.5 k northeast of town). Rooms: 410 ☎ *526 51; Telex 56288.* This Mediterranean-looking, self-contained resort complex offers pools, tennis and squash courts, saunas, gym and restaurant. The idea is that you never need leave. Nor did you have to fly to Portugal for this. It is not even on the beach.

EXPENSIVE ($100-200)

Sol e Mar ### 1st-class ★★★
Rua João Bernardino de Sousa (at the west end of the town, above the beach). Rooms: 74. ☎ *58 67 21; FAX 58 70 36.* An ordinary two stories in front hide much more behind where four additional stories descend a cliff to the beach. There sits a swimming pool to guild the lily of a hotel that is literally on the shore. While rooms are nothing wonderful, they are comfortable enough, and the location is ideal for beach and city. All bedrooms include balconies, the majority with unobstructed ocean views. Prices just enter the expensive category.

Clube Mediterrâneo da Balaia
Praia Maria Luisa (7k. east). Rooms: 300. ☎ *58 66 81; FAX 53 78 47* *(Reservations should be made through Clube Mediterrâneo do Viagens Av. António de Aguiar 24 in Lisbon;* ☎ *53 83 09.)* This is a Club Med facility, with every activity imaginable and communal dining. The price includes all meals and there is a minimum stay of a week.

MODERATE ($50-99)

Estalagem do Cerro ### E1st-class ★★
Rua Samor Barros. Rooms: 83. ☎ *58 61 91; FAX 58 61 74; Telex 56211.* Half of this hotel is modern, half more rustic, but altogether the accommodations offer much more than expected in the price range, including sauna, Jacuzzi, Turkish bath, and gym. Of course there is a pool too. It perches atop a hill for views, which means a steep 10-minute walk to the beach and a longer walk back. The decor is slightly tacky, but we've seen worse.

Rocamar ### 2nd-class ★
Largo Jacinto d'Ayet (along Rua Samora Barros). Rooms: 83. ☎ *58 69 90; FAX 58 69 98; Telex 56211.* Out of town far enough for quiet but near the best beach, this modern angular hotel offers standard rooms but nice views.

Baltum ### 3rd-class ★
Av. 25 de Abril (near the main beach). Rooms: 50. ☎ *58 91 02; FAX 58 61 46.* How about modern conveniences and a quieter location than most for reasonable rates? Here it is. There is a too-noisy annex in the village that we would avoid.

INEXPENSIVE (-$50)

Villa Recife   R2nd-class ★★

R. Miguel Bombarda, 6 (up the hill a few steps from the Sol e Mar above). Rooms: 92. ☎ 58 67 47; Telex 58316. The location is super for beach and town. The entrance, set back from the street past a lawn lined with bougainvillea, is a cozy introduction. The first part of the hotel is a former villa, the rest is a modern addition. While the rooms are not large, the hotel is fun and its location and price are hard to beat.

WHERE TO EAT

Restaurants are everywhere in this village; the cheapest ring the harbor.

EXPENSIVE ($40+)

Vila Joya   ★★★★★

Praia da Gale, Apartado 120, 8200 Albufeira (head west along the coast for 6 1/2 k to Praia da Gale, near the Salgados Praia golf course). ☎ 59 17 95; FAX 59 12 01. Closed from the middle of January to the middle of February and from the second week in November to the middle of December. Not only is the food here sublime, it is also the invention of an Austrian chef who puts Portuguese ingredients to new uses. Lunches are served on a patio overlooking a garden and the sea, dinners in a cozy white room with arched brick ceiling, fireplace and one huge marble table for large parties with smaller tables for the rest of us. Although the service is professional, it is relaxed. Food recommendations are difficult because the menu changes daily and everything is delicious, but if the *cherne ao basilic* is available, go for it. Desserts are a specialty, naturally, for an Austrian chef. The problem with Vila Joya is its popularity. Dinner reservations are difficult because the hotel guests all take their meals here; lunch reservations used to be relatively easy, but Michelin has just awarded the restaurant a coveted star which is sure to draw crowds even at midday.

Amex, MasterCard and Visa accepted.

MODERATE ($15-$30)

Montinho   ★★

In Montechoro, 3.5 k northeast. ☎ 51 39 59. Closed Sun., and from the second week of January through the first week of February, and from the middle of November to the middle of December. The French-influenced cuisine here is the second-best food near Albufeira. It is served in a converted old farmhouse that has been tastefully restored with rustic accents. A reasonably priced *menu de degustation* is the best way to sample the chef's specialties. Reservations are strongly advised.

Amex, MasterCard and Visa accepted.

Cabaz da Praia   ★

Pr. Miguel Bombarda, 7 (west near the tunnel down to the beach). ☎ 51 21 37. Closed Sat. lunch and Sun. The style of this little place will first attract you, then as you go further in and see nothing but beach and sea through the windows, you'll be awed. Finally you'll be pampered with delicious food. Dishes come with a French sensibility and cover more than just the expected fish. Not to depreciate a well-grilled fish, but sometimes a guy hankers for a souffle. Here you can have either in a lovely atmosphere. Reservations are recommended for this small place.

No credit cards.

A Ruína ★

Cais Herculano (near the fisherman's beach). ☎ 51 20 94. Despite the rustic atmosphere of its bare stone walls, wood tables, and dripping candles, to call this restaurant a "ruin" is true hyperbole. The customers come for the seafood, which is incredibly fresh and fairly priced.

Diners and MasterCard accepted

EXCURSIONS

The major excursions closest to Albufeira are Slide and Splash **water park** and the lovely church in **Almancil**. Slide and Splash is located on N-125 near Lagoa, 19 k west. It offers six different water chutes, bumper rafts and a mini-moto course. Almancil, 27 k east along N-125, is described in the Faro "Excursions."

VILAMOURA ★

*From **Albufeira** Vilamoura is 4 k north to N-125, then 12 k to the turnoff for this resort. From **Faro** it is 23 k west along N-125.*

Vilamoura is the most ambitious golfing resort in Portugal and perhaps all Europe. It consists of not one championship golf course but three, and boasts manicured lawns, gardens, a casino, and spanking luxury hotels vying to outdo one another in opulence. Every comfort is available at a price. The scenic beauty is Portugal's as is the land, but a guest has to remind himself that he is neither in the U.S. nor in several similar complexes around the world. Costs are high—all the hotels charge 20,000$00-35,000$00 for a double more or less, except the two finds we list below. Breakfast and golf privileges are included, as they should be. Although views over the ocean are dramatic, the nearest beach is 4 k away at Quarteira. That beach is all right, but its scenery consists of high-rise apartments and hotels.

WHERE TO STAY

VERY EXPENSIVE ($200+)

Vilamoura Marinotel Deluxe ★★★

Beside the marina. Rooms: 387. ☎ 38 99 88; FAX 38 98 69; Telex 58827. This huge complex is insistently ultramodern, with every gadget a hotel can have. Views of the marina and sea are lovely.

THE ALGARVE

EXPENSIVE ($100-200)

Dom Pedro Golf　　　　　　　　　　　　　　1st-class ★★
　Rooms: 261. ☎ 38 96 50; FAX 31 54 82; Telex 56870.

Dom Pedro Marina　　　　　　　　　　　　　1st-class ★★
　Rooms: 155. ☎ 38 98 02; FAX 31 32 70; Telex 56307.

Atlantis Vilamoura　　　　　　　　　　　　　1st-class ★★
　Rooms: 313. ☎ 38 99 37; FAX 38 98 69; Telex 56838.

Ampalius　　　　　　　　　　　　　　　　　　1st-class ★★
　Rooms: 150. ☎ 38 80 08; FAX 38 09 11.

Although the preceding are separate hotels, they are similar enough that comments about one apply to the others. All are first class in every modern way and sit amid lovely lawns and gardens. The Dom Pedro Golf is closest to the Casino; the Dom Pedro Marina, naturally, is by the harbor with views; the Atlantis is Moorish in decor and close to a passable beach; the Ampalius is next to both the beach and the casino.

MODERATE ($50-99)

Estalagem da Cegonha　　　　　　　　　E2nd-class ★★★★
　Centro Hipico de Vilamoura (soon after the turn from N-125 toward Vilamoura). Rooms: 10. ☎ 30 25 77. Situated right beside Vilamoura's stables, this inn covered in bougainvillea was the birthplace of the woman loved by the great Portuguese poet Camões. She was born in 1536. What you see today is not quite that old, but utterly wonderful parts go back to the 17th century. In particular, the cathedral ceiling in the dining room is formed of rafters a few centuries old. Decor is according to various whims, but generally has to do with horses. Everything is wood, and dark, for the wood is ancient. Rooms are charming, comfortable, each unique and the greatest bargain in Vilamoura. There is no obligation that you ride, but if you do, rentals are reasonable.

Motel Vilamoura Golf　　　　　　　　　　　1st-class ★★
　On the Pennick golf course grounds). Rooms: 52. ☎ 30 29 77; FAX 38 00 23 Telex 15872. Despite the name, this is not a motel. It is a modern, low-slung hotel surrounding a patio with two pools and decorated in tiles and mosaics. It is impossible to get any closer to the golf course, and tennis is nearby. In such a luxurious area, this "motel" is a bargain indeed.

QUARTEIRA

Population: 8905
Area code: 089; zip code: 8125

16 k west from Faro along N-125, a 6 k feeder road leads toward the coast and this resort. From Albufeira the direc-

tions to Vilamoura will lead to Quarteira in 4 k additional.

Quarteira's blessing and curse is that it contains one of the longe[st] pure beaches on the coast. The original fishing village now is lo[st] among blocks of high rise apartment buildings, and the beach [is] barely discernible between the crowd of sunning bodies. With s[o] many lovely areas along the coast, it is something of a mystery wh[y] people choose this place. Whatever the reason, it is difficult for a[n] overnight visitor to find accommodations because the high-rise[s] consist of apartments leased by the week or month, leaving few tru[e] hotels. About the only reason for selecting Quarteira we can think o[f] is to play golf at the spectacular courses in Vilamoura, 4 k away with[-] out paying the prices of the luxury hotels there.

WHERE TO STAY

As noted above, the choices are few.

MODERATE ($50-99)

Dom José 2nd-class

Av. Infante de Sagres. Rooms: 134. ☎ 30 27 50; FAX 30 27 55. Th[is] modern nine-story hotel is a walled complex with more convenience[s] than its rating would suggest. Its good value makes it popular an[d] thus difficult to book.

Atis 2nd-clas[s]

Av. Infante de Sagres. Rooms: 72. ☎ 38 97 71; FAX 38 97 74; Tel[ex] 56802. This hotel is tucked into the rows of high rises, but, with [a] beach-view balcony, accommodations should prove acceptable.

FARO

Population 28,622
Area Code 089; zip code 8000

From **Albufeira** go north for 7 k to the autoestrada IP-1, then 33 k to the Faro exit where N-2 goes south to Faro in another 11 k. From **Olhão** go west on N-125 for 8 k. From **Tavira** go west on N-270 to the autoestrada IP-1, then west to the Faro exit in 18 k. A final leg south on N-2 for 11 k completes the trip. From the **Spanish border** Spain's N-431 joins the Portuguese IP-1 north of Ayamonte for a fast trip of 55 k to the Faro exit.

Because Faro is the capital of the Algarve and serves as the airpor[t] for the area, it crowds with tourists. What it offers is a beach near [a] true city. Its harbor area is attractive, and an interesting old town i[s] reached through ancient city walls, but a shantytown rings its outskirts.

Although more attractive towns exist elsewhere in the Algarve, accommodations in Faro are generally scarce because many of those who land here venture no further. As a result, its island beach, although attractive, is covered with sunbathers. Bus #16 serves this beach from the Office of Tourism in the harbor. The better shops congregate on the pedestrian Rua Santo António that goes west from the harbor.

WHERE TO STAY

Reservations anywhere along the Algarve are strongly advised in high season, but nowhere is this admonition more important than for Faro, even for a stay of one night.

VERY EXPENSIVE ($200+)

La Réserve   1st-class ★★★★

Estrada de Esteval. (Take N-125 northwest past the airport for 8 k to a right turn toward Loulé. In one mile comes Esteval where a right turn toward Santa Barbara de Nexe brings the hotel in 2 k.) Rooms: 20 apartments. ☎ 904 74; FAX 904 02; Telex 56790 FUCHS P. Closed from the second week of November through the first week of December. For those familiar with the Relais et Chateaux association, it is sufficient to say that this hotel is a member, one of two in Portugal. The association is comprised only of elegant, luxury estates. This hotel is uncharacteristically modern, rather than one of the historic properties usually affiliated with the group, but it is luxurious anyway. Apartments have a distant sea view; the gardens are lovely. Two swimming pools and a tennis court complete the complex. Understand, however, that La Réserve is located inland, not near any beach. Prices are high, but the comfort and elegance provided are higher for there are no more relaxing accommodations in the Algarve. Conveniently alongside stands one of the finest restaurants (described below) in Portugal. Note, credit cards are not accepted.

EXPENSIVE ($100-200)

Eva   1st-class ★★

Av. da República (occupying the north end of the harbor). Rooms: 150. ☎ 80 33 54; FAX 80 23 04; Telex 56524. This eight-story modern hotel overlooks the yacht harbor and beyond. Bedrooms are pleasant, the management efficient, and there is a rooftop pool. The hotel is also a bargain because prices for rooms with a sea view just touch the expensive category.

MODERATE ($50-99)

Casa de Lumena   2nd-class ★★

Pr. Alexendre Herculano, 27 (two blocks east of the harbor). Rooms: 12.

☎ *80 19 90; FAX 80 40 19.* The hotel was the home of Portugal's sardine king over a century ago who was the richest man in town. It sits on a lovely quiet square. Although by no means grand, it is tastefully restored and dotted with fine furniture. Each bedroom is different but all are appealing, and the most expensive remains well within the moderate-price category. The establishment is run by an English couple who keep it spotless. All told, the hotel is a pleasure to stay at and a great bargain.

Faro 2nd-class ★

Pr. Don Francisco Gomes, 2 (at the center of the harbor). Rooms: 52. ☎ *80 32 76; FAX 80 35 46; Telex 56108.* This is a grey, factorylike modern building whose bedrooms are comfortable if unimaginative. Rooms with balconies overlooking the harbor are best. The price is a bargain even with the $10 supplement for a sea view, given the location.

INEXPENSIVE (UNDER $50)

Condado R2nd-class ★

R. Conçalo Barreto, 14. (Go north along R. de Alportel for 7 blocks from the harbor to its intersection with R. da Trindade. Turn left for two streets, then left again.) Rooms: 16. ☎ *82 20 81; FAX 82 77 55.* The bedrooms are perfectly clean, and the price should not hurt anyone.

WHERE TO EAT

Restauranteurs in Faro act as though the tourists will come whether they try hard or not, so most do not. The following are the only restaurants that can be recommended.

EXPENSIVE ($40+)

La Réserve ★★★★

Estrada do Esteval (see the hotel of the same name above). ☎ *902 34; FAX 904 02; Telex 56790. Closed Tuesday, and from the second week of November through the first week in December.* This restaurant ranks with the finest in the country, both for the quality of its French-inspired dishes and the elegance of their presentation. Salmon marinated in mustard and duck Vendome are memorable, as is the smoked scabbard fish. Furthermore, two can dine and be pampered for the cost of one at a fine Lisbon restaurant. Reservations are required. *No credit cards are accepted.*

Cidade Velha ★★

Rua Domingos Guieiro, 19 (beside the city hall and cathedral, through the old city walls 1 block east of the port). ☎ *271 45. Closed for Saturday lunch, and Sunday.* This is the leading restaurant in Faro proper. It is a romantic place installed in a former bishop's mansion, decorated with pink tablecloths and fresh flowers under soft lighting. The food is inventive and very good indeed. All that prevents us from recommending it more strongly is the fact that a few dollars more would buy a meal at La Réserve above. *MasterCard and Visa accepted.*

DIRECTORY

AIRPORT • Faro Airport (☎ *81 82 81*) is 10 k west of the city and serves Europe. A bus connects with Faro for 100$00; a taxi should cost no more than 1000$00. TAP is located on *R. D. Francisco Gomes, 8* at the beginning of the harbor garden (☎ *221 41*).

INFORMATION • *R. da Misericórdia 8-12* (☎ *80 36 04*), in the city walls across from the harbor garden.

SHOPPING • Crafts, ceramics and other things line the pedestrian R. de Santo António which leaves the harbor at the garden.

TRAINS and BUSES • Faro is a hub for good transportation. The train station (☎ *226 53*) is in Largo Estação in the harbor area to the north. Connections can be made to anywhere in the country. The bus station (☎ *299 92*) for connections throughout the Algarve is on Av. da República, behind the hotel Eva between the harbor and the train station.

EXCURSIONS

Tiny Almansil contains an appropriately tiny church, stunningly covered in azulejos. Loulé is a crafts town.

Almansil lies 16 k west on N-125 past the airport. So small is the church of São Lourenço that the inside startles. It glistens and dances in azulejos covering every inch, including an amazing ceiling.

Loulé is located northwest of Faro. Take N-125 past the airport for a sign for Loulé in about 8k, which lies inland along N-125-4 for another 7 k. Loulé is a center for baskets, mats, and hats of palm and esparto, as well as for copperware, fine wrought iron, some pottery, and beautiful colored harnesses (although the latter are hard to find these days). It is no chore to search through the shops that huddle under the ancient fortress in the center of the town. While there, notice the lacy chimneys that seem almost artworks, certainly with that order of individuality. Saturday is market day, but individual craftspeople in the town sell every day but Sunday.

OLHÃO

Population: 34,573
Area code: 089; zip code: 8700

8 k east of **Faro** *on N-125. From* **Tavira** *go west on N-125 for 22 k.*

Olhão is the largest fishing port in the Algarve, and consists of long rows of cubical houses, some with external stairs and roof terraces, causing the town to be referred to as a cubist city. Olhão contains poor sections, and the town is dreary, but so far tourists are few and three superb beach islands wait nearby—Ilha da Armona, Ilha do Farol and Ilha da Cualatra, with the first two being the best. Ferries leave the harbor frequently during the season. The problem is that, with so few tourists, not many hotels have been built, and those that exist are not particularly appealing. We would leave this town to its fishermen.

WHERE TO STAY

MODERATE ($50-99)

Ria-Sol — 3rd-class

Rua General Humberto Delgado, 37. Rooms: 52. ☎ 70 52 67; Tele 56923. This hotel is a step up from the pensãos, but not distinguished.

INEXPENSIVE (UNDER $50)

Bicuar — 3rd-class

Rua Vasco da Gama, 5 (about 2 blocks from the Office of Tourism). Rooms: 12. ☎ 71 48 16. Rooms at this tiny establishment are small but tasteful, and most provide small terraces.

Helena — 3rd-class

Rua Dr. Miguel Bombarda, 42 (down the street and left from the Office of Tourism). Rooms: 20. ☎ 70 26 34. Bedrooms are large for the price, but the place shows wear.

TAVIRA ★★

Population: 7282
Area code: 081; zip code: 8800

*Tavira is 22 k east from **Olhão** along N-125; 30 k east of **Faro**, and 31 k west of the border with **Spain**.*

There is no prettier town on the coast or any less crowded with tourists. Glistening white houses sprawl along the Gilão River then rise up a gentle hill, while twenty charming churches punctuate the scene. A pedestrian bridge on Roman foundations spans the river; the ruins of a Moorish alcázar, with gardens inside, crown the hill, and an offshore sandspit provides 10 k of beach opportunities to stay far from the madding crowd. The bus marked "Quatro Aguas" leaves from the movie house in the Pr. de República for a five-minute ride to the ferry. Santa Luzia, 1 k south, is an even nicer, less crowded beach. Last, but not least, the Ria Formosa nature reserve lies just outside of town.

WHERE TO STAY

You can't have your cake and eat it too. When a resort is unspoiled, it can't have wonderful accommodations. This is Tavira's debit. While there

MODERATE ($50-99)

...inta do Caracol 3rd-class ★ ★ ★

Bairro do São Pedro (off R. Dr. Miguel Bombarda, the main road into town). Rooms: 7 apartments. ☎ *224 75; FAX 231 75.* Eccentric white bungalows surround a large patio and wading pool for the most pleasant accommodations in Tavira. There are two aviaries, a feel of comfortable community, and cooking facilities in each apartment. A swimming pool of sorts and tennis court complete the list. You'll like the place and wish it were just a tad closer to town, but, thinking of everything, the management rents bikes.

...vira Garden 2nd-class ★ ★

Quinta das Oliveiras (3 k east on N-125, next to the Eurotel). Rooms: 100 apartments. ☎ *32 55 08; FAX 32 55 09.* This Swedish-owned condominium development rents about 50 rooms at any time. All are Algarve white, roomy and decorated in pastels. Cooking facilities are incorporated and the price is a steal for this level of convenience. But it is two miles outside the town.

...rotel Tavira 2nd-class ★

Quinta das Oliveiras (3 k east on N-125). Rooms: 80. ☎ *32 43 24; FAX 32 55 71; Telex 562 18.* A modern complex presents a pool and tennis courts. Prices are low for the type and facilities. However, package tours often book every room, the setting is a bit desolate and it's two miles to town.

INEXPENSIVE (UNDER $50)

...incesa do Gilão R3rd-class ★

R. Borda de Agua de Aguiar, 10 (just across the river on the esplanade). Rooms: 14. ☎ *226 65.* Clean rooms with tiled floors and nice views of the village make this a pleasant place. And it is very inexpensive.

...goas Bica P3rd-class ★

Rua Candido dos Reis, 24 (cross the "Roman" bridge, continue for one block, then right). Rooms: 17. ☎ *222 82.* This pension has spotless rooms and cheerful management. It is also incredibly inexpensive. The restaurant serves very inexpensive, yet decent food.

WHERE TO EAT

You will get authentic, fresh food in Tavira for reasonable prices.

MODERATE ($15-$30)

...Águas ★

On the quay. ☎ *32 53 29.* This is the new king in town, a barn of a place where the waiter wears black tie. The atmosphere seems almost too elevated for simple fresh fish, but that is what they do best, along with arroz de marisco. *MasterCard and Visa accepted.*

INEXPENSIVE (under $15)

Restaurant Avenida
Av. Dr. Mateus T. de Acevedo (2 blocks south of Pr. da República via R. Liberdade). ☎ 811 13. Closed Mon. and May. Here is the old favori still producing respectable food. Grilled tuna is a specialty both of t restaurant and of the town.

Amex, Diners, MasterCard and Visa accept

DIRECTORY

INFORMATION • Located in the Pr. da República, the main square by t "Roman" bridge (☎ 225 11).

THE SOUTHWEST

Here are resort alternatives to the Algarve. During July and A gust when the Algarve is full, this west coast often retains rooms, f it is little known to any but the Portuguese.

Development has not hit yet, for the money usually comes fro elsewhere in Europe. This means that accommodations are less th grand, but the area has much to recommend it both for scenery an compared to more international Algarve resorts, for a genuine tas of Portugal. There are scenic coves, expansive beaches and adorab villages, which is not a shabby list.

The southwestern coast begins below Sines, a dreary refinery tov 100 miles south of Lisbon, and runs all the way south to the weste Algarve. N-120 is the major artery that follows the coast, connecti with beaches by feeder-roads. We describe the beaches going sou for about 60 kilometers, beginning with lovely Porto Covo.

PORTO COVO ★★

Population: 429
Area code: 069; zip code: 7520

From **Lisbon** *the autoestrada A-2 reaches* **Setubal** *in 50 k. From there N-10 east for 21 k reaches Marateca to join N-5 south for 31 k to Alcaçer do Sal and a change in its designation to N-120. Bear right in 18 k to continue on N-120 toward Sines. 34 k later the express N-261-3 toward Sines is entered. Turn to skirt Sines in 10 k onto N-120-1 toward Cercal. In 8 k, after crossing the Morgavel River, turn off to Porto Covo along a 6 k feeder-road. From* **Évora** *take N-114 west toward Montemor-o-Novo in 30 k. There take N-4 west toward Vendas Novas and Cruzamento de Pegões* *in 37 k. Take N-10 south to Marateca and follow the Lisbon directions thereafter.*

Low, long beach stretches for 7 k to either side of Porto Covo, but e coast at the village itself is wildly dramatic. A few houses huddle a promontory from the edge of which one looks down on little ves (whence the name). Faced by strong seas, and almost hidden surrounding cliffs, Praia dos Buizinhos is secluded and less than 0 ft long, but protected from the wind by intimate rocks. The enery reminds of the Maine coast, with a dash of the Monterez ninsula. That is to say, it is dramatic rather than pretty.

The village is all Portuguese. Low, whitewashed houses whose or- and window-ways are bordered in cerulean shine in the hot n. All is peaceful and utterly undeveloped.

The best beach for swimming lies three kilometers south at Praia Ilha Pessegueiro, named for a little island offshore topped by a ru- ed Renaissance fort. It is a fine long dune beach with its own 7th-century fortress behind it for exploring. There is a restaurant o, with windows to take advantage of the views.

WHERE TO STAY

Exactly two residentials provide only 12 very basic rooms between them. e better bet is a faded camping park, just outside of town. Forget com- rt.

INEXPENSIVE (-$50)

mpismo da Ilha do Pessegueiro   **P3rd-class**
On the road into town. Rooms: 30. ☎ 951 78. This is basic accommodations in long bungalows with no views. They are not as cramped as the rooms in town and have cooking facilities for the low price.

elha   **R3rd-class**
R. Vasco de Gama, 40. Rooms: 10. ☎ 951 08. You would not want to spend a lot of time in such small rooms, but they will do for sleeping.

a Esperança   **R3rd-class**
No address, but on the edge of town. Rooms: 2. ☎ 951 09. Two apartments are rented in this family house. One has two small bedrooms, the other one very small bedroom without a window.

WHERE TO EAT

The best restaurant is at Praia da Ilha, 3 k south of the village.

INEXPENSIVE (under $15)

staurante a Ilha   ★
On Ilha beach. Thatched roof and a terrace make this nicely beachy. The food is simple and good.

VILA NOVA DE MILFONTES ★

Population: 3442
Area code: 083; zip code: 7645

N-120-1 reaches Cercal in 14 k south of the turn-off for **Porto Covo**. Go west on N-390 for 12 k to Milfontes.

The Portuguese have discovered Milfontes; new villas spring daily. They come for the long beaches that line both sides of the M River estuary. Blindingly white houses create the feeling of a Gre island village and, as opposed to neighbor Porto Covo, decent commodations are available.

WHERE TO STAY

Popularity with the Portuguese means that hotel space grows preci during July and August. Rooms should be available at other times.

MODERATE ($50-99)

Castelo de Milfontes — P2nd-class

In the main square. Rooms: 7. ☎ 961 08. Since this is a genui 16th-century fort, it has to be the most unusual accommodations town. The building was bought from the government at the turn the century and made over into a hotel about 50 years ago. You en over an appropriate drawbridge into a rather dark reception area. F tunately the rooms are brighter and have views over the estuary.

Hotel Social — 2nd-class

Av. Marginal. Rooms: 45. ☎ 965 17; FAX 965 17. The hotel is mode white, spotless, has views of the estuary and is incredibly inexpensi The reason for the low prices, in part, is that it is owned by the soci ist political party, although that should not affect your stay.

INEXPENSIVE (-$50)

Residential Mil-Réis — R1st-class

Largo de Rossio (2 blocks from the main square). Rooms: 12. ☎ 962 While the rooms are small, they are cheerful and a bargain.

ALMOGRAVE ★

Population: 351
Area code: 083; zip code: 7645

You can drive from Milfontes along the beach road N-393, looking for a right turn to Almograve in about 17 k. From N-120, the right turn to Almograve is at São Luís, 17 k after Cercal.

The beach at Almograve reminds of Porto Covo in that cliffs fo dramatic coves. But here the coves are wider, the cliffs lower a backed by huge sand dunes. There is no town at all within one kilometer of the beach, but a changing area is provided.

Almograve is tiny and undiscovered. When we were there last April, hardly a soul was around to supply telephone numbers, although you can write. **Residential Luna Praia**, R2nd-class, is a new inn 100 yards up the beach road. It is tiled in white with balconies facing the road. By all external appearances, it should be cozy and cheap. **Pensão Paul Carlos**, on R. Antonio Pacheco, the main street in town rents small rooms inexpensively.

ODECEIXE ★

Population: 893
Area code: 083; zip code: 7645

The village of Odeceixe is on N-120 42 k south of São Luís, the turn-off for Almograve. It is 46 k north of Lagos on that same N-120.

The only reason for mentioning Odeceixe is that it will be a resort some day. But not yet. No accommodations exist except private rooms. The beach lies 4 k from the village through a valley that held a mighty river in prehistoric times but now is a lush canyon ending in a horseshoe bay. Dune beaches run north for three kilometers of solitary shore. If staying in Sagres, or near it, take a run up N-120 to look at Odeceixe.

THE PORTUGUESE LANGUAGE

It should be some consolation that even the Portuguese recognize that their language is incomprehensible to anyone else. No one expects you to speak it, but they will be thrilled by any effort. If you memorize the phrases, for "good day" (there are three, depending on the time), "thank you" and "excuse me," you will win the Portuguese over.

In written Portuguese many words will be recognized because all Romance languages contain similarities. Knowledge of Spanish will serve you well. It is spoken Portuguese that is the problem, for it sounds like some unfamiliar Eastern European language. As far as attempts to speak are concerned, have no hesitation, for the Portuguese will be pleased by the effort and strain hard to grasp your point. Understanding the natives is another matter. The language is nasal and filled with hisses and "shs" that make even words spelled the same as the Spanish equivalent sound entirely different.

A tilde over a vowel, as in ã, indicates a nasal sound with a hint of an *n* at the end. Informação, for example is pronounced almost as we say "information," though nasal and with the final *n* more hinted-at than vocalized.

As that example shows, a cedilla beneath a *c* makes it sound like *sh*. Otherwise a *c* is hard, as if it were a *k*, unless it precedes an *e* or an *i* which turns it soft and sibilant. The sound of the letter *j* is surprising for it is pronounced as if it were *sh*. The letter *g* is pronounced with the same *sh* sound when it precedes an *e* or an *i*, but otherwise is hard as if it were our *g*. You begin to see why the language is so full of sibilant sounds. Further, an *s* before a constant or at the end of a word is pronounced like *sh*, as is an *x* anywhere.

Thus, Lisboa (the Portuguese name for Lisbon) sounds like "Lishbo" (with the final "a" almost silent), Lagos is "Lagosh," Cascais is "Kashkays."

The combination *nh* produces the same sound as the Spanish ñ—that of the *ny* in English ca*ny*on—so Portuguese *senhor* sounds like the Spanish *señor*. The combination *lh* makes for a sound similar to the *ll* in bi*ll*ion, so we would think *Batalha* were spelled *Batalla*. The stress within a word follows much the same principles as Spanish, that is to say that the last syllable receives the emphasis unless an accent elsewhere indicates stress at that place.

Somehow every tourist manages to communicate with and understand the Portuguese. English will be spoken at almost every hotel and understood in most restaurants. Incidentally, any French you know is likely to serve well because it is the second language of Portugal.

WORDS AND PHRASES

ENGLISH	PORTUGUESE
Good morning (afternoon/evening)	Bom dia (boa tardes/boa noite)
Goodbye	Adeus
Hello	Ola
How are you?	Como vai?
Please/thank you	Por favor/obrigado
Yes/no	Sim/não
Pardon me	Perdão
I do not speak Portuguese	Não falo Português
Do you speak English?	Fala inglês?
I do not understand	Não compreendo
Miss	Menina
Madam	Senhora (married)
Mister	Senhor
Open/closed	Aberto/fechado
Entrance/exit	Entrada/saida
Push/pull	Empurrar/puxar
Today/yesterday/tomorrow	Hoje/ontem/amanha
Where is...	Onde éstão ...?
the toilet	os casa de banho
the train station	a estação de trem
the drug store	farmácia
How much is it?	Quanto custa?

NUMBERS

ENG.	PORT.	ENG.	PORT.	ENG.	PORT.
1	um(a)	11	onze	21	vinte e um
2	dois	12	doze	30	trinta
3	três	13	treze	31	trinta e um
4	quatro	14	catorze	40	quarenta
5	cinco	15	quinze	50	cinquênta
6	seis	16	dezaseis	60	sessenta
7	sete	17	dezasete	70	setenta
8	oito	18	dezóito	80	oitenta
9	nove	19	dezanove	90	noventa
10	dez	20	vinte		
100	cem	101	cento e um		
200	duzentos				
300	trezento				
1000	mil	2000	dois mil		
0	cero				

DAYS

ENGLISH	PORT.	ENGLISH	PORT.
Monday	Segunda-feira	Friday	Sexta-feira
Tuesday	Terça-feira	Saturday	Sábado
Wednesday	Quarta-feira	Sunday	Domingo
Thursday	Quinta-feira		

MONTHS

ENGLISH	PORT.	ENGLISH	PORT.
January	Janeiro	July	Julho
February	Fevereiro	August	Agosto
March	Março	September	Setembro
April	Abril	October	Outubro
May	Maio	November	Novembro
June	Junho	December	Dizembro

AT THE HOTEL

ENGLISH	PORTUGUESE
I have a reservation	Mandei reservar
I would like...	Queria...
a single room	um quarto simples
a double room	um quarto duplo
a quiet room	um quarto tranquilo
with bath	com banho
with a shower	con duche
with air conditioning	com ar acondicionado
for one night only	so uma noite
for two nights	por dios noites

ON THE ROAD

ENGLISH	PORTUGUESE
north (south/east/west)	norte (sul/este/oeste)
right (left)	direita (esquerda)
straight ahead	em frente
far (near)	longa (perto)
gas station	estação de serviço
tires	pneus
oil	o óleo
danger (caution)	perigo
detour	desvio
Do not Enter	Entrada Proibida
No parking	Estacionamento Proibido
No passing	Proibido Ultrapassar
One Way	Sentido Único
Reduce Speed	Devagar
Stop	Alto
Toll booth	Pedagio

    A list of Portuguese words for commonly available foods follows on the next page, arranged by the categories on most menus. Still, a pocket guide to Portuguese food will prove helpful since the available variety is large.

COMMONLY USED WORDS AND PHRASES

PORTUGUESE	ENGLISH
SOPAS	**SOUPS**
Caldeirada	fish chowder
Caldo verde	potato and kale soup
Canja de galenha	chicken and rice soup
Sopa a alentejana	garlic soup with egg
Sopa de feijão	bean soup
Sopa de marisco (or de peixes)	seafood bisque
OVAS	**EGGS**
Ovos cozido	hard boiled
Ovos mal pasados (or quentes)	soft boiled
Ovos estrelados	fried eggs
Ovos escalfados	poached eggs
Ovos mexidos	scrambled eggs
PEIXE E MARISCOS	**FISH AND SHELLFISH**
Amêijoas	clams
Anchovas	anchovies
Arenques	herring
Atum	tuna
Bacalhau	codfish
Camarões	shrimp
Caranguejo	crab
Carabineiros (or gambas)	prawns
Cataplana	clams stewed with sausage and bacon
Eiros	eel
Espadarte	swordfish
Linguado	sole
Mexilhões	mussels
Ostras	oysters
Pescada	hake
Robalo	sea bass
Salmão	salmon
Salmonete	red mullet
Sardinhas	sardines
Truta	trout

COMMONLY USED WORDS AND PHRASES

PORTUGUESE	ENGLISH
CARNE	**MEAT**
Assado	roasted
Chouriço:	spicy smoked sausage
Cordeiro	lamb
Costeleta	chop
Cozido	boiled
Figado	liver
Grelhado	grilled
Panado	fried in breadcrumbs
Porco	pork
Presunto	cured ham similar to prosciutto
Rim	kidney
Salsicha	fresh sausage
Salteado	sautéed
Vitela	veal
AVES E CACA	**POULTRY AND GAME**
Faisão	pheasant
Frango	chicken
Ganso	goose
Pato	duck
Veado	venison
LEGUMES	**VEGETABLES**
Alcachofra	artichoke
Alface	lettuce
Alho	garlic
Arroz	rice
Batata	potato
Beringela	eggplant
Broculos	broccoli
Cenoura	carrot
Cogumelos	mushrooms
Couve	cabbage
Ervilhas	peas
Espinafre	spinach
Feijae	beans
Salada	salad

COMMONLY USED WORDS AND PHRASES
PORTUGUESE — ENGLISH

SOBREMESA — **DESSERT**

Arroz doce	rice pudding
Bolos	pastries
Flão	creme caramel
Gelado	ice cream
Pudim	pudding

FRUTA — **FRUIT**

Ananás	pineapple
Cerejas	cherries
Figos	figs
Framboesas	raspberries
Laranja	orange
Limão	lemon
Maçã	apple
Melão	melon
Morangos	strawberries
Pêssgo	peach
Pêra	pear
Toranja	grapefruit
Uvas	grapes

HOTEL QUICK REFERENCE LIST
(By Region)

Because dollar prices vary as the peseta floats internationally and as local ordinances change, instead of specific dollar amounts we use the following price-categories:

Very Expensive (VExp)...............$200-299 per double per night

Expensive (Exp) ....$100-199 per double per night

Moderate (Mod) ....$51-99 per double per night

Inexpensive (Inexp) ....$50 or less per double per night

LISBON

Hotels	Ph./FAX #	Class	Price	Rooms	Stars
01+					
Albergaria da Senhora do Monte Calçada do Monte, 39 Lisboa 1100	886 60 02 87 77 83	1st	Mod	28	★★★★★
Altis R. Castilho, 11 Lisboa 1200	52 24 96 54 86 96	1st	Exp	307	
Avenida Palace R. 1 de Dezembro, 123 Lisboa 1100	346 01 54 342 22 84	1st	Exp	100	★★★
As Janelas Verdes R. das Janelas Verdes, 47 Lisboa 1200	396 81 43 398 81 44	R1st	Exp	17	★★★
Capitol R. Eça de Queiroz, 24 Lisboa 1000	53 68 11 352 61 65	2nd	Mod	58	★
Da Lapa, Hotel R. Pau de Bandeira, 4 Lisboa 1200	395 00 05 395 06 65	Deluxe	VExp	86	★★★★★
Dom Carlos Av. Duque de Loule, 121 Lisboa 1000	53 90 71 352 07 28	2nd	Mod	73	★★★

LISBON

Hotels	Ph./FAX #	Class	Price	Rooms	Stars
Dom Manuel I Av. Duque d'Ávila, 189 Lisboa 1000	57 61 60 57 69 85	2nd	Exp	64	★★★
Horizonte Av. António Agusto de Aguiar, 42 Lisboa 1100	53 95 26 56 25 29	R2nd	Inexp	52	
Imperador Av. 5 de Outubro, 55 Lisboa 1000	352 48 84 352 65 37	R3rd	Inexp	43	★
Lisboa Plaza Travessa do Salitre, 7 Lisboa 1200	346 39 22 347 16 30	1st	Exp	112	★★
Lisboa Sheraton R. Latino Coelho, 1 Lisboa 1097	57 57 57 54 71 64	1st	VExp	385	★★
Meridien Lisboa, Le R. Castiho, 149 Lisboa 1000	69 09 00 69 32 31	1st	VExp	331	★★★
Mundial R. Dom Duarte, 4 Lisboa 1100	886 31 01 87 91 29	1st	Exp	147	★★
Nazareth Av. António Agusto de Aguiar, 25 Lisboa 1000	54 20 16 356 08 36	R2nd	Inexp	32	
Príncipe Av. Duque d'Ávila, 301 Lisboa 1000	53 61 51 53 42 14	2nd	Mod	68	★
Príncipe Real R. da Alegría, 53 Lisboa 1200	346 01 16 342 21 04	2nd	Exp	24	★★★
Ritz R. Rodrigo da Fonseca, 88 Lisboa 1093	69 20 20 69 17 83	1st	VExp	310	★★★★
Roma Av. de Roma, 33 Lisboa 1700	796 77 61 793 29 81	2nd	Mod	265	★
Tivoli Jardim R. Julio Cesar Machado, 7 Lisboa 1200	53 99 71 355 65 66	1st	Exp	119	★

LISBON

Hotels	Ph./FAX #	Class	Price	Rooms	Stars
Torre, Da R. dos Jerónimos, 8 Lisboa 1400	363 62 62 364 59 95	2nd	Mod	50	★
Veneza Av. da Liberdade, 189 Lisboa 1200	352 26 18 352 66 78				
York House R. das Janelas Verdes, 32 Lisboa 1200	396 25 44 397 27 93	R1st	Exp	45	★★★★

ENVIRONS OF LISBON

Hotels	Ph./FAX #	Class	Price	Rooms	Stars
Alcobça	**062+**				
Corações Unidos R. Frei António Brandão, 39 Alcobça 2460	421 42	P2nd	Inexp	16	
Santa Maria R. Dr. Zagalo Alcobça 2460	59 73 95 59 67 15	2nd	Mod	31	★
Batalha	**044+**				
Pousada do Mestre Afonso Domingues Batalha 2440	962 60 962 60	1st	Exp	21	★★
Quinta do Fidalgo	961 14 76 74 01		Exp	5	★★★
Cascais	**01+**	\multicolumn{4}{l}{(See also Praia do Guincho)}
Albatroz R. Frederico Arouca, 100 Cascais 2750	248 28 21 284 48 27	Deluxe	VExp	40	★★★★★
Casa da Pérgola Av. Valbom, 13 Cascais 2750	484 00 40	2nd	Mod	10	★★★
Cidadela Av. 25 de Abril Cascais 2750	483 29 21 486 72 26	1st	Exp	130	★★

ENVIRONS OF LISBON

Hotels	Ph./FAX #	Class	Price	Rooms	Stars
Estalagem Senhora da Guia Estrado do Guincho Cascais 2750	486 92 39 486 92 27	1st	Exp	28	★★★
Estoril	**01+**	\multicolumn{4}{l}{(See also Praia do Guincho)}
Palácio R. do Parque Estoril Estoril 2765	468 04 00 468 48 67	Deluxe	VExp	162	★★★★
Smart R. José Viana, 3 Estoril 2765	468 21 64	R3rd	Inexp	16	★
Mafra	**061+**				
Albergaria Castelão Av. 25 de Abril Mafra 2640	81 20 50 516 98	3rd	Mod	35	★
Nazaré	**062+**				
Maré R. Mouzinho de Albuquerque, 8 Nazaré 2450	56 12 26 56 17 50	2nd	Mod		
Priaia Av. Vieira Guimarães, 39 Nazaré 2450	56 14 23 56 14 36	2nd	Mod	40	
Riba-Mar R. Gomes Freire, 9 Nazaré 2450	51 11 58	P3rd	Mod	23	★
Óbidos	**062+**				
Albergaria Rainha Santa Isabel R. Direita Óbidos 2510	95 91 15 95 91 15	3rd	Mod	20	★★
Estalagem do Convento R. Dom João de Ornelas Óbidos 2510	95 92 17 95 91 59	2nd	Mod	31	★★
Pousada do Castelo Paço Real Óbidos 2510	95 91 05 95 91 48	1st	Exp	9	★★

HOTEL QUICK REFERENCE LIST 321

ENVIRONS OF LISBON

Hotels	Ph./FAX #	Class	Price	Rooms	Stars
Palmela	**065+**				
Pousada do Castelo de Palmela Palmela 2950	235 12 26 233 04 40	1st	Exp	28	★★★★
Praia do Guincho	**01+**				
Do Guincho Praia do Guincho Cascais 2750	487 04 91 487 04 31	Deluxe	Exp	31	★★★★
Queluz	**01+**				
Poma e Restaurant Via Prado Tercena, Queluz 2745	437 27 45 560 81 86	2nd	Mod	50	
Sesimbra	**065+**				
Espadarte Av. 25 de Abril Sesimbra 2970	223 31 89	3rd	Mod	80	
Do Mar R. Combatentes do Ultamar, 10 Sesimbra 2970	223 33 26 223 38 88	1st	Exp	168	★★
Setúbal	**065+**				
Pousada de São Filipe R. São Filipe Setúbal 2900	52 38 44	1st	Exp	14	★★
Sintra	**01+**				
Casa Adelaide Av. Guilherme Gomes Fernandes, 11 Sintra 2710	923 08 73	R3rd	Inexp	10	★
Central Pr. da República, 35 Sintra 2710	923 09 63	3rd	Mod	14	★
Estalagem da Raposa R. Dr. Alfredo Costa, 3 Sintra 2710	923 04 65	4th	Mod	8	★★
Palácio de Seteais Av. Bocage, 8 Seteais 2710	923 32 00 923 42 77	Deluxe	VExp	30	★★★★★

ENVIRONS OF LISBON

Hotels	Ph./FAX #	Class	Price	Rooms	Stars
Quinta da Capela Estrada de Monserrate Seteais 2710	929 34 05 929 34 25	2nd	Exp	10	★★★★
Quinta de São Thiago Estrada de Monserrate Seteais 2710	923 29 23	2nd	Exp	14	★★★
Tivoli Sintra Pr. da República Sintra 2710	923 35 05 923 15 72	1st	Exp	75	★

Tróia 065+

Aparthotel Tróia Tróia Setúbal 2900	442 22	2nd	Mod		
Magnoliamar Tróia Setúbal 2900	441 51	2nd	Mod		
Rosamar Tróia Setúbal 2900	441 51	2nd	Mod		

NORTHERN PORTUGAL

Hotels	Ph./FAX #	Class	Price	Rooms	Stars

Águeda 034+

Palácio de Águeda Quinta da Borralha Águeda 3750	60 19 77 60 19 76	1st	Exp	48	★★★

Áveiro 034+

Arcadia R. Viana do Castelo, 4 Aviero 3800	230 01 218 86	3rd	Mod	49	★
Estalagem Riabela Torreira Murtosa 3870	481 37 481 47	2nd	Mod	35	★★
Imperial R. Dr. Nascimento Leita Aviero 3800	221 41 241 48	1st	Mod	107	★

HOTEL QUICK REFERENCE LIST

NORTHERN PORTUGAL

Hotels	Ph./FAX #	Class	Price	Rooms	Stars
Paloma Blanca Rua Luís Gomes de Carvalho, 23 Aviero 3800	38 19 92 38 18 44	R1st	Mod	50	★★★★
Pousada da Ria Bico do Muranzel Murtosa 3870	483 32 483 33	2nd	Exp	19	★★★

Braga   053+

Hotels	Ph./FAX #	Class	Price	Rooms	Stars
Carandá Av. da Liberdade, 96 Braga 4700	61 45 00 61 45 50	2nd	Mod	100	★★
Do Elevador Bom Jesus Braga 4700	67 66 11 67 66 79	1st	Mod	67	★★
Do Parque Bom Jesus Braga 4700	67 66 79 67 66 79	1st	Mod	49	★
Turismo Dom Pedro Praceta João XXI Braga 4700	61 22 00 61 22 11	1st	Mod	132	★

Bragança   073+

Hotels	Ph./FAX #	Class	Price	Rooms	Stars
Albergaria Santa Isabel Rua Alexandre Herculano, 67 Bragança 5300	224 27 269 37	R1st	Inexp	67	
Bragança Av. Dr. Francisco de Sá Carneiro Bragança 5300	225 79	2nd	Mod	42	★
Pousada de São Bartolomeu Estrada de Truismo Bragança 5300	224 93 234 53	1st	Mod	16	★★
São Roque Rua da Estacada, 26-7 Bragança 5300	234 81 269 37	R2nd	Inexp	36	★

Buçaco   031+

Hotels	Ph./FAX #	Class	Price	Rooms	Stars
Palace Hotel do Buçaco Foresta do Buçaco Buçaco 3800	93 01 01 936 09	1st	Exp	62	★★★

NORTHERN PORTUGAL

Hotels	Ph./FAX #	Class	Price	Rooms	Stars
Caniçada	**053+**				
Pousada de São Bento Caniçada 4850	64 73 17 64 78 67	2nd	Mod	29	★★
Castelo do Bode	**049+**				
Pousada de São Pedro Tomar 2300	38 22 74 38 11 76	2nd	Mod	15	★★
Cernache do Bonjardim	**039+**				
Estalagem Vale da Ursa Sertá 6100	995 11 995 94	R1st	Mod	12	★★
Coimbra	**039+**				
Almedina Av. Fernão de Magalhães, 203 Coimbra 3000	291 61	R2nd	Inexp	43	
Astória Av. Emidio Navarro, 21 Coimbra 3000	220 55 220 57	2nd	Mod	64	★★★
Bragança Largo das Ameias, 10 Coimbra 3000	221 71 361 35	2nd	Mod	83	
Dom Luís Quinta da Verzea Coimbra 3000	44 15 10 81 31 96	2nd	Mod	104	★
Domus Rua Adelino Veiga, 62 Coimbra 3000	285 84	R3rd	Inexp	20	★
Oslo Av. Fernão de Magalhães, 25 Coimbra 3000	290 71 206 14	2nd	Mod	30	
Tiroli Coimbra R. João Machado, 4 Coimbra 3000	269 34 268 27	1st	Exp	90	★★
Condeixa	**033+**				
Pousada do Sta. Cristina condeixa-a-Nova 3000	94 40 25 94 30 97	2nd	Mod	45	★★★★

HOTEL QUICK REFERENCE LIST

NORTHERN PORTUGAL

Hotels	Ph./FAX #	Class	Price	Rooms	Stars
Figeira da Foz	**033+**				
Aparthotel Atlântico Av. 25 de Abril Figeira da Foz 3080	240 45 224 20	2nd	Mod	70	★
Grande Hotel da Figueira Av. 25 de Abril Figeira da Foz 3080	221 46 224 20	1st	Exp	91	★
Nicola Rua Bernardo Lopes, 36 Figeira da Foz 3080	223 59	R1st	Mod	24	
Gerês	**053+**				
Hotel das Termas Gerês 4845	39 11 43	3rd	Mod	31	
Hotel do Parque Gerês 4845	67 65 48	3rd	Mod	60	★
Guimarães	**053+**				
Fundador Dom Pedro Av. Don Afonso Henriques, 740 Guimarães 4800	51 37 81 51 37 86	1st	Mod	63	
Pousada de Santa Marinha da Costa Guimarães 4800	51 44 53 51 44 59	Deluxe	Exp	50	★★★★★
Pousada de Santa Maria da Oliveira Rua Santa Maria Guimarães 4800	51 41 57 51 42 04	1st	Exp	16	★★★
Porto	**02+**				
Albergaria Girassol Rua do da Bandeira, 133 Porto 4000	200 18 91	R1st	Inexp	18	★
Albergaria Miradouro Rua da Alegría, 598 Porto 4000	57 07 17 57 02 06	R1st	Mod	30	★★
Albergeria São José Rua da Alegria 172 Porto 4000	208 02 61 32 04 46	2nd	Mod	43	★★

NORTHERN PORTUGAL

Hotels	Ph./FAX #	Class	Price	Rooms	Stars
Castor Rua das Doze Casas, 17 Porto 4000	57 00 14 56 60 76	2nd	Mod	63	★
Dom Henrique Rua Guedes de Azevedo, 179 Porto 4000	200 57 55 201 94 51	1st	Exp	112	★★★
Grand Hotel do Oporto Rua de Santa Catarina, 197 Porto 4000	200 81 76 31 10 61	2nd	Mod	100	★
Infante de Sagres Pr. Dona Filipa de Lencastre, 62 Porto 4000	201 90 31 31 49 37	Deluxe	Exp	74	★★★★★
Méridien Porto, Le Av. da Boavista, 1466 Porto 4100	600 19 13 600 20 31	Deluxe	Exp	232	★★★
Peninsular Rua do da Bandeira, 21 Porto 4000	200 30 12 38 49 84	3rd	Inexp	50	★
Porto Sheraton Av. da Boavista, 1269 Porto 4100	606 88 22 609 14 67	Deluxe	Exp	253	★★
Rex Pr. da República, 117 Porto 4000	200 45 48 38 38 82	R1st	Inexp	21	★★★
Tomar	**049+**				
Dos Templários Largo Candido dos Reis, 1 Tomar 2300	32 17 30 32 21 91	1st	Mod	84	★
Pensão Luanda Av. Marquês de Tomar, 13-15 Tomar 2300	31 29 29	R2nd	Inexp	14	★
Residencial Trovador Rua Dr. Joaquim Ribeiro Tomar 2300	32 25 67 32 21 94	R1st	Mod	30	
Residencial União Rua Serpa Pinto, 91 Tomar 2300	31 28 31	R2nd	Inexp	21	★

HOTEL QUICK REFERENCE LIST

NORTHERN PORTUGAL

Hotels	Ph./FAX #	Class	Price	Rooms	Stars
Viseu	**032+**				
Avenida Av. Alberto Sampaio, 1 Viseu 3500	42 34 32 267 43	R3rd	Inexp	40	★
Grão Vasco Rua Gaspar Barreiros Viseu 3500	42 35 11 270 47	1st	Mod	100	★
Moinho de Vento Rua Paulo Emilio, 13 Viseu 3500	42 41 16 42 96 62	R2nd	Mod	30	★
Viana do Castelo	**058+**				
Pousada Santa Luzia Viana 4900	82 88 90 82 88 92	1st	Exp	55	★★★
Viana Mar Av. dos Combatentes da Grande Guerra, 215 Viana 4900	82 89 62 82 98 62	R2nd	Inexp	36	★
Viana Sol Largo Vasco da Gama Viana 4900	82 89 95 82 89 97	1st	Mod	65	★

EASTERN PORTUGAL

Hotels	Ph./FAX #	Class	Price	Rooms	Stars
Elvas	**068+**				
Dom Luís Av. de Badajoz Elvas 7350	62 27 56 62 07 33	1st	Mod	90	★
Estalgem Don Sancho II Pr. da República, 20 Elvas 7350	62 26 86 62 47 17	R2nd	Inexp	26	★
Pousada do Santa Luzia Av. de Badajoz Elvas 7350	62 21 94 62 21 27	1st	Mod	16	★★

EASTERN PORTUGAL

Hotels	Ph./FAX #	Class	Price	Rooms	Stars
Estremoz	**068+**				
Pousada da Reinha Santa Isabel Largo Dom Dinis Estremoz 7100	226 18 239 82	1st	Exp	23	★★★★
Évora	**066+**				
Albergaria Vitória Rua Diana de Lis Évora 7000	271 74 298 80	R1st	Mod	48	★
Eborense, O Largo da Misericordia, 1 Évora 7000	220 31	R2nd	Inexp	29	★★★
Evorahotel Quinta do Cruzeiro Évora 7000	73 48 00 73 48 06	2nd	Mod	114	★
Planicie Largo Álvaro Velho, 40 Évora 7000	240 26 298 80	2nd	Mod	33	★★
Policarpo Rua da Freiria de Baixo, 16 Évora 7000	224 24	R3rd	Inexp	16	★
Pousada dos Lóios Largo Conde de Villa Flor Évora 7000	240 51	1st	Exp	32	★★★
Riviera Rua 5 de Outubro, 49 Évora 7000	233 04 204 67	R1st	Mod	22	★★
Santa Clara Travessa da Milheira, 19 Évora 7000	241 41	2nd	Inexp	51	
Guarda	**071+**				
Filipe Rua Vasco da Gama, 9 Guarda 6300	21 26 58 21 64 02	R1st	Mod	45	★
Pousada São Lourenço Manteigas 6260	(075) 98 24 50 (075) 98 24 53	2nd	Mod	20	★★★

HOTEL QUICK REFERENCE LIST

EASTERN PORTUGAL

Hotels	Ph./FAX #	Class	Price	Rooms	Stars
Turismo, De Av. Coronel Orlindo de Carvalho Guarda 6300	21 22 05 21 22 04	1st	Mod	105	★

Marvão 045+

Estalagem Dom Dinis Rua Dr. Matos Magalhães Marvão 7330	932 36	R2nd	Inexp	8	★
Pousada de Santa Maria R. 24 de Janeiro, 7 Marvão 7330	932 01 934 40	2nd	Mod	29	★★★

Redondo 066+

Convento de São Paulo Aldeia da Serra Redondo 7170	99 91 00 99 91 04	1st	Exp	21	★★★★★

ALGARVE

Hotels	Ph./FAX #	Class	Price	Rooms	Stars

Albufeira 089+

Baltum Av. 25 de Abril Albufeira 8200	58 91 02 58 61 46	3rd	Mod	50	★
Clube Mediterrâneo da Balaia Praia Maria Luisa Albufeira 8200	58 66 81 53 78 47	NR	Exp	300	
Estalagem do Cerro Rua Samor Barros Albufeira 8200	58 61 91 58 61 74	E2nd	Mod	83	★★
Montechoro Montechoro Albufeira 8200	526 51	1st	VExp	410	★
Rocamar Largo Jacinto d'Ayet Albufeira 8200	58 69 90 58 69 98	2nd	Mod	83	★

ALGARVE

Hotels	Ph./FAX #	Class	Price	Rooms	Stars
Sheraton Algarve Praia da Falésia Apartado 644 Albufeira 8200	50 19 99 50 19 50	Deluxe	VExp	215	★★★
Sol e Mar Rua João Bernardino de Sousa Albufeira 8200	58 67 21 58 70 36	1st	Exp	74	★★★
Vila Joya Praia da Gale Albufeira 8200	59 17 95 59 12 01	E1st	VExp	16	★★★★
Villa Recife R. Miguel Bombarda, 6 Albureira 8200	58 67 47	R2nd	Inexp	92	★★

Alvor 082+

Hotels	Ph./FAX #	Class	Price	Rooms	Stars
Alvor Praia Praia dos Três Irmãos Portimão 8500	45 89 00 45 89 99	Deluxe	Exp	217	★★
Aparthotel Alvor Jardim Sítio de São Pedro Portimão 8500	76 34 58 45 80 24	2nd	Mod	28	★★
Delfim Praia dos Três Irmãos Portimão 8500	45 89 01 45 89 70	1st	Exp	312	★
Praiha Club Hotel Praia dos Três Immãos Apartado 25 Portimão 8500	76 34 58 45 95 69	Deluxe	Exp	300	★★

Armação de Pêra 082+

Hotels	Ph./FAX #	Class	Price	Rooms	Stars
Algar Av. Beira Mar Armação de Pêra 8365	31 47 10 31 49 56	2nd	Mod	47	★
Garbe Av. Marginal Armação de Pêra 8365	31 51 87 31 50 87	1st	Exp	140	★★
Do Levante Sitio das Quintas Armação de Pêra 8365	31 49 00 31 49 99	1st	Exp	41	★

HOTEL QUICK REFERENCE LIST

ALGARVE

Hotels	Ph./FAX #	Class	Price	Rooms	Stars
Viking Praia Senhora da Rocha Armação de Pêra 8365	31 48 76 31 48 52	Deluxe	Exp	184	★★
Vilalara Alporchinhos Armação de Pêra 8365	31 49 10 31 49 56	Deluxe	Exp	130	★★★★★
Vila Vita Parc Alporchinhos Armação de Pêra 8365	31 53 41 31 53 33	Deluxe	VExp	194	★★★★

Faro 089+

Hotels	Ph./FAX #	Class	Price	Rooms	Stars
Casa de Lumena Pr. Alexendre Herculano, 27 Faro 8000	80 19 90 80 40 19	2nd	Inexp	12	★★★
Condado R. Conçalo Barreto, 14 Faro 8000	82 20 81 82 77 55	R2nd	Inexp	16	★
Eva Av. da República Faro 8000	80 33 54 80 23 04	1st	Exp	150	★★
Faro Pr. Don Francisco Gomes, 2 Faro 8000	80 32 76 80 35 46	2nd	Mod	52	★
Réserve, La Estrada de Esteval Faro 8000	904 74 904 02	1st	VExp	20	★★★★

Lagos 082+

Hotels	Ph./FAX #	Class	Price	Rooms	Stars
Casa de S. Gonçalo de Lagos Rua Cândido dos Reis, 73 Lagos 8600	76 21 71	R1st	Mod	13	★★
Golfinho Praia Dona Ana Lagos 8600	76 99 00 76 99 99	Deluxe	Exp	262	
Lagos, De Rua Nova da Aldeia Lagos 8600	76 99 67 76 99 20	1st	Exp	317	★★
Lagosmar Rua Dr. Faria e Silva, 13 Lagos 8600	76 37 22 76 73 24	R2nd	Mod	45	★

ALGARVE

Hotels	Ph./FAX #	Class	Price	Rooms	Stars
Marazul Rua 25 de Abril 20, 13 Lagos 8600	76 91 43 76 99 60	R3rd	Mod	18	★★
Meia Praia Meia Praia Lagos 8600	76 20 01	2nd	Mod	66	
São Cristovão Rossio de São João Lagos 8600	76 30 51	2nd	Mod	80	★
Sole Praia Praia Dona Ana Lagos 8600	76 20 76 76 02 47	2nd	Mod	80	★
Olhão	**089+**				
Bicuar Rua Vasco da Gama, 5 Olhão 8700	71 48 16	R3rd	Inexp	12	
Helena Rua Dr. Miguel Bombarda, 42 Olhão 8700	70 26 34	R3rd	Inexp	20	
Ria-Sol Rua General Humberto Delgado, 37 Olhão 8700	70 52 67	3rd	Mod	52	
Porto Covo	**069+**				
Abelha R. Vasco de Gama, 40 Porto Covo 7520	951 08	R3rd	Inexp	10	
Boa Esperança Porto Covo 7520	951 09	R3rd	Inexp	2	
Campismo do Alho do Pessequeiro Porto Covo 7520	951 78	P3rd	Inexp	30	
Praia da Luz	**082+**				
Ocean Club Praia da Luz 8600	78 94 72 78 97 63	1st	Mod	250	★★

HOTEL QUICK REFERENCE LIST

ALGARVE

Hotels	Ph./FAX #	Class	Price	Rooms	Stars
Praia da Rocha	**082+**				
Algarve Av. Tomás Cabreira Portimão 8500	41 50 01 41 59 99	1st	VExp	220	★★
Apartamento Oriental Av. Tomás Cabreira Portimão 8500	41 30 00 41 24 13	1st	VExp	85	★★★★
Albergaria Vila Lido v. Tomás Cabreira Portimão 8500	241 27 242 46	A1st	Mod	10	★★★★★
Avenida Praia Av. Tomás Cabreira Portimão 8500	41 77 40 41 77 42	2nd	Mod	61	★
Bela Vista Av. Tomás Cabreira Portimão 8500	240 55 41 53 69	1st	Exp	14	★★★
Júpiter Av. Tomás Cabreira Portimão 8500	41 50 41 41 53 19	1st	Exp	180	★
Residencial Solar Penguin Portimão 8500	243 08	R2nd	Inexp	14	★★
Residential Toca R. Engenheiro Francisco Bivar Portimão 8500	240 35	R2nd	Inexp	14	★★
Quartiera	**098+**				
Atis Av. Infante de Sagres Quartiera 8125	38 97 71 38 97 74	2nd	Mod	72	
Dom José Av. Infante de Sagres Quartiera 8125	30 27 50 30 27 55	2nd	Mod	134	★
Sagres	**082+**				
Aparthotel Navigator R. Infante D. Henrique Sagres 8650	643 54 643 60	A2nd	Mod	56	★★
Baleeria Sagres 8650	642 12	2nd	Exp	118	★

ALGARVE

Hotels	Ph./FAX #	Class	Price	Rooms	Stars
Dom Henrique Sítio da Mareta Sagres 8650	641 33	R2nd	Mod	15	★★★
Motel Os Gambozinos Praia do Martinhal Sagres 8650	643 18	3rd	Mod	17	★★
Pousada do Infante Ponta da Atalaia Sagres 8650	642 22 642 25	1st	Exp	23	★★★
Salema	**082+**				
Estalagem Infante do Mar Praia da Salema Sagres 8650	651 37 574 51	E1st	Mod	16	★★
Residêncial Salema R. 28 de Janeiro Salema 8650	653 28 553 29	R2nd	Mod	32	★
Tavira	**081+**				
Eurotel Tavira Quinta da Oliveiras Tavira 8800	32 43 24 32 55 71	2nd	Mod	80	★
Lagoas Bica Rua Candido dos Reis, 24 Tavira 8800	222 82	R3rd	Inexp	17	★
Princesa do Gilão Rua Borda de Agua de Aguiar, 10 Tavira 8800	226 65	R3rd	Inexp	14	★
Quinta do Carcol Bairro do São Tavira 8800	224 75 231 75	3rd	Mod	7	★★★
Tavira Garden Quinta das Oliveiras Tavira 8800	32 55 08 32 55 09	2nd	Mod	100	★★
Vilamoura	**089+**				
Ampalius Vilamoura 8129	38 80 08 38 09 11	1st	Exp	150	★★
Atlantis Vilamoura Vilamoura 8125	38 99 37 38 98 69	1st	Exp	313	★★

HOTEL QUICK REFERENCE LIST

ALGARVE

otels	Ph./FAX #	Class	Price	Rooms	Stars
om Pedro Golf lamoura 8125	38 96 50 31 54 82	1st	Exp	261	★★
om Pedro Marina lamoura 8125	38 98 02 31 32 70	1st	Exp	155	★★
stalagem da Cegonha entro Hipico de Vilamoura lamoura 8125	30 25 77	2nd	Mod	10	★★★★
otel Vilamoura Golf lamoura 8125	30 29 77 38 00 23	1st	Mod	52	★★
lamoura Marinotel lamoura 8125	38 99 88 38 98 69	Deluxe	Mod	387	★★★

Vila Nova de Milfontes 083+

astelo de Milfontes ossio ilfontes 7645	961 08	P2nd	Mod	7	★
otel Social v. Marginal ilfontes 7645	965 17	2nd	Moc	45	★
esidential Mol-Reis argo de Rossio ilfontes 7645	962 23	R1st	Inexp	12	★

SPECIAL RESTAURANTS
(By Region)

NOTE: Because restaurant prices are not fixed, we use the following price categories:

Very Expensive (VExp).... $50+ for dinner for one with house wine

Expensive (Exp)............. $40+ for dinner for one with house wine

Moderate (Mod)............ $15–30 for dinner for one with house wine

Inexpensive (Inexp)....... $15 or less for dinner for one with house wine

Closing days are indicated by the obvious day abreviations of M, etc., with Su for Sunday and Th for Thursday. In some cases an establishment closes only for lunch or only for dinner, which we indicated with M/l (*closed Monday for lunch*), or T/d (*closed Tuesday for dinner*).

Note, most resort restaurants close for one month or for the season in winter, while other restaurants generally close for one month in summer. Check the listing in the text for specifics.

LISBON

Restaurants	Phone #	Price	Stars	Closed
Lisbon	**01+**			
Aviz R. Serpa Pinto, 12-B	32 83 91	Exp	★★	Su, S/l
Bonjardim Traversa de Santo Antõa, 11	342 74 24	Inexp	★	
Bota Alta Travessa da Queimada, 35	32 79 59	Inexp	★★	Su
Casa da Comida Travessa das Amoreiras, 1	388 53 76	Exp	★★★★★	Su, S/l
Cervejaria da Trindade R. Nova de Trindade, 20-B	342 35 06	Inexp	★	
Comida de Santo Calçada do Eng. Miquel Pais, 39	396 33 39	Mod	★	

LISBON

Restaurants	Phone #	Price	Stars	Closed
Conventual Pr. das Flores, 45	60 91 96	Exp	★★★★	Su, S/l
Exbaixada R. Pau de Bandeira, 4	395 00 05	Exp	★★★	
Gambrinus R. das Portas de Santo Antão, 25	32 14 66	Exp	★★★	
Great American Disaster Pr. Marquês de Pombal, 1	51 61 45	Inexp		
Numero Um R. Dom Francisco de Malo, 44A	68 43 26	mod	★	Su, S/l
Pap'Açorda R. da Atalaya, 57	346 48 11	Mod	★★	Su
Pastelaria Bénard R. Garrett, 104	347 31 33	Inexp	★	Su
Restaurante 33 R. Alexandre Herculano, 33A	54 60 79	Mod	★	Su, S/l
Sancho Travessa da Gloria, 14	346 97 80	Mod	★	Su
Sua Excelencia R. do Conde, 42	60 36 14	Mod	★★	W, S/l
Tágide Largo da Academia Nacional de Belas Artes, 18	347 18 80	Exp	★★★★	Su, S/d
Xêlê Bananas Pr. des Flores, 29	395 25 15	Inexp	★	Su, S/l

ENVIRONS OF LISBON

Restaurants	Phone #	Price	Stars	Closed
Alcobaça	**062+**			
Trindade Pr. Dom Afonso Henriques, 22 Alcobaça	423 97	Mod	★	

SPECIAL RESTAURANTS

ENVIRONS OF LISBON

Restaurants	Phone #	Price	Stars	Closed
Batalha	**044+**			
Pousada do Mestre Afonso Domingues Batalha	962 60	Mod		
Gambrinus R. das Portas de Santo Antão, 25	32 14 66	Exp	★★	
Cascais	**01+**			
Albatroz R. Federico Arouça	483 28 21	Exp	★★★	
Jardim dos Frangos Av. Marginal	438 06 75	Inexp	★★	
Mafra	**061+**			
Albergaria Castelão Av. 25 de Abril	81 20 50	Mod	★	
Nazaré	**062+**			
Arte Xavega Calçada do Sitio	55 21 36	Mod	★	M
Beira-Mar Av. da República, 40	56 13 58	Inexp		
Mar Bravo Pr. Sousa Oliveira, 75	55 11 80	Inexp		
Óbidos	**062+**			
Alcaide R. Direita	95 92 20	Mod	★	M
Praia do Guincho	**01+**	(See also Cascais and Estoril)		
Porto de Santa Maria Estrada do Guincho	487 02 40	Exp	★★★★	M
Queluz	**01+**			
Cozinha Velha Largo do Palácio	435 02 32	Exp	★★	
Sintra	**01+**			
Alcobaça R. da Padarias, 7	923 16 51	Inexp	★	W
Galeria Real R. Tude de Sousa	923 16 61	Mod	★	M

ENVIRONS OF LISBON

Restaurants	Phone #	Price	Stars	Closed
Palácio de Seteais Av. Bocage, 8	923 32 00	Exp	★★★	

NORTHERN PORTUGAL

Restaurants	Phone #	Price	Stars	Closed
Aveiro	**034+**			
Centenario Largo do Mercado, 9	227 98	Mod	★★	T
Braga	**053+**			
Abade de Priscos Pr. Mousinho de Albuquerque, 7	766 50	Mod	★★	
Inácio, O Campo das Hortas, 4	61 32 25	Mod	★★	T
Bragança	**073+**			
Lá em Casa Rua Marquês de Pombal	221 11	Mod		M
Plantório Estrada Cantarias	224 26	Mod		
Coimbra	**039+**			
Alfredo, O Av. João das Regras, 32	44 15 22	Inexp	★	
Dom Pedro Av. Emidio Navarro, 58	291 08	Inexp		M
Pedro dos Leitões Mealhada	220 62	Inexp	★★	
Trovador Largo da Sé Velha, 17	254 75	Inexp	★	M
Ze Manuel Beco do Forno, 12	237 90	Inexp	★★★	
Figeira da Foz	**033+**			
Tamargueira Estrada do Cabo Mondeo	225 14	Mod	★	
Tubarão Av. 25 de Abril	234 45	Mod	★	

SPECIAL RESTAURANTS

NORTHERN PORTUGAL

Restaurants	Phone #	Price	Stars	Closed
Guimarães	**053+**			
Pousada de Santa Maria da Oliveira Rua Santa Maria	51 41 57	Mod	★	
Montemor-o-Velho	**039+**			
Ramalhão R. Tenente Valadim, 24	68 94 35	Exp	★★★★	Su/M
Porto	**02+**			
Aquário Marisqueiro Rua Rodriques Sampaio, 179	200 22 31	Mod	★	Su
Chez Lapin Cais da Ribeira, 42	264 18	Inexp	★★	
Escondidinho, O Rua de Passos Manuel, 144	200 10 79	Mod		Su
Mesa Antiga Rua de Santo Ildefonso, 208	200 64 32	Mod	★★	S
Porta Nobre, A Largo do São Francisco, 133	38 49 42	Exp	★★★	
Portucale Rua da Alegria, 598	57 07 17	Exp	★★★	
Standard Bar Rua Infante Dom Henrique, 43	239 04	Inexp	★	Su
Taverna de Bebobos Cais da Ribeira, 25	31 35 65	Inexp	★★	Su
Tomar	**049+**			
Chez Nous Rua Dr. Joaquim Jacinto, 31	31 47 43	Mod	★	T
Chico Elias Algarvias	310 67	Mod	★★	T
Viana do Castelo	**058+**			
3 Potes, Os Beco dos Fornos, 7	82 99 28	Mod	★★	M

NORTHERN PORTUGAL

Restaurants	Phone #	Price	Stars	Closed
Viseu	**032+**			
Cacimbo Rua Alexandre Herculano, 95	228 94	Inexp	★	
Cortiço, O Rua Augusto Hilário, 43	42 38 53	Mod	★	
Trave Negra Rua dos Loureiros, 40	261 38	Mod	★	

EASTERN PORTUGAL

Restaurants	Phone #	Price	Stars	Closed
Elvas	**068+**			
Don Quixote On N-4	62 20 14	Mod	★	
Estalgem Don Sancho II Pr. da República, 20	62 26 86	Inexp	★	
Pousada de Santa Luzia Av. de Badajoz	62 21 94	Mod	★	
Évora	**066+**			
Cozinha de Santo Humberto Rua da Moeda, 39	242 51	Mod		Th
Fialho Travessa das Mascarenhas, 14	230 79	Mod	★	M
Guião Rua da República, 81	224 27	Mod		M
Guarda	**071+**			
Filipe Rua Vasco da Gama, 9	21 26 58	Mod	★	
Marvão	**045+**			
Pousada de Santa Maria Rua 24 de Janeiro, 7	932 01	Mod	★	

SPECIAL RESTAURANTS

Restaurants	ALGARVE Phone #	Price	Stars	Closed
Albufeira	**089+**			
Ruína Cais Herculano	51 20 94	Mod	★	
Cabaz da Praia, o R. Miguel Bombarda, 7	51 21 37	Mod	★	
Montinho, O Montechoro	51 39 59	Mod	★★	Su
Vila Joya Praia da Gale	59 17 95	Exp	★★★★★	
Armação de Pêra	**082+**			
Flor do Campo, A N-125	31 49 64	Inexp		
Santola Largo da Fortaleza	31 23 32	Mod	★	
Lagos	**082+**			
Alpendre Rua António Barbosa Viana, 17	76 27 05	Exp	★	
Arcos, Os R. 25 de Abril, 30	76 32 10	Mod		
Dom Henrique R. 25 de Abril, 75	76 35 63	Mod	★	
Dom Sebastião Rua 25 de Abril 20, 20-2	76 27 95	Mod	★	
Hasan's Doner Kebab R. Silva Loper, 27	76 46 82	Inexp	★	
Faro	**089+**			
Cidade Velha Rua Domingos Guieiro, 19	271 45	Exp	★★	Su, S/l
Réserve, La Estrada do Esteval	902 34	Exp	★★★★	T
Porto Covo	**069+**			
Restaurant a Ilha Praia da Ilha		Inexp	★	

ALGARVE

Restaurants	Phone #	Price	Stars	Closed
Praia da Luz	**082+**			
Poço, O Av. dos Pescadores	78 91 89	Mod	★	
Sagres	**082+**			
Fortaleza do Beliche Cabo Vicente	641 34	Mod	★	
Tasca, A In the port	641 77	Mod		
Salema	**082+**			
Atlântico On the beach		Inexp	★★	
Taveira	**081+**			
4 Aguas On the quay	32 53 29	Mod	★	
Restaurant Avenida Av. Dr. Mateus T. de Acevedo	811 13	Inexp	★	M

INDEX

A

commodations, 18–23
  Albufeira (Algarve), 293–294
  Alcobaça (Environs of
    Lisbon), 129
  Alvor (Algarve), 286–287
  Armação (Algarve), 291–292
  Aveiro (North), 166–168
  Batalha (Environs of Lisbon), 132
  Braga (North), 172–173
  Bragança (North), 179–180
  Buçaco Forest (North), 193
  Cascais (Environs of
    Lisbon), 135–137
  Coimbra (North), 187–188
  Condeixa (North), 191
  Elvas (East), 240
  Estoril (Environs of
    Lisbon), 135–137
  Estremoz (East), 243
  Évora (East), 251–252
  Faro (Algarve), 299–300
  Figueira da Foz (North), 194
  Guarda (East), 257
  Guimarães (North), 199
  House exchanges, 22
  Lagos (Algarve), 283–285
  Lisbon, 103–108
  Mafra (Environs of Lisbon), 139
  Marvão (East), 262
  Nazaré (Environs of
    Lisbon), 140–141
  Óbidos (Environs of
    Lisbon), 143–144
  Olhão (Algarve), 302
  Outstanding, 21
  Palmela (Environs of Lisbon), 148
  Peneda Gerês Park (North), 201
  Porto (North), 208–210
  Porto Covo (Southwest), 305
  Pousadas, 18
  Praia da Luz (Algarve), 281
  Praia da Rocha
    (Algarve), 288–290
  Private homes, 19
  Quarteira (Algarve), 298
  Queluz (Environs of Lisbon), 146
  Redondo (East), 255
  Sagres (Algarve), 278–279
  Salema (Algarve), 280
  Setúbal (Environs of
    Lisbon), 147–148
  Sintra (Environs of
    Lisbon), 153–154
  Tavira (Algarve), 302–303
  Tomar (North), 217–219
  Tróia (Environs of Lisbon), 148
  Viana do Castelo (North), 176
  Vila Nova de Milfontes
    (Southwest), 306
  Vilamoura (Algarve), 296–297
  Viseu (North), 223
Afonso Henriques. *See* Afonso I
Afonso I (King), 56, 82, 158,
    159–160, 181
  birthplace, 195
  tomb of, 186
Afonso II (King), 161
Afonso III (King), 82, 161
Afonso IV (King), 120
Afonso V (King), 123, 130, 142
Afonso VI (King), 228
Afonso, Jorge (painter), 70
Águeda (North), 166
  accommodations, 166
Ajimese, 64
Albufeira (Algarve), 292–296
  accommodations, 293–294
  excursions, 296
  restaurants, 295
Alcobaça (Environs of
    Lisbon), 126–129
  accommodations, 129
  directory, 129
  excursions, 129
  history of, 120, 126
  Mostario de Santa Maria, 127
  sights, 127–128

Alentejo, 235
Alfama (Lisbon), 90–92
Algarve, 267–304
    Albufeira, 292–296
    Alvor, 286–287
    areas, 273–276
    Armação, 290–292
    Faro, 298–301
    history, 267–271
    Lagos, 282–286
    name of, 159
    Olhão, 301–302
    Praia da Luz, 281–282
    Praia da Rocha, 287–290
    Quarteira, 297
    Sagres, 276–279
    Salema, 280–281
    Tavira, 302–303
    Vilamoura, 296–297
Aljubarrota (battle of), 130, 131, 171
Almeida (East), 260
Almograve (Southwest), 306
Almourol. *See* Tomar excursions.
Álvares Pereira, Nuno (general), 131
Alvor (Algarve), 286–287
    accommodations, 286–287
    restaurants, 287
Amarante (North), 200
Architecture, 63–72
    Arte Deco, 68
    Baroque, 67, 172
    Castles, 65
    Fortresses, 65
    Gothic, 66
    Manueline, 66, 124, 131, 217
    Modern, 68
    Moorish, 64
    Neoclassic, 67
    Pombaline, 67
    Roman, 184, 191, 249
    Romanesque, 64–65, 185
    Victorian, 67, 152
Armação (Algarve), 290–292
    accommodations, 291–292
    directory, 292
    restaurants, 292
Arraiolos (East), 236
    history, 236
    shopping, 236
    sights, 236

Art, 63–72
    Azulejos, 71–72
    Painting, 70–71
    Sculpture, 68–69
    Victorian, 67
ATMs, 24
Aveiro (North), 164–168
    accommodations, 166–168
    beaches, 166
    Convento de Jesús, 165
    directory, 168
    history, 164
    restaurants, 168
    shopping, 168
    sights, 165–166
Avís, *see* House of Avís
Azulejos, 71–72

B

Baixa (Lisbon), 92–94
Barcelos (North), 174–175
Baroque architecture, 67
    Bom Jesus (Braga), 67
    Mafra, 67
    Queluz, 67
Batalha (Environs of Lisbon), 129–1
    accommodations, 132
    excursions, 133
    history of, 130
    Mostairo de Santa Maria da
        Vitoria, 131–132
    restaurants, 133
Beaches, 47–48
    Albufeira (Algarve), 293
    Almograve (Southwest), 306
    Alvor (Algarve), 286
    Armação (Algarve), 290
    Aveiro (North), 166
    Carrapateira (Algarve), 277
    Cascais (Environs of Lisbon), 13
    Estoril (Environs of Lisbon), 134
    Faro (Algarve), 298
    Figueira da Foz (North), 194–1
    Lagos (Algarve), 282
    Odeceixe (Southwest), 307
    Olhão (Algarve), 302
    Porto Covo (Southwest), 305
    Praia da Luz (Algarve), 281
    Praia da Rocha (Algarve), 288

INDEX

Praia do Guincho Environs of Lisbon), 135
Quarteira (Algarve), 298
Sagres (Algarve), 277
Salema (Algarve), 280
Tavira (Algarve), 302
Viana do Castelo (North), 176
Vila do Bispo (Algarve), 277
Vila Nova de Milfontes (Southwest), 306
Belém (Lisbon), 96–99
Belmonte (East), 258
Books, 37
Borba (East), 238
    shopping, 238
    sights, 238
Bosch (painter), 70
Boytac, Diogo (architect), 97, 147
Braga (North), 169–174
    accommodations, 172–173
    Bom Jesus, 172
    cathedral, 170–171
    Citânia de Briteiros, 172
    directory, 174
    excursions, 174
    history, 169
    Museu Biscainhos, 171
    restaurants, 173–174
    sights, 170
    walking tour, 170
Bragança
    House of, 59–61
Bragança (North), 176–180
    accommodations, 179–180
    restaurants, 180
    sights, 177–179
Bravães (North), 175
Brazil, 124
Buarcos (North), 194
    See Figueira da Foz.
Buçaco Forest (North), 193
    accommodations, 193
    See also Luso
Bullfighting, 114
Buses, 27

C

Cabral, Pedro Alvares (explorer), 171, 272
Caetano, Marcelo (politician), 61, 233
Camões (poet), 98
Caravel (ship), 270
Carlos I (King), 231
Carlos V (King of Spain), 124
Carlota (Queen), 145
Cars
    Rentals, 15, 16
    See Travel (in Portugal)
    See Travel (to Portugal)
Cascais (Environs of Lisbon), 134–138
    accommodations, 135–137
    restaurants, 137–138
Cash advances. *See* ATMs
Casino
    Estoril (Environs of Lisbon), 135
Castelo Branco (East), 264
    shopping, 264
Castelo do Bode (North), 218
Castelo Melhor (East), 260
Castelo Rodrigo (East), 260
Castelo de Vide (East), 264
Castilho, João and Diogo (sculptors), 184
Castles, 48–49, 65
    Almourol (North), 65, 220
    Elvas (East), 240
    Estremoz (East), 242
    Evoramonte (East), 254
    Guimarães (North), 196
    Leiria, 65
    Monsaraz (East), 254
    Óbidos, 142–144
Castro, Joaquim Machado de (sculptor), 69, 93
Celtiberian, 54, 172, 198
Celts, 54
Cernache do Bonjardim (North), 218
Chanterene, Nicolas (sculptor), 69, 97, 184, 186
Charola (Templar church), 216
Chaucer, Geoffry, 122
Churches
    Aveiro (North), 165
    Braga (North), 170, 171, 172
    Carmo, do (Lisbon), 95
    Coimbra (North), 185
    Évora (East), 247
    Guarda (East), 257
    Guimarães (North), 197, 198
    Lisbon Cathedral, 92

348   *FIELDING'S PORTUGAL*

Madre de Deus (Lisbon), 102
Porto (North), 206
São Roque (Lisbon), 95
Tomar (North), 216–217
Viseu (North), 222, 223
Citânia de Briteiros (North), 172, 198
Climate and seasons, 12
Clothes and packing, 17
Coelho, Gaspar and Domingos (sculptors), 69
Coimbra (North), 180–190
    accommodations, 187–188
    directory, 189
    excursions, 190–195
    history, 181
    Mosteiro de Santa Cruz, 186
    Museu Machado de Castro, 184
    restaurants, 188–189
    Se Velha, 185
    shopping, 189
    sights, 182–187
    Velha Universidade, 182–183
Colonies, 84, 232
Columbus, 58, 124, 271
Communists, 233
Condeixa (North), 190–192
    accommodations, 191
    Conimbriga, 191
    directory, 192
    shopping, 192
Conimbriga (North), 64, 181, 191
    See Coimbra excursions
Costs, 11
Credit cards, 24
Crime, 36–37
Crusades, 82, 215
Customs requirements, 16

D

Dias, Bartolomeu, 124, 270
Dinis I (King), 57, 161, 215, 261
Directory
    Alcobaça (Environs of Lisbon), 129
    Armação (Algarve), 292
    Aveiro (North), 168
    Braga (North), 174
    Coimbra (North), 189
    Condeixa (North), 192
    Elvas (East), 241

Estremoz (East), 243
Évora (East), 253
Faro (Algarve), 301
Lisbon, 115–116
Porto (North), 212–213
Sintra (Environs of Lisbon), 155
Tavira (Algarve), 304
Viseu (North), 224
Domingues, Afonso (architect), 130
Duarte I (King), 123, 130
Dürer, Albrecht (painter), 70, 100

E

Eastern Portugal
    Almeida, 260
    area, 235
    Arraiolos, 236
    Belmonte, 258
    Borba, 238
    Castelo Branco, 264
    Castelo de Vide, 264
    Castelo Melhor, 260
    Castelo Rodrigo, 260
    Elvas, 238–241
    Estremoz, 241–245
    Évora, 245–255
    Evoramonte, 253
    Flor de Rosa, 263
    Guarda, 256–261
    Marialva, 260
    Marvão, 261–265
    Monsanto, 259
    Monsaraz, 254–255
    Portalegre, 263
    Redondo, 255
    Sabugal, 259
    sights, 235
    Sortelha, 259
    Trancoso, 261
    Vila Viçosa, 244–245
Economy, 42
Electricity, 32
Elvas (East), 238–241
    accommodations, 240
    Castle, 240
    directory, 241
    history, 239
    restaurants, 241
    sights, 239–240
Entertainment

INDEX

fado, 114
Lisbon, 113–115
Environs of Lisbon, 126–156
    Alcobaça, 126–129
    Batalha, 129–133
    Cascais, 134–138
    Estoril, 134–137
    Fátima, 133–134
    Mafra, 138–139
    Nazaré, 139–141
    Óbidos, 142–144
    Palmela, 148
    Praia do Guincho, 136
    Queluz, 144–146
    Serra de Arrábida, 148
    Sesimbra, 149
    Setúbal, 146–149
    Sintra, 149–156
    Tróia, 148
Erasmus (philosopher), 182
Estoril (Environs of Lisbon), 134–137
    accommodations, 135–137
    restaurants, 137
Estrela, Serra da, 235
Estremoz (East), 241–245
    accommodations, 243
    castle, 242
    directory, 243
    excursions, 243
    sights, 242–243
Évora (East), 245–255
    accommodations, 251–252
    Cathedral, 247
    directory, 253
    excursions, 253
    history, 246
    restaurants, 252–253
    sights, 247–250
Evoramonte (East), 253
    castle, 254
Excursions
    Albufeira (Algarve), 296
    Alcobaça (Environs of Lisbon, 129
    Batalha (Environs of Lisbon), 133
    Braga (North), 174
    Coimbra (North), 190–195
    Estremoz, 243
    Évora (East), 253
    Faro (Algarve), 301
    Guarda (East), 258–261

    Guimarães (North), 200
    Lisbon, 116–117
    Marvão (East), 263–265
    Porto (North), 213–214
    Sintra (Environs of Lisbon), 156
    Tomar (North), 219
    Viseu (North), 225
Eyck, Jan van (painter), 70, 100

F

Fado, 114
Faro (Algarve), 298–301
    accommodations, 299–300
    directory, 301
    excursions, 301
    restaurants, 300–301
Fátima (Environs of Lisbon), 133–134
Felipe II, of Spain, 60, 227
Ferdinand and Isabella, 59, 123, 124, 270
Fernandes, Mateus (architect), 131
Fernandes, Vasco. *See* Vasco Fernandes
Fernando I (King), 152
Figueira da Foz (North), 194–195
    accommodations, 194
    restaurants, 195
Flor de Rosa (East), 263
Flower Revolution, 61, 233
Food and drink, 73–78
    bread, 74
    breakfast, 74
    cheese, 76
    coffee, 76
    cover-charge, 74
    desert, 76
    dinner, 74
    fish, 75
    lunch, 74
    meat, 75
    port wine, 77–78, 207
    soup, 74
    wine, 76–78
Fortresses, 65
    Almeida (East), 260
    Belmonte (East), 258
    Castelo Melhor (East), 260
    Castelo Rodrigo (East), 260
    Elvas (East), 240
    Guarda (East), 257
    Marialva (East), 260

Monsanto (East), 259
Sabugal (East), 259
Sortelha (East), 259
Trancoso (East), 261
Franco, Francisco, 232

G

Gama, Vasco da, 58, 82, 98, 124, 271
Geography, 39–42
Golf, 33–34
Gonçalves, Avelino (poitician), 233
Gonçalves, Nuno (painter), 70, 100
Goya, Francisco (painter), 71
Grand Vasco. *See* Vasco Fernandes.
Guarda (East), 256–261
    accommodations, 257
    Cathedral, 257
    excursions, 258–261
    fortress, 257
    fortresses nearby, 258–261
    restaurants, 258
Guimarães (North), 195–200
    accommodations, 199
    Castelo, 196
    excursions, 200
    history, 195
    Nossa Senhora da Oliveira, 197
    Paço dos Duques de Braganza, 196
    restaurants, 200
    São Francisco, 198
    sights, 196–198
Guincho, Praia do (Environs of Lisbon), 134, 135
    restaurants, 137
Gulbenkian, Calouste, 71, 101

H

Hannibal, 54
Henri of Burgundy, 56, 159, 195
    tomb of, 171
Henrique I (King), 125
Henry the Navigator, 58, 70, 122–123, 215, 217, 268–270, 277
    tomb of, 131
Heronymite Monestery (Lisbon), 97–98
Hiking, 34
History

    Burgundian Dynasty, 56–57
    Early, 53–56
    Henri of Burgundy, 56
    Henrique, Afonso, 56
    Henry the Navigator, 58
    House of Avís, 58–59
    House of Bragança, 59–61
    João I, 57
    João II, 58
    João IV, 60
    João V, 60
    José I, 60
    Manuel I, 58
    Moors, 55–57
    Pedro I, 57
    Republic, the, 61–62
    Sabastião I, 59
History, *see also* proper names of Kings
Holidays and special events, 13–14
    Fairs, 14
    Regional, 13
Hotels and restaurants
    Hotel classes, 3
    prices, 3
    ratings, 2–3
Houguet (architect), 130
House of Avís, 58–59, 120–125
House of Burgundy, 159–161

I

Iberians, 54
Industrial Revolution, 84
Inês de Castro, 120, 128, 178, 186
Inquisition, 59
Isabella (Queen), 161
Isabella. *See* Ferdinand and Isabella
Itineraries, 50–52

J

Jews, 124, 264
João I (King), 57, 120–123, 130, 150, 268
    tomb of, 131
João II (King), 58, 123, 178, 271
João III (King), 98, 124, 130, 182, 215, 217
João IV (King), 60, 228
João V (King), 60, 138, 183, 228
João VI (King), 230
John of Gaunt, Duke of Lancaster, 121

sé I (King), 60, 83, 228

K

nights Templar, 215, 216, 220

L

agos (Algarve), 282–286
    accommodations, 283–285
    restaurants, 285
isbon, 85–118
    accommodations, 103–108
    airport (Portela), 115
    Alfama, 90–92
    Baixa, 92–94
    Barrio Alto, 94
    Belém, 96–99
    Belém Tower, 96
    buses, 88
    capture of, 82, 160
    Castelo de São Jorge, 90
    Cathedral, 92
    directory, 115–116
    earthquake, 83
    entertainment, 113–115
    excursions, 84, 116–117
    fado, 114
    Heronymite Monastery, 82
    Igreja do Carmo, 95
    Igreja São Roque, 95
    layout, 88
    Madre de Deus, 102
    Mosteiro dos Jerónimos, 97–98
    Museu Calouste
        Gulbenkian, 101–102
    Museu de Arte Popular, 96
    Museu Nacional de Arte
        Antiga, 99–101
    Museu Nacional dos Coches, 99
    name of, 82
    Parque Eduardo VII, 94
    population, 82, 84
    post office, 116
    Praça do Comércio, 83, 93
    restaurants, 108–112
    Rossio, 93
    shopping, 112–113
    sights, 89–103
    taxis, 88
    tours, 115
    train stations, 116
    walking tours, 90–96
Lopes, Gregorio (painter), 70
Luis I (King), 231
Lusitanians, 54, 158
Luso (North), 192–193
    accommodations, 193

M

Mafra (Environs of Lisbon), 138–139
    accommodations, 139
    Mosteiro de Mafra, 138
Mail, 31–32
Manuel I (King), 58, 82, 97, 98, 123,
    130, 150, 215, 271
Manuel II (King), 231
Manueline architecture, 66, 124, 131,
    217
    Batalha, 66
    Belém, 66
    Setúbal, 66
    Sintra, 66
    Tomar, 66
Maria (Queen), 145
Maria II (Queen), 152, 231
Marialva (East), 260
Market
    Barcelos (North), 174
Marvão (East), 261–265
    accommodations, 262
    excursions, 263–265
    restaurants, 263
    sights, 262
Mashrabiyas, 170
Mateus (North), 213–214
    See also Porto excursions
Measurements, metric, 32
Methuen Treaty, 203
Miguel I (King), 203, 230
Modern architecture, 68
Money, 23–24
Monsanto (East), 259
Monsaraz (East), 254–255
    castle, 254
Montemor-o-velho (North)
    restaurants, 188
Moors, 55, 55–57
    Architecture, 64
Mudejar, 64, 150
Museu do Abade de Baçal
    (Bragança), 178

N

Napoléon, 60
Nazaré (Environs of Lisbon), 139–141
    accommodations, 140–141
    restaurants, 141
Neoclassic architecture, 67
Northern Portugal, 162–225
    , 192–193
    Amarante, 200
    Aviero, 164–168
    Barcelos, 174–175
    Braga, 169–174
    Bragança, 176–180
    Bravães, 175
    Buçaco Forest, 193
    Castelo do Bode, 218
    Cernache do Bonjardim, 218
    Coimbra, 180–190
    Condeixa, 190–192
    Figueira da Foz, 194–195
    Guimarães, 195–200
    Mateus, 213–214
    Peneda Gerês Park, 200–201
    Porto, 202–214
    Tomar, 214–220
    Trofa, 200
    Viana do Castelo, 175–176
    Viseu, 220–225

O

Óbidos (Environs of Lisbon), 142–144
    Accommodations, 143–144
    history, 142
    restaurants, 144
Óbidos, Josefa de (painter), 143
Odeceixe (Southwest), 307
Olhão (Algarve), 301–302
    accommodations, 302
Oporto. *See* Porto

P

Packaged tours. *See* Travel (to Portugal)
Palaces
    Guimarães (North), 196
    Palácio Nacional da Pena
        (Sintra), 152
    Palácio Real (Sintra), 150–151
    Vila Viçosa (East), 244
Palmela (Environs of Lisbon), 148
Parks

Peneda Gerês, 200–201
Passports, 14–15
Pedro I (King), 57, 120, 127, 128, 178
Pedro IV (King), 203, 230, 254
Pedro V (King), 231
Peneda Gerês Park (North), 200–201
    accommodations, 201
    sights, 201
Peninsular War, 230
Philippa of Lancaster (Queen), 58, 12
    tomb of, 131
Phoenicia, 54, 81
Phrases, commonly used, 309–312
PIDE (secret police), 232
Planes, 5–??
    see Travel (to Portugal)
Pombal (Marquis of)
    architecture, 67
    See also Architecture, Pombaline
Pombal, (Marquis of), 83, 92, 228–229
Population, 42
Portalegre (East), 263
    shopping, 263
Portimão (Algarve). *See* Praia da Rocha (Algarve)
Porto (North), 202–214
    accommodations, 208–210
    airport (Pedras Rubras), 212
    Cathedral, 206
    directory, 212–213
    excursions, 213–214
    history, 202–204
    restaurants, 210–212
    São Francisco, 206
    Shopping, 212
    sights, 204–208
    Vila Nova de Gaia, 207
Porto Covo (Southwest), 305
    accommodations, 305
    restaurants, 305
Portugal
    language, 309–312
    name of, 159
Pousadas, 18
Praia da Luz (Algarve), 281–282
    accommodations, 281
    restaurants, 281
Praia da Rocha (Algarve), 287–290

accommodations, 288–290
restaurants, 290
Praia do Guincho (Environs of Lisbon), 136
restaurant, 136
Prices
hotels and restaurants, 3

Q

Quarteira (Algarve), 297
accommodations, 298
Queluz (Environs of Lisbon), 144–146
Accommodations, 146
history, 144–145
Palácio Real, 145
Restaurants, 146

R

Ratings
hotels and restaurants, 2–3
Redondo (East), 255
accommodations, 255
shopping, 255
Republic, the, 61–62, 231
Restaurants, 27–29
Albufeira (Algarve), 295
Alvor (Algarve), 287
Armação (Algarve), 292
Aveiro (North), 168
Batalha (Environs of Lisbon), 133
Braga (North), 173–174
Bragança (North), 180
Cascais (Environs of Lisbon), 137–138
Coimbra (North), 188–189
Elvas (East), 241
Estoril, 137
Évora (East), 252–253
Faro (Algarve), 300–301
Figueira da Foz (North), 195
Guarda (East), 258
Guimarães (North), 200
Lagos (Algarve), 285
Lisbon, 108–112
Marvão (East), 263
Montemor-o-velho (North), 188
Nazaré (Environs of Lisbon), 141
Óbidos (Environs of Lisbon), 144
Porto (North), 210–212
Porto Covo (Southwest), 305
Praia da Luz (Algarve), 281
Praia da Rocha (Algarve), 290
Praia do Guincho (Environs of Lisbon), 137
Queluz (Environs of Lisbon), 146
Sagres (Algarve), 279
Salema (Algarve), 280
Sintra (Environs of Lisbon), 154
superior, 28
Tavira (Algarve), 303–304
Tomar (North), 219
Viana do Castelo (North), 176
Viseu (North), 224
Retornados (Returners), 84
Robillion, Jean-Baptiste (architect), 145
Roman, 55, 90, 191, 249
Romanesque architecture, 64–65

S

Sabugal (East, 259
Sagres (Algarve), 276–279
accommodations, 278–279
directory, 279
restaurants, 279
Salazar, Dr. António de Oliveira, 61, 182, 231–233
Salema (Algarve), 280–281
accommodations, 280
restaurants, 280
Sancho I (King), 160
tomb of, 186
Sebastião I (King), 59, 98, 125, 282
Sequeira, Domingos António (painter), 71, 100
Serra de Arrábida (Environs of Lisbon), 148
Sesimbra (Environs of Lisbon), 149
accommodations, 149
Setúbal (Environs of Lisbon), 146–149
accommodations, 147–148
excursions, 148–149
Igreja de Jesus, 147
Shopping, 29–30
Arraiolos (East), 236
Aveiro (North), 168
Borba (East), 238
Castelo Branco (East), 264
Condeixa (North), 192
Lisbon, 112–113

Portalegre (East), 263
Porto, 212
Redondo (East), 255
Sintra (Environs of Lisbon), 155
Sightseeing
  Lisbon, 89–103
Sintra (Environs of Lisbon), 149–156
  accommodations, 153–154
  directory, 155
  excursions, 156
  Palácio Nacional da Pena, 152
  Palácio Real, 150–151
  restaurants, 154
  shopping, 155
Slaves, 270, 283
Soares, Mario (politician), 233
Sortelha (East), 259
Spinola, General (poitician), 233
Sports, 33–34
  golf, 33–34
  hiking, 34
  tennis, 34
Star ratings, 2
Student travel, 35
Swabians, 55, 158, 169

T

Tagus River. *See* Tejo River
Tavira (Algarve), 302–303
  accommodations, 302–303
  directory, 304
  restaurants, 303–304
Tejo River, 81
Telephones, 32
Teles de Meneses, Leonor, 57, 121
Tennis, 34
Time zone and official hours, 31
Tipping, 30–31
Tomar (North), 214–220
  accommodations, 217–219
  Almourol, 220
  Convento de Cristo, 216–217
  excursions, 219
  history, 214
  restaurants, 219
  sights, 216–217
Trains, 26–27
  See Travel (to Portugal)
Trancoso (East), 261
Travel (in Portugal), 24–27

Buses, 27
Car rentals, 15, 16
Cars, 24–26
CarsTravel (in Portugal)
  Cars, 16
Gas, 25
Planes, 26
student, 35
Trains, 26–27
Travel (to Portugal), 5–11
  baggage allowances, 7
  Cars, 8
  Package tours, 9–11
  Planes, 5–8
  Trains, 8–9
Trofa (North), 200
Tróia (Environs of Lisbon), 148

V

van Eyck. *See* Eyck.
Vasco Fernandes (painter), 71, 221, 222
Vauban (defenses), 65, 260
Vespucci, Amerigo, 272
Viana do Castelo (North), 175–176
  accommodations, 176
  restaurants, 176
Victoria (Queen of Britain), 152
Victorian architecture, 67, 152
  Palace of Pena (Sintra), 68
Vila Nova de Milfontes (Southwest), 306
  accommodations, 306
Vila Viçosa (East), 244–245
  Paço Ducal, 244
Vilamoura (Algarve), 296–297
  accommodations, 296–297
Villa Nova de Gaia. *See* Porto
Villages, 49–50
Virianthus (Lusitanian general), 54, 158
Viseu (North), 220–225
  accommodations, 223
  Cathedral, 222
  directory, 224
  excursions, 225
  Igreja de Misericordia, 223
  Museu Grão Vasco, 222–223
  restaurants, 224
  sights, 221–223

Visigoths, 55, 90

W

Wellesly, Arthur. *See* Wellington, Duke of
Wellington, Duke of, 60, 230
Where to go
    beaches, 47–48
    Castles, 48–49
    Itineraries, 50–52
    Portugal, 45–52
    Villages, 49–50
Wine, *see* Food and Drink
Women travelers, 36

Z

Zêzere, River. *See* Tomar accommodations

Get the latest travel & entertainment information faxed instantly to you for just $4.95*

The new Fielding's fax-on-demand service.

Now get up-to-the-minute reviews of the est dining, lodging, local attractions, or ntertainment just before your next trip. hoose from 31 U.S. and international destiations and each has five different category uides.

Take the guesswork out of last-minute avel planning with reliable city guides sent any fax machine or address you choose. elect just the information you want to be ent to your hotel, your home, your office or ven your next destination.

All category guides include money-saving best buy" recommendations, consensus ar-ratings that save time, and cost omparisons for value shopping.

Fielding's Cityfax™ now combines the nmediacy of daily newspaper listings and eviews with the wit and perspective of a ielding Travel Guide in an easy-to-use, onstantly updated format.

Order a minimum of two or all five ategory guides of the destination of your hoice, 24 hours a day, seven days a week. All ou need is a phone, a fax machine, and a redit card.

5 different category guides for each destination

❶ Restaurants
❷ Hotels & Resorts
❸ Local Attractions
❹ Events & Diversions
❺ Music, Dance & Theater

Choose from 31 destinations

1 Atlanta
2 Baltimore
3 Boston
4 Chicago
5 Dallas
6 Denver
7 Detroit
8 Hawaii
9 Houston
10 Kansas City
11 Las Vegas
12 L.A.: Downtown
13 L.A.: Orange County
14 L.A.: The Valleys
15 L.A.: Westside
16 Miami
17 New Orleans

18 New York City
19 Orlando
20 Philadelphia
21 Phoenix
22 San Diego
23 San Francisco
24 San Jose/Oakland
25 Santa Fe
26 Seattle
27 St. Louis
28 Tampa/St.Pete
29 Washington DC

INTERNATIONAL
30 London
31 Paris

Order each category guide faxed to you for $4.95, or order all five guides delivered by U.S. Priority Mail for just $12.95 (plus $3.50 shipping and handling), a savings of $8.30!

Fielding's Cityfax

CALL: 800-635-9777 FROM ANYWHERE IN THE U.S.
OUTSIDE THE U.S. CALL: 852-172-75-552
HONG KONG CALLERS DIAL: 173-675-552

Introducing first hand, "fresh off the boat" reviews for cruise fanatics.

Order Fielding's new quarterly newsletter to get in-depth reviews and information on cruises and ship holidays. The only newsletter with candid opinions and expert ratings of: concept, ship, cruise, experience, service, cabins, food, staff, who sails, itineraries and more. Only $24 per year.

- Star-ratings by region, type of ship and more
- No holds barred straight to the po[int]
- Rip-offs, scams and other warnings
- No fluff. No filler.
- A real lifesaver.
- In-depth, first-ha[nd] reviews
- Written and shipped within 4 weeks
- Hot off the presses!

Fielding's "Cruise Insider" Newsletter is a 50-plus page quarterly publication, available at an annual subscription rate of only $24.00, limited to the first 12,000 subscribers.

Call 1-800-FW2-GUIDE to reserve your subscription today.
(VISA, MasterCard and American Express accepted.)

Order Your Fielding Travel Guides Today

BOOKS	$ EA.
Amazon	$16.95
Australia	$12.95
Bahamas	$12.95
Belgium	$16.95
Bermuda	$12.95
Borneo	$16.95
Brazil	$16.95
Britain	$16.95
Budget Europe	$16.95
Caribbean	$18.95
Europe	$16.95
Far East	$19.95
France	$16.95
Hawaii	$15.95
Holland	$15.95
Italy	$16.95
Kenya's Best Hotels, Lodges & Homestays	$16.95
London Agenda	$12.95
Los Angeles Agenda	$12.95
Malaysia and Singapore	$16.95
Mexico	$16.95
New York Agenda	$12.95
New Zealand	$12.95
Paris Agenda	$12.95
Portugal	$16.95
Scandinavia	$16.95
Seychelles	$12.95
Southeast Asia	$16.95
Spain	$16.95
The World's Great Voyages	$16.95
The World's Most Dangerous Places	$19.95
The World's Most Romantic Places	$16.95
Vacation Places Rated	$19.95
Vietnam	$16.95
Worldwide Cruises	$17.95

To order by phone call toll-free 1-800-FW-2-GUIDE
(VISA, MasterCard and American Express accepted.)

*To order by mail send your check or money order,
including $2.00 per book for shipping and handling (sorry, no COD's) to:
Fielding Worldwide, Inc. 308 S. Catalina Avenue, Redondo Beach, CA 90277 U.S.A.*

**Get 10% off your order by saying "Fielding Discount"
or send in this page with your order**